OXFORD WORLD'S CLASSICS

ROME'S MEDITERRANEAN EMPIRE
BOOKS FORTY-ONE TO FORTY-FIVE
AND THE *PERIOCHAE*

TITUS LIVIUS (LIVY), the historian, was born in Patavium (modern
Padua) in 64 or 59 BCE and died in 12 or 17 CE in Patavium, surviving therefore into his late seventies or early eighties. He came to
Rome in the 30s BCE and began writing his history of Rome not long
after. There is no evidence that he was a senator or held other governmental posts, although he was acquainted with the emperor
Augustus and his family, at least by his later years. He appears to
have had the means to spend his life largely in writing his huge history of Rome, *Ab Urbe Condita* or 'From the Foundation of the
City', which filled 142 books and covered the period from Rome's
founding to the death of the elder Drus us (753–9 BCE). Thirty-five
books survive: 1–10 (753–293 BCE) and 21–45 (218–167 BCE).

JANE D. CHAPLIN is Professor of Classics at Middlebury College,
Vermont, and author of *Livy's Exemplary History* (2000).

OXFORD WORLD'S CLASSICS

For over 100 years Oxford World's Classics have brought readers closer to the world's great literature. Now with over 700 titles—from the 4,000-year-old myths of Mesopotamia to the twentieth century's greatest novels—the series makes available lesser-known as well as celebrated writing.

The pocket-sized hardbacks of the early years contained introductions by Virginia Woolf, T. S. Eliot, Graham Greene, and other literary figures which enriched the experience of reading. Today the series is recognized for its fine scholarship and reliability in texts that span world literature, drama and poetry, religion, philosophy and politics. Each edition includes perceptive commentary and essential background information to meet the changing needs of readers.

OXFORD WORLD'S CLASSICS

LIVY

Rome's Mediterranean Empire

Books Forty-One to Forty-Five
and the *Periochae*

Translated with an Introduction and Notes by
JANE D. CHAPLIN

OXFORD
UNIVERSITY PRESS

OXFORD
UNIVERSITY PRESS

Great Clarendon Street, Oxford OX2 6DP
Oxford University Press is a department of the University of Oxford.
It furthers the University's objective of excellence in research, scholarship,
and education by publishing worldwide in

Oxford New York

Auckland Cape Town Dar es Salaam Hong Kong Karachi
Kuala Lumpur Madrid Melbourne Mexico City Nairobi
New Delhi Shanghai Taipei Toronto

With offices in

Argentina Austria Brazil Chile Czech Republic France Greece
Guatemala Hungary Italy Japan Poland Portugal Singapore
South Korea Switzerland Thailand Turkey Ukraine Vietnam

Oxford is a registered trade mark of Oxford University Press
in the UK and in certain other countries

Published in the United States
by Oxford University Press Inc., New York

© Jane D. Chaplin 2007

The moral rights of the author have been asserted
Database right Oxford University Press (maker)

First published as an Oxford World's Classics paperback 2007

British Library Cataloguing in Publication Data

Data available

Library of Congress Cataloging in Publication Data

Livy.
[Ab urbe condita. Liber 41–45. English]
Rome's Mediterranean empire: books forty-one to forty-five, and the Periochae / Livy; translated
with an introduction and notes by Jane D. Chaplin.
(Oxford world's classics)
Includes bibliographical references and index.
1. Rome—History. 2. Livy.—Translations into English. I. Chaplin, Jane D.,
1964– II. Titi Livi periochae. English III. Title.
PA6452. A9C48 2007   937′.02—dc22   200701507
ISBN-13. 978–0–19–283340–2 (alk. paper)

Typeset by Cepha Imaging Private Ltd., Bangalore, India
Printed in Great Britain
on acid-free paper by
Clays Ltd, St Ives plc.

ISBN 978–0–19–283340–2

1

CONTENTS

INTRODUCTION

Livy's Life and Work

As is the case with many ancient authors, no one bothered to write a biography of Livy (59 BCE – 17 CE).[1] Fortunately, his intellectual productivity made him well known during his lifetime, and from snippets in his contemporaries and subsequent writers it is possible to construct a general picture of his life. For example, the later historian Cremutius Cordus is reported to have said that the emperor Augustus (63 BCE – 14 CE) referred to Livy as a 'Pompeian' because of Livy's praise for Pompey; Pompey was the great rival of Augustus' adoptive father Julius Caesar, but according to Cremutius Cordus the partiality was not a bar to friendship between Livy and Augustus.[2] Familiarity with the emperor can be inferred also from the fact that Livy encouraged Claudius, a great-nephew of Augustus and a future emperor himself, to write history.[3] There is also information about Livy's personal life. He came from Patavium (modern Padua), and the *Patavinitas* of his style was criticized by another Roman historian (though the exact purport of the remark is unclear).[4] A gravestone has survived at Padua, listing a Titus Livius, two sons, and a wife.[5] He had a daughter as well, who married a minor rhetorician.[6] These bits and pieces of information have led to the general view that Livy moved to Rome at some point, became known to the imperial family through his writing, and returned to Padua before his death.

Livy is unusual among Roman historians for having played no role in public life, either the army or politics. Instead, he seems to have dedicated himself to writing. His philosophical works and an essay on style addressed to one of his sons are now lost,[7] but his reputation has always rested on his monumental history of Rome. The elder

---

[1] These dates are based on Jerome, *Chronicles*, p. 164 H; the alternative dates of 64 BCE–12 CE were proposed by R. Syme, 'Livy and Augustus', *Harvard Studies in Classical Philology*, 64 (1959), 40–2.

[2] Tacitus, *Annals* 4.34.3.

[3] Suetonius, *Claudius* 41.1.

[4] Asinius Pollio, quoted in Quintilian 1.5.56.

[5] The text of the epitaph can be found in *Corpus Inscriptionum Latinarum*, vol. 5, no. 2975.

[6] For Livy's son-in-law, see Seneca the Elder, *Controversiae* X, proem 2.

Pliny, a voluminous writer himself, admired Livy's observation that, even when he had already achieved enough fame, he continued to write because the restlessness of his intellect drove him on.[8] Livy's renown was evidently widespread. There is a charming story about a man from Cadiz who travelled to Rome just to see Livy and, having done so, turned around and went home.[9]

Livy's history of Rome is known in Latin as *Ab Urbe Condita* ('From the Foundation of the City') and originally consisted of 142 'books' (the longest is about sixty-five pages in English). He begins with Aeneas' flight to Italy after the Trojan War. Book 120 ends in 43 BCE with the death of Cicero, which may originally have been intended as the conclusion. Livy eventually went at least as far as 9 BCE; the death of Augustus' stepson Drusus in that year was included in Book 142. Of the original work, Books 1–10 and 21–45 survive. The rest were lost before the manuscripts of late antiquity and the Middle Ages were published in modern book form during the Renaissance. Almost the entirety of *Ab Urbe Condita*, however, is preserved in summaries. Within a century of Livy's death, there was at least one abbreviated version in circulation.[10] Currently, two sets of summaries are known: one, referred to as the *Periochae* and varying in length from a few pages to a few sentences per book, covers all but Books 136 and 137; the second, the 'Oxyrhynchus' epitomes, is incomplete and fragmentary. The present translation contains what remains of Books 41–5 and the *Periochae*.

Ancient Historical Writing

To appreciate Livy's work, it helps if we understand the differences between ancient and modern historical writing. As a genre of literature, ancient historiography had distinct conventions. For example, it was acceptable and even expected that the historian would craft speeches for his historical actors, despite neither having heard them nor having any transcript of their words. Further, there are no footnotes or bibliographies; in fact, ancient historians tend to note their sources

---

[7] Seneca the Younger, *Epistles* 100.9, is the source for the philosophical dialogues; Quintilian 10.1.39 for Livy's letter on style to his son.

[8] Pliny the Elder, *Natural History* preface 16.

[9] Pliny the Younger, *Epistles* 2.3.8.

[10] Martial 14.190–1.

(if at all) only when they disagree with them or when the sources themselves are in conflict. The kind of archival work done by professional historians now did not play a prominent part in ancient historical research; classical historians relied on written accounts, testimony of eyewitnesses, their own experiences, monuments, tradition, and the occasional document, in varying degrees. Furthermore, for the Romans, the very nature of historical writing was different: history was moralistic and didactic; it was supposed to teach, and its readers were supposed to learn, not just what happened, but how to behave in similar situations.

Within ancient historiography, Livy's chosen genre was what is called 'annalistic history', that is, a narrative of the past organized chronologically, year by year, rather than focused on a particular event or a theme. Annalistic history has certain formal elements unfamiliar to twenty-first-century readers, and these are worth noting since they recur throughout Books 41–5. The annalistic year contained all the events of Roman public life. Every year the citizenry elected officials to one-year terms, most of which began on 15 March (the Ides). The two most important magistrates were the consuls, and each year they and the Senate, an advisory body comprising roughly 300 men who had already held at least one magistracy, determined what areas required direct administration. These areas of responsibility, or provinces, were normally assigned randomly by lot to the consuls and the six praetors (the next most senior magistrates). Troops were allocated as needed to the various magistrates, and any conscription necessary took place. Other political and military material included the sending and receiving of embassies as well as the creation of senatorial commissions for special tasks such as allocating conquered territory to settlers.

Religion was a large part of public life. Before the consuls departed for their provinces, at least one of them had to preside over another annual event, the Latin Festival. This ceremony had its origins in Rome's relations with the neighbouring communities of Latium and was sacred to the god Jupiter. Major public rituals of this kind feature regularly in annalistic historiography, as does other religious material. One of the elements most foreign to a modern readership is the recording of what are known as 'prodigies'. Unusual episodes, generally involving the natural world, were reported to the Senate, which determined whether or not they should be officially recognized as prodigies and what kind of remedy should be sought. The remedies were prescribed by various groups of priests. In many cases, priests were actually members of the Senate, since at Rome people with religious authority were from families of secular importance. The first prodigy list in this volume appears early in Book 41 (chap. 9). Livy reports that a rock fell from the sky, that a boy was born without all four limbs, that a snake with four legs was seen, that buildings at Capua and ships at Puteoli had been struck by lightning, and, finally, that a wolf ran through Rome the day the prodigies were announced. All these unusual events required expiation as they indicated divine displeasure. The death of a priest and the appointment of his successor were also matters for public record.

Every five years the Romans elected two censors. Over the course of eighteen months these officials revised the membership of the Senate and the equestrian 'order' (the second wealthiest property class), conducted an investigation of public morals, gave out contracts for public works, counted the number of Roman citizens, and performed a ritual purification of the city (*lustrum*).

In writing annalistic history, then, Livy took these yearly events—elections, assignment of duties, recruiting, embassies, religious developments—and the periodic activities of the censors and used them as the foundation of his narrative. They serve as a *basso continuo*, an underlying rhythm that orients the reader to the passage of time. But all these various elements of annalistic historiography make Livy's narrative very different from what twenty-first-century readers might expect from an account of the Romans' history.

Furthermore, for modern students of ancient history who want to know what really happened, there is the additional difficulty that Livy was writing for the benefit of his contemporaries, not to inform people in an unimaginably different future. Although he occasionally pauses to explain a foreign place or practice to his Roman audience, Livy does not aim to lay out the political structures, inter-state relations, and warfare of the past in a way that would make them readily intelligible to readers as unfamiliar as we are with the basic geopolitical terrain of the Roman Republic. Consequently, rulers and events, both past and present, routinely appear in the narrative without explanation, and the modern reader must assemble the pieces. It is thus worth sketching a backdrop for the period covered in Books 41–5.

The Historical Background and Livy's Sources

Books 41–5 centre around what is known as the Third Macedonian War (171–168), in which the Romans defeated Perseus, the last king of Macedonia. Ancient Macedonia was the territory to the north and east of Greece on the northern Aegean. (The coastal area of the ancient kingdom is part of modern Greece.) The royal family was Greek in origin; the ethnicity of the general population, the Macedones, is disputed, but they were probably Greek as well. Several strong kings (most notably Philip II and his son Alexander the Great in the fourth century) transformed Macedonia into a world power. Alexander's successors divided up his conquests, from Greece and Macedonia, south and east to Egypt and India, into separate kingdoms. Over the course of the third century, the Ptolemaic dynasty in Egypt, the Seleucid dynasty in Asia Minor, the Middle East, and Mesopotamia, and the Lagid dynasty in Macedonia (and sometimes Greece) dominated the eastern Mediterranean. In addition to these powers, there were smaller, independent communities: for example, the kingdom of Pergamum in western Asia Minor, the island city-state of Rhodes, the Balkan kingdoms of Epirus and Illyricum, Greek federations such as the Achaean and Aetolian Leagues, and some historically significant though militarily weak places such as Athens and Delphi. In the century after Alexander's death this complex patchwork of powers large and small achieved an effective balance of power. Whenever any single political entity became disproportionately dominant, other states formed alliances and contained it.

In this same period, Rome was growing from a major city-state on the Italian peninsula to the military powerhouse of the western Mediterranean. Initially, the Hellenistic kingdoms attempted to incorporate Rome into their network of alliances. The Romans, however, took a different view of inter-state relations and rather than participating in maintaining stability, gradually defeated one Hellenistic state after another until they controlled the Mediterranean. Why this happened is a vigorously debated question that goes back to Polybius (c.200–118 BCE). A Greek statesman and historian from Achaea in the northern Peloponnese, Polybius lived through and witnessed Rome's great period of expansion; and he made it the theme of his forty-book history, stating in the preface that 'There can surely be nobody so petty or so apathetic in his outlook that he has no desire to discover by what means and under what system of government the

Romans succeeded in less than fifty-three years in bringing under their rule almost the whole of the inhabited world, an achievement which is without parallel in human history'.[11] The fifty-three years run from 220, just before the Romans' biggest war with Carthage, to 167, just after the defeat of Perseus and Macedonia at Pydna in 168. After Pydna, Polybius himself was taken to Rome as a hostage (since the Achaeans had not supported the Romans in the war). Polybius was thus superbly placed to gather information and to write a largely firsthand account of Rome's expansion.

Much of that account of this period is now lost, but Polybius was Livy's chief source for the Third Macedonian War. By contemporary standards, Polybius is the superior historian. His approach appears modern because he lays out his methodology and offers overt analysis of historical causality. Further, he had direct knowledge of the subject and thus is a primary source. Despite these advantages, Polybius cannot be treated as a neutral authority. He had his own aims and interests, and where excerpts of Polybius have survived, it is generally valuable to compare the two historians for the light they shed on one another. Some of the explanatory notes to this translation point out how Livy adapts Polybius to his own purposes. For example, in pursuing his vision of the past the Roman historian often sets aside the explicitly theoretical approach that makes Polybius attractive to modern readers.

Livy's other main set of sources is earlier Roman annalists, of whom he mentions Claudius Quadrigarius and Valerius Antias by name in this pentad. Unfortunately, apart from the fact that they lived in the first century, very little is known about either of them, and their narratives are lost. Thus it is not possible to compare their approach to Livy's in the way that one can with Polybius. Other Roman sources Livy used include the speeches of Cato the Elder (234–149 BCE and thus also contemporaneous with the Third Macedonian War) and monuments in the city of Rome. Drawing on this array of sources presented Livy with compositional challenges. To note one problem, Polybius organized material by Olympiads, the four-year periods from one celebration of the Olympic Games to the next, and his chronology does not map well onto the Roman political year which, as discussed above, was the temporal underpinning of

[11] Polybius 1.1.5, trans. Ian Scott-Kilvert as *The Rise of the Roman Empire*, Penguin Books (London, 1979).

annalistic historiography. Livy occasionally reports information twice, once from Polybius and once from his annalistic sources. Overall, however, his narrative of the Romans' war with Perseus is a skilfully constructed narrative.

The Structure of Books 41–5

Ancient or modern, all writers of history share at least one hurdle: how to demarcate beginnings and ends. Livy carefully distributes his material within and across books. Unfortunately, Books 41–5 do not offer good material for analysing the structure of individual books. They were preserved in just one manuscript, and only Book 42 is complete. Book 41 is missing the first sixth and another quarter or so in the middle. Over half of Book 43 is lost. Book 44 is missing eleven pages, and Book 45 three.

We can, however, see that together the books form a coherent whole and, as such, are consistent with Livy's practice in the preceding books. He organized his narrative into groups of five and ten books, referred to nowadays as 'pentads' and 'decades'. Some people think that the groups of five were further combined into units of fifteen, or 'pentakaidecades'. So, for example, the first pentad (Books 1–5) covers the years from the Trojans' arrival in Italy to the sack of Rome by the Gauls, traditionally dated to 390 BCE and recognized by the Romans as a major event in their past. Books 21–30, the third decade, are devoted to the war with Hannibal (218–202). In other words, Livy used book divisions to indicate what he saw as distinct periods in Roman history. These divisions are not hard and fast: even as he relates one historical segment, Livy is laying the groundwork for the next. For instance, although the Hannibalic war is the main storyline of Books 21–30, during the war the Romans formed a retaliatory alliance against Hannibal's ally, Philip V of Macedonia. Livy uses this historical 'subplot' as a quiet prelude to the Second Macedonian War (200–196) in Books 31–5, which in turn sets the stage for the Third Macedonian War, treated in 41–5.

The ninth pentad (Books 41–5) has been seen both as potentially attached to the lost tenth pentad, and as a pendant to Books 31–40, forming with them a pentakaidecade. There are certainly good arguments for the latter view, since Livy emphasizes the connections between the Second and Third Macedonian Wars. The relationship

between the ninth and tenth pentads is harder to assess since the
tenth pentad no longer exists. The *Periochae* for Books 46–50, however, reveal that they covered the years 167–148 and that Book 50
included the defeat of Andriscus, a pretender to the Macedonian
throne. His revolt is known as the Fourth Macedonian War, and so
it is possible to view the fifth decade as dedicated as a whole to
Rome's gradual absorption of Macedonia.

Regardless of these potential connections to the preceding and
succeeding books, Books 41–5 stand on their own as an unusually
well-designed and coherent section, even by Livy's high standards of
composition. He singled out the Third Macedonian War as a crucial
period in Rome's moral development. First, working within an annalistic framework, Livy manipulates Perseus' reign so that it can occupy
a full pentad and underscore the significance of the fall of Macedonia.
Perseus inherited the Macedonian throne in 179 when his father,
Philip, died. The war, however, did not break out until 171. Livy
accordingly compresses events before the hostilities. The main purpose of the now fragmentary Book 41 was to move the reader briskly to
the eve of war. Book 41 originally covered five years; this total contrasts
sharply with the rest of the pentad: there are two and a half years
in 42, two years in 43, and Books 44 and 45 each have parts of 169–167.
In fact, Book 41, in stretching from 178 to 174, contains more complete annalistic years than any other book between 21 and 45.

The actual warfare takes place in the three central books, and Livy
appears to have structured them to coincide with alternations in the
fortunes of the Romans and the Macedonians. In Book 42, for example,
Perseus has his only notable victory while the Romans achieve just
minor success in skirmishes. Book 43 contains several Roman rever-
sals and disgraces. As Book 44 begins, the Romans manage, through
what is represented as Perseus' incompetence, to regain the upper
hand, and the book ends with their decisive victory at Pydna. Book 45
provides a meditation on the immediate fallout from the campaign:
reactions at Rome, shifts in inter-state relations in the eastern
Mediterranean, and the juxtaposed fates of Perseus and the Roman
general Lucius Aemilius Paullus. In sum, Livy went to considerable
effort to find, organize, and distribute material to fill the five books.[12]

---

[12] On the preceding interpretation of the structure of Books 41–5, see T. J. Luce,
Livy: The Composition of his History (Princeton, 1977), 115–22.

Leadership and Lessons

The pentad thus achieves one historiographical purpose in marking off a self-standing and consequential war in Roman history. But, as noted previously, Roman historians and their audiences valued moral didacticism. In the Preface to *Ab Urbe Condita*, Livy states morality's centrality to his perception of his undertaking:

The following matters are the ones that I think each person should sharply scrutinize: what the way of life and traditions were, through which men and by what abilities both civic and military the empire was created and expanded; next, as discipline gradually gave way, he should mentally trace those morals, first as they were undermined, then how they subsided further and further, and then began to tumble headlong, until we have come to our current straits, where we can endure neither our disorders nor their remedies. For in the study of history it is especially healthful and fruitful to contemplate examples of every kind of behaviour, set up on a clear monument. From it you can extract for yourself and your common-wealth both what is worthy of imitation and what you should avoid because it is rotten from start to finish. (Preface 9–10)

What makes the Third Macedonian War truly important is not its his-torical consequences, but its moral richness. Livy shapes his account in a way that illustrates how attention to traditional Roman ways promotes not just military and political supremacy, but moral betterment. A brief survey of five magistrates from these books shows that Roman success depends on old-fashioned conduct and piety.

In the 170s the Romans were campaigning mainly in Spain, Sardinia, and Gaul (northern Italy). One of the consuls for 178, Aulus Manlius, was assigned to this last area but moved into the northern Adriatic. The extant text opens with a surprise attack by the Istrians against Manlius and his troops in their camp. Though Manlius even-tually regains control of the situation, the conflict is perpetuated into the following year and one of the incoming consuls, Gaius Claudius Pulcher, is allotted it as his province. His predecessors, however, have remained in Istria and appear so close to victory that Claudius hurriedly departs from Rome to ensure his participation in the conflict. Livy describes Claudius' attempt to take command of the army as a shamefully impious and shambolic power-play. Neglecting all the usual ceremonies, including the official assumption of martial attire and, most important, the pronouncing of vows to the gods, Claudius rushes to Istria. He antagonizes his predecessor and the troops, and they refuse to acknowledge his authority until he has returned to Rome and performed the appropriate ceremonial departure (41.10). Livy emphasizes two points: Claudius' speed (a hasty nocturnal departure for the province, the equally hasty exodus from the camp, the near-instantaneous return to Rome, and the rapid trip back to the province); and, even more marked because the exact words are used four times, Claudius' neglect of the traditional rituals (the pronouncing of vows on the Capitoline and the formal assumption of military garb by the consul and his official attendants, known as lictors). The repeated emphasis on Claudius' bypassing of procedure indicates Livy's disapproval. Morally, then, the pentad begins at a low point: in his eagerness to assume command and receive credit for a victory, presumably so that he can hold a triumph, Claudius disregards tradition and the respect due to the gods.

The censorship of Quintus Fulvius Flaccus in 174 provides a further example of magisterial weakness in this period. As a general in Spain in 180, Flaccus was caught in a fierce battle and vowed a temple to Fortuna Equestris, the patron goddess of the cavalry, if she should help him to victory (40.40); a cavalry manoeuvre then carried the day. As censor, Fulvius fulfilled his promise and, wanting his building to outshine existing ones, he appropriated roof-tiles from a temple of Juno in southern Italy, with disastrous consequences. Although he tried to keep secret the source of the tiles (and his theft of them), word leaked out. The Senate took him to task for abusing his power; in representing the vituperation to which Fulvius was subjected, Livy dwells especially on the irony of a magistrate who, elected to oversee morals, acts with outrageous immorality himself. Fulvius was forced to return the tiles, but Livy concludes the episode with the even grimmer irony that no one could devise a way to restore the tiles to their original position and so they were simply left next to the temple (42.3). Flaccus, like Claudius before him, violates traditional practice and insults the gods.

Little of what remains of Book 43 reflects well on the Romans. One nexus of disgrace centres on the praetor in charge of the fleet in 170: Lucius Hortensius. After capturing and looting the Greek city of Abdera in Thrace, he demands cash and food from the locals. They appeal for time to send envoys both to the consul and to the Senate in Rome. Shortly after reaching the former, the envoys learn that

Hortensius has already beheaded the leading citizens and sold the rest of the population into slavery. The envoys continue on to Rome to lay their complaints before the senators, who are appalled by Hortensius' conduct. While this episode lacks the religious element and the violation of tradition found in the previous two cases, it shows how Hortensius' attack on Abdera belongs to a pattern of abuse by Roman magistrates. Livy begins by noting the transfer of negative publicity from the praetor of the previous year to Hortensius; the Senate's response to Hortensius' misconduct is to follow the procedure established when the consul of the previous year, Publius Licinius, assaulted another ally, Coronea. That episode thus belongs to a series in Book 43, which has justifiably been characterized as a low point in Roman morality.[13]

Livy's treatment of Quintus Marcius Philippus evidences a preference for consistency of theme over consistency of character. In Book 42, when the Romans are preparing for war with Perseus, the Senate buys time by sending an embassy to negotiate with him. Philippus is one of the two leaders who proudly announce that they have tricked Perseus, making him think that war could be avoided. According to Livy, the reaction in the Senate is mixed: a majority of the senators approves of the deceitful stratagem while the older men deplore the use of cunning, which Livy has them characterize as 'new and excessively clever wisdom', in contrast to 'traditional ways' (42.47). Here Philippus is manifestly aligned with the disgraceful, modern approach to warfare. Just two years later, however, at the beginning of his campaign against Perseus, Philippus' age and dedication to military service receive the emphasis. Contrasting the Macedonian king and the Roman consul, Livy describes Philippus as assiduous and committed, engaged in every aspect of his military duties (44.4). So in this episode it is clear that Livy wants his audience to focus on Philippus' virtues, not the cunning he displayed in the earlier negotiations.

Livy's purpose is to demonstrate, via the admirable characteristics of their commander, that the Romans' character in general is on the mend. In the first third of Book 44, Livy stresses Philippus' attentiveness to the gods: he invokes them in his address to the troops (44.1); and when the Roman army seizes the Macedonian city of Dium, Philippus takes care that the temple is not violated (44.7). In other

<hr/>

[13] D. S. Levene, *Religion in Livy* (Leiden, 1993), 115.

words, Philippus' behaviour during his consulship in 169 is not consistent with his conduct as an envoy in 171; but the shift in the way he is depicted signals the Romans' return to righteousness.

Lucius Aemilius Paullus is in many ways the hero of the ninth pentad, which, as readers have noticed, contrasts Paullus' virtues with the failings of his predecessors[14] and treats Perseus as a foil for Paullus.[15] Stretching over nearly two books, Livy's handling of Paullus is intricate and well developed. Two of his most prominent attributes are important for the leaders already considered: piety and respect for tradition.

Livy depicts Paullus as belonging firmly to the old school. Before departing for Macedonia, he addresses the citizenry in Rome and inveighs against civilian gossip and criticism of generals. Invoking the strength of mind of Quintus Fabius Cunctator, an early hero of the war against Hannibal, Paullus says that not everyone has Fabius' ability to put the best conduct of public affairs above reputation and to ignore the malicious talk of the people. Paullus urges anyone who thinks he knows anything about the proper conduct of the campaign to join it and not to engage in idle talk in the city (44.22). When Paullus takes charge of the army, he reiterates this position and explains to the troops his approach to generalship; he so impresses even the veterans that they say that for the first time they understand military matters (44.34).

The reference to Fabius Cunctator and the emphasis on Paullus' military expertise resurface in a speech delivered once Paullus has won the war. When his right to a triumph is challenged, his defence is taken up by Marcus Servilius. Servilius attributes the soldiers' complaints about Paullus' stinginess to the strictness he imposed on them. Servilius argues that the imposition of traditional military discipline prevented mutiny and saved the Romans in battle: Paullus' old-fashioned discipline prevented harmful words and actions. Servilius too invokes Fabius and his ability to ignore the talk of the crowd (45.37). So these two particular traits serve to align Paullus with the past and tradition. Towards the end of what remains of his speech Servilius stresses the gods' role in triumphs (45.39); this part of the argument highlights true Roman religiosity, another attribute conscientiously displayed by Paullus throughout the campaign.

---

[14] W. Reiter, *Aemilius Paullus, Conqueror of Greece* (New York, 1988), 71–80.
[15] Luce, *Livy*, 115 n. 3.

Servilius prevails, and Paullus celebrates a triumph. Servilius' speech, written by Livy of course, illustrates how an annalistic historian can interweave themes from year to year. The speech incorporates the moral concerns raised in the pentad. One particularly nice touch is that, by having Servilius dwell on the proper way for a consul to set out on campaign, Livy implicitly contrasts Paullus with Claudius, the self-promoting consul of 178. The ninth pentad thus comes full circle with Paullus' propriety. These five books have many more themes and topics than can be mentioned here. Nonetheless, consideration of these five magistrates reveals how Livy emplots history within an annalistic framework: Rome's leaders in this pentad descend from bad to worse before being redeemed by Paullus' traditionalism, in warfare, politics, and the observance of sacred custom, which are all mandatory subjects of annalistic historiography.

Past and Present: Livy's Contemporary Context

In the middle of what remains of Book 43, Livy famously articulates part of his attitude towards Rome's past:

> I am not unaware that the heedlessness underlying the widespread modern refusal to believe that gods issue portents also causes prodigies no longer to be announced in public or included in the historical record. Nevertheless, as I write about bygone affairs, my mind in some way takes on an antique cast, and a certain spirit of religious respect prevents me from regarding as unworthy of recording in my history matters that the deeply sagacious men of old deemed meritorious of public attention. (43.13)

The phrase 'as I write about bygone affairs, my mind in some way takes on an antique cast' has been cited as general evidence for Livy's idealization of the past.[16] The most important study of religion in Livy, however, argues that the passage must be taken in context, which is the nadir of the Romans' moral fortunes, and that this emphatic introduction to the unusually long prodigy list that follows is, if anything, embarrassingly present-minded: Livy laments the signs of the loss of the gods' favour in the past even as he detects its absence in the Rome of his own day.[17]

---

[16] e.g. P. G. Walsh, *Livy: His Historical Aims and Methods* (Cambridge, 1961), 62.

[17] Levene, *Religion in Livy*, 113–16.

As the passage previously quoted from the Preface shows, Livy undertook to write the Romans' history at what he considered their lowest point. While the exact date of the Preface's composition is disputed, the very broadest parameters put it some time between 35 and 25 BCE, well before anyone could have anticipated the eventual fruits of Augustus' reign. In fact, the first third of Livy's lifetime was a tremendously unsettled period. The Senate had lost the control it was exercising during the Mediterranean phase of Roman imperialism, and a series of powerful individuals competed to fill the vacuum. In the years immediately before Livy began writing, Augustus (at that time still Octavian), Mark Antony, and Aemilius Lepidus banded together against Julius Caesar's assassins in the name of restoring public order. Their alliance degenerated into a civil war between Octavian and Antony. This background explains Livy's dispirited view of Rome's position when he wrote the Preface.

But given the moral programme he lays out there, the extraordinary appeal of the Third Macedonian War period also becomes manifest. The ninth pentad models how the Romans can reset their moral compasses and chart a better course. Greedy, corrupt, abusive, cruel, and stupid as Claudius, Flaccus, Hortensius, and to some extent Philippus appear to be, ultimately they are offset by the unflinchingly upright Paullus. Taken together, these leaders demonstrate how Romans who have succumbed to corruption can turn themselves around. What the Third Macedonian War lacks in actual warfare Livy compensates for by having Rome's leaders enact moral decline and redemption, and the ninth pentad offers his readers not so much a war narrative as illustrations of the bad and good behaviour that ensures failure or success.

The timing of the composition of Books 41–5 is also impossible to pin down, with the years 20–10 BCE as the likely limits. By that stage, Augustus' efforts and some of his success at halting the chaos of the civil war years must have been apparent. Intriguingly, Augustus advertised his policies and actions as a return to the past. His overt traditionalism and piety resonate harmoniously with the ideals Livy enacts in the ninth pentad. The emperor and the historian, survivors of years of political turmoil and desirous of civil order, sought moral reform each in his own way.

The Periochae

The history of the various summaries and epitomes of Livy is obscure. As noted above, there was an abbreviated version of Livy's massive narrative within a century of his death, and more than one summary was made. The *Periochae* (a noun derived from a Greek verb meaning to travel all over) may be as early as the second century CE, but are usually dated to the fourth. They have generally been read for two purposes. On the one hand, they are a storehouse of information such as census figures, which the epitomator(s) regularly culled from Livy's original. Those data are invaluable since no other source contains them. On the other hand, scholars have scrutinized the *Periochae* to determine how Livy shaped and interpreted Roman history from 167 on. This enterprise is trickier, and no consensus has been achieved.[18]

Reading through the *Periochae* and considering Livy's distribution of textual space to historical material, however, allows one to appreciate at least partially his vision of Roman history. Roughly speaking, it forms a pyramid, from the condensed treatment of the early years at the peak to the expansive treatment of the first century at the bottom. For example, the entire monarchy, from 753 to 510, is in Book 1 while, as we have seen, the Third Macedonian War receives an entire pentad, and individual years (e.g. 82, 42), where civil war was raging, consume multiple books. Two conclusions suggest themselves. First, throughout *Ab Urbe Condita*, Livy made careful decisions about the amount of coverage he devoted to events and episodes; and secondly, the preservation of the early books creates a distorted impression of the relative weight Livy gave to the distant and recent past.

However one uses the *Periochae* to interpret Livy's historical project, it is important to keep in mind that they reflect the interests and emphases of their author(s) at least as much as those of Livy. For the books we have, the *Periochae* do not follow the sequence of events as Livy narrates them, and they highlight some episodes and skip over others. Sometimes they do not correspond to Livy's narrative: for example *Per.* 44 reports that, before Lucius Aemilius Paullus left

---

[18] See 'Works on the *Periochae*' in the Select Bibliography; esp. Syme, 'Livy and Augustus', and Luce, *Livy*.

Rome for his campaign against Perseus, he prayed that any imminent disaster might befall his own household rather than the Roman people; in Livy, Paullus reveals this wish in Book 45, after he has returned from Macedonia.

Because of the ways that the *Periochae* diverge from what we know about the surviving books, it is often as rewarding to read them for their own sake as for what they may or may not reveal about Livy. Their author(s) had independent ideas about what was valuable in Livy's text. For instance, Cato seems to have exerted a certain fascination; attention is drawn to his speeches and views throughout. The varying length of the *Periochae* is also intriguing. While there is a tendency towards increasing brevity, the progression is uneven. And leaving aside the pedestrian possibility that the author(s) ran out of steam—since it seems unlikely that having condensed volume after volume someone would give up at the very end—how do we explain the telegraphic nature of the final summaries? Did Livy write less about years he lived through? Is deliberate or unconscious censorship at work? Did the epitomator(s) find these years less interesting or less important?

Ultimately, then, the *Periochae* may raise more questions than they can answer, at least about Livy, but since he assumed that the rewards of history lay in considering its meaning, their fragmentary state may unintentionally contribute to his moral programme, if not to the complete satisfaction of our own curiosity about the Romans' past.

NOTE ON THE TEXT AND TRANSLATION

The translation of Books 41–5 is based on John Briscoe's 1986 Teubner edition. There is only one manuscript for these books. It was written in the fifth century, but there were already mistakes in the text. Furthermore, the manuscript suffered further, physical damage before the first printed edition appeared in 1531. The first editor, Simon Grynaeus, and many others have done their best to make sense of the text where there is a gap (known as a lacuna), where it is clearly spurious, or where the script is hard to read. Briscoe elected to produce a conservative text, reproducing readings of the manuscript (known as V) even where he believed them corrupt, rather than emending it speculatively. For the purpose of preparing a coherent translation, I tried to use the simplest conjecture possible and to give some context in the explanatory notes when difficulties in the text are consequential for our understanding of what Livy wrote. For the longer gaps in the manuscript I have supplied some content from other sources to maintain the flow of the narrative. I occasionally consulted the facsimile edition of V, but the reader should be aware that I was working as a translator, not an editor, and that simplicity, rather than editorial expertise, dictated my choices. In some cases, I have followed Briscoe in simply marking a lacuna with the conventional punctuation <. . .>. In a very few places, where Briscoe has marked the text as spurious with an obelus (†), I have also followed him and not attempted a translation. The Appendix is based on the apparatus in Briscoe's edition, and readers interested in greater detail should consult it.

The translation of the *Periochae* is based on Paul Jal's 1984 Budé and follows it almost without exception, including the occasional conjecture he supplies for his translation.

Every translation exists on a continuum between the literal and the free; this one errs in both directions at different points. My highest priority was to reproduce in English Livy's gift for narrative because I regard his ability to captivate his reader as the most distinctive attribute of his style. Livy's writing is characterized above all by variety; pace, diction, tone are all attuned to the shifts in subject matter. The far more plodding quality of the *Periochae*, which were compiled by an unknown epitomator (who gives no sign of being a master of

Latin prose!), may be the easiest way to gain some sense of the contrasting vibrancy of Livy's Latin in Books 41–5.

These five books have not received the scholarly attention they deserve. In particular, they lack a modern commentary. I consulted the Weissenborn–Müller long-authoritative but now outdated edition, but often found that other translations were more helpful interpretations of Livy's meaning. In many ways the present translation is in a conversation with the corresponding volumes of the Loeb, translated by Evan Sage and A. C. Schlesinger, and the Revd Canon Roberts' Everyman edition. The Loeb has the advantage of showing which text is being translated; the Everyman is a model of lucid, elegant English. As a translator I miss the scholar's luxury of the footnote; it is impossible to document my debt to these works.

The translation of the *Periochae* is primarily intended to allow more access to the full scope of Livy's conception of the Romans' history. The explanatory notes are minimal; truly appropriate annotation would require a full scholarly commentary. (And with the exception of these notes, the ancillary material is intended primarily for use with the translation of Books 41–5.)

It is a pleasure to acknowledge all the people who have helped me. This translation would neither have been undertaken nor completed without the efforts and support of Eve Adler, David Levene, Bill Nelson, Peggy Nelson, and Tony Woodman. I owe special thanks to David and Tony for their constant willingness to respond to the multifarious queries of a novice translator. Michael Crawford, Noel Lenski, Stephen Oakley, and Robert Parker read portions at various stages. The translation is the better for their input, though doubtless still not free from error. Josh Drake did the initial work on the maps, Elizabeth Stratford put exceptional care into the preparation of the manuscript for publication. The generosity of Judy DeLottie of the University of Connecticut Library was above and beyond the call of duty. Institutional support came from the Faculty Professional Development Fund of Middlebury College and from Fondation Hardt. There is no way to thank sufficiently the three dedicated readers who pored over every word, often more than once: Justin Bennett, John Briscoe, and Christopher Pelling. Last and most, I thank Judith Luna for providing everything one could want or need from an editor.

SELECT BIBLIOGRAPHY

Texts

Livius: Ab Vrbe Condita, Libri XLI–XLV, ed. J. Briscoe (Stuttgart: Teubner, 1986).

Abrégés des livres de l'histoire romaine de Tite-Live, ed. P. Jal, Collection Budé (Paris: Belles Lettres, 1984), 2 volumes.

Other Editions

Liuius: Codex Vindobensis Lat. 15, phototypice editus, ed. C. Wessely (Leiden, 1907).

Titi Livi ab urbe condita libri, ed. W. Weissenborn and H. J. Müller (1880–1924) (Berlin, repr. 1967).

Translations

Rome and the Mediterranean, trans. H. Bettenson, ed. A. H. McDonald, Penguin Classics (London, 1976).

Livy: Books XL–XLII, trans. E. Sage and A. C. Schlesinger, Loeb Classical Library (Cambridge, Mass., 1938).

Livy: Books XLIII–XLV, trans. A. C. Schlesinger, Loeb Classical Library (Cambridge, Mass., 1951).

Livy: Summaries, Fragments, and Obsequens, trans. A. C. Schlesinger, Loeb Classical Library (Cambridge, Mass., 1959, rev. repr. 1967).

The History of Rome by Livy, vol. 6, trans W. M. Roberts, Everyman Library (New York and London, 1924).

Works on Livy

Chaplin, J. D., Livy's Exemplary History (Oxford, 2000).

—— and Kraus, C. S., Oxford Readings in Classical Studies: Livy (Oxford, forthcoming).

Dorey, T. A. (ed.), Livy (London and Toronto, 1971).

Feldherr, A., Spectacle and Society in Livy's History (Berkeley, 1998).

Jaeger, M., Livy's Written Rome (Ann Arbor, 1997).

Kraus, C. S., and Woodman, A. J., Latin Historians, Greece and Rome, New Surveys in the Classics, 27 (Oxford, 1997).

Levene, D. S., Religion in Livy (Leiden, 1993).

—— 'History, Metahistory, and Audience Response in Livy 45', Classical Antiquity, 25 (2006), 73–108.

Luce, T. J., Livy: The Composition of his History (Princeton, 1977).

Miles, G. B., *Livy: Reconstructing Early Rome* (Ithaca, NY, and London, 1995).

Syme, R., 'Livy and Augustus', *Harvard Studies in Classical Philology*, 64 (1959), 27–87; repr. in *Roman Papers*, vol. 1, ed. E. Badian (Oxford, 1979), 400–454.

Walsh, P. G., *Livy: His Historical Aims and Methods* (Cambridge, 1961).

Works on the Periochae

Begbie, C. M., 'The Epitome of Livy', *Classical Quarterly*, 17 (1967), 332–8.

Brunt, P. A., 'On Historical Fragments and Epitomes', *Classical Quarterly*, 30 (1980), 477–94.

Stadter, P. A., 'The Structure of Livy's History', *Historia*, 21 (1972), 287–307.

Works on Polybius

Eckstein, A. M., *Moral Vision in the Histories of Polybius* (Berkeley, 1995).

Sacks, K. S., *Polybius on the Writing of History* (Berkeley, 1981).

Walbank, F. W., *A Historical Commentary on Polybius*, 3 vols. (Oxford, 1957–79).

—— *Polybius* (Berkeley, 1972).

—— *Polybius, Rome and the Hellenistic World: Essays and Reflections* (Cambridge, 2002).

Works on Roman Culture and History

Astin, A. E., *Cato the Censor* (Oxford, 1978).

—— '*Regimen Morum*', *Journal of Roman Studies*, 78 (1988), 14–34.

Badian, E., *Foreign Clientelae, (264–70 B.C.)* (Oxford, 1958).

Beard, M., North, J., and Price, S., *Religions of Rome*, 2 vols. (Cambridge, 1998).

Bickerman, E. J., *Chronology of the Ancient World*, rev. edn. (London, 1980).

Broughton, T. R. S., *The Magistrates of the Roman Republic*, 3 vols. (New York and Athens, Ga., 1951–86).

Brunt, P. A., *Italian Manpower 225 B.C.–A.D. 14* (Oxford, 1971, repr. 1987).

Eckstein, A. M., *Senate and General: Individual Decision Making and Roman Foreign Relations, 264–194 B.C.* (Berkeley, 1987).

Errington, R. M., *The Dawn of Empire. Rome's Rise to World Power* (Ithaca, NY, 1972).

Harris, W. V., *War and Imperialism in Republican Rome 327–70 B.C.*, rev. edn. (Oxford, 1985).

Keppie, L., *The Making of the Roman Army: From Republic to Empire*, rev. edn. (London, 1998).

Lintott, A., *The Constitution of the Roman Republic* (Oxford, 1999).

Platner, S. B., and Ashby, T., *A Topographical Dictionary of Ancient Rome* (Oxford, 1926).

Reiter, W., *Aemilius Paullus, Conqueror of Greece* (New York, 1988).

Richardson, J. S., *The Romans in Spain* (Oxford, 1996).

Rosenstein, N., *Imperatores Victi: Military Defeat and Aristocratic Competition in the Middle and Late Republic* (Berkeley, 1990).

Scullard, H. H., *Roman Politics, 220–150 B.C.* (Oxford, 1951).

—— *The Elephant in the Greek and Roman World* (Ithaca, NY, 1974).

—— *Festivals and Ceremonies of the Roman Republic* (Ithaca, NY, 1981).

Sherk, R. K., *Roman Documents from the Greek East: Senatus Consulta and Epistulae to the Age of Augustus* (Baltimore, 1969).

Sherwin-White, A. N., *The Roman Citizenship*, rev. edn. (Oxford, 1973).

Taylor, L. R., *Roman Voting Assemblies from the Hannibalic War to the Dictatorship of Caesar* (Ann Arbor, 1966).

Versnel, H. S., *Triumphus: An Inquiry into the Origin, Development and Meaning of the Roman Triumph* (Leiden, 1970).

Works on Macedonia and the Hellenistic World

Allen, R. E., *The Attalid Kingdom: A Constitutional History* (Oxford, 1983).

Berthold, R. M., *Rhodes in the Hellenistic Age* (Ithaca, NY, 1984).

Errington, R. M., *A History of Macedonia* (Berkeley, 1990).

Green, P., *Alexander to Actium: The Historical Evolution of the Hellenistic Age* (Berkeley, 1990).

Gruen, E. S., *The Hellenistic World and the Coming of Rome* (Berkeley, 1984).

Hammond, N. G. L., *Epirus* (Oxford, 1967; repr. New York, 1981).

—— *A History of Macedonia*, vol. 1 (Oxford, 1972, repr. New York, 1981).

—— *The Macedonian State: Origins, Institutions, and History* (Oxford, 1989).

—— and Griffith, G. T., *A History of Macedonia*, vol. 2 (Oxford, 1979).

—— and Walbank, F. W., *A History of Macedonia*, vol. 3 (Oxford, 1988; repr. 2001).

Larsen, J. A. O., *Greek Federal States* (Oxford, 1968).

Mørkholm, O., *Antiochus IV of Syria* (Copenhagen, 1966).

Hölbl, G., *A History of the Ptolemaic Empire* (London and New York, 2001).

Walbank, F. W., *The Hellenistic World*, rev. edn. (Cambridge, Mass., 1981).

—— *Philip V of Macedon* (Cambridge, 1940).

Wilkes, J., *The Illyrians* (Oxford, 1992).

Further Reading in Oxford World's Classics

Caesar, Julius, *The Civil War*, trans. John Carter.

—— *The Gallic War*, trans. Carolyn Hammond.

Livy, *The Rise of Rome*, Books 1–5, trans. T. J. Luce.

—— *Hannibal's War*, Books 21–30, trans. J. C. Yardley, ed. Dexter Hoyos.

Livy, *The Dawn of the Roman Empire*, Books 31–40, trans. J. C. Yardley, ed. Waldemar Heckel.

Plutarch, *Roman Lives: A Selection of Eight Lives*, trans. R. Waterfield, ed. P. A. Stadter.

Tacitus, *The Histories*, trans. W. H. Fyfe, rev. and ed. D. S. Levene.

A CHRONOLOGY OF EVENTS

All dates are BCE.

Background

264–241 First Punic War.

229–228 First Illyrian War.

219 Second Illyrian War.

218–201 Second Punic War.

214–205 First Macedonian War.

200–196 Second Macedonian War.

192–189 War with Antiochus.

Book 41

178 *Consuls: Marcus Junius Brutus (Liguria), Aulus Manlius Vulso (Gaul)*. Manlius campaigns against the Istrians and is joined by Junius after an initial defeat. The Senate receives a Lycian embassy complaining about Rhodes. Triumphs for Tiberius Sempronius Gracchus and Lucius Postumius Albinus for campaigns in Spain.

177 *Consuls: Gaius Claudius Pulcher (Istria; Liguria), Tiberius Sempronius Gracchus (Sardinia)*. Embassy from the Latins about migration to Rome and recruitment. Claudius initially fails to take command, then subdues the Istrians and is reassigned to Liguria. Campaigning in Sardinia. Claudius' two triumphs.

176 *Consuls: Gnaeus Cornelius Scipio Hispallus (Pisa; died and replaced), Quintus Petillius Spurinus (Liguria; killed in battle); suffect consul: Gaius Valerius Laevinus (Liguria)*. The year begins with various bad omens. Scipio Hispallus dies, and Valerius Laevinus is elected in his place. The Ligures revolt again. Tiberius Sempronius is victorious in Sardinia. Petillius dies in a Roman defeat of the Ligures.

175 *Consuls: Publius Mucius Scaevola (Liguria), Marcus Aemilius Lepidus (Liguria)*. Campaigning in northern Italy. First complaints are brought against Perseus, for fomenting conflict between the Bastarnae and the Dardani. Account of their fighting. Description of Antiochus.

174 *Consuls: Quintus Mucius Scaevola and Spurius Postumius Albinus (provinces not in text)*. Plague at Rome. The envoys return from Africa. Perseus campaigns against the Dolopes and returns to Macedonia via

Delphi and Thessaly; he attempts to win over the Greeks. The Achaeans debate repealing their embargo of Macedonia and decide to continue it. Catalogue of troubles among foreigners. Roman campaign against the Celtiberi. Activities of the censors.

Book 42

173 *Consuls: Lucius Postumius Albinus (Liguria), Marcus Popillius Laenas (Statellates in Liguria).* The Senate's envoys return from failed embassy to Perseus. Fulvius and the temple of Fortuna Equestris. Diplomatic activity at Rome and in Greece. The Senate dispatches another embassy to Perseus. Popillius' controversial treatment of the Statellates. Activities of the censors.

172 *Consuls: Gaius Popillius Laenas (brother of consul of 173; Liguria), Publius Aelius Ligus (Liguria).* The consuls and Senate debate the Ligurian situation. Eumenes visits Rome to urge war against Perseus. The Senate receives an embassy from Perseus. Attempted assassination of Eumenes at Delphi. The embassy returns from Macedonia and reports to the Senate. The Senate decides on war. Senatorial reaction to treatment of the Statellates. Embassies from the Carthaginians and Masinissa. The envoys report Perseus' hostile behaviour. Accusations against Gentius. Mobilization begins.

171 *Consuls: Publius Licinius Crassus (Macedonia), Gaius Cassius Longinus (Italy; attempted invasion of Macedonia).* Attitudes around the Mediterranean towards the war. The Romans declare war on Perseus. Conscription (speech of Spurius Ligustinus). The Senate dismisses Perseus' envoys. Roman diplomacy in Greece. Conference of Quintus Marcius Philippus and Perseus at the Peneus. Dissolution of Boeotian League. Roman and Macedonian diplomacy in the eastern Mediterranean. Marcius' report in the Senate. Licinius' departure for Macedonia. Perseus musters his forces and starts the campaign. First campaign season. Perseus' victory over the Romans at Callinicus. The Romans reject Perseus' peace overtures. Minor Roman successes.

Book 43

Cassius' unauthorized march into Illyricum. Embassies from Spain.

170 *Consuls: Aulus Hostilius Mancinus (Macedonia), Aulus Atilius Serranus (Liguria and Gaul).* Complaints against Roman magistrates. Return of representatives from Masinissa and the Carthaginians. Appius Claudius campaigns in Illyricum.

169 *Consuls: Quintus Marcius Philippus (Macedonia), Gnaeus Servilius Caepio (Italy).* Activities of the censors. Perseus' campaign in Illyricum; his

failed negotiations with Gentius. Appius Claudius' campaign in Illyricum.

Book 44

169 *Consuls: Quintus Marcius Philippus (Macedonia), Gnaeus Servilius Caepio (Italy).* Quintus Marcius Philippus invades Macedonia over the shoulder of Mount Olympus, unnerves Perseus, but returns to Thessaly because of inadequate supply-lines. Activities of the Roman fleet. The Rhodians tell the Romans to come to terms; the Senate's response. Activities of the censors.

168 *Consuls: Lucius Aemilius Paullus (Macedonia), Gaius Licinius Crassus (Italy).* An Alexandrian embassy seeks Roman help. Paullus receives a report from Macedonia and addresses the Romans. Perseus and Gentius form an alliance. Failed negotiations between Perseus and Eumenes. Failed alliance between Perseus and the Gauls. Macedonian naval activities. Anicius' campaign in Illyricum results in the defeat of Gentius. Lucius Aemilius Paullus establishes his command and reorganizes the army. He defeats the Macedonians at Pydna. Perseus flees, eventually to Samothrace.

Book 45

News of victory reaches Rome. Perseus surrenders. Gaius Popillius' embassy to Antiochus and the 'Day of Eleusis'. The Senate receives the embassies. Activities of the censors.

167 *Consuls: Quintus Aelius Paetus (Liguria), Marcus Junius Pennus (Liguria).* The Senate decides on general terms for Macedonia. Attalus in Rome. The Rhodians attempt to defend their actions. Anicius' operations in Illyricum. Paullus tours Greece. The partitioning of Macedonia. The sack of Epirus. Gentius, Perseus, and leading Greeks sent to Rome. The Senate votes triumphs for Anicius (Illyricum), Octavius (fleet), and Paullus (Macedonia). Resistance to Paullus' triumph stirred up by Galba. Servilius' speech supporting the triumph. Paullus' triumph and speech. Triumphs of Octavius and Anicius. Prusias of Bithynia visits Rome.

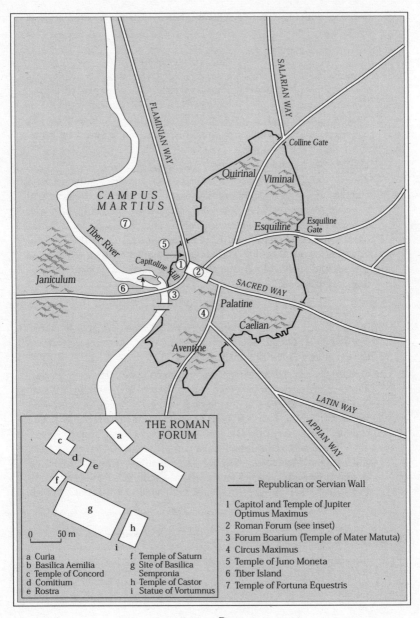

MAP I. Rome

MAP 2. The Italian peninsula

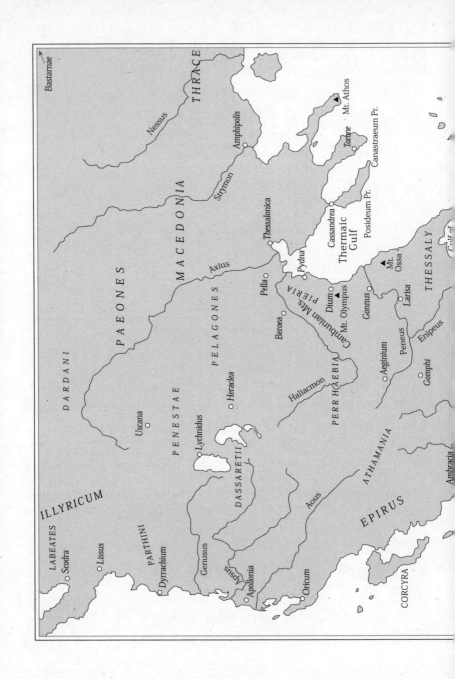

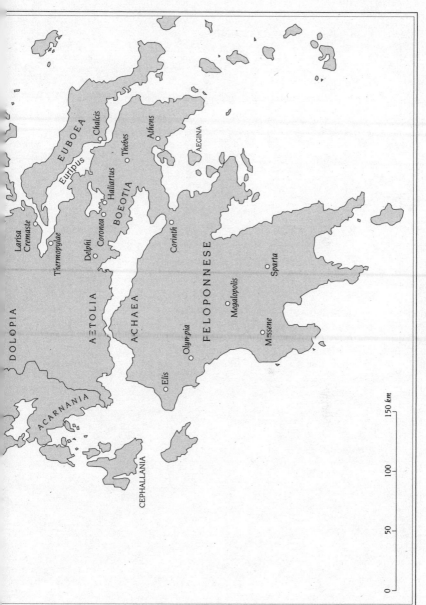

MAP 3. Macedonia and Greece

MAP 4. The Mediterranean

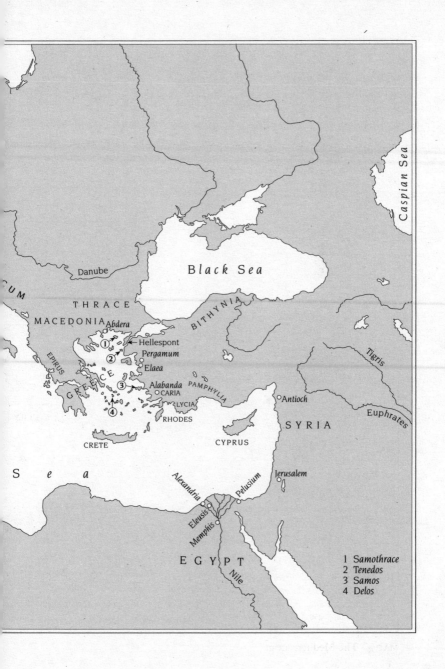

Caspian Sea

Danube

Black Sea

THRACE

MACEDONIA

BITHYNIA

Abdera

① ← Hellespont

Pergamum

②

Elaea

Tigris

EPIRUS

GREECE

Alabanda

PAMPHYLIA

③

CARIA

Antioch

④

LYCIA

RHODES

Euphrates

SYRIA

CRETE

CYPRUS

Sea

Jerusalem

Alexandria

Pelusium

Eleusis

Memphis

EGYPT

Nile

1 Samothrace
2 Tenedos
3 Samos
4 Delos

ROME'S MEDITERRANEAN EMPIRE

BOOK FORTY-ONE

[The first sixth of Book 41 was lost well before the first printed edition appeared in 1531, and so the beginning of the narrative here is misleadingly abrupt. The contents of the lost portion, however, can be reconstructed from the *Periocha* for Book 41. In addition to the prelude to the war against Perseus, it notes, among other topics, the Roman campaigns in Spain, the succession of Antiochus Epiphanes to the kingdom of Syria, the census of 179, and the passing of the *lex Voconia* (a law preventing women in the top property class from being instituted as heirs). Some of the material pertaining to Antiochus Epiphanes appears in the extant text (chap. 20 below). The narrative here begins with the Roman campaign against the Istrians, who inhabited a peninsula in what is now Croatia. They had previously clashed with the Romans just before the outbreak of the Second Punic War (*Per.* 20). The source of the trouble here is Istrian opposition to the Romans' new colony at Aquileia (40.26 and 40.34). The text begins in the middle of a sentence, and the name of the Istrians' chief, Aepulo, has to be supplied from further on in the text (chap. 11).]

1. The story goes that the Istrians had been a peaceful people under Aepulo's father, and that it was Aepulo who had given them weapons. In this way, supposedly, he ingratiated himself with the younger men, who were eager for plunder.

The consul* held a conference of war about the Istrians. Some of his advisers thought it should be fought immediately, before the enemy could assemble its forces, others that the Senate should be consulted first. Those who opposed delay prevailed.

The consul left Aquileia and made camp at Lake Timavus, which is not far from the sea. He was joined there by ten ships under the command of Gaius Furius, one of the *duumviri* who had been appointed to deal with the Illyrian fleet. Using Ancona as their focal point, they were supposed to divide up the coast of the Adriatic and protect it with twenty ships. Lucius Cornelius was responsible for the right-hand side of the coast, down to Tarentum, and Gaius Furius for the left-hand side, up to Aquileia. His ships were sent to the closest harbour in Istrian territory; they had cargo-vessels and a large store of supplies with them. The consul followed with the legions and made camp about five miles from the sea.

In no time at all there was a busy trading post at the harbour. Everything was transported from there to the camp. To make the transportation of goods more secure, detachments were posted all around the camp. The main stronghold faced Istria, and an emergency cohort from Placentia was stationed there. Marcus Aebutius, a military tribune from the second legion, was ordered to take two maniples of soldiers to the area between the camp and the sea and also to protect the water-carriers around the stream. The third legion was supposed to protect the men who were foraging for food and wood, so the military tribunes, Titus and Gaius Aelius, had led the soldiers along the road to Aquileia. Roughly a mile from this area was a camp of Gauls where a minor king named Catmelus had under his command at most 3,000 armed men.

2. As soon as the Romans established their camp at Lake Timavus, the Istrians themselves occupied a place hidden behind a hill. From then on they shadowed the Roman troops by zigzagging paths, alert for any opportunity. None of the activity in the camp or on the water escaped their notice. When they observed that the detachments in front of the camp were weak and that the crowds of unarmed traders in the busy commercial area between the camp and the shore had no protection from the land or the sea, the Istrians attacked two outposts simultaneously. Their targets were the cohort from Placentia and the maniples of the second legion.

An early morning mist had concealed the beginning of the Istrians' enterprise. This lifted with the first warmth of the sun, but even as the light grew somewhat brighter, it was still murky (as is often the case) and magnified the size of everything. The Romans were deceived into thinking that the enemy force was much larger than it actually was. The soldiers of both detachments were terrified. They fled to the camp in a great panic and compounded the fear their initial stampede had provoked when they were unable to explain their flight or indeed to answer any questions at all.

Then an outcry was heard from the camp's entrances since there was no detachment to fend off an attack. Rushing about in the darkness had caused the Romans to bump into one another so much that it was unclear whether or not the enemy was within the rampart. Amidst the shouting, a single voice was heard: 'To the sea!' This chance, ill-considered outburst from one man reached every corner of the camp. And so men began to run down to the shore just as if they had been ordered to do so. At first it was only a few, and although some were armed, most had no weapons. Then more men joined them. Finally, practically everyone did, including the consul himself. His efforts to recall the fleeing men had proved useless: they ignored his orders and his authority and even his begging.

One man alone held his ground; this was Marcus Licinius Strabo, a military tribune from the third legion, who had been left behind with three maniples from his legion. The Istrians made an assault into the empty camp and, encountering no other opposition, over-whelmed him in front of the general's headquarters even as he was marshalling his men and shouting out encouragement to them. The fight was disproportionately fierce considering the small number of defenders involved, and it lasted until the tribune and all of those who had stood by him were slaughtered.

The Istrians tore down and ransacked the general's headquarters. Then they made their way to the quaestor's quarters, the meeting area, and the trading district. There they came across all the supplies neatly arranged and exposed to view, and in the quaestor's quarters they discovered couches set up for a meal. Their king immediately lay down and began to eat. It did not take all the others long to forget about the fighting and the enemy and to do the same. Unaccustomed to the rather luxurious fare, they greedily loaded down their bodies with food and drink.

3. Far different was the scene among the Romans at that particular moment: panic reigned on land and sea. The sailors were taking down their tents, gathering up the supplies that lay exposed on the shore, and carrying them to the ships. Terrified soldiers were rushing into rowing boats and the sea. Alarmed that the boats might fill up, some of the sailors obstructed the soldiers while others pushed the boats away from the shore and into deeper water. The ensuing brawl soon turned into a full-scale battle between navy and infantry, including an exchange of wounds and casualties. It ended only when the consul ordered the fleet out to sea.

The consul then began to separate out the armed men from those without weapons. Out of the entire group, scarcely 1,200 had weapons; and very few of the cavalry turned out to have brought their horses with them. The rest resembled a shapeless mass of camp followers and servants; no doubt they would have been captured as spoils of war, if the enemy had remembered there was a war going on.

Finally, a messenger was sent to recall the third legion and the garrison of the Gauls. At the same time a move began on all sides to regain the camp and erase the disgrace of having lost it. The military tribunes of the third legion told the foragers to abandon the food and wood they had collected; and they directed the centurions, once the pack animals had been unloaded, to mount two of the older soldiers on each animal, and each of the cavalry to take up one of the younger infantrymen on his horse. The tribunes went on to say how glorious the reputation of the third legion would be if the soldiers proved brave enough to regain the camp that had been lost by the cowardice of the second—and the camp could easily be recovered if they surprised the barbarians in the act of plundering and overwhelmed them quickly. In short, they could take the camp in the same way it had been taken from them. The soldiers heard these heartening words with great eagerness. The standard-bearers started off at once, and the troops did not delay them. Even so, the consul and the troops he had re-marshalled from the shore reached the rampart first.

The speech of Lucius Atius, first tribune of the second legion, went beyond mere encouragement. He pointed out to his troops that if the Istrians intended to defend the camp with the same forces with which they had just successfully seized it, first they would have pursued their ousted enemies down to the sea and then they would at least have posted detachments before the rampart. He concluded that it was very likely they were lying around overcome by wine and sleepiness.

4. No sooner had he finished than he ordered his standard-bearer, Aulus Baeculonius (a man known for his bravery), to lead the charge. Baeculonius said that if the rest would follow him alone, his pace would be all the faster, and with a mighty effort he hurled his standard over the rampart and was the first to enter the gate. Titus and Gaius Aelius, military tribunes of the third legion, approached from the other direction with the cavalry. Right behind them were the soldiers whom they had doubled up on the pack animals, and the consul with the full battle-column.

Nevertheless, the few Istrians who had drunk only moderately had the presence of mind to flee. As for the rest, somnolence merged imperceptibly into death. The Romans recovered all their belongings except for the food and drink that had been consumed. Once they realized their comrades were within the rampart, even the wounded soldiers, who had been left behind in the camp, seized their weapons and contributed a large share to the slaughter. Everyone else was outdone by the performance of a cavalryman, Gaius Popillius, with the *cognomen* of Sabellus. Although he had been left behind because of a wound in his foot, he accounted for the largest number of casualties by far. About 8,000 Istrians were killed. There were no prisoners: a combination of anger and outrage made the Romans overlook potential profit. The king of the Istrians, however, escaped; drunk from the banquet as he had been, his men had hastily loaded him on a horse. On the winning side 237 men were lost, of whom more died in the early morning scramble than in the recovery of the camp.

5. Gnaeus and Lucius Gavillius Novellus of Aquileia happened to be on their way to deliver supplies to the camp and, unaware of the situation, nearly entered it when it was in Istrian hands. They dropped their loads and fled back to Aquileia where they filled everyone with fear and consternation. They caused the same reaction at Rome too a few days later. There the story spread that the camp had been taken by the enemy and that the Romans had run away; this part was true enough, but it was also said that all was lost and that the entire army had been wiped out.

And so the standard emergency measures were taken. Special levies were announced at Rome as well as throughout Italy. Two legions of Roman citizens were enlisted, and 10,000 infantry and 500 cavalry were called up from the Latin and Italian allies. The consul Marcus Junius was directed to cross into Gaul and to drum up from the towns there as many troops as each could muster. At the same time it was decreed that the praetor Tiberius Claudius should order the soldiers of the fourth legion, along with 5,000 infantry and 250 cavalry from the Latin and Italian allies, to assemble at Pisa and that he should look after the province in the consul's absence. The praetor Marcus Titinius was to tell the first legion to gather at Ariminum with the same number of allied infantry and cavalry.

Nero* donned his military cloak and set out for his command at Pisa. Titinius remained at Rome to conduct the draft and sent a military tribune named Gaius Cassius to Ariminum to take charge of his legion. Marcus Junius, the consul, crossed from Liguria to the province in Gaul. As soon as he had ordered auxiliary forces from the local communities and additional manpower from the colonies, he went on to Aquileia. Since he was informed there that the army was in no danger, he sent a letter to Rome to end the state of emergency, dismissed the Gallic auxiliaries he had requisitioned, and set out to join his colleague.

At Rome there was tremendous rejoicing over the unexpected outcome. The levy was abandoned, those who had taken the oath were released from it, and the troops at Ariminum (where they had been stricken with the plague) were sent home. When the Istrians, who were encamped in large numbers near the consul's camp, heard about the arrival of the other consul with fresh forces, they slipped away by various routes to their towns. The consuls led the legions back into winter quarters at Aquileia.

6. When the emergency caused by the Istrians finally ended, the Senate decreed that the consuls should decide between themselves which of them should return to Rome to hold the elections. In his absence, Manlius was the object of a savage attack launched by two tribunes of the plebs at public meetings. Licinius Nerva and Gaius Papirius Turdus promulgated a motion that Manlius not keep his *imperium* past the fifteenth of March, despite the fact that the consuls' commands had already been extended for a year. That way, once he was out of office, he could be put on trial immediately.* The tribunes' colleague, Quintus Aelius, vetoed the motion. After extended arguments, he managed to prevent its passage.

In this same period Tiberius Sempronius Gracchus and Lucius Postumius Albinus returned to Rome from Spain. Marcus Titinius, the praetor, held a meeting of the Senate in the temple of Bellona so that they could render an account of their actions and lay claim to the rewards owed to them.*

Also at this time there was news of a serious emergency on Sardinia.* A report from the praetor there, Titus Aebutius, had been delivered to the Senate by his son. The Ilienses, reinforced by their allies the Balari, had attacked his peaceful province. The army had been weakened and in large part wiped out by a plague and could put up no resistance. Emissaries from the Sardinians told the same tale and beseeched the Senate at least to provide aid to the towns; they had already despaired of their farms. Their embassy and everything pertaining to Sardinia were referred to the incoming magistrates.

There was an equally piteous delegation from the Lycians, protesting against the cruelty of the Rhodians, in whose control they had been placed by Lucius Cornelius Scipio.* They said that they had been under Antiochus' dominion, but that their former servitude to a king seemed like glorious freedom compared to their current state. For not only were they oppressed by Rhodian rule in their civic life, but as individuals they endured virtual slavery: their wives and children were abused; their own backs and bodies were treated with violent savagery; and—a shameful business—their reputation was stained and dishonoured. The Rhodians committed patent atrocities merely for the sake of exercising their rights: they intended to make it clear that there was no difference between the Lycians and slaves that had been bought and paid for.

The Senate felt the force of this appeal and entrusted the Lycians with a letter* for the Rhodians stating that the enslavement of the Lycians to the Rhodians, or indeed of any freeborn men to anyone, did not meet with the Senate's approval; and further, the Lycians had the same standing under the Rhodians' control and protection as allied cities under Roman dominion did.

7. Then there were two triumphs, one after the other, both for campaigns in Spain. That of Sempronius Gracchus took place first; he triumphed over the Celtiberi and their allies. On the following day Lucius Postumius held his triumph over the Lusitani and other Spanish peoples in the same area. In Gracchus' procession, 40,000 pounds of silver were conveyed; in Albinus' 20,000. Both distributed twenty-five *denarii* to each soldier, twice as much to the centurions, and three times as much to the cavalry; the allies received the same as the Romans.*

In this same period Marcus Junius the consul returned to Rome from Istria to hold the elections. The tribunes, Papirius and Licinius, pestered him endlessly in the Senate about what had happened in Istria and then brought him before a public meeting. By way of defence, the consul said that he had spent not more than eleven days in that province and that he too, just as they did, had to rely on hearsay for what had happened in his absence. Then the tribunes continued by asking why Aulus Manlius had not himself come to Rome to explain in full to the Roman people why he had left Gaul, the province he had received by lot, and crossed over into Istria. When had the Senate decreed a war with the Istrians? When had the Roman people authorized it? Well then, by Hercules, suppose he were to claim that even if he started the war on his own initiative, he fought it with intelligence and courage! Quite the opposite. It was impossible to say which was worse: the impropriety of starting the war or the totally injudicious way he waged it. Two detachments had been unexpectedly overwhelmed by the Istrians; the Romans' camp taken; the cavalry and infantry in the camp had been killed; the rest, unarmed and routed, had fled; the consul himself had led the way in the mad dash to the sea and the ships. Since Manlius had refused to give a full explanation while he was still consul, he would have to do so when he became a private citizen again.

8. Then the elections were held. Gaius Claudius Pulcher and Tiberius Sempronius Gracchus were elected consuls; and on the following day the praetors were chosen: Publius Aelius Tubero (for the second time), Gaius Quinctius Flamininus, Gaius Numisius, Lucius Mummius, Gnaeus Cornelius Scipio, and Gaius Valerius Laevinus. Tubero received urban jurisdiction as his lot; Quinctius received peregrine jurisdiction. Sicily fell to Numisius and Sardinia to Mummius. But the latter was designated a consular province because of the extent of the hostilities there. Gracchus received it by lot while Claudius received Istria. Scipio and Laevinus both received Gaul, which was divided into two separate spheres of command.

On the fifteenth of March, when Sempronius and Claudius took up their consular duties, the subject of the provinces of Sardinia and Istria and the enemies who had disrupted the peace in them was merely broached. The following day the Sardinian emissaries, who had had to wait for the new magistrates, and Lucius Minucius Thermus, who had been a junior officer of the consul Manlius in Istria, were admitted to the Senate and reported on the gravity of the conflicts in their respective provinces.

The envoys from the Latin allies made a significant impression on the Senate. They were admitted to the Senate only after their tireless appeals had worn down the censors and the previous consuls. The essence of their complaint was that a great number of their fellow citizens were registered at Rome* and had moved there. If this practice were allowed to continue, it would not be many census periods before their towns and farms would be deserted and incapable of providing troops. The Samnites and the Paeligni also complained that 4,000 families had left them and moved to Fregellae, and yet that change had not resulted in the Samnites and the Paeligni supplying fewer men or the Fregellani more for the conscription of troops.

Individuals had engaged in two kinds of fraud to change citizenship. The law entitled the Latin allies to become Roman citizens as long as they left a son of their own at home. In abusing this law some men committed an injustice against the allies and some against the

Roman people. To avoid the necessity of leaving a son at home, men would hand their sons over as slaves to anyone with Roman citizenship, on the condition that the sons would be manumitted; as freedmen they would become citizens. Men with no offspring to leave behind adopted sons in order to become Roman citizens.* After a while people dispensed with even these legal charades, and ignoring the law and their offspring alike, they made a general practice of changing citizenship by moving to Rome and being counted in the census.

The ambassadors sought to put an end to all this. They asked the Senate to direct the allies to go back to their cities; they asked also that legal provision be made against the acquisition or renunciation of offspring for the sake of changing citizenship; and that if anyone should become a Roman citizen by these means, he should not be one. The Senate granted these requests.

9. Then Sardinia and Istria, the provinces with ongoing hostilities, were assigned to the consuls. For Sardinia, orders were given that two legions be enrolled. Each legion was to have 5,200 infantry and 300 cavalry; 12,000 infantry and 600 cavalry were to be enrolled from the Latin and Italian allies; ten quinqueremes were also to be made ready for removal from the dockyards, in case this became desirable. Exactly the same numbers of infantry and cavalry were ordered for Istria. The consuls were also directed to send one Roman legion, with 300 cavalry, and 5,000 allied infantry and 250 allied cavalry to Marcus Titinius in Spain.

Before the consuls drew lots for their provinces, prodigies were announced:* in the territory of Crustumine a rock had fallen from the sky and landed in the grove of Mars; in Roman territory a male child was born without all his limbs, and a four-legged snake was seen; and at Capua several buildings in the forum had been struck by lightning; at Puteoli two ships were struck by lightning and incinerated. Even while these events were being announced, a wolf was chased through Rome itself in broad daylight; it came in by the Colline Gate and escaped by the Esquiline, with great uproar from the pursuers. To expiate these prodigies, the consuls sacrificed full-grown animals, and there was a one-day supplication* at all the sacred couches. Once the sacrifices had been properly performed, the provinces were assigned by lot: Istria fell to Claudius and Sardinia to Sempronius.

Then, with the authorization of the Senate, Gaius Claudius carried a law about the allies. He issued an edict that those of the Latin allies

who had been registered as such or whose ancestors had been registered as such during the censorship of Marcus Claudius and Titus
Quinctius* or at any point from then on should return to their own
cities before the first of November. The praetor Lucius Mummius*
was assigned to look into the cases of those who did not comply. The
Senate added its own decree to the consular law and edict: if anyone
should ask a senior magistrate, present or future, to perform a manumission or a vindication of free status, the dictator, consul, interrex,
censor, or praetor now or in the future should require the petitioner to
take an oath that the purpose of the manumission was not to alter civic
status; in any case where there was no such oath, the Senate forbade
the manumission.* These precautions were taken for the future; and
by the edict of the consul Gaius Claudius <. . .> it was decreed by
Claudius.

10. These were the events in Rome. Meanwhile, Marcus Junius and
Aulus Manlius, the consuls of the previous year, had spent the winter
at Aquileia, but at the beginning of spring they led their forces into
Istrian territory and raided far and wide. The Istrians watched the
destruction of their land, and though they had no great expectation
that their manpower would suffice against two armies, grief and outrage drove them to action. From every community the younger men
came together. In the initial assault their rough and ready army fought
with more vigour than staying power. Approximately 4,000 of them
were killed in battle; the rest gave up the fight and dispersed in disorder
to their towns. From there, they first dispatched ambassadors to the
Roman camp to seek peace and then sent hostages when these were
demanded.

When a dispatch from the proconsuls made these events known at
Rome, the consul, Gaius Claudius, was terrified that these developments
might perhaps deprive him of his province and his army. Without
pausing to pronounce vows, or to have his lictors put on their military
cloaks, or even to tell anyone other than his immediate colleague, he
left under cover of night and rushed precipitately to his province.*

His conduct there showed even less good sense than his journey had.
He called a general meeting and proceeded to castigate Aulus Manlius
for fleeing the camp. The soldiers listened belligerently, for of course
they had been the first to run. Then Claudius heaped reproaches on
Marcus Junius for making himself a partner to his colleague's shameful behaviour. He ended by ordering both men to leave the province.

They retorted that they would heed the consul's order only when he had taken his leave from Rome in the proper ancestral fashion, including pronouncing vows on the Capitol and properly cloaked lictors. Claudius, enraged, summoned the man serving as Manlius' quaestor and demanded that he bring chains; he threatened to send Junius and Manlius to Rome shackled. The man in question also spurned the consul's order, and he drew the confidence to disobey from the surrounding soldiers, who took the part of the generals and showed hostility to the consul.

In the end, the butt of constant mockery and exhausted by the taunts and insults of one and all, Claudius returned to Aquileia in the same ship that had brought him. From there he sent word to his colleague to announce that the new recruits destined for Istria should assemble at Aquileia. In this way nothing at Rome would keep him from leaving the city as soon as he had pronounced the vows and adopted military attire. This task his colleague duly undertook, and a day in the near future was announced for the troops to assemble.

Claudius followed on the heels of his own letter, and as soon as he arrived, held a public meeting about Manlius and Junius. He spent no more than three days in Rome; then, lictors cloaked and vows pronounced on the Capitol, he went back to his province as fast as he had raced there the first time.

11. A few days earlier, Junius and Manlius had mounted an all-out attack on the town of Nesactium, where the Istrian leaders and their king, Aepulo himself, had withdrawn. Claudius brought his two new legions there and sent the old army and its leaders home. He invested the town and prepared to launch an attack with siege-equipment. The river flowing past the town was simultaneously a barrier to the besiegers and a source of water for the Istrians. After many days' work, Claudius managed to have the river diverted and drawn off into a new channel.

The diversion of the water-flow terrified the barbarians as if it were some wondrous thing. Not even then, however, did they think of peace, but instead turned to slaughtering their wives and children. Further, to make a display of their foul deed for their enemies, they committed the massacre in full view on the walls and then threw the bodies over. Amidst the shrieking of the women and children and the unspeakable slaughter, the Roman soldiers scaled the wall and entered the town. The king took the terrified cries of the fugitives as a signal that the town had been captured, and he drove a sword through his heart to avoid being taken alive. Everyone else was captured or killed.

Two more towns, Mutila and Faveria, were then seized and destroyed. The booty, which was greater than the poverty of the people would have led anyone to expect, was all shared out to the soldiers; 5,632 captives were sold as slaves. The men responsible for the war were flogged and beheaded. The destruction of the three towns and the death of their king led to the pacification of the Istrians; the rest of the population handed over hostages and put themselves under Roman jurisdiction.

Towards the end of the war in Istria, the Ligures began to hold councils of war.* 12. Tiberius Claudius, who had been a praetor the year before and was now proconsul, was in charge of the garrison at Pisa with a single legion. His dispatches informed the Senate of the situation. The Senate decided to refer them to Gaius Claudius, who had already crossed over to Sardinia. Appended to the dispatches was senatorial authorization for Claudius, if he saw fit, to lead his troops against the Ligures since the province of Istria had been pacified. At the same time, a two-day supplication was decreed in response to the dispatches that Claudius had written about his activities in Istria.

The other consul, Tiberius Sempronius, in Sardinia, also met with success. He advanced his army into the territory of the Sardinian Ilienses. Large numbers of the Balari had come to the aid of the Ilienses, and so the consul fought a pitched battle against both peoples. The enemy were routed, put to flight, and deprived of their camp; 12,000 armed men were killed. The following day the consul ordered the weaponry to be gathered and stacked in a pile, which he then burned as an offering to Vulcan. Then he led his victorious army back into winter quarters in allied towns.

Gaius Claudius, having received the dispatches from Tiberius Claudius and the Senate's decree, transferred his troops from Istria to Liguria. The enemy had marched as far as the Scultenna river and established a camp in the fields. The battle against them took place there. There were 15,000 casualties, more than 700 men were captured either in the battle or in the camp (for this was taken too), and also fifty-one of the enemy's military standards were captured. The Ligures who survived the massacre took refuge in the hills, and there was no further sign of hostilities as the consul raided farms across the plains. And so, victorious over two peoples in a single year and, what others had rarely done, having pacified two provinces in a single consulship, Claudius returned to Rome.

13. Prodigies were reported that year: in Crustumine a 'sanqualis' bird (the local term for a kind of vulture) had made a crack in a sacred stone with its beak; a cow in Campania had spoken; in Syracuse a wild bull had wandered away from its herd, mounted a bronze statue of a cow, and spattered semen on it. In Crustumine there was a one-day supplication on the spot; in Campania the cow was handed over to be maintained at public expense; and the Syracusan prodigy was expiated by supplication to gods named by the *haruspices*.

A priest died that year, Marcus Claudius Marcellus, who had been a consul and a censor; his son Marcus Marcellus took his place in the priesthood. Also in that year a colony of 2,000 Roman citizens was established at Luna. A three-man commission consisting of Publius Aelius, Marcus Aemilius Lepidus, and Gnaeus Sicinius oversaw the establishment of the colony. Each colonist got fifty-one and a half *iugera* of land.* The land had been seized from the Ligures; before the Ligures it had belonged to the Etruscans.

The consul Gaius Claudius returned to the city. After he described his successful activities in Istria and Liguria to the Senate, he was granted the triumph he requested. Still in his magistracy, he celebrated a double triumph over the two peoples. He had 307,000 *denarii* and 85,702 *victoriati* conveyed in the procession. The soldiers each received fifteen *denarii*; the centurions twice that; and the cavalry three times. The allies got only half as much as those with Roman citizenship, and so they followed Claudius' chariot in such silence that you could feel their resentment.*

14. As this triumph was being celebrated over them, the Ligures shed their fear when they realized that not only had the consul's army been marched back to Rome, but that Tiberius Claudius had dismissed his legion from Pisa. Secretly they recruited an army and made their way over the mountains along side trails down to the plains. After raiding the territory around Mutina, they seized the colony itself in a surprise attack.

When this news was brought to Rome, the Senate directed the consul Gaius Claudius to hold the elections at the very first opportunity and, once the magistrates were chosen for the year, to return to the province and wrest the colony back from the enemy. The elections were held in accordance with the Senate's decree. Gnaeus Cornelius Scipio Hispallus and Quintus Petillius Spurinus were elected consuls; then Marcus Popillius Laenas, Publius Licinius Crassus, Marcus Cornelius Scipio, Lucius Papirius Maso, Marcus Aburius, and Lucius Aquillius Gallus were chosen as the praetors. The consul Gaius Claudius' command was extended for a year, with Gaul as his province. And to prevent the Istrians from doing precisely what the Ligures had done, he was to dispatch to Istria the Latin and Italian allies whom he had brought back from the province for his triumph.

On the day when the consuls Gnaeus Cornelius and Quintus Petillius took up their duties, they each sacrificed a cow to Jupiter, according to custom. The liver of the victim that Quintus Petillius killed was found not to have a head.* When he reported this to the Senate, he was ordered to repeat the ritual until he received a favourable omen. Then, when the Senate was consulted about the provinces, Pisa and Liguria were chosen for the consuls; whichever of the two received Pisa as his lot was directed to return for the elections when the time came for choosing magistrates. It was also decided that each of the consuls should enrol two new legions and 300 cavalry; and that each should enlist 10,000 infantry and 600 cavalry from the Latin and Italian allies. Tiberius Claudius' command was extended until whenever the consul should reach his province.

15. While the Senate was engaged in these matters, Gnaeus Cornelius was called away by a public messenger. He left the temple and returned a little later with a troubled expression. He explained to the conscript fathers* that the liver of the *sescenaris** cow he had sacrificed had dissolved; he himself could so little believe the attendant who informed him that he had ordered the water to be poured out of the pot in which the entrails were being cooked; then he had seen that every other part was intact, but that an indescribable wasting process had consumed the liver.

The senators were alarmed by this prodigy, and the other consul added to their anxiety when he reported that he had failed to receive a favourable omen from three sacrificial animals, in each of which the liver had no head. The Senate ordered him to go on sacrificing full-grown victims until he obtained a positive outcome. It is said that Petillius eventually achieved a successful result in sacrificing to the rest of gods, but not with the goddess of Safety.

Then the consuls and praetors drew lots for their provinces. Gnaeus Cornelius received Pisa, and Petillius the Ligures. Of the praetors, Lucius Papirius Maso received urban jurisdiction and Marcus Aburius jurisdiction involving foreigners. Farther Spain fell to Marcus Cornelius Scipio Maluginensis, and Sicily to Lucius Aquillius Gallus. Two of the praetors requested not to go to their provinces. In the case of Marcus Popillius, it was Sardinia: his argument was that Gracchus was establishing order there, and the Senate had sent the praetor Titus Aebutius to him as an assistant; it was extremely inefficient to disrupt the way he was handling matters, in the prosecution of which continuity was the most vital factor; opportunities for successful operations were often lost in the transition of power and in a successor's lack of familiarity with the situation, which inevitably required a training period before necessary measures could be taken. Popillius' request for a dispensation was upheld. Publius Licinius Crassus (to whose lot Nearer Spain had fallen) asserted that the performance of customary rituals* prevented him from going to his province. He was ordered either to go or to swear in a public meeting that such a ritual prohibited his departure. When this was approved in Publius Licinius' case, Marcus Cornelius asked that they accept the same oath from him so that he could avoid going to Farther Spain. Both praetors swore an oath by the very same formula. Marcus Titinius and Titus Fonteius, the proconsuls, were directed to stay in Spain with the same authority as before; and reinforcements consisting of 3,000 Roman citizens with 200 cavalry and 5,000 Latin and Italian allies with 300 cavalry were to be sent to them.

16. The Latin Festival took place on the fifth of March. There were religious misgivings because a magistrate of Lanuvium had not offered a prayer on behalf of the Roman people, the Quirites, when sacrificing one of the victims. When this was reported to the Senate, and the Senate had referred it to the college of priests, the latter decided that the Latin Festival should be repeated since it had not been celebrated properly and that the people of Lanuvium should supply the victims since it was because of them that the ceremony had to be repeated.

The sense of disquiet intensified after the consul Gnaeus Cornelius collapsed as he was returning from the Alban Mount and suffered a partial seizure. He went to Aquae Cumanae, but his condition grew worse, and he died at Cumae.* His body was taken back to Rome where, after the cortège, it was interred in a magnificent funeral. He had been a priest also.

The other consul, Quintus Petillius, was directed to hold elections as soon as the auspices permitted so that a new colleague could be chosen for him; he was also supposed to announce the new date for the Latin Festival. He set the elections for the third of August and the Latin Festival for the thirteenth of August. While everyone's mind was full of superstition, further prodigies were reported: a comet had been seen in the sky at Tusculum; lightning had struck the temple of Apollo and several private homes at Gabii, as well as the walls and gate of Graviscae. The senators directed that these prodigies be handled however the priests should see fit.

So it was that at first the consuls were busy with religious affairs, and then the death of one of them, as well as the election and the repetition of the Latin Festival, kept his colleague occupied. In the meantime, Gaius Claudius transferred his army to Mutina, which the Ligures had seized the previous year. Within three days of beginning the siege he took the town from the enemy and restored it to the colonists. Eight thousand Ligures were cut down within the walls, and the consul immediately wrote a letter to Rome in which he not only described the operation, but also boasted that because of his personal valour and good fortune not a single enemy of the Roman people remained this side of the Alps, and a considerable amount of land had been taken that could be subdivided into plots for many thousands of men.

17. Also at this time Tiberius Sempronius subjugated the Sardinians with a series of victories on the island. There were 15,000 casualties; all the Sardinian peoples who had defected were brought back under control. Previous tributaries were compelled to pay twice as much in taxes as before; the rest contributed grain. Once the province had been pacified and 230 hostages assembled from all over the island, envoys were sent to Rome to announce the news and to seek from the Senate that the gods be officially thanked for the successes achieved under the leadership and auspices of Tiberius Sempronius and that he be allowed to leave his area of command and to bring his army back with him. When the envoys delivered their report in the temple of Apollo, the senators decreed that there should be a two-day thanksgiving and that the consuls should sacrifice forty full-size animals, but that the procon-sul Tiberius Sempronius and his army should remain in the province for the year.

Then the election for a single consul that had been announced for the third of August was completed on that very day. Quintus Petillius presided over the appointment of Gaius Valerius Laevinus as his colleague; the latter was to enter office immediately. Fortunately for Laevinus, who had long been yearning for a provincial command, bulletins comporting to his desire arrived: the Ligures had revolted.

On the fifth of August, he assumed full military attire and departed for his province. After hearing his reports, the Senate ordered the third legion to set out to join the proconsul Gaius Claudius in Gaul in response to this uprising; further, naval *duumviri* were to go with the fleet to Pisa to patrol the coast of Liguria and present a threat by sea. The consul, Quintus Petillius, had set a day for the army to assemble, also at Pisa, and the proconsul Gaius Claudius, as soon as he heard about the rebellion of the Ligures, held an emergency draft for soldiers to supplement those he had with him at Parma and led his army to the borders of the Ligures' territory.

18. At the approach of Gaius Claudius the Ligures remembered how at the Scultenna river he had recently defeated them and caused them to flee. And so, determined to use geography rather than arms to defend themselves against his painfully familiar strength, they took over two mountains, Letum and Ballista, and encircled them with a wall in addition. About 1,500 Ligures left the plains too late and were trapped and killed; but the rest kept to the mountains. Even in this state of fear, their innate barbarity asserted itself, and they vented their savage anger on what they had seized from Mutina: the prisoners were unspeakably mutilated and killed, and the animals were butchered all around the shrines rather than properly sacrificed. Once the Ligures had had their fill of killing the live booty, they smashed the inanimate plunder against a wall, though these were not decorative vessels, but useful containers of all kinds.

Quintus Petillius, the consul, unwilling to have the war concluded in his absence, sent a dispatch to Gaius Claudius directing the latter and his army to join him in Gaul where he would await Claudius at Campi Macri. Upon receipt of this message Claudius broke camp in Liguria and turned his army over to the consul at Campi Macri. The other consul, Gaius Valerius, arrived there a few days later. They divided up the forces on the spot and performed a joint *lustrum* of both armies before departing. Having agreed to attack the enemy from different directions, they determined by lot where they would each go. There was general agreement that Valerius had cast his lot in the correct religious fashion because he had been within a sacred area. In Petillius' case, however, the augurs subsequently pronounced that the procedure had been carried out in a flawed manner: namely that after the lot had been placed in the sortition urn, within the sacred precinct, Petillius himself had remained outside it although he too should have entered the sacred precinct.

The consuls then set off for their respective territories. Petillius encamped opposite the ridge between Mount Ballista and Mount Letum, which linked them with a continuous spine. The story goes that while he was giving a speech to his soldiers in a public meeting, he had no thought for the possible ambiguity of his words when he predicted that 'Letum' would be his that day.* He began the assault up the mountains with two divisions simultaneously. The first, of which he himself was a member, advanced briskly. When the other division was repulsed by the enemy, the consul rode over to restore the deteriorating situation. Although he rallied his men, he himself, carelessly riding out in front of the standards, was struck by a javelin and killed.

The enemy did not notice the general's death, and the few of his own men who had seen it carefully concealed the corpse since they knew that victory turned on doing so. The remaining forces of infantry and cavalry overwhelmed the enemy and took the mountains without their leader. About 5,000 Ligures were killed; the Roman army lost fifty-two men. In addition to such an obvious fulfilment of the evil omen, the *pullarius** also reported that there had been a problem with the auspices of which the consul had been fully aware. Gaius Valerius, what had been heard <. . .>

[The text breaks off with this incomplete sentence. More or less the middle third of Book 41 is missing and with it Livy's handling of the outcome of Petillius' generalship. Other sources record that the troops were blamed and fined for not preventing Petillius' death (see Valerius Maximus 2.7.15d and Frontinus, *Strategemata* 4.1.46). Other material almost certainly in the lost pages includes the election of the magistrates for 175. (The consuls were Publius Mucius Scaevola and Marcus Aemilius Lepidus; the praetors were probably Publius Aelius Ligus, Quintus Baebius Sulca, Appius Claudius Centho, Servius Cornelius Sulla, Gnaeus Lutatius Cerco, and Gaius Popillius Laenas.) Further, Livy probably mentioned the dispatch of an embassy to Perseus, the Macedonian king, and an investigation into the complaints of the Dardani about the incursions of the Bastarnae. (See Polybius 25.6 on this episode; the Dardani were an Illyrian tribe living to the north-west of Macedonia; the Bastarnae were nomadic and of obscure origin.)

Surviving from this section are two manuscript pages, labelled as chaps. 19 and 20 below, and a single sentence, preserved in the sixteenth-century grammarian Priscian. The latter can be securely assigned to this part of Livy because of the unique circumstances under which the consuls died. The translation resumes with this isolated sentence and then picks up the thread of the narrative with the campaigns of the consuls Marcus Aemilius and Publius Mucius in Gaul and Liguria.]

Experts in religious and public law said that in a year where the two regular consuls died (one from disease and the other from death in battle), a suffect consul could not legitimately hold the elections.*

19. <. . . Marcus Aemilius . . .> led away. The Garuli, Lapicini, and Hergates used to live on the near side of the Apennines, and the Briniates on the far side, within the Audena river. Publius Mucius campaigned against those who had sacked Luna and Pisa; once they were completely subjugated, he stripped them of their weapons. For these victories in Gaul and Liguria, achieved under the leadership and auspices of the two consuls, the Senate decreed a three-day thanksgiving and a sacrifice of forty animals.

And in fact the Gallic and Ligurian revolt, which had arisen early in the year, was suppressed quickly and easily. But there was already an undercurrent of anxiety about war with Macedonia. Perseus was stirring up trouble between the Dardani and the Bastarnae, and the envoys who had been sent to investigate the situation in Macedonia now returned to Rome and announced that war had broken out in Dardania. At the same time spokesmen came from King Perseus to disclaim any responsibility on his part for provoking the Bastarnae or instigating their behaviour in any way. The Senate neither exonerated nor convicted him of any fault in the matter; it simply directed that a warning should be given to Perseus: it should be his constant concern that he could be seen to be honouring his treaty with the Romans.

With the recognition that the Bastarnae were not just failing to leave their territory, as the Dardani hoped, but were becoming more oppressive all the time, and were aided and abetted by their neighbours the Thracians and Scordisci, the Dardani thought bold action was called for, even if it were foolhardy. And so, resorting to arms, they assembled from all sides at their settlement closest to the camp of the Bastarnae. It was winter, and they had chosen that time of year with the hope that the Thracians and the Scordisci might go back home. When they heard that this had happened and that the Bastarnae were now on their own, the Dardani divided their forces in two: one group was to take the direct route and make an open assault; the other was to circle around via a remote pass and attack from the rear. Before the latter group managed to encircle the enemy camp, however, the battle was over. The Dardani were defeated and driven back into their town, which was about twelve miles from the camp of the Bastarnae. The victors followed directly and surrounded the town, confident that they would take it the following day by force or that the enemy would be intimidated into surrendering. Meanwhile, the other band of Dardani, the group that had circled around, unaware of the disaster to their side, <. . .> the abandoned and undefended camp of the Bastarnae <. . .>

[Here is the second part of the large gap. It must have included the eventual undoing of the Bastarnae who, according to the fifth-century writer Orosius, were almost entirely wiped out when they subsequently tried to cross the Danube and the ice proved insufficiently thick to bear their weight (*Seven Books against the Pagans* 4.20). Livy almost certainly discussed in addition the dispatch of an embassy to North Africa; the return of the ambassadors is treated in chap. 22. Also in the missing text must have been the introduction of Antiochus Epiphanes, the Seleucid king who is best known for his assault on Jerusalem; see the hostile portrait in 1 Maccabees (chaps. 1–6). The text of Book 41 resumes with a sketch of his eccentricities.]

20. <. . .> King Antiochus dispensed justice in the Roman fashion, sitting in an ivory chair, where he arbitrated disputes of the least consequence. His mind did not adhere to any particular worldly status, flitting amongst all stations in life so much that neither he nor others could be entirely certain what sort of man he was.* He did not talk to his friends, he gave ready smiles to those he barely knew, he made fools of himself and others with his inconsistent generosity: to some men, those of noble birth who held themselves in great esteem, he gave childish gifts such as food and toys; others, who expected nothing, he made into wealthy men. And so he seemed to some men not to know what he wanted; some said that he was playing about in a simple-minded way; others were convinced of his insanity.

But in two great and worthy areas his mind was truly royal: benefactions to cities and worship of the gods. He promised the people of Megalopolis in Arcadia that he would encircle their city with a wall, and he donated the larger part of the money; at Tegea he began to have a magnificent theatre built out of marble; at Cyzicus, he contributed to the *prytaneum* (that is, one of the inner buildings of the city, the dining place of those who have the right to eat at public expense) a golden dinner service for one table. To the Rhodians he presented not any single gift that was particularly remarkable, but rather all sorts, whatever their way of life called for. His generosity to the gods is manifest in the temple of Olympian Jupiter at Athens which, though unfinished, is the only one in the world commensurate with the greatness of the god. In addition, the king adorned Delos with remarkable altars and an abundance of statuary, and at Antioch he promised a magnificent temple to Capitoline Jupiter, with a panelled ceiling of gold and walls entirely gilded as well. And, though in the very brief period of his reign he did not complete them, yet he pledged many other things in many other places.

He also surpassed earlier kings in the magnificence of his spectacles of every kind, mostly traditional entertainments with a generous supply of Greek performers, with one exception: gladiatorial games in the Roman fashion (at first more to the horror than the delight of his people, who were unfamiliar with this kind of show*). By then sponsoring performances with increasing frequency, at times limited to flesh wounds and at others with no quarter allowed, he accustomed their eyes to this spectacle and made it a pleasurable one. In this way he roused in many young men a passion for fighting. And so he, who had initially been accustomed to import trained gladiators from Rome at great cost, soon from his own <. . .>

[Another gap in the text follows. It probably contained an account of the passing of the *lex Voconia*, the law preventing men in the top property class from instituting women as heirs.]

21. <. . .> Lucius Cornelius Scipio had received as his lot jurisdiction involving foreigners. Although Marcus Atilius had received Sardinia as his province, he was ordered to cross over to Corsica with the new legion (consisting of 5,000 infantry and 300 cavalry) that the consuls had conscripted. So while Atilius was fighting there, Cornelius' term of command was extended so that he could take charge of Sardinia. Gnaeus Servilius Caepio in Farther Spain and Publius Furius Philo in Nearer Spain were voted 3,000 Roman infantry, 150 Roman cavalry, and 5,000 infantry and 300 cavalry from the Latin and Italian allies. Lucius Claudius was given Sicily without reinforcements. In addition, the consuls were directed to enrol two legions, with the regular numbers of infantry and cavalry, and to levy 10,000 infantry and 600 cavalry from the allies.

Conducting the draft was very difficult for the consuls because the plague that had attacked cattle the previous year took the form of human diseases that year. Those who succumbed were hard-pressed to survive past the seventh day; those who survived became ill subsequently with a long-lasting disease, usually quartan fever.* Slaves died in the greatest numbers, and their unburied bodies lay piled up on every road. There were insufficient means to bury even the freeborn. Putrefaction consumed the corpses, left untouched by the dogs and vultures, and in fact people agreed that for those two years there was not a vulture to be seen anywhere, despite such heaps of beasts and men.

The public priests* who died of the plague were the pontifex Gnaeus Servilius Caepio, father of the praetor, and Tiberius Sempronius Longus, son of Tiberius, a decemvir for sacred rites, and the augur Publius Aelius Paetus, and Tiberius Sempronius Gracchus, and Gaius Mamilius Atellus, the curio maximus, and the pontifex Marcus Sempronius Tuditanus. The substitute *pontifices* were Gaius Sulpicius Galba in the place of Caepio and <. . .> in the place of Tuditanus. Titus Veturius Gracchus Sempronianus filled Gracchus' place as augur, and Quintus Aelius Paetus filled Publius Aelius'. Gaius Sempronius Longus became the decemvir for sacred rites, and Gaius Scribonius Curio replaced the curio maximus.

With no end to the plague to be found, the Senate decreed that the decemvirs should consult the Sibylline oracles. These men in turn decreed a one-day supplication, and with Quintus Marcius Philippus leading the responsive prayers, the people undertook a vow in the Forum, that if sickness and plague should leave Roman territory, they would hold two days of festival and supplication.

A two-headed boy was born in the district of Veii, and one with only one hand in Sinuessa, and a baby girl with teeth at Auximum. On a clear day and in broad daylight, a rainbow appeared over the temple of Saturn in the Roman Forum, and three suns shone simultaneously; that very night there were multiple shooting stars. Further, the people of Lanuvium and the Caerites claimed that a crested serpent, dotted with golden spots, had appeared in their towns, and it was generally agreed that in Campanian territory an ox talked.

22.* On the seventh of June the envoys returned from Africa* where they had met with Masinissa before going on to Carthage; their understanding of what had happened there came more from the king than the Carthaginians themselves. Nevertheless they confirmed as fact that ambassadors had come from King Perseus and that they had been granted a meeting with the senate* at night in the temple of Aesculapius. Masinissa had also asserted that ambassadors had been sent from Carthage to Macedonia, a fact that the Carthaginians denied, though not terribly firmly. The Senate decided to send envoys to Macedonia too: there were three of them, Gaius Laelius, Marcus Valerius Messalla, and Sextus Digitius.

Around this time Perseus set out with an army and compelled the entire race of the Dolopes to submit to his authority and jurisdiction, for some of them were defying him and referring their legal disputes to the Romans instead. He then crossed the Oetaei Mountains and made his way up to Delphi in order to consult the oracle about certain religious matters that were weighing on him. His unexpected appearance in the centre of Greece provoked great terror not only in the neighbouring towns, but also emergency messengers were sent to Asia to King Eumenes. Perseus spent no more than three days in Delphi and then returned to his own kingdom without harming or disrupting the communities through whose territory he travelled, Phthiotic Achaea and Thessaly. Not satisfied with ingratiating himself only with those cities he was going to pass through, he also sent around ambassadors and letters asking that memories of the quarrels with his father be forgotten (for these had not been so heated that they could not and should not come to an end with him); indeed they could start with an entirely clean slate and pursue friendly relations with every confidence.

Above all, he was looking for a way to win back the favour of the Achaeans. **23.** Only this people, out of all the Greeks, and the Athenians,* had reached such a point of animosity that they had sealed their borders to Macedonians. As a result, Macedonia was a refuge for any slaves fleeing from Achaea: as long as their borders were closed to Macedonians, the Achaeans did not themselves dare to cross the frontiers of the Macedonians' kingdom. Once Perseus had noticed this, he apprehended the slaves and <. . .> a letter * with a warning that it was the Achaeans' responsibility to devise a way to prevent a similar exodus of slaves in the future.

When this letter was read out by the praetor Xenarchus (who was looking for an opportunity to gain the king's personal gratitude), it was generally considered to have been written in a restrained and well-intentioned way, especially by those who were, against all hope, about to regain their renegade slaves. But Callicrates, who belonged to the group that thought their well-being as a people depended on respecting their treaty with the Romans, spoke as follows:

'To some, Achaeans, the matter at issue seems trifling or not terribly significant; for my part, I think that not only are we dealing with a most serious and weighty matter, but in some sense we have already dealt with it. For we, who had closed our borders to the kings of Macedonia and even the Macedonian people, and we, who know that this decree remains in order not to admit envoys and messengers of the king, who might change some minds among us, we are listening to the king, who is thus practically pleading his case in our midst, even though he isn't even here, and—heaven help us—we are responding with approval!

'Further, while wild animals generally shun food set out to entrap them and run away, we, on the contrary, blinded at the sight of a minuscule advantage, are enticed to eat, and for the hope of retrieving some pathetic slaves of minimal value, we allow our freedom to be sapped and undermined. For who does not see that the king seeks a road to alliance with us and that it will be the ruination of our treaty with the Romans, the very treaty on which our entire existence depends? Or is there anyone who cannot tell that war between the Romans and Perseus is inevitable? Expected in Philip's lifetime and postponed by his death, it will come to pass now that he is dead.

'Philip, as you know, had two sons, Demetrius and Perseus. Demetrius was far the superior because of his maternal ancestry, his virtue, his character, and his popularity among the Macedonians. But Philip, having decided to dispose of his kingdom as if it were a prize for hating the Romans, killed Demetrius simply for being on friendly terms with them. Knowing that Perseus would embark on war with the Romans practically before taking up his inheritance, Philip made Perseus his successor.

'And so what has Perseus done since his father's death other than prepare for war? First, to the consternation of all, he sent the Bastarnae against the Dardani: for if they had taken over that territory, they would have proved more dangerous neighbours for Greece than the Gauls* were for Asia. Deprived of this hope, he still did not abandon his warmongering plans but, if we are to tell the truth, he has already begun the war. He forcibly subdued the Dolopes, ignoring their pleas to submit their disagreements to the Roman people for arbitration. Then he crossed Oeta so that he could suddenly materialize in the very heart of Greece, and he made his way up to Delphi. How do you interpret this assertion of the right to take a little-used route? Next he swept through Thessaly: since he did this without harming any of those he hated, I fear it all the more as an attempt to win people over. Then he sent a letter to us under the semblance of a favour, and directs us to contrive a way to avoid the need for this favour in the future—that is to say that we should repeal the decree that excludes Macedonians from the Peloponnese. Let us once again see royal ambassadors and hospitality shared between our leaders, and soon the Macedonian army, and Perseus crossing from Delphi to the Peloponnese—for how wide is the strait between? Let us intermingle ourselves with the Macedonians as they arm themselves against the Romans.

'My opinion is that we should make no new decision; everything should stay as it is until it is definitely established whether this concern of mine is justified or empty. If the peace between the Macedonians and the Romans persists, we too may enter into diplomatic and commercial relations; but for the time being, to come to a decision in this matter seems risky and premature.'

24. After Callicrates, Archo, the brother of Xenarchus the praetor, spoke as follows:

'Callicrates has made speaking difficult for me and everyone who disagrees with him: for by arguing the case of the Roman alliance himself, by saying it is being assailed and attacked—though no one is assailing or attacking it—he causes anyone who disagrees with him to seem to be speaking against the Romans. First of all, just as if he had not been here with us, but was coming from the Curia of the Roman people or was present at the innermost councils of the king, he knows everything and reports what took place in secret. He even divines what would have happened had Philip lived, why Perseus inherited the kingdom as he did, what the Macedonians have in hand, and what the Romans are thinking. But we, who have no idea why or how Demetrius died, nor what Philip would have done had he lived, we must base our plans on what is happening openly.

'And we know that Perseus was recognized as king by the Roman people when he inherited the kingdom; we hear that Roman envoys went to King Perseus, and that he welcomed them warmly. I consider all these things indeed to be indicators of peace, not war; nor do I think the Romans can be offended if we imitate them as purveyors of peace just as we followed them into war. For I do not see why we alone of all people should wage war relentlessly against the kingdom of Macedonia. Are we vulnerable because of our very proximity to Macedonia? Or are we so terribly feeble, like those Dolopes whom he recently subdued? On the contrary, thanks to the gods, we are protected in these matters by our own strength and our distant location. But suppose that we are as exposed to danger as the Thessalians and the Aetolians; have we no more credit and weight with the Romans, we who were always their allies and friends, than the Aetolians, who were their enemies only a little while ago? Whatever the legal bond between the Macedonians and the Aetolians, the Thracians, the Epirotes—in short, all the rest of Greece—let us enjoy the same. Why should this execrable collapse, as it were, of human ties be unique to us? Suppose Philip's behaviour did prompt us to outlaw him when he was armed and engaged in war: why does Perseus, a new king, innocent of any wrongdoing, reversing his father's enmities with his own generosity, deserve that we alone of all peoples should be his enemies?

'And I could have said this too, that previous Macedonian kings performed so many good services for us that they eclipse the wrongful conduct of Philip, if by chance there was any—especially after his death. You remember that when the Roman fleet was at Cenchreae and the consul at Elatia with his army, we spent three days in a meeting, discussing whether we would side with the Romans or Philip.* Even if the imminent danger from the Romans did not sway our judgement, there was certainly something that made our deliberations so lengthy, and this was our long-standing association with the Macedonians as well as the considerable favours of their kings of old. Let these same factors prevail even now, not so that we become their allies especially, but so that we are not especially their enemies either.

'And let us not pretend, Callicrates, that something is under discussion when it isn't. No one advocates drawing up a new alliance or treaty that might rashly place us under an obligation, but only that we show reciprocity in legal matters, and not bar our people and ourselves from their kingdom by refusing them access to our territory; in that way our slaves would have no place of refuge. How is this in contravention of the treaty with the Romans? Why do we make a small and open matter of public business into something huge and suspicious? Why do we provoke needless hysteria? Why must we render others suspect and odious in order to have our own opportunity to humour the Romans? If there is a war, Perseus can have no doubt that we will follow the Romans; as long as there is peace, let our animosities be put aside, even if they are not resolved.'

Although this speech pleased the same men who had been favourably inclined to the king's letter, the decision was postponed because the leaders were insulted that Perseus should achieve with a brief letter something that he had not considered worthy of an official embassy.

Subsequently the king did send ambassadors, when the Achaeans were meeting at Megalopolis, but those who feared offending the Romans were careful not to allow the ambassadors into the meeting.

25. In this same period the senselessly destructive passion of the Aetolians turned against itself, and it seemed that mutual slaughter had brought them to the brink of genocide. But then exhaustion set in; and the two parties sent envoys to Rome and began negotiations between themselves to restore harmony. Then a new outrage intervened and stirred up the old hatred again. Eupolemus, a leading citizen, had given his word of honour in guaranteeing a safe return home to eighty distinguished men of Proxenus' faction, who were in exile from Hypata. When they returned, Eupolemus came out with a crowd to greet them, and there was a warm reception and handshakes all around; once within the gates, however, the men were cut down, calling to no avail on Eupolemus' word of honour and the gods who witnessed it. Then the war burst into violent flames all over again.

The Senate dispatched Gaius Valerius Laevinus, Appius Claudius Pulcher, Gaius Memmius, Marcus Popillius, and Lucius Canuleius. They went to Delphi where delegates from both sides presented their positions in a heated debate. Proxenus appeared to prevail, both for his case and for his eloquence. A few days later he was poisoned by his wife Orthobula, who was convicted and exiled.

The Cretans were in the grips of the same kind of insane rage when, with the arrival of Quintus Minucius, the envoy from Rome who had been sent with ten ships to settle their conflicts, they achieved some hope of peace. But the truce was for a mere six months, at which point the war flared up all the more violently. Also at this time the Lycians were being harassed by the Rhodians. But there is no point in tracing in detail the internal fighting of foreigners, exactly what happened and how, when there is more than enough labour involved in setting down the history of the Roman people.*

26. In Spain, the Celtiberi, who had surrendered to Tiberius Gracchus after he defeated them in battle, had remained peaceful while the province was under the governance of the praetor Marcus Titinius; but they rebelled when Appius Claudius arrived. They started the conflict with a surprise attack on the Roman camp. It was just dawn, and the guards were at their posts along the wall and at the watchtowers of the gates. The moment they spotted the enemy approaching in the distance, they gave the call to arms. Appius Claudius had the signal for

battle raised, encouraged the soldiers with a brief speech, and launched the attack from all three gates simultaneously. The Celtiberi blocked their exit, and at first the battle was even on both sides since not all the Romans could fight in the narrow spaces of the passageways. But then, despite jostling one another, as they crossed beyond the wall, they were able to spread out their line of battle and draw up level with the wings of the enemy line that was encircling them. They charged forward so suddenly that the Celtiberi could not sustain the onslaught. They were driven back before the second hour;* about 15,000 men were killed or captured, and thirty-two standards seized. Their camp was taken, and the war was over that day, for the survivors slipped away to their own towns. Then they submitted quietly to Roman control.

27. The censors elected that year, Quintus Fulvius Flaccus and Aulus Postumius Albinus, conducted a review of the Senate. Marcus Aemilius Lepidus, the pontifex maximus, was chosen as the leader of the Senate; and nine men were expelled. Of these the most noteworthy were Marcus Cornelius Maluginensis, who had been a praetor in Spain two years earlier, Lucius Cornelius Scipio, who was the peregrine praetor at the time, and Lucius Fulvius, the censor's full brother and, according to Valerius Antias,* his partner in the management of their patrimony.

The consuls made their vows on the Capitol and set out for their provinces. To one of them, Marcus Aemilius,* the Senate gave the task of suppressing an uprising among the people of Patavium* in Venetia; envoys of these people had reported that factional strife had flared up into civil war. The envoys who had gone to Aetolia to suppress similar disturbances announced that there was no way to contain the people's insanity. The consul's arrival was the salvation of the people of Patavium, and since he had nothing else to do in his province, he returned to Rome.

The censors were the very first to give contracts for paving the streets of Rome with flint and for spreading roads outside the city with gravel and edging them, as well as for building bridges in many places. The censors gave a contract also for providing the aediles and praetors with a stage for theatrical performances. And they gave out contracts for starting gates in the Circus, egg-shaped markers* for enumerating the laps, posts for the turning point, and iron cages through which the wild beasts could be released. <. . .>* for the consuls for festivals on the Alban Mount. Further, they oversaw the paving with flint of the ascent from the Forum to the Capitoline, as well as the construction of a colonnade from the temple of Saturn to the Capitoline as far as the *senaculum** and then right on up to the Curia;* and they paved the marketplace outside the Trigemina Gate with paving-stones and enclosed it with fencing. They also undertook repairs to the Aemilia colonnade, and they made a set of steps up from the Tiber to the market. Inside the Trigemina Gate they paved the road to the Aventine with flint, and they built a colonnade on Publicius street to the temple of Venus. They also gave out contracts for walls to be built around Calatia and Auximum; and they spent the income from the sale of public places on surrounding both forums with shops.

Of the two censors, Postumius announced that he would not give out contracts for anything other than what the Senate or Roman people ordered, but Fulvius Flaccus* used their money to have a temple of Jupiter built at Pisaurum and Fundi as well as an aqueduct at Potentia, and he paved with flint a road at Pisaurum. At Sinuessa he gave contracts for the installation of drains, the construction of a wall to encircle the town, and the enclosing of the forum with colonnades and shops; and he had three statues of Janus made. The colonists were extremely grateful to the one censor for these public works. It was also a rigorous and severe censorship as far as the regulation of morals was concerned: many men lost their equestrian status.

28. When the year was almost at an end, there was a one-day supplication for the successful conduct of affairs in Spain, under the leadership and auspices of the proconsul Appius Claudius; and twenty full-grown victims were sacrificed. Also, on another day, there was a supplication at the temple of Ceres, Liber, and Libera because word had come from Sabine territory that a powerful earthquake had destroyed many buildings.

When Appius Claudius returned to Rome from Spain, the Senate decreed that he should have an ovation upon his entry to the city. The consular elections were already drawing near, and the competition was fierce because many men pursued the office, but Lucius Postumius Albinus and Marcus Popillius Laenas were elected. Next the praetors were chosen: Numerius Fabius Buteo, Gaius Matienus, Gaius Cicereius, and, for the second time, Marcus Furius Crassipes, Aulus Atilius Serranus, and Gaius Cluvius Saxula. Once the elections were over, Appius Claudius Centho celebrated his ovation over the Celtiberi upon his entry into the city. He had 10,000 pounds of silver and 5,000 pounds of gold carried to the public treasury. Gnaeus Cornelius was installed as *flamen Dialis*.

That same year a tablet was set up in the temple of Mater Matuta with the following inscription: 'Under the command and auspices of Tiberius Sempronius Gracchus a legion and an army of the Roman people subjugated Sardinia. More than 80,000 of the enemy were captured or killed in that province. Once his public charge had been successfully carried out, the allies liberated, and taxes reinstituted, he brought home his army, safe, sound, and liberally supplied with booty. He entered the city of Rome in a triumph for a second time. For this reason he has dedicated this stone tablet as an offering to Jupiter.' On the tablet were a map of the island of Sardinia and pictures of the battles.

There were several other small gladiatorial shows that year, but Titus Flamininus' stood out from the rest; because of his father's death he gave one lasting four days and including a banquet with a sacrificial feast and theatrical shows. The height of the entertainment, which was lavish for its time, was that seventy-four gladiators fought over the course of three days.

BOOK FORTY-TWO

1. When the consuls Lucius Postumius Albinus and Marcus Popillius Laenas brought the disposition of provinces and armies before the Senate, both men were assigned to Liguria. They were also directed to conscript troops: two new legions of Roman citizens apiece and 10,000 infantry and 600 cavalry from the Latin and Italian allies to use in governing their province, as well as reinforcements for Spain consisting of 3,000 Roman infantry and 200 cavalry. In addition, they were instructed to draft 1,500 Roman infantry and 100 cavalry for the praetor assigned to Sardinia; he was to take these and cross over to Corsica and conduct the military operations there. In the interim the former praetor, Marcus Atilius, would continue to govern Sardinia.

Then the praetors drew lots for their areas of responsibility: Aulus Atilius Serranus drew urban jurisdiction, and Gaius Cluvius Saxula jurisdiction involving Romans and foreigners; Numerius Fabius Buteo drew Nearer Spain, and Gaius Matienus Farther Spain; Marcus Furius Crassipes drew Sicily, and Gaius Cicereius Sardinia.

Before the magistrates set out for their provinces, the Senate agreed that the consul Lucius Postumius should go to Campania to establish boundaries between public and private land. It was well known that some individuals had gradually encroached on the former and were now treating it as their own.*

Postumius had a grudge against the citizens of Praeneste* for not having honoured him publicly or privately when he had gone as a private citizen to sacrifice at their temple of Fortuna. So before he set out from Rome, he sent a dispatch to Praeneste: the chief magistrate was to meet him along the way, to provide, at public expense, a place for him to stay, and to supply pack animals upon his departure. Before this consul, no one was ever an expense or a burden to the allies in any way.* Magistrates were supplied with pack animals and tents and all other military equipment expressly so that they would not make such demands on the allies. They did partake of private hospitality, which they cultivated readily and graciously; and they hosted at Rome the people who customarily lodged them when they were on the road.* Envoys on emergency business might require a single mule from the towns through which they had to travel, but the allies incurred no other cost because of Roman magistrates. Even if the consul's wrath was justified, he should not have vented it during his magistracy. At the same time, the passivity of the Praenestini, whether born of too much restraint or too much fear, in effect gave Roman magistrates the right to make increasingly burdensome demands, as if this precedent conferred legitimacy on them.

2. At the beginning of this year, the ambassadors who had been sent to Aetolia and Macedonia* reported that they had not been able to meet with Perseus: they had been told by some people that he was away while others claimed with equal falsity that he was ill. Just the same, it had been readily apparent that preparations for war were under way and that the king would no longer postpone recourse to arms. Also, factional strife among the Aetolians was intensifying by the day, and the ambassadors had not been able to use their authority to bring to heel the instigators of the dissension.

With war against Macedonia on the horizon, it was decided to expiate all prodigies and to use the prayers prescribed in the oracular books to seek reconciliation with the gods before hostilities could begin. It was reported that at Lanuvium a vision of an enormous fleet had been seen in the heavens, and at Privernum dark-coloured wool had sprouted from the ground; at Remens in the Veientine district there had been a shower of stones; the whole of the Pomptine area had been enveloped in clouds—so to speak—of locusts; and ploughing anywhere in the Gallic territory had turned up fish in the freshly dug soil. These were the prodigies for which the oracular books were consulted. The decemvirs decreed which victims should be offered to which gods. Their decree further called for a supplication to expiate the prodigies, and another prayer (following the one of the previous year) for the health of the people, and a festival. These ceremonies took place in accordance with the decemvirs' written instructions.

3. It was this year also that the temple of Juno Lacinia was stripped of its roof. Quintus Fulvius Flaccus, the censor, was building a temple for Fortuna Equestris that he had vowed* when fighting against the Celtiberi during his praetorship in Spain. Driven by competitive zeal, he wanted his temple to be larger and more magnificent than any other in Rome. Thinking that marble roof-tiles would be a great adornment to the temple, he went to Bruttium and stripped the temple of Juno Lacinia of half its roof—calculating that this would suffice to cover the one he was constructing. The ships for loading

and transporting the tiles were standing by, and his authority as censor deterred the terrified allies from preventing the sacrilege.

When Fulvius returned to Rome, the tiles were unloaded from the ships and carried to the temple. Despite the silence surrounding their origin, it could not be kept secret. There was an uproar in the Curia, and on all sides the cry went out that the consuls should bring the matter before the Senate for a formal discussion. When the censor responded to the summons to the Curia, one and all attacked him to his face with greater venom for thinking that the only proper way to desecrate the most sacred temple in the area—one which neither Pyrrhus nor Hannibal* had desecrated—was to strip the roof and leave the temple practically ruined. Fulvius had removed the tiles and left the untiled sub-roof open to the eroding force of the rain. And this was a man who had been appointed censor to regulate others' conduct? He had been charged to enforce the maintenance of public shrines and to <. . .> places that were supposed to be protected in accordance with ancestral custom? Fulvius, the one who wandered about the towns of the allies, ruining their temples and exposing the sub-roofs of sacred buildings? Treating the allies' homes in this fashion would be outrage enough, but he was wrecking temples of the immortal gods! Building temples from the ruins of temples, he brought sacrilege on the Roman people—as if the immortal gods were not the same everywhere, as if it were right for some to be worshipped and honoured with the spoils of others!

Although the sentiments of the senators were apparent before the matter was put to a vote, when it was they voted unanimously that the roof-tiles should be taken back and reinstalled and that sacrifices should be offered to appease Juno. The religious ceremony was carried out carefully; but the contractors who returned the tiles reported that they had been left in the temple precinct since no artisan could devise a way to reattach them.

4. Among the praetors who had departed for provinces abroad Numerius Fabius died at Massilia, while travelling to Nearer Spain. When messengers from Massilia brought the news, the Senate decided that his predecessors, Publius Furius and Gnaeus Servilius, should determine by lot which of them would stay on in Spain with an extended command. The fortunate outcome of the lot was that Publius Furius, who had been in charge of the province previously, remained there.

That same year the Senate decreed that the land captured in Ligurian and Gallic territory should be divided up into individual plots since much of it was unoccupied. In accordance with the Senate's decree, the urban praetor, Aulus Atilius, appointed a commission of ten men: Marcus Aemilius Lepidus, Gaius Cassius, Titus Aebutius Parrus, Gaius Tremellius, Publius Cornelius Cethegus, Quintus and Lucius Appuleius, Marcus Caecilius, Gaius Salonius, and Gaius Munatius. They distributed ten *iugera* to each citizen and three *iugera* to the Latin allies.

At the same time these matters were going on, there arrived at Rome ambassadors from Aetolia with news of internal quarrels and upheaval, and ambassadors from Thessaly bringing word about events in Macedonia.

5. Perseus was turning over in his mind the war that Philip had planned before his death. By sending embassies and making promises (without actually acting on them), Perseus was ingratiating himself with all the Greek peoples and cities. Moreover, a large segment of the population was sympathetic to him. In fact, they tended to prefer him to Eumenes, although all the cities of Greece and most of the leading men were bound to Eumenes by his gifts and benefactions, and he ruled in such a way that the cities under his control did not wish to exchange their position for that of any free state.

Perseus, by contrast, was rumoured to have killed his wife with his own hand after the death of his father; further, as for Apelles,* once he had been Perseus' confederate in the assassination of his brother, and for that reason Philip sought to bring him to justice. Apelles went into exile, but was summoned back after Philip's death and promised great rewards for having done such a deed; then Perseus secretly had him killed. Besides, although Perseus was notorious for many assassinations, of both Macedonians and foreigners, and lacked any commendable quality, the cities generally favoured him over King Eumenes, who was pious to his relatives, just to his subjects, and generous to all. They may have been swayed by the reputation and grandeur of the Macedonian kings and scorned the newly created kingdom,* or perhaps they desired a change of circumstances, or perhaps they did not wish to become subject to the Romans.

The Aetolians, moreover, were not the only ones in internal conflict because of a crushing weight of debt; the case was the same with the Thessalians.* And this evil, like a contagious disease, had also spread to Perrhaebia. When it was reported that the Thessalians were in arms, the Senate sent Appius Claudius as an envoy to assess the situation and resolve it. First he rebuked the leaders of both sides. Then, with the acquiescence of the creditors, who had encumbered their loans with unfair interest rates, he reduced the debt load and made the legally owed amount payable in instalments over ten years. Appius also resolved the problems in Perrhaebia in the same way. Meanwhile, at Delphi, Marcus Marcellus listened to the arguments of the Aetolians, who argued as fiercely as they had engaged in civil war. Perceiving that the two parties were well matched in reckless- ness and effrontery, he was not inclined to issue a decree to lessen or increase the burden for either side; rather, he sought from both that they stop fighting, resolve their quarrels, and then put the whole matter behind them. Confidence in the reconciliation was strength- ened on both sides by an exchange of hostages; by mutual agreement these were to be kept at Corinth.

6. After the conference with the Aetolians at Delphi, Marcellus crossed to Aegium in the Peloponnese where he had convened a meet- ing with the Achaeans. After commending them for holding fast to their old decree banning the Macedonian kings from crossing their borders, he emphasized the Romans' hatred of Perseus. Wishing to fan the flames of this, Eumenes came to Rome, bringing with him a report he had com- piled from an investigation into Perseus' military preparations. At the same time five ambassadors were sent to the king to assess the state of affairs in Macedonia. The same men were directed to go on to see Ptolemy in Alexandria and renew the alliance with him. These ambas- sadors were Gaius Valerius, Gnaeus Lutatius Cerco, Quintus Baebius Sulca, Marcus Cornelius Mammula, and Marcus Caecilius Denter.

Around the same time ambassadors came from King Antiochus. Their leader, one Apollonius, was granted an audience with the Senate. He gave many valid reasons for the king's tardy payment of tribute,* and he explained that he had brought all of it with him so that the king need be granted no special treatment other than the grace- period. Moreover, he had also brought a gift of gold vases weighing 500 pounds; the king sought, he said, to renew for himself the alliance and treaty that had existed with his father and to request the Roman people to ask of him whatever should be required of a king who was a good and loyal ally; he would stop at nothing in the execution of his duty. During Antiochus' stay in Rome,* Apollonius added, the

Senate had treated him so honourably and the young men with such kindness that in all levels of society he had been regarded as a king and not a hostage.

The embassy was favourably received, and the urban praetor Aulus Atilius was directed to renew with Antiochus the alliance that had been in effect with his father. The urban quaestors accepted the tribute, and the censors took the gold vases, which they were charged with placing in whichever temples they thought appropriate. The ambassador was sent a gift of 100,000 *asses*,* and he was granted a house without rent where he could be a guest, with his expenses taken care of while he remained in Italy. (The envoys who had been in Syria had announced that he was highly esteemed by the king and most favourably disposed to the Roman people.)

7. The provincial activities of the year were as follows. Gaius Cicereius, the praetor in Corsica,* fought a pitched battle in which 7,000 Corsicans were killed and more than 1,700 captured. During the battle the praetor vowed a temple to Juno Moneta. The Corsicans subsequently sued for peace and were assessed 200,000 pounds of wax. Having subjugated Corsica, Cicereius crossed over to Sardinia.

Fighting also took place in Liguria outside Carystus, a town in the territory of the Statellates where a large army of Ligures had gathered. When the consul Marcus Popillius first approached, they stayed within the walls, but once they perceived that the Roman was about to attack the town, they marched out and drew up their battle line before the gates. This had been the consul's aim in threatening the assault, and he began it immediately. The battle went on for more than three hours with no prospect of victory on either side. When the consul realized that the Ligurian standards were holding on every front, he ordered the cavalry to mount and make a simultaneous three-pronged push to create maximum chaos. A sizeable group of horsemen forced back the middle of the line and drove behind the ranks. Then, thrown into panic, the Ligures turned and fled in every direction. The Roman cavalry had concentrated on blocking the route into the town, and only a very few Ligures slipped through. Many of them had been killed in the lengthy battle, and others were cut down in the random retreat. The reported totals are 10,000 killed, more than 700 captured, and eighty-two battle standards seized. Nor was it a bloodless victory: the Romans lost over 3,000 soldiers since those in the front lines had fallen when both sides were refusing to yield.

8. After the battle the Ligures who had scattered in flight regrouped and surrendered. They recognized that their casualties outnumbered the survivors: no more than 10,000 men remained. In fact they did not negotiate at all, hoping rather that the consul would not treat them any more savagely than previous commanders had. But he stripped them all of their weapons, destroyed their town, and sold them and their belongings. Then he sent a letter to the Senate reporting on his accomplishments.

The other consul, Postumius, had become utterly immersed in the investigation of landownership in Campania, and so the praetor Aulus Atilius read Popillius' letter out in the Curia. The Senate was appalled: the Statellates, the only Ligurian tribe that had not taken up arms against the Romans, had been attacked when they were not themselves starting a war; afterwards, when they entrusted themselves to the good faith of the Roman people, they had been tortured and killed with the most extreme cruelty; thousands upon thousands of innocent people had been sold into slavery even as they invoked the good faith of the Romans. The worst possible precedent had been set, a warning against anyone ever again daring to surrender. These peaceable people had been dispersed here and there as slaves to men who had recently been Rome's real enemies.

For all these reasons the Senate agreed that the consul Marcus Popillius should give back the money he had received for the Ligures and liberate them, and that he should undertake to restore their property, to the extent that he was able to retrieve it. Their weapons were to be returned, and these steps were to be taken at the very first opportunity. Further, the consul was not to leave his province until he had re-established in their own homes the Ligures who had voluntarily surrendered. The consul was additionally reminded that a victory acquired glory from the defeat of aggressors, not from abuse of the crushed.*

9. The consul exhibited the same intemperate rage in defying the Senate as he had in his savagery towards the Ligures. He immediately sent his legions into winter quarters at Pisa and returned to Rome, angry at the senators and furious with the praetor. He summoned the Senate at once to a meeting in the temple of Bellona, where he attacked the praetor at length: Atilius ought to have brought a motion before the Senate to honour the immortal gods officially for a great military accomplishment; instead, he had initiated a senatorial decree

against the consul and in favour of the enemy; thus had Popillius' victory been handed to the Ligures, to whom Atilius, a praetor, had practically ordered the consul to surrender himself. So Popillius was fining the praetor and demanding that the senators revoke the decree passed against him and order a thanksgiving. This they ought to have voted upon in his absence when he had sent the letter about what he had done for the commonwealth. They ought to do it now, primarily to honour the gods but also to indicate at least a modicum of respect for him.

Several senators rebuked him as harshly as they had in his absence, and he returned to his province having achieved neither aim.

The other consul, Postumius, spent the summer investigating landownership and returned to Rome for the elections without even having seen his province. He presided over the selection of Gaius Popillius Laenas and Publius Aelius Ligus as consuls. The praetors then chosen were Gaius Licinius Crassus, Marcus Junius Pennus, Spurius Lucretius, Spurius Cluvius, Gnaeus Sicinius (for the second time), and Gaius Memmius.

10. A *lustrum* was conducted that year. The censors were Quintus Fulvius Flaccus and Aulus Postumius Albinus; the latter conducted it. The number of Roman citizens was 269,015. The reduced total reflected the consul Lucius Postumius' public declaration that the Latin allies who had been obliged, in accordance with Gaius Claudius' decree,* to return to their own cities be counted there and not in Rome. The census was conducted harmoniously and to the benefit of the common good.* The censors ranked as *aerarii* and removed from their voting tribe all those whom they demoted from the Senate or stripped of equestrian status; and neither censor vetoed a decision of the other to demote someone. Fulvius dedicated the temple of Fortuna Equestris seven years after he had vowed it while fighting the Celtiberi in Spain as a proconsul, and he put on theatrical shows for four days, with another day in the Circus.

That year Lucius Cornelius Lentulus, the decemvir for sacred rites, died, and Aulus Postumius Albinus was appointed in his place. An unexpected infestation of locusts came in such numbers from the sea that their swarms smothered the fields of Apulia. The incoming praetor, Gnaeus Sicinius, was specially empowered to go there to free the crops of this plague; even after a large group of men was mustered, it took him rather a long time to remove the insects.

The beginning of the following year, in which Gaius Popillius and Publius Aelius were consuls, was taken up with residual conflicts from the previous year. The senators wished to discuss the Ligurian situation again and to renew the resolution they had passed in response to it; accordingly, the consul Aelius brought the matter before them. Popillius pleaded with both his colleague and the Senate on behalf of his brother, stating openly that he would veto any decree against the latter. His colleague was deterred, but the senators stood their course all the more, now equally opposed to both consuls. And so when the subject of the provinces arose and Macedonia seemed desirable because of the impending war with Perseus, both consuls were instead appointed to Liguria: the senators refused to assign Macedonia unless the matter of Marcus Popillius was put before them. Furthermore, the consuls' requests for permission to recruit new armies or to reinforce the old were both rejected. Reinforcements were also denied to the praetors who were seeking them for Spain (Marcus Junius for Nearer Spain and Spurius Lucretius for Farther Spain). Gaius Licinius Crassus had drawn urban jurisdiction and Gnaeus Sicinius jurisdiction involving foreigners. Gaius Memmius drew Sicily, and Spurius Cluvius Sardinia. The consuls, enraged at the Senate's decisions, set the Latin Festival for the first possible day and announced that they were on the verge of departing for their province and would conduct no public business other than what pertained to the administration of the provinces.

11. According to Valerius Antias, during this consulship King Eumenes' brother Attalus came to Rome as an ambassador to lay charges against Perseus and to disclose his preparations for war. The annals of most historians* and especially those whom you would prefer to believe report that Eumenes himself came. So, when Eumenes arrived in Rome, he was received with great honour, because people considered this treatment consistent with his own merits as well as with the innumerable favours that had been heaped upon him. The praetor brought him before the Senate where he explained that his reason for coming to Rome—beyond a desire to see the gods and men whose generosity had placed him in circumstances beyond his most impossible dreams—had been to forewarn the Senate lest Perseus' enterprises proceed unimpeded.

Consequently, Eumenes related first Philip's schemes: Perseus' brother Demetrius, who had opposed attacking Rome, had been murdered; the Bastarnae, who could assist in the crossing to Italy, had been roused from their homes. Death had caught up with Philip while he was contemplating this project, and he had left his kingdom to the person whom he had perceived to be the most hostile to the Romans. Thus it was that Perseus inherited not just the monarchy but also the war his father had left behind, and for a long time now his every thought had been revolving around nurturing and fostering it.

Macedonia, Eumenes went on to say, was full of young men, the fruit of the long peace, and Perseus' resources were at their peak. He too was in the prime of life: his body was strong and vigorous, and his mind deeply familiar with age-old theoretical and practical aspects of warfare. Already as a boy he had shared his father's tent, and the latter had sent him on many different missions, not just in border conflicts, but even in the war against Rome. So, from the time when he had inherited the kingdom he had achieved with remarkable success many objectives that had eluded Philip, though the latter had tried every form of force and cunning alike. Perseus' power had accrued the kind of authority that results from numerous important benefactions over a long period of time.

12. Indeed, Eumenes said, all the Greek and Asian cities held Perseus' majesty in awe. Eumenes himself could not see which favours or what generosity had achieved such regard for Perseus, nor say for certain whether he obtained it through good fortune or, reluctant as Eumenes was to suggest it, whether resentment of the Romans enhanced Perseus' popularity. Even among kings Perseus' standing was remarkable. Not as the wooer but as the wooed had he married the daughter of Seleucus; and he had given his sister in marriage to Prusias in response to earnest appeals from the latter. Both weddings were celebrated with felicitations and gifts from countless delegations, and the most prominent peoples joined the processions to lend their blessing.

Philip, Eumenes said, had sought to win over the Boeotians, but they could never be induced to sign a treaty of alliance with him; now their treaty with Perseus was inscribed on stone in three places, one at Thebes, the second at Dium in its extremely holy and renowned temple, and the third at Delphi. Indeed, unless a few men at the council of the Achaeans had held out the threat of Roman force, the matter of Perseus' entrée to Achaea would have been nearly assured. But by Hercules, as for the honours these people had conferred on

Eumenes—and it was difficult to say whether his public or personal services to them were the greater—some of these had lapsed through disregard and neglect, while others had been eliminated out of hostility. Was there anyone now, Eumenes asked, who did not know that during their internal conflict the Aetolians had turned to Perseus instead of the Romans? And though he could rely on these friendships and alliances, Perseus had made such preparations for war at home that he did not need outsiders. He would not need provisions from his own or enemy territory because he had amassed enough food to support 30,000 infantry and 5,000 cavalry for ten years. His finances were such that in addition to the Macedonian forces he had pay ready for 10,000 mercenaries also for ten years, and this did not include the annual revenue from the royal mines. In his armouries he had accumulated weaponry for three such armies. And should Macedonia prove lacking, he had at his disposal the youth of Thrace, which he could draw upon as if from a spring that never runs dry.

13. The rest of Eumenes' address was an exhortation:

'I am not tossing around rumours of doubtful veracity in presenting this information to you, conscript fathers; nor do I believe it more readily because I would prefer accusations made against a personal enemy of mine to be true. On the contrary, they have been investigated and thoroughly looked into, just as if you had dispatched me as a spy and I were reporting on matters I had seen with my own eyes. Nor would I have abandoned my kingdom, which owes its greatness and distinction to you, to cross a vast expanse of water in order to discredit myself by reporting groundless stories. Rather, I have observed the most brilliant cities of Asia and Greece revealing their intentions more and more as each day passes; should this be allowed to continue, they will reach the point of no return and no repentance. I have also observed that Perseus is not restricting himself to Macedonia: some places he has taken by force and others, which could resist his physical might, he has enfolded in embraces of partiality and benevolence.

'I saw too the disparity of circumstance: as he pursued war with you, you held out the security of peace to him (though it certainly seemed to me that he was not just preparing for war but virtually waging it). Abrupolis,* your friend and ally, he expelled from his kingdom; Arthetaurus* the Illyrian, another friend and ally of yours, Perseus had killed because he learned of messages Arthetaurus sent you; the Thebans Eversa and Callicritus* also, leaders of their city, he had eliminated for having denounced him rather freely in the Boeotians' council, saying that they would report to you what was transpiring. He aided the Byzantines in violation of your treaty; he attacked the Dolopes; intending to use the lower orders to destroy their betters in a civil war, he brought his army into Thessaly and Doris. In Thessaly and Perrhaebia, he disrupted everything and created universal confusion by feeding the expectation that debts would be cancelled; his purpose was to crush the aristocrats with men who would then be personally indebted to him. Since he did these things while you stood by and did not interfere, and since he perceives that you have conceded Greece to him, he takes for granted that he will encounter no armed opposition before he crosses into Italy. You will judge just how safe and honourable this is for you; for my part I thought it positively shameful that Perseus should reach Italy in arms before I, your ally, could do so to warn you. Now that I have fulfilled my duty and in some sense have released myself from my obligation, what more can I do than beseech the gods and goddesses that you take thought for yourselves and your state and us, your allies and friends, who depend on you?'

14. This speech disturbed the conscript fathers. At the time, however, the Curia had been veiled in such silence that no one knew anything except that the king had been there. Only when the war was finally over did the king's words and the reply leak out.

A few days later Perseus' ambassadors were granted a meeting with the Senate, but the ears and thoughts of the latter had already been pre-empted by Eumenes' words. The ambassadors' excuses and entreaties were totally rejected. Especially grating was the arrogance of Harpalus, the leader of the embassy. He said that the king yearned and strove to be believed when he pleaded that he had never said or done anything with hostile intent; at the same time, if he should detect a relentless hunt for a motive for war, he would defend himself with a bold spirit. War was an impartial business, Harpalus ended, and its outcome never certain.

Every city in Greece and Asia was deeply concerned about what Perseus' envoys and Eumenes had said in the Senate. Eumenes' arrival prompted the majority of them to send their own envoys, ostensibly for other reasons, but with the thought that his presence would precipitate a change of one kind or another. The leader of the

Rhodians' embassy was hot-tempered and not about to promote fal-
sities as true. He was convinced that Eumenes had implicated their
city in his accusations against Perseus, and so, relying on his host and
patrons, he tried every possible means to get a chance to debate the
king in the Senate. Having failed to gain his object, he inveighed
against the king in an uncontrolled and reckless speech: Eumenes
had stirred up the Lycians against the Rhodians and been more
burdensome than Antiochus to Asia. Although popular in appeal and
not displeasing to the common people of Asia (where Perseus' popularity had also spread), the speech was anathema to the Senate and
disadvantageous to the Rhodian and his city. In fact, the general
hostility towards Eumenes enhanced the Romans' partiality for him;
they decorated him with every honour and showered him with
magnificent gifts, including a curule chair and an ivory staff.*

15. The moment the embassies were dismissed Harpalus rushed
hastily back to Macedonia to inform the king that he had left the
Romans not yet actually marshalling for war but so antagonistic that
obviously there would be no further delay. Perseus himself, aside
from the fact that he was expecting this to happen, now actively
desired it since he believed he was at the height of his power.

He detested Eumenes above all others. Choosing him as the first
casualty of the war, Perseus arranged his assassination at the hands
of one of the allied commanders, a Cretan named Evander, and three
Macedonians who were used to this kind of dirty work. Perseus gave
them a letter of introduction to his guest-friend Praxo, an important
and wealthy woman at Delphi. It was generally known that Eumenes
was on his way up there to sacrifice to Apollo. Having arrived ahead
of him, Evander and the conspirators scouted the area thoroughly in
search of a suitable location for the execution of their task. Along the
ascent to the temple from Cirrha, before one reaches the part that is
more crowded with buildings, on the left there was a stone wall along
the path, which was almost flush with the base of the wall, and
passers-by had to go in single file; on the right-hand side an earthslide
had created a steep slope of some height. The assassins concealed
themselves behind the wall, where they had built up steps so that they
could attack Eumenes as if from a rampart when he approached.

A crowd of friends and attendants surrounded Eumenes as he
began the climb from the sea, but the narrow passageway eventually
thinned them into a column. When they reached the point where

it was necessary to go in single file, a prominent Aetolian named Pantaleon, with whom the king had started a conversation, led the way along the path. At that moment the assassins jumped up and sent two huge boulders rolling down. One struck the king in the head and the other in the shoulder; knocked unconscious, Eumenes slipped off the path and down the slope and lay collapsed under a heap of rocks. The rest of the friends and attendants, seeing him fall, took flight, but Pantaleon courageously stayed behind to protect him.

16. The brigands could have easily slipped around the wall and rushed down to finish off the wounded king, but instead they fled to the top of Mount Parnassus as if they had completed their task. Their pace was such that when one of them had difficulty following the steep, pathless flight and slowed down the escape, his comrades killed him to prevent his being captured and exposing the plot.*

As for the king, his friends, followed by his attendants and slaves, came running back to his body. When they lifted him, they realized from the warmth of his body and his breathing that he was alive, though still senseless and stunned from the blow. Hope of survival was minimal, practically non-existent. Some of the attendants pursued the tracks of the assassins, but after an exhausting climb to the top of Parnassus they returned empty-handed. The Macedonians had undertaken the enterprise with as much careful thought as audacity, but they abandoned it in a careless and craven manner.

The king had already recovered his senses the very next day, and his friends transferred him to a ship. They sailed to Corinth, where the ship was dragged across the neck of the Isthmus,* and continued over to Aegina.* There he was nursed in such secrecy and seclusion that a rumour that he had died made its way to Asia. His brother Attalus accepted the report with more haste than was compatible with true brotherly feeling and addressed Eumenes' wife and the head of the palace guard as if he had indisputably inherited the kingdom. This came to Eumenes' attention later on, and although he had initially decided to dissemble and keep it quiet, at their first meeting he did not refrain from accusing his brother of courting his wife with unseemly speed.* The rumour about Eumenes' death reached Rome as well.

17. About the same time Gaius Valerius came back from Greece. He was the envoy who had gone to investigate the conditions in that region and to look into King Perseus' plans. Everything he reported concurred with the charges levelled by Eumenes. He had also

brought back with him Praxo from Delphi, whose house had sheltered the assassins, and Lucius Rammius of Brundisium, who disclosed the following information. Rammius was a leading citizen of Brundisium who was accustomed to hosting all the Roman generals and their envoys, as well as important foreigners, especially those associated with kings. That had been the origin of his acquaintance with Perseus, whom he had not then met directly. Lured by a letter that promised closer ties and consequently enormous wealth, he went to visit the king. Rammius rapidly began to be considered an intimate and to be drawn deeper than he wished into secret conversations. For the king promised great rewards and then started asking him—since all those Roman generals and envoys routinely availed themselves of Rammius' hospitality—to undertake to poison any of them Perseus instructed him to. Perseus knew that the preparation of poison involved much trouble and risk, that many people would necessarily be involved, and that the results were unpredictable: the poison might or might not be powerful enough to do its job; it might or might not safely escape detection. But he said he would supply some that would not leave a trace during or after its administration. Rammius was terrified that if he refused, he might be the first to have the poison tested on him, so he promised to do it and left for Brundisium. He did not wish to return there before making contact with Gaius Valerius, who was reported to be near Chalcis. Having first disclosed the plot to Valerius, Rammius then accompanied him to Rome at his behest. Rammius was admitted to the Senate and revealed what had happened.

18. This information, on top of what Eumenes had said, hastened the decision to declare Perseus a public enemy: they could see that he was not just preparing war with the mind of a king, but that he was proceeding with all the underhanded and criminal activities of assassins and poisoners.

The conduct of the war was referred to the new consuls; for the time being, however, the decision was made that the praetor Gnaeus Sicinius, who had jurisdiction involving Romans and foreigners, should recruit soldiers to be marched to Brundisium at the very first opportunity so that they could be taken across to Apollonia in Epirus to occupy the coastal cities. There, whichever consul was allotted Macedonia would be able to put in safely with the fleet and conveniently disembark his troops.

Eumenes was detained for a considerable time at Aegina by his recuperation, which was fraught with difficulty. He set out for Pergamum as soon as it was safe and prepared for war with the utmost energy, for the recent attack had reinvigorated his old hatred of Perseus. Ambassadors from Rome went to him there to offer congratulations on his escape from such grave danger.

As the Macedonian war had been postponed for a year, when the rest of the praetors had already set out for their provinces, Marcus Junius and Spurius Lucretius, who had been assigned to Spain, went on importuning the Senate with the same petition. Finally they succeeded in obtaining reinforcements for their armies: they were directed to conscript 3,000 infantry and 150 cavalry for the Roman legions, and the allies were to supply 5,000 infantry and 300 cavalry for their troops. This force was transported to Spain along with the new praetors.

19. That same year, after the consul Postumius' investigation had recovered for the state a considerable amount of Campanian territory which private individuals had appropriated as their own, Marcus Lucretius, a tribune of the plebs, proposed a law that the censors should rent out this land for cultivation. Because this had not been done in all the many years since the fall of Capua, the greed of private citizens had been let loose on the unregistered territory.

Though there had not yet been a formal declaration of war, nevertheless the decision had been made, and the Senate was waiting to see which of the kings would side with them and which with Perseus. At this juncture ambassadors from King Ariarathes* came to Rome bringing with them the king's young son. They said that the king had sent his son to Rome to be educated so that from boyhood on he would be familiar with the Romans and their customs; the king sought their willingness not just to put him in the care of personal friends but also to treat him as a public charge, as if he were a ward of the state.* The embassy pleased the Senate, and it was decided that the praetor Gnaeus Sicinius should give a contract for the furnishing of a house where the king's son and his companions could live.

Ambassadors from some of the Thracian tribes were granted the official alliance and friendship that they had come for, as well as a gift of 2,000 *asses* each. The formation of an alliance with these people in particular caused general rejoicing since Thrace lay to the rear of Macedonia. At the same time, however, in order to explore the state of affairs in Asia and the islands, Tiberius Claudius Nero and Marcus Decimius were dispatched as envoys with orders to go to Crete and Rhodes, where they could simultaneously renew alliances and observe whether Perseus had been meddling with the allies' state of mind.

20. On a stormy night, while the city was taut with suspense because of the impending war, a bolt of lightning struck and destroyed the *columna rostrata*;* it had been set up on the Capitoline during the First Punic War to commemorate the victory of the consul Marcus Aemilius (the one whose colleague was Servius Fulvius). This event was regarded as a portent and reported to the Senate. The senators ordered the matter to be referred to the *haruspices* and also directed the decemvirs to consult the sacred books. The decemvirs proclaimed that the city had to undergo a ceremonial cleansing, that a supplication and public appeal to the gods were necessary, and that there should be a sacrifice with full-grown victims both at Rome on the Capitoline and in Campania on the promontory of Minerva; in addition, there should be a ten-day festival for Jupiter Optimus Maximus as soon as possible. All these procedures were carefully carried out. The *haruspices* answered that the divine sign would turn out to be for the good and that it portended territorial expansion and the death of enemies since the ships' prows knocked over by the storm had been enemy spoils. Other events combined to heighten the atmosphere of superstition: it had been announced that at Saturnia it had rained blood in the town centre for three days in a row; at Calatia a donkey was born with three legs, and a bull and five cows had been killed by a single stroke of lightning; at Auximum it had rained earth. In response to these prodigies too, divine rites were performed, there was a one-day supplication, and a holiday was observed.

21. The consuls still had not departed for their province, because they would not comply with the Senate's desire to discuss Marcus Popillius and the senators in turn had resolved not to make decisions about anything else first. Resentment towards Popillius was further increased by his dispatches reporting that in his capacity as proconsul he had fought the Ligurian Statellates again and had killed 6,000 of them. This unjustified act of war drove the rest of the Ligures to arms. So then a protest was launched in the Senate, not just against the absent Marcus Popillius who, in contravention of human and divine law, had made war on people who had surrendered and had driven peaceful people to rebellion, but also against the consuls, who had not gone to their province. Prompted by the unanimous reaction of the senators, two tribunes of the plebs, Marcus Marcius Sermo and Quintus Marcius Scylla, warned that they would fine the consuls unless they went to their province. They also read out in the Senate the motion they intended to promulgate with respect to the defeated Ligures. It prescribed that if any one of the defeated Statellates had not been restored to freedom by the first of August next, the Senate was on oath to appoint someone to investigate the matter and punish whoever had been responsible for this malicious enslavement. Once they had the backing of the Senate, the tribunes promulgated their motion.

Before the consuls left, Gaius Cicereius, who had been a praetor the year before, was granted an audience with the Senate in the temple of Bellona. He recounted what he had accomplished in Corsica. When his request for a triumph was denied, he held one on the Alban Mount, which had become the customary ceremony in the absence of public authorization. The plebs approved and voted almost unanimously for the Marcian motion about the Ligures. In accordance with the plebiscite the praetor Gaius Licinius asked the Senate who it wished to conduct the investigation specified by the resolution; the senators directed him to undertake it himself.

22. Then at last the consuls set out for their province and took over the army from Marcus Popillius. He, however, dared not to return to Rome because he might have to stand trial, in the face of the Senate's hostility and the even greater animosity of the general population, before the praetor who had referred to the Senate the investigation now threatened against him. The tribunes of the plebs countered Popillius' recalcitrance with the announcement of a second motion to the effect that if he did not come back to the city before the thirteenth of November, Gaius Licinius would judge and sentence him in his absence. Thus ensnared, Popillius returned to Rome and entered the Senate amidst a sea of resentment. There, many people lambasted him viciously, and the Senate passed a decree that the praetors Gaius Licinius and Gnaeus Sicinius should have responsibility for liberating those Ligures who had not been in arms after the consulship of Quintus Fulvius and Lucius Manlius,* and that the consul Gaius Popillius should give them land on the other side of the Po. In accordance with this decree many thousands of men were freed, taken across the Po, and given land. In accordance with the Marcian resolution, Marcus Popillius stood trial before Gaius Licinius for two days. On the third day, the praetor, succumbing to the influence of the absent consul and the entreaties of Popillius' family, ordered the defendant to return on the fifteenth of March. On that day new magistrates would take up their duties, and Licinius would return to private life and not have to pass judgement. With this deceitful manoeuvre he evaded the resolution about the Ligures.

23. Ambassadors from Carthage and Masinissa's son Gulussa were in Rome at this time, and they had a heated argument at a meeting of the Senate. The Carthaginians' complaint was that Masinissa, in addition to the land investigated on the spot by the envoys earlier sent from Rome, had forcibly taken possession of more than seventy towns and strongholds in Carthaginian territory in the past two years. He had done this lightly, free from scruples. The Carthaginians said too that they were bound by their treaty and did not retaliate; they were forbidden to bear arms outside their territory; although they knew that fending off Numidian incursions would not take them outside their own territory, they were deterred by a clause of the treaty that was crystal clear: they were expressly forbidden to wage war with the allies of the Roman people. But now the Carthaginians could no longer endure Masinissa's arrogance, cruelty, and greed. The ambassadors said that they had been sent to beseech the Senate to grant them one of three things: either that the Senate establish, on equal terms between the allied king and their people, what belonged to each; or that the Carthaginians might be allowed to engage in limited, defensive warfare against unfair attacks; or finally, if political favouritism mattered more than the truth to the Senate, that they might establish once and for all what they wished to give Masinissa from other people's territory. While Masinissa would make no boundary except at the caprice of his own pleasure, no doubt the senators would be less open-handed, and the Carthaginians themselves would know exactly what had been given away. If the Carthaginians could obtain none of these objects, if they had committed some injury since the treaty established by Publius Scipio,* then let the Romans themselves exact the punishment. They preferred the security of Roman domination to a freedom vulnerable to Masinissa's assaults: ultimately, they said, they preferred to die rather than to draw breath only at the whim of a viciously savage butcher. With tears forming as they spoke, the ambassadors prostrated themselves

and, thus crouched on the ground, they roused pity for themselves and antagonism towards the king in equal measure.

24. The Senate decided to ask Gulussa for his response to the Carthaginians, unless he preferred to explain first what business had brought him to Rome. Gulussa replied that it was difficult for him to discuss matters on which he had no instructions from his father; nor would it have been easy for his father to issue such instructions since the Carthaginians had not announced what they intended to do or even that they were going to Rome at all. Their leaders had held clandestine meetings for several nights in the temple of Aesculapius, and no information had leaked out except that ambassadors were being sent to Rome with secret instructions. This was the reason his father had sent him to Rome—to entreat the Senate not to accept accusations made against Masinissa by their mutual enemies, who hated Masinissa solely for his unwavering fidelity to the Roman people.

When both sides had been heard out and the Senate was asked for a judgement on the Carthaginian demands, the following response was resolved upon: it was agreed that Gulussa should set out for Numidia immediately and tell his father both to send envoys as quickly as possible to the Senate to reply to the Carthaginians' complaints and to alert the Carthaginians to come to Rome to dispute the issue. The senators said that they had acted and would act out of respect for Masinissa in whatever other matters they could; but that partiality would not substitute for justice. They wished everyone to keep possession of what was rightfully his and intended not to create new boundaries but rather to respect the old ones: they had granted to the defeated Carthaginians both their city and their lands, but not permission to seize unlawfully in peacetime what they had not taken by right of war. The prince and the Carthaginians were then sent away. According to custom, gifts were conferred on both parties, and they were also courteously treated to other traditional forms of hospitality.

25. This same period saw the return of Gnaeus Servilius Caepio, Appius Claudius Centho, and Titus Annius Luscus, the envoys who had been sent to Macedonia to demand reparations and renounce the alliance with the king. Their systematic report of what they had heard and observed further enflamed the Senate, which was already fuming against Perseus of its own accord. The envoys had seen for themselves that mobilization was proceeding at full strength in every Macedonian town. When they had reached the king, they had been denied access to him day after day; in the end, they gave up hope of talking with him and left. Then at last, while already en route, they were recalled and brought to see him. The essence of their remarks to him had been that a treaty had been struck with Philip and renewed with Perseus after his father's death; according to it he was expressly forbidden to bear arms beyond the borders of his kingdom and to attack allies of the Roman people. The envoys next laid out what they had recently heard when Eumenes presented all his well-corroborated findings in the Senate. To these they added the secret meetings at Samothrace that the king had held for many days with delegations from the cities of Asia. In conclusion, the envoys gave the Senate's opinion that by all rights satisfaction should be given for these violations and that anything Perseus held in contravention of the treaty should be returned to the Romans and their allies.

The king's immediate reaction was rage, and he spoke with intemperate fury, accusing the Romans of greed and arrogance and ranting that embassy after embassy came to spy on his words and deeds because, in the Romans' view of what was right, he was supposed to talk and act completely in accordance with their imperial whims; finally, after a long, shrill tirade, he had told the envoys to come back the next day as he wished to give them his response in writing. The document they subsequently received went as follows: the treaty made with his father had nothing to do with him; he had suffered its renewal not because it had met with his official approval but because upon first inheriting the kingdom he had been in no position to reject anything. If they wished to make a fresh treaty with him, they ought first to agree on its terms. If they could accept that the treaty must be based on equality, he would see what it entailed for him, and he imagined that the Romans would consult their public interest. At this point Perseus had started to sweep out, and there had been a move to clear everyone from the palace. So then the envoys had renounced the friendship and the alliance. Perseus, infuriated by this announcement, had stopped short and declared to them in ringing tones that they had three days to get themselves out of his kingdom. And so they left him, having met with no civility or hospitality during their stay or upon their departure.*

After the subsequent audience with the Thessalian and Aetolian envoys, the Senate sent a message to the consuls: the Senate wished whichever of the consuls was available to come to Rome and hold the elections so that the senators could know as soon as possible which leaders would next be at the disposal of the state.

26. The consuls of that year engaged in no public activities worthy of record;* it had seemed more beneficial to the general welfare that the Ligures, now thoroughly outraged, should be brought under control and appeased.

While the Macedonian war was still pending, envoys from Issa* brought under suspicion the Illyrian king Gentius also, simultaneously complaining that he had ravaged their borders and reporting that the Macedonian and Illyrian kings were of one mind: by common consent they were mustering for war against Rome, and the Illyrians in Rome under the guise of an embassy were actually spies sent by Perseus to discover what was going on. The Illyrians were summoned before the Senate. When they said that they had been sent by their king to defend any charges that the Issaei might bring against him, they were asked why they had not then presented themselves to a magistrate; in this way they might receive lodging and entertainment, as was customary, and their presence and the purpose of their visit might be known. When they fumbled for an answer, they were directed to leave the Curia, and it was agreed not to grant them an official reply, such as genuine envoys received, since they had not sought an audience with the Senate. The senators decided to send envoys to the king to report the allies' complaints to him and the fact that the Senate did not think it right for him to inflict harm on Roman allies. Aulus Terentius Varro, Gaius Plaetorius, and Gaius Cicereius were dispatched on this mission.

The envoys who had been sent to make the circuit of allied kings returned from Asia and reported that they had met with Eumenes in Aegina, Antiochus in Syria, and Ptolemy in Alexandria. All three had been solicited by delegations from Perseus, but remained steadfast in their loyalty, and promised to deliver everything the Roman people asked of them. The envoys had also visited the allied cities and found them generally loyal, except for the Rhodians, who were wavering, infected with Perseus' scheming. Rhodian ambassadors had come to defend their city against the rumours they knew were being bandied about. The Senate, however, refused to grant them a hearing until the new consuls had entered their magistracies.

27. The senators resolved not to postpone mobilization. The praetor Gaius Licinius was assigned the task of refitting and equipping

for use fifty ships from the old quinqueremes in the dockyards at
Rome. If it was not possible to reach this total, he should write to his
colleague Gaius Memmius in Sicily to refit and prepare for action the
ships there in order to send them to Brundisium at the very first
opportunity. For twenty-five of the ships the praetor Gaius Licinius
was ordered to recruit crews of Roman citizens of freedmen status;
Gnaeus Sicinius was to muster from among the Latin and Italian
allies the same size crews for the other twenty-five. The latter praetor was also to requisition 8,000 infantry and 400 cavalry from the
Latin and Italian allies. Aulus Atilius Serranus, who had been a praetor the year before, was selected to take charge of this force at
Brundisium and conduct it to Macedonia. In order for the praetor
Gaius Sicinius to have the army ready for the crossing, the praetor
Gaius Licinius wrote, by order of the Senate, to the consul Gaius
Popillius that he should order both the second legion, which was the
most experienced in Liguria, and 4,000 infantry and 200 cavalry
from the Latin and Italian allies to be at Brundisium by the thirteenth of February. Gnaeus Sicinius was ordered to contain the
situation in Macedonia with this fleet and army until his successor
should arrive, and his authority was extended for the year.

Everything the Senate voted on was carried out vigorously.
Thirty-eight quinqueremes were brought out of the dockyards;
Lucius Porcius Licinius was put in charge of conducting them to
Brundisium. Twelve were sent from Sicily. Three envoys—Sextus
Digitius, Titus Juventius, and Marcus Caecilius—were sent to Apulia
and Calabria to buy grain for the fleet and the army. Gnaeus Sicinius
assumed military attire and left Rome for Brundisium where every-
thing was in readiness.

28. Towards the end of the year the consul Gaius Popillius
returned to Rome. He was rather later than the Senate had recom-
mended; the idea had been that with such a serious war pending, it
would be in the public interest if the magistrates were elected at the
very first opportunity. And so the Senate was by no means a sympathetic audience when the consul described in the temple of Bellona
his actions in Liguria. There were frequent shouts of disapproval as
well as questions as to why he had not freed the Ligures who had
been victimized by his brother's wickedness.

The consular elections were held on the eighteenth of February,
as had been announced. Publius Licinius Crassus and Gaius Cassius

Longinus were elected as consuls. The next day the praetors were chosen: Gaius Sulpicius Galba, Lucius Furius Philus, Lucius Canuleius Dives, Gaius Lucretius Gallus, Gaius Caninius Rebilus, and Lucius Villius Annalis. They were given for their areas of responsibility the two juristic positions in Rome, Spain, Sicily, and Sardinia; one man's duties thus remained unspecified and left to the Senate's discretion.

The Senate directed the incoming consuls, on the day they entered office, to make appropriate sacrifices with full-grown victims and to pray for a successful conclusion to the war that the Roman people intended to wage. The Senate decreed on the same day that the consul, Gaius Popillius, should vow ten days of games to Jupiter Optimus Maximus as well as gifts at all the sacred couches, if the Republic should remain in the same condition for ten years. Thus, in accordance with this decree, the consul gave his oath on the Capitol for the holding of games and the distribution of gifts, at whatever cost the Senate chose, provided that at least 150 senators were in attendance at the time.* This vow was made with Lepidus, the pontifex maximus, pronouncing the formulaic prayer.

Two public priests died that year: Lucius Aemilius Papus, a decemvir for sacrifices, and Quintus Fulvius Flaccus, the pontifex who had been censor the year before. This man came to a shameful end.* Of his two sons, who were fighting in Illyricum at the time, it was reported that one had died, and the other was dangerously ill with a serious disease. Grief and fear combined to overwhelm Fulvius' mind; the next morning, upon entering the bedroom, the household slaves found him dangling from a noose. It was the received opinion that he was less than sane after his censorship; the general belief was that an enraged Juno Lacinia had driven him mad for violating her temple. The decemvir appointed in Aemilius' place was Marcus Valerius Messalla; and Gnaeus Domitius Ahenobarbus, an exceptionally young man for a priesthood, was appointed to replace Fulvius.

29. During the consulship of Publius Licinius and Gaius Cassius not just the city of Rome, nor the Italian peninsula, but every king and city in Europe and Asia had become preoccupied with the war between the Macedonians and the Romans. Eumenes was motivated not just by his long-standing hatred, but also by the fresh cause for anger: Perseus' villainy at Delphi had nearly caused him to be slaughtered like a sacrificial animal. Prusias, king of Bithynia, had decided to stay neutral and await the outcome, for he concluded that

the Romans could not think it right for him to take up arms against his brother-in-law, and if Perseus should win, his sister could arrange for him to be pardoned. Ariarathes, the Cappadocian king, aside from the fact that he had pledged auxiliary troops to the Romans in his own name, had shared strategy with Eumenes in all matters concerning war and peace ever since they had become related by marriage.

Antiochus, it is true, had designs on Egypt, having a low opinion of the king's youth and his guardians' lack of initiative; he thought that by provoking a quarrel over Coele Syria,* he could furnish himself with grounds for war, and that he could wage it without interference since the Romans would be busy with their own war against the Macedonians. Even so, both through a delegation of his own men to the Senate and in person to the Senate's envoys, he had gone to great lengths in pledging everything for that war. Ptolemy still had guardians at the time because of his youth, and they prepared for the war against Antiochus to maintain the claim to Coele Syria while simultaneously promising the Romans everything regarding the Macedonian war.

Masinissa assisted the Romans with grain and undertook to send his son Misacenes and auxiliaries with elephants to join the fight. At the same time, he arranged his plans to suit every possible outcome: if the Romans should win, his standing with them would remain the same and he would not attempt further incursions since the Romans would not permit any aggression against the Carthaginians; if the might of Rome—which was shielding the Carthaginians—should be crushed, then all Africa would be his. The Illyrian king Gentius had certainly managed to make the Romans mistrust him, but he had not determined which side he would support, and it seemed likely that some impulse, rather than careful thought, would attach him to one side or the other. Cotys the Thracian, king of the Odrysae, was on the side of Macedonia.

30. Such were the sentiments of the various kings towards the war. Of the autonomous communities and peoples, almost everywhere the masses favoured the less desirable elements—as is generally the case— and tended to side with Macedonia and its king. Among the more important citizens you might observe a range of positions. Some people had been so effusive towards the Romans that their boundless partisanship undermined their credibility; a few of these were attracted by the justice of Roman rule, but most calculated that a display of dedication would promote their position in their own cities.

Other people fawned on the king: dire financial straits and the hopelessness of their own affairs should there be no change drove some men headlong into any new enterprise; and some capricious spirits turned to Perseus because the wind of popularity was blowing his way. A third group, the best and most thoughtful, preferred to be under Roman rule rather than that of the king, if it were simply a case of picking the more powerful master; given a choice of destinies, however, they wished that neither side would topple the other and emerge on top, but rather that each might maintain its strength and thus yield a lasting peace through a balance of power. For the cities, poised between Rome and Macedonia, this arrangement would be the best set of circumstances since one power would constantly protect the weak from the aggression of the other. Those who felt this way observed silently and safely from afar the rivalries among the supporters of the two sides.

In accordance with the Senate's decree, on the day they entered office the consuls made offerings of full-size victims around all the shrines where there was customarily a *lectisternium* for the better part of the year.* Having concluded from the omens that the gods were pleased with the offerings, they reported to the Senate that the sacrifices and prayers pertaining to the war had been properly performed. The *haruspices* responded that any new undertaking embarked on should be hastened: victory, a triumph, the expansion of the empire lay in the portents. The senators, offering a prayer for the prosperity and good fortune of the Roman people, directed the consuls to assemble the Roman people in the *comitia centuriata** on the first possible day and to put to them the following: whereas Perseus, the son of Philip and the king of Macedonia, had attacked allies of the Roman people, in contravention of the treaty made with Philip and renewed with Perseus after Philip's death, whereas he had devastated lands and occupied cities, and whereas he had entered into plans to prepare war against the Roman people, readying weapons, an army, and a fleet to this end, unless he should give satisfaction for these actions, they would go to war with him. This motion was brought to the people.

31. Then the Senate decreed that the consuls should either settle between themselves or determine by lot which of them was to have Italy as his province and which Macedonia. The one responsible for Macedonia was to prosecute the war against Perseus and his followers

if they refused to give satisfaction to the Roman people. It was agreed
that four new legions should be enrolled, two for each of the consuls.
Special arrangements were made for Macedonia. While in keeping
with established practice, the other consul would have 5,200 infantry
assigned to each legion, for Macedonia 6,000 infantry and 300 cavalry were ordered to be enlisted for each legion. The second consul
was also to have additional forces from the allies: he was to take
to Macedonia 16,000 infantry and 800 cavalry in addition to the
600 cavalry Gnaeus Sicinius had taken there. For Italy, 12,000 allied
infantry and 600 cavalry seemed sufficient. Another special arrangement made for Macedonia involved the draft: the consul could enlist
as he pleased veteran centurions and soldiers up to the age of fifty.
The Macedonian war led that year to an innovation regarding the
military tribunes: by senatorial decree the consuls proposed to the
people that the military tribunes for the year not be chosen by popular
vote, but that the selection be left to the discretion and judgement of
the consuls and practors.

Among the practors, areas of command were divided in the following manner: the one whose lot it was to go wherever the Senate
decided was sent to the fleet at Brundisium to inspect the crews.
He was to dismiss men who appeared to be unfit, select freedmen as
substitutes, and see to it that there was a balance of two Roman citizens for every ally. It was further decided that the two practors who
drew Sicily and Sardinia should be charged with extracting a second
tithe from the islands so that the supplies for the fleet and the army
might come from them. This food was to be transported to the
troops in Macedonia. Gaius Caninius Rebilus drew Sicily, and
Lucius Furius Philus Sardinia. Lucius Canuleius Dives drew Spain.
Gaius Sulpicius Galba drew urban jurisdiction, and Lucius Villius
Annalis jurisdiction involving foreigners. Gaius Lucretius Gallus
drew the lot to remain at the Senate's disposal.

32. Between the consuls there was not so much a fully fledged
argument as some quibbling about the provinces. Cassius said that he
was prepared to claim Macedonia without any drawing of lots and
that his colleague could not draw lots without violating his oath. For
when Licinius had been a practor, in order to avoid going to his
province he had sworn publicly that there were sacrifices for him to
perform in a particular place on particular days and that these could
not be done properly in his absence.* In Cassius' view, these rites

could no more be done properly in Licinius' absence if he were a consul than if he were a praetor—unless of course the Senate decided to have a higher regard for Licinius' wishes as a consul than for his oath as a praetor; Cassius, however, would leave his fate in the hands of the Senate. After deliberating, the senators deemed it arrogant to deny a province to a man whom the Roman people had chosen to entrust with the consulship, and so they directed the consuls to draw lots. Macedonia fell to Publius Licinius and Italy to Gaius Cassius. Then the legions were assigned by lot: the first and third were to cross to Macedonia, the second and fourth to remain in Italy.

The consuls conducted the draft much more scrupulously than at other times. Licinius mustered veteran centurions and soldiers as well, and large numbers volunteered since they saw that those who had served in the earlier Macedonian war and against Antiochus in Asia had become wealthy men. Since the military tribunes were enrolling centurions in order of arrival rather than by experience,* twenty-three men who had held the position of chief centurion appealed to the tribunes of the plebs. Two from their college, Marcus Fulvius Nobilior and Marcus Claudius Marcellus, referred the matter to the consuls on the grounds that it should be investigated by the men who had been given responsibility for the levy and the war. The other tribunes said they themselves would look into the case of anyone who appealed and come to the aid of their fellow citizens if there were any injustice.

33. The inquiry took place in front of the official seats of the tribunes;* it was attended by Marcus Popillius as a consular representative for the centurions, the centurions, and the consul. The consul insisted on a public debate, and so a meeting of the people was convened. Marcus Popillius, who had been consul two years previously, spoke on behalf of the centurions in the following fashion. He said that these military men had honourably completed full terms of service and worn out their bodies with age and constant work; nevertheless, they were not at all unwilling to make their contribution for the state; their only request was not to be assigned to a rank lower than what they had held while on active service.

The consul Publius Licinius called for a public reading of the Senate's decrees: first, its vote for war against Perseus; second, the decision that as many veteran centurions as possible should be enlisted for this war and that there should be no exemption from military service for anyone under fifty. He then pleaded that in a new war, so close to Italy, against an unusually powerful king, the tribunes of the plebs should not hinder the military tribunes as they conducted the draft, nor prevent the consul from assigning each man to the position where he would be most useful to the state. If any of this was unclear, they should refer it to the Senate.

34. After the consul said what he had wanted to, Spurius Ligustinus, one of those who had appealed to the tribunes, asked the consuls and the tribunes for permission to say a few words to the crowd. When this was granted he spoke as follows:

'Citizens of Rome, I am Spurius Ligustinus, a Sabine by birth, of the Crustuminian tribe.* My father left me a *iugerum* of land and the small cottage in which I was born and brought up, and I live there to this day. As soon as I came of age, my father married me to the daughter of his brother. She brought nothing with her but her free-born status and her chastity, together with a fecundity sufficient for even a wealthy home. We have six sons, and two daughters, both of whom are already married. Four of my sons have assumed the *toga virilis*, and two wear the *toga praetexta*.*

'I became a soldier in the consulship of Publius Sulpicius and Gaius Aurelius.* As an ordinary infantryman in the army that was taken to Macedonia I served for two years against King Philip; in the third year, because of my bravery, Titus Quinctius Flamininus raised me to the rank of centurion of the tenth company of *hastati*.* When Philip and the Macedonians were defeated and we were brought back to Italy and discharged, I immediately set out for Spain as a volunteer with the consul Marcus Porcius.* Of all generals alive, he was a harsher critic and judge of personal courage, as men who have known him and other leaders, who have their own extensive military experience, acknowledge. This general considered me worthy of promotion to first centurion of the first company of the *hastati*. The third time when, again as a volunteer, I enlisted in the army sent against the Aetolians and King Antiochus, I was made first centurion of the *principes* by Manius Acilius. After King Antiochus had been driven out and the Aetolians subdued, we were brought back to Italy; and then I served twice when legions were called up for a year's campaigning. Then I fought twice in Spain, once with the praetor Quintus Fulvius Flaccus, and then again under the praetor Tiberius Sempronius Gracchus.* I was chosen by Flaccus to be among those who, because of their bravery, accompanied him from the province to participate in his triumph; I returned to the province at Tiberius Gracchus' request.

'Four times within a few years I was chief centurion; thirty-four times I was recognized by my generals for bravery; I have been awarded six civic crowns.* I have served twenty-two years in the army, and I am over fifty years old. But even if I had not served all these years and even if my age did not exempt me, it would still be fair to excuse me, Publius Licinius, since I can give you four soldiers to take my place.* But I prefer that you take these words as spoken for my case: I myself, as long as a recruiter judges me fit to fight, will never seek to exempt myself. The military tribunes have the power to place me at whatever rank they think fit; it is up to me to see that no one in the army outstrips me in courage: both my generals and my comrades stand as witnesses that I have always served in this fashion. You too, my fellow soldiers, though you act lawfully in exercising your right to appeal, still it is fitting that just as when you were young men you never challenged the authority of the magistrates and the Senate, now also you should submit to the power of the consuls and the Senate, and you should regard as an honour any way you can defend your country.'

35. After this speech the consul, Publius Licinius, showered Spurius with praise and brought him from the public meeting to the Senate. There the Senate also officially conferred its gratitude on him, and in recognition of his bravery, the military tribunes made him chief centurion of the first legion. The rest of the centurions withdrew their appeal and complied obediently with the draft.

The Latin Festival took place on the first of June so that the consuls could leave earlier for their provinces.* Once the ceremony was over, the praetor Gaius Lucretius left for Brundisium where everything necessary for the fleet had been sent in advance. In addition to the forces that the consuls were mustering, the praetor Gaius Sulpicius Galba had been entrusted with enlisting four city legions,* with the usual number of infantry and cavalry, and he was also supposed to select from the Senate four military tribunes to be the commanders. He was to order up 15,000 infantry and 1,200 cavalry from the Latin and Italian allies; this army was to be ready for deployment wherever the Senate should decide.

In response to a request from the consul Publius Licinius, his Roman and allied forces were augmented with auxiliaries: 2,000 Ligures,

Cretan archers—the exact number the Cretans supplied when asked for auxiliaries is uncertain—and also Numidian cavalry and elephants. Lucius Postumius Albinus, Quintus Terentius Culleo, and Gaius Aburius were sent to Masinissa and the Carthaginians to obtain these. It was agreed also that three envoys should go to Crete; these were Aulus Postumius Albinus, Gaius Decimius, and Aulus Licinius Nerva.

36. Also at this time envoys from King Perseus arrived.* The decision was made not to receive them within the city since the Senate had decided on war against the Macedonians and their king and the Roman people had ratified the decision. The envoys, brought before the Senate in the temple of Bellona, spoke as follows. King Perseus was wondering why forces had been sent to Macedonia; if he could convince the Senate to recall them, the king would, at the Senate's discretion, make amends for the commission of any injuries the allies complained about.

Spurius Carvilius had been sent back from Greece by Gnaeus Sicinius for this very purpose and was at the meeting of the Senate. He brought forward as accusations the hostile invasion of Perrhaebia, the conquest of several cities in Thessaly, and the other activities that the king was engaged in or was setting into motion.* The ambassadors were ordered to reply to these points. When they hesitated, claiming that they had not been empowered to handle anything else, they were told to report back to their king that the consul Publius Licinius would shortly be in Macedonia with his army; if the king intended to make reparations, he could send his envoys to Licinius. It was, moreover, pointless to send them to Rome, for none of them would be permitted to travel through Italy. With this the ambassadors were dismissed. The consul Publius Licinius was instructed to tell them to leave Italy within fifteen days and to send Spurius Carvilius to keep them under observation until they boarded ship.

These were the events at Rome before the consuls left for their provinces. Gaius Sicinius had been sent ahead to the fleet and troops at Brundisium before the expiration of his magistracy. Having conveyed 5,000 infantry and 300 cavalry to Epirus, he set up camp at Nymphaeum in the territory of Apollonia. From there he dispatched military tribunes with 2,000 soldiers to occupy the fortresses of the Dassaretii and the Illyrians since these people were seeking help in guarding themselves against an attack from their neighbours the Macedonians.

37. A few days later, Quintus Marcius, Aulus Atilius, Publius and Servius Cornelius Lentulus, and Lucius Decimius, the envoys sent to Greece, sailed to Corcyra with 1,000 soldiers. There they apportioned amongst themselves both the regions that each would visit and the troops. Decimius was sent to Gentius, the Illyrian king; if he discovered that Gentius had any regard for his friendship with the Roman people, his mission was to try in addition to coax him into a military alliance. The Lentuli were sent to Cephallania so that they could cross to the Peloponnese and make the rounds of the western coast before winter. Marcius and Atilius were assigned to travel around Epirus, Aetolia, and Thessaly; from there, they were to look into the situation in Boeotia and Euboea and then to cross to the Peloponnese. They agreed to rejoin the Lentuli there.

Before the envoys left Corcyra, a letter arrived from Perseus asking what could be the Romans' reason in coming to Greece or for occupying its cities. A formal written response seemed undesirable; instead, the messenger who had brought the letter was given a verbal reply to the effect that the Romans were acting to protect these cities.

The Lentuli made the circuit of the towns in the Peloponnese, encouraging all the communities, without distinction, to assist the Romans against Perseus with the same spirit and loyalty with which they had helped in the wars against first Philip and then Antiochus. The result was muttering amongst the crowds. The Achaeans were upset that although they had stood by the Romans in every way from the beginnings of the war with Macedonia and had fought against Philip and the Macedonians, their status was no higher than that of the Messenians and the Eleans, who had fought for Antiochus against the Roman people; and the Messenians and the Eleans, who had recently been incorporated into the Achaean League, were complaining that they were actually being handed over to the victorious Achaeans as spoils of war.*

38. Marcius and Atilius made their way up to Gitana, an Epirote city ten miles from the sea. At the meeting with the Epirotae, they were heard with great approval on all sides, and these people sent 400 of their young men to serve as a garrison for the Orestae,* who had been liberated from the Macedonians. The envoys continued on into Aetolia and waited there a few days until a successor was installed to replace the chief magistrate, who had recently died. Once Lyciscus, a man well known to favour the Roman side, took up his duties, the Romans moved on to Thessaly.

Representatives from the Acarnanians* and Boeotian exiles* came to them there. The Acarnanians were given a message to take home: this was their opportunity to atone for what they had done to the Roman people in the wars against Philip and Antiochus when they had been duped by the kings' promises; where they had once met with Roman forbearance when they little deserved it, they would now find generosity if they truly deserved it. The Boeotians were reproved for having made an alliance with Perseus. They cast the blame on Ismenias, the leader of the other faction, and said that some cities had been drawn into the matter against their will. Marcius replied that these circumstances would come out into the open because the Romans were about to grant each city autonomy.*

A council of the Thessalians took place at Larisa. On both sides there were abundant grounds for gratitude: the Thessalians were grateful for the gift of their freedom;* and the Roman envoys because the Thessalian people had assiduously rendered aid first in the war against Philip and then again in the war against Antiochus. After a reminder of shared service, the general population was eager to decide in favour of everything the Romans wanted.

After this meeting envoys from King Perseus came, private individuals relying particularly on the guest-friendship between Perseus' father and Marcius. The envoys started with a reminder of this relationship and requested that the king be given an opportunity to come and confer with Marcius. Marcius replied that he too had heard from his father of the bond of amity and of the guest-friendship with Philip,* indeed that he had undertaken this embassy with that relationship in mind. As for a conference, were his health sufficiently good, he would not have postponed it; so now, as soon as he could, the Romans would go to the Peneus river, at the crossing from Homolium to Dium, and messengers would be sent in advance to alert the king.

39. And so for the time being, because Marcius, in saying that he had undertaken the embassy on Perseus' behalf, had cast a faint whisper of hope in his direction, Perseus withdrew from Dium to the inner recesses of his kingdom. A few days later they met at the appointed place. A great retinue of his companions and attendants accompanied the king, crowding around him. The Roman ambassadors arrived with an equally large throng, composed of many escorts from Larisa as well as delegations from the cities; these people had

converged on Larisa and wished to report at home whatever trust-
worthy information they could glean. There was an innate element of
curiosity for ordinary mortals in witnessing a meeting between the
famous king and the representatives of the greatest people on earth.
When they stood within eyesight, separated by the river, there was a
brief delay for an exchange about which party should make the crossing. The royal party thought this was owed to the majesty of the
king; the Romans considered that it was, on the contrary, owed to the
name of the Roman people, especially since Perseus had requested
the conference. At last Marcius ended the delay with a joke, saying,
'Let the younger come to the elder,' and, because his *cognomen* was
Philip, 'Let the son come to the father.' The king was easily won over
by this. Then there was a second dispute as to the number of men
that should accompany him. The king thought that crossing with his
entire retinue was fair; the Roman ambassadors told him to come with
three men, or if he wished to bring such a throng, to give hostages to
prevent any trickery during the conference. So he handed over as
hostages Hippias and Pantauchus, his chief companions and the same
men whom he had sent as his ambassadors. The hostages had been
required less as a pledge of good faith than to show the allies that
the king was not meeting with the Roman ambassadors on an equal
footing. Nevertheless, the greeting was not antagonistic, but rather
cordial and welcoming; then they took the seats arranged for them.

40. After a brief silence Marcius said: 'I imagine that you expect
us to reply to the letter that you sent to Corcyra, in which you questioned why we came as we did, ambassadors accompanied by soldiers,
and why we are spreading garrisons among individual cities. I am
apprehensive both about not responding to your query, lest you
think this arrogance, and about telling the truth, lest when you hear
it, you think it excessively harsh. But since a reprimand, whether
physical or verbal, is justified when a person violates a treaty, just as
I would prefer war against you to be entrusted to someone other than
myself, so I will submit to the painful experience of saying unpalat-
able things to a guest-friend, no matter what; in the same way do
doctors apply bitter-tasting remedies to effect physical well-being.

'The Senate believes that ever since you inherited the throne, you
have only once acted as you ought to have done: you sent ambassadors to Rome to renew the treaty. And yet the Senate thinks that you
would have done better not to renew it at all rather than to do so only

to violate it. You expelled Abrupolis, a friend and ally of the Roman people, from his kingdom; by granting refuge to Arthetaurus' murderers after they had killed the king who was, of all the Illyrians, the Romans' most faithful adherent, you gave the impression—I won't put it more strongly than that—that you were pleased by his assassination; in contravention of the treaty, you went to Delphi with an army by way of Thessaly and Malian territory; also in contravention of the treaty you sent auxiliary forces to Byzantium; with the Boeotians, our allies, you struck a secret treaty under oath, which was not permitted; and I prefer to ask rather than to make an accusation about who killed the Theban envoys Eversa and Callicritus when they were on their way to us. Does it seem possible that the civil war and assassination of leading men in Aetolia could have arisen through agents other than yours? The Dolopes were wiped out by you personally. King Eumenes, when he was returning from Rome to his kingdom, was nearly slaughtered at Delphi, just like a sacrificial victim, in a holy area before the altar; I shrink from stating whom he blames; as for the secret crimes which your host at Brundisium has revealed—no doubt all has been described to you in letters from Rome and reported by your envoys as well. In one way only could you have prevented me from saying these things, and that is by not asking why our troops are being transported to Macedonia or why we are sending garrisons to the cities of our allies. Since you ask, I should have been more arrogant in keeping quiet than in telling you the truth. Indeed, because of the hospitality between our fathers, I am receptive to what you have to say, and I hope that you will supply me with some means of putting your case before the Senate.'

41. The king replied: 'I could make a good case if I were arguing it before impartial arbitrators, not men who are the accusers as well as the arbitrators. As for the charges made against me, however, some of them I think perhaps I should glory in, not blush to confess, and some, consisting of words, can be refuted by words. For what, if I were a defendant under your laws today, could either your Brundisian informant or King Eumenes charge me with such that they could represent themselves as accusers rather than muckrakers? No doubt Eumenes is on bad terms with no one other than me—even though he has made a burden of himself to so many men, whether in affairs of state or personal matters; and no doubt I could not find anyone more suited to be my accomplice in criminal activities than

Rammius, a man whom I had never seen before and was not to see afterwards. I am also supposed to account for the deaths of the Thebans who, all agree, were lost at sea, and of Arthetaurus for whom there is, however, no charge other than that his murderers went into exile in my kingdom. I will not mount a defence against this unfair argument as long as you also agree to accept responsibility for any crimes committed by men who have gone into exile in Italy or Rome. If you and everyone else in the world refuse to adopt this view, then I will count myself among the rest of you. And by Hercules, what good does it do to offer a man exile if there is no place for him to go into exile?* Nevertheless, as soon as I learned from your warning that those men were in Macedonia, I had them hunted down and ordered them to leave, forever banned from my kingdom.

'Those are the points on which I have actually been charged, as if I were defending myself in a criminal prosecution; but the following matters are brought against me as a king, and involve a difference of opinion over my treaty with you. For if the treaty was drawn up in such a way that I am not allowed to protect myself and my kingdom even if someone attacks me, I must confess that I violated the treaty in using force to defend myself against Abrupolis, an ally of the Roman people. But if, on the contrary, both the treaty and the principles of international law permit answering force with force, what then was it right for me to do, when Abrupolis laid waste to areas of my kingdom as far as Amphipolis, and carried off many free citizens, a large number of slaves, and many thousand cattle? Should I have kept quiet and been passive until, armed to the hilt, he made his way to Pella and right into my palace? Grant that I was justified in fighting,* was it somehow unacceptable that he was defeated and suffered everything else that befalls the defeated? When I, the person who was attacked, had to endure the consequences, how can he, the person who started the war, complain of what happened to him?

'I am not about to defend myself in the same way, Romans, for coercing the Dolopes into submission: even if they did not deserve it, I acted within my rights, since they were within my kingdom and my jurisdiction, assigned to my father by your decree. Moreover, if it were necessary to justify my situation not to you, and not to your allies, but to people who condemn the harsh and unjust exercise of power even over slaves, I would still not be considered to have vented my rage against them beyond what is reasonable and fair: given the way they

killed Euphranor, the governor I appointed for them, death was the
lightest of punishments for them.

42. 'But then when I had gone to visit Larisa and Antronae and
Pteleon, by a route near Delphi, I continued on up to Delphi to offer
sacrifices and release myself from vows made long ago. For the sake of
exaggerating my guilt, these circumstances have been linked with the
fact that I travelled with my army—as if I went to occupy cities and
install garrisons in their citadels, exactly the actions I now object to
your taking. Summon a meeting of the Greek cities through which
I passed; should anyone at all complain of an injury from one of my
soldiers, then shall I accept that I gave the impression of pretending to
offer sacrifice while pursuing another goal. I sent garrisons to the
Aetolians and the Byzantines, and I made a treaty of friendship with
the Boeotians. These activities, whatever their nature, my representatives not only announced, but repeatedly justified to your Senate,
where, Quintus Marcius, I have critics who are not so well inclined
towards me as you, my supporter and guest-friend by birth. But
Eumenes had not yet come to Rome to make his accusations; it was he
who made everything suspicious and odious by misrepresenting and
twisting it around; and it was he who attempted to persuade you that
Greece could not be free and enjoy your favour as long as the kingdom
of Macedonia remained secure in its position. But the wheel will come
full circle: soon someone will assert that the removal of Antiochus
beyond the Taurus Mountains was to no avail; that Eumenes is a much
greater threat to Asia than Antiochus was; that your allies will not be
able to sleep at night as long as the royal house of Pergamum stands;
its citadel sits in surveillance over the heads of the neighbouring states.

'Quintus Marcius and Aulus Atilius, I know that the things of which
you have accused me or against which I have defended myself will be
defined by the ears and thoughts of those listening, and that what matters is not what I did or to what end, but whatever view you take of it.
I know full well that I have not intentionally done anything wrong and
if, through a lapse of judgement, I have, I know that I can be set straight
and put on the right course by your reproaches. Certainly I have done
nothing irreparable, nor anything you could think necessitates the
forceful reprisals of war; or your reputation for clemency and upright-
ness has spread through the world to no purpose, if for reasons that
scarcely constitute grounds for grievance or complaint, you take up
arms and make war on kings who are your allies.'

43. Marcius listened to the king's speech with approval and proposed sending envoys to Rome. Since the king's friends also thought that every possibility should be tested to the fullest and that nothing that gave grounds for hope should be passed over, the rest of the conference concerned which route would be safe for the messengers. For this purpose, although the request for a truce seemed unavoidable under the circumstances and although Marcius had wanted and sought nothing else from the conference, he granted it in a grudging way, as if it were a great favour to the petitioner. For at the time the Romans had nothing—no army, no general—sufficiently prepared for the war while Perseus had everything completely ready and in order: had not the fruitless hope of peace blinded him, he could have commenced hostilities at a time entirely advantageous to him and inopportune for his enemies.

Pledges to honour the truce were exchanged, and the Roman embassy immediately left the conference and went to Boeotia. An uprising had recently begun there. Certain groups were seceding from the federation of the united league of Boeotians because the Roman ambassadors' response—that it would be clear exactly which peoples found the formation of an alliance with the king unacceptable—had been made public.* First envoys from Chaeronea and then some from Thebes met the Romans along the way, claiming that they had not been at the meeting when this alliance was voted on. Giving these envoys no immediate reply, the Romans directed them to follow along to Chalcis.

At Thebes, an enormous fracas had arisen from a different factional quarrel.* At the elections of the praetor and the boeotarchs, the defeated party, as revenge for the humiliation, got together a herd of voters and issued an order at Thebes barring the boeotarchs from the cities. These men all retreated into exile at Thespiae; they were readily taken in there, only to be recalled to Thebes once popular opinion changed. Back at Thebes, they decreed that a punishment of exile should be imposed on the twelve men who had convened the assembly and the council on their personal authority alone. Then the new praetor, Ismenias, an influential man from a noble family, condemned them to death after they had left. They had fled to Chalcis, and from there they had set out to meet the Romans at Larisa where they had accused Ismenias of being behind the alliance with Perseus. These party politics were the source of the fracas. Representatives from each party approached the Romans, the exiles and Ismenias' accusers on the one side and Ismenias himself on the other.

44. After their arrival in Chalcis, in a move that was extremely gratifying to the Romans, one by one leaders from the other cities issued proclamations rejecting the alliance with the king and attached themselves to the Romans; and Ismenias reached the decision that committing the Boeotian people as a whole to the Romans was the right course of action. This provoked a fight, and had he not escaped to the Roman ambassadors' headquarters, he would have been killed by the exiles and their supporters. Thebes itself, too, the principal city in Boeotia, was in a state of tremendous upheaval, with some tugging the city towards the king and others towards the Romans. Further, a crowd of Coronaei and Haliarti* had gathered there to defend the resolution to ally with the king. The steadfastness of their leaders, however, who kept pointing to the calamitous fates of Philip and Antiochus to illustrate the extent of the Romans' power and good fortune, finally overcame the common people, and they decreed that the alliance with the king should be abolished. They sent to Chalcis those who had supported making the alliance so that they could effect a reconciliation with the Roman embassy, and they directed that the city be entrusted to the good faith of the ambassadors. Marcius and Atilius listened to the Thebans with pleasure and advised both them and each of the other cities to send ambassadors to Rome to renew friendly relations. Above all, they ordered the exiles reinstated and issued their own decree condemning those who supported the alliance with the king. And so, having achieved their greatest desire, namely the dissolution of the Boeotian League, they set out for the Peloponnese after they had summoned Servius Cornelius to Chalcis.

An assembly was arranged for them at Argos, where they asked the Achaeans for nothing except a contribution of 1,000 soldiers. This garrison was sent to protect Chalcis while the Roman army was on its way to Greece. As winter set in, Marcius and Atilius returned to Rome with their mission accomplished.

45. Around the same time a delegation was dispatched from Rome to travel throughout Asia and the islands; the three ambassadors were Tiberius Claudius, Spurius Postumius, and Marcus Junius. They went around encouraging the allies to join the Romans in undertaking the war against Perseus. The wealthier the city, the more carefully the ambassadors proceeded, for the smaller ones tended to be influenced by the authority of the greater ones. The Rhodians were considered to be of the greatest importance in every way, since they could not simply support the war, but also promote it actively with their own resources. On the proposal of Agesilochus, they had forty ships prepared. When he was their chief magistrate—what they call the prytanis—he had persuaded the Rhodians with speech after speech to abandon the hope of supporting kings, which they knew from experience to be useless, and to keep the Roman alliance, the only one in the world at that time to be counted on for strength or reliability; war with Perseus was imminent; the Romans would require the same naval equipment that they had seen in the previous war against Philip and more recently Antiochus; unless the Rhodians themselves had already started to repair the ships and to fit them out with crews, they would have to rush about madly if the fleet suddenly had to be made ready and dispatched all at the same time; it was all the more important to act vigorously so that the irrefutable testimony of their actions could disprove the accusations brought by Eumenes. Roused by these speeches, the Rhodians displayed their fleet of forty ships, equipped and furnished, to the Romans when they arrived so that it was obvious that no exhortations were needed. This delegation did much to tip the balance when it came to winning over minds among the cities of Asia. Only Decimius, tainted with the suspicion of having taken bribes from the Illyrian kings,* went back to Rome without having achieved anything.

46. When Perseus returned to Macedonia after his conference with the Romans, he sent ambassadors to Rome to pursue the peace negotiations he had embarked on with Marcius. Also, he wrote letters to Byzantium, Rhodes, and other cities and gave them to envoys to deliver. The substance of the letters was the same for everybody: that he had spoken with the Romans' delegation; what had been said on both sides was presented in such a way as to make it seem that he had got the better in the debate. To the Rhodians, Perseus' envoys added their complete confidence that there would be peace, on the grounds that Marcius and Atilius had authorized the sending of ambassadors to Rome; if the Romans continued to stir up war in contravention of the treaty, then the Rhodians should strive, with all their influence and with every resource, to re-establish the peace; if they accomplished nothing by entreaty, they would have to act to

prevent the regulation and domination of the whole world from passing into the hands of a single people. This was advantageous for everyone else, but especially for the Rhodians inasmuch as they surpassed other cities in standing and resources; if everybody looked to the Romans alone, the Rhodians' assets would become subject to Roman control.

The warmth of the reception for the ambassadors' letter and speeches exceeded their weight in changing people's minds: the influence of the nobles' party had begun to prevail. The official response was that the Rhodians favoured peace: if there were a war, that the king should seek and expect nothing from the Rhodians that would sever the long-standing friendship between them and the Romans, forged by many great services in peace and war.

On the way back from Rhodes the envoys also went to the cities of Boeotia—Thebes,* Coronea, and Haliartus—thinking that these had been forced against their will to renounce the alliance with the king and attach themselves to the Romans. The Thebans did not yield an inch, although they were furious with the Romans for having condemned their leaders and having had the exiles recalled. The Coronaei and Haliarti, because of a certain inherent fondness for kings, sent envoys to Macedonia to request a garrison with which they could defend themselves against the Thebans' wanton arrogance. This delegation was told by the king that he could not send a garrison because of the truce he had made with the Romans; but he urged them to avenge the Thebans' transgressions in any way they could, provided that the Romans were not given reason to retaliate.

47. Upon their return to Rome, Marcius and Atilius made a formal report on their embassy on the Capitoline; they boasted above all that they had tricked the king with a truce and the hope of peace. For while they were completely unprepared for war, he had been so thoroughly ready that he could have seized all the key locations well before a Roman army reached Greece. But now, after the interval of a truce, they would meet on equal terms: the king would be no more prepared, and the Romans could start the war better equipped in every respect. They also boasted that they had skilfully fragmented the Boeotians' league so that they could never again be linked to the king by mutual consent.

Most of the Senate approved of these actions as products of the highest strategic thinking; the older men and those who remembered traditional ways said that they could not recognize Roman practices in this embassy.* Their ancestors had not conducted war with trickery and nocturnal battles, nor by false retreats and the sudden resumption of fighting when the enemy had relaxed his guard, nor in order to glory in guile more than genuine courage; they were accustomed to declare war before waging it, even to announce and sometimes specify the place where they intended to fight.* In the same spirit of good faith Pyrrhus' doctor was denounced to the king when he was plotting against his life; in the same spirit of good faith the betrayer of their children was bound and turned over to the Falisci.* These were the ways of the Roman, not the cunning of the Carthaginians nor the craftiness of the Greeks, for whom it was more glorious to fool an enemy than to overcome him by force. Occasionally, deceit can be momentarily more profitable than courage; but a man's spirit is fully conquered only when he has been made to acknowledge that he has been defeated not by artifice* or misfortune, but in a just and righteous war where one force is pitted directly against the other. This was the opinion of the older men, who found the new and excessively clever wisdom less pleasing; but that part of the Senate for whom expediency mattered more than honour prevailed. Consequently, Marcius' earlier embassy was approved, and he was also sent back to Greece with <. . .> quinqueremes and directed to do whatever else seemed to him to be in the best interests of the state. The senators also dispatched Aulus Atilius to occupy Larisa in Thessaly, fearing that if the time limit on the truce should expire, Perseus could send a garrison there and have the capital of Thessaly under his control. Atilius was directed to requisition 2,000 infantry from Gnaeus Sicinius to handle this assignment. Publius Lentulus, who had come back from Achaea, was given 300 Italian soldiers to try to keep Boeotia under control from Thebes.

48. Once these arrangements were made, the Senate agreed to give an audience to Perseus' envoys,* despite the fact that plans for the war had been fixed. The envoys said almost exactly what the king had in the conference. They answered the charge of the conspiracy against Eumenes' life with the greatest thoroughness but the least plausibility, for the case was clear. Everything else was an earnest entreaty. Their auditors' minds, however, were incapable of being persuaded or swayed, and the Senate warned the delegation to remove itself beyond the city walls immediately and depart from Italy within thirty days.

Next, Publius Licinius, the consul who had been put in charge of Macedonia, was instructed to name the earliest possible day for the army to assemble. Gaius Lucretius, the praetor responsible for the fleet, set out from Rome with forty quinqueremes, as it had been agreed that some of the refurbished ships should be left near the city for other purposes. The praetor sent his brother, Marcus Lucretius, with a single quinquereme and instructions to join the fleet at Cephallania with ships collected from the allies, in accordance with the treaty. Gathering one trireme from Rhegium, two from Locri, and four from the territory of Uria, Marcus sailed along the shore of Italy, past the farthest promontory of Calabria and crossed the Ionian Sea to Dyrrachium. There he collected ten small craft from the Dyrrachini themselves, twelve from the Issaei, and fifty-four from King Gentius (accepting the pretence that they had been made ready for Roman use), and took all these to Corcyra two days later; from there he crossed directly to Cephallania. The praetor, Gaius Lucretius, set out from Naples, crossed the straits of Sicily, and arrived at Cephallania four days later. The fleet stood at anchor there, waiting until the land forces made the crossing and the supply ships that had fallen out of line while at sea should catch up.

49. In that same period, as it happened, the consul Publius Licinius pronounced vows on the Capitol, adopted military attire, and set out from the city. Such a departure is always conducted with great solemnity and majesty; it especially attracts people's gaze and thoughts when they escort a consul setting out against an enemy who is endowed with consequence and renown, either for his innate character or for his good fortune. Not just respect for the office draws people, but also a passion for the spectacle itself, so that they can see the leader to whose authority and judgement they have entrusted the supreme defence of the state. Then their minds dwell on the hazards of war, the uncertainty of fortune, and the danger of combat for both sides: they think of defeats and victories, the disasters too often caused by imprudence and rashness on the part of leaders, but also the successes brought about by the virtues of foresight and courage. What mortal can know the character and luck of the consul they are sending to war? Will they soon see him holding a triumph and climbing the Capitol with his victorious army, on his way back to the same gods who attended his departure? Or will they be offering that joy to their enemies? In this particular case, he was being sent against

King Perseus, who derived his reputation from the Macedonian people, renowned in war, and from his father Philip, distinguished for his many successful actions, even in the war with the Romans; from the time when Perseus had inherited the kingdom, his name and predictions of war had been constantly and inseparably discussed.

With such thoughts did men of every class accompany the consul on his departure. Two men of consular rank were sent with him as military tribunes, Gaius Claudius and Quintus Mucius; there were three prominent young men as well, Publius Lentulus and the two Manlii Acidini, one the son of Manius Manlius and the other of Lucius Manlius. Accompanied by them, the consul went to the army at Brundisium, and from there he crossed with his total force at Nymphaeum in the territory of Apollonia where he pitched camp.

50. A few days earlier Perseus held a council, once the ambassadors had returned from Rome and cut short any hope of peace. There were differing views, and the debate went on for some time. Some thought that some kind of indemnity should be paid, if the Romans assessed it, or that some territory had to be conceded, if the penalty took this form; in short, whatever had to be endured for the sake of peace should not be rejected; nor should the king undertake anything where he would be risking himself and his kingdom on a throw of the dice, since the stakes were so high. As long as his right to the kingdom remained undisputed, then many events could bring the time and day when, as well as recovering his losses, he could also become a source of fear to the very people whom he currently feared.

But a significant majority was of a more belligerent cast of mind.* They claimed that whatever concession he made, he would immediately have to concede his kingdom too. For the Romans did not need money or land; but they knew this, that everything mortal, most especially powerful kingdoms and empires, was susceptible to much misfortune: they themselves had smashed the might of the Carthaginians and placed them under the yoke of an overwhelmingly powerful king on their border; they had banished Antiochus and his descendants beyond the Taurus Mountains; the kingdom of Macedonia alone remained both close to them and seemingly capable, if the Roman people's good fortune should fail them anywhere, of reanimating its kings with the spirit of yesteryear. So, while his resources were unimpaired, Perseus ought to make up his mind whether he preferred to concede everything bit by bit, until he was reduced to his last penny and an exile from his kingdom, or to beg the Romans to let him grow old, scorned and impoverished, on Samothrace* or some other island, a private citizen who had outlived his kingdom; or whether he chose to take up arms in defence of his station and his dignity—as was becoming to a man of courage—and either suffer whatever misfortune the war brought or, should he prove the victor, to liberate the world from Roman domination. It was no less unthinkable for the Romans to be driven out of Greece than that Hannibal was forced out of Italy. And, by Hercules, they did not see how it was consistent for him to have used force to pre-empt his brother's unlawful attempt to take over the kingdom* and to yield it to outsiders after securing it for himself. Ultimately, their discussion of war and peace was predicated on the universal agreement that nothing is more shameful than to have surrendered without a fight, and that nothing is more glorious than to have risked everything for the sake of dignity and majesty.

51. The council was at Pella, the ancient royal seat of the Macedonians. The king proclaimed, 'So then let us make war, since this seems best, and may the gods be favourable!' He sent word to his governors and assembled all his forces at Citium, a town in Macedonia. He himself offered a sacrifice on a royal scale, with 100 animals for Minerva, whom the Macedonians call Alcidemos,* and then, with a band of courtiers* and bodyguards, he set out for Citium.

All the Macedonian and allied forces had gathered there. Perseus pitched his camp in front of the city and lined up all the soldiers in a plain.* The sum total of the forces was 43,000; nearly half of them were the phalanx troops commanded by Hippias of Beroea. From all the peltasts, there was a select force of 2,000 especially strong and youthful troops; this division is known as the 'agema'* and was led by Leonnatus and Thrasippus, both Eulyestae.* Antiphilus of Edessa was in charge of the remaining peltasts, about 3,000 men. The Paeones from both Paroria and Parstrymonia—which lie on the edge of Thrace—and the Agrianes, mixed together with native Thracians, numbered about 3,000 also. These men had been armed and assembled by Didas of Paeonia, the person who had killed the young Demetrius.*

There were also 2,000 Gauls under arms, commanded by Asclepiodotus from Heraclea Sintice. The 3,000 free Thracians had their own general. About the same number of Cretans were under their own generals, Susus of Phalasarna and Syllus of Gnossus. And Leonides the Lacedaemonian was in charge of a mixed force of 500 Greeks. He was reputedly from the royal family, and had been sentenced to exile at a full meeting of the Achaeans, after his letters to Perseus were intercepted. The Achaean Lycon was in charge of the Aetolians and the Boeotians, who numbered at most 500 altogether. This mixture of so many peoples and so many races comprised an auxiliary force of approximately 12,000 soldiers.

The cavalry, drawn from all over Macedonia, numbered 3,000. Cotys, too, was there, the son of Seuthes and king of the Odrysae people; he had 1,000 select horsemen and nearly the same number of infantry. So the total of the entire army was 39,000 infantry and 4,000 cavalry. It was generally agreed that, except for the army Alexander the Great took to Asia, no Macedonian king had ever possessed so much manpower.

52. It was now the twenty-sixth year since Philip had sued for and been granted peace. Throughout this whole time Macedonia had remained free from war, producing a new generation, most of which was now of military age and, having engaged in skirmishes with their Thracian neighbours, had been tested but not worn out by nearly constant military activity. Since first Philip and then Perseus had long contemplated war against Rome, everything had been brought to the peak of readiness.

The troops were lined up for battle and went through a brief practice manoeuvre, not a fully fledged one, but enough to show that they had done more than stand at arms; and exactly as they were, in full battle gear, they were summoned by Perseus to an assembly. He stood on the tribunal with his two sons at his side: the elder was Philip, who was his brother by birth but a son by adoption; the younger one, known as Alexander, was his biological child. Perseus urged the soldiers on to war. He recalled the Romans' insulting behaviour towards him and his father: how all these indignities had driven the latter to rise up against his conquerors, and how Philip had been overtaken by fate in the midst of his preparations for war; as for Perseus himself, the Romans had simultaneously sent ambassadors to him and soldiers to occupy the cities of Greece. Then the winter had been taken up with a misleading conference,* ostensibly for the sake of re-establishing peace, but actually so that they would have time to prepare. Now the consul was on his way with two Roman legions, each consisting of

6,000 infantry and 300 cavalry, and nearly the same number of allied foot and horse. Supposing in addition there were auxiliary troops from the kings, Eumenes and Masinissa, there would be no more than 27,000 infantry and 2,000 cavalry.

Now that they had heard about the enemy numbers, Perseus said, the Macedonian forces should consider their own army, specifically how superior they were in both number and quality to those raw recruits hastily pressed into service. They themselves had been trained from boyhood in the art of fighting and had been disciplined and toughened by so many campaigns. The Roman auxiliaries were Lydians and Phrygians and Numidians while theirs were Thracians and Gauls, the fiercest of all races. Among their opponents, each poverty-stricken soldier had what weaponry he could provide for himself; the Macedonians were equipped from the royal stockpiles, accumulated over many years through his father's care and outlay. The Romans' supplies would be coming to them from a great distance, subject to all the accidents that happen at sea; but he had set aside ten years' worth of both money and grain, in addition to the profits from the mines. Everything that could be prepared with the gods' favour and the king's care, the Macedonians had in full and abundant supply. So, said Perseus, it was up to them to show that same spirit possessed by their ancestors, who subjugated Europe completely before crossing to Asia and opening up by military force a world unknown even by word of mouth; they had not stopped conquering until there was nothing this side of the Red Sea* left for them to conquer.

But now, by Hercules, Fortune had announced a competition not for the most remote shores of India but for control of Macedonia itself. The Romans, when they fought against his father, had flaunted a specious banner about the liberation of Greece; now they openly sought to enslave Macedonia so that there would not be a king on the border of their empire and no race distinguished in warfare could retain a military arsenal. For if the Macedonians wished to refrain from war and give in to the Romans' demands, they would have to hand over to arrogant masters not just their king and their kingdom, but also their weapons.

53. Throughout the speech Perseus was applauded enthusiastically at frequent intervals. But at that moment there arose such a roar from the men—simultaneously threatening and full of indignation,

but partly also urging the king to have confidence—that Perseus brought his words to a close and ordered the troops to prepare for the march; for word was already going around that the Romans were moving out from their encampment at Nymphaeum.

After dismissing the assembly, Perseus turned to receiving delegations from the cities of Macedonia. These had come to promise for the war grain and whatever cash each one could. He thanked them all but refused every offer, saying that the royal stockpiles were sufficient for his needs. He requisitioned only vehicles to transport the catapults, the huge supply of missiles already prepared, and other military equipment.

Then he set out with his entire army for Eordaea; they made camp at the lake known as Begorritis; the following day he advanced into Elimea to the Haliacmon river. Then he traversed the so-called Cambunian Mountains through a narrow pass and made his way down to Azorus, Pythium, and Doliche; the locals call them Tripolis. These three towns hesitated for a time because they had given hostages to the people of Larisa,* but faced with an immediate threat they surrendered. Perseus spoke to them in a friendly way. He was convinced that the Perrhaebi too would choose surrender; the inhabitants exhibited no hesitation, and he took over the city of <. . .> as soon as he arrived. He was forced to assault Chyretiae and moreover was driven back on the first day by a fierce onslaught of soldiers at the gate; the following day, he attacked in full strength and received everyone's capitulation by nightfall.

54. The next town, Mylae, was so thoroughly fortified that insuperable confidence in the fortifications made the residents more aggressive; not satisfied with barring the gates before the king, they hurled impudent insults at him and the Macedonians. Since this behaviour made the invaders all the more keen to attack, the defenders, with no hope of mercy, were forced to become yet more active in their own self-protection. And so for three days the city was besieged and defended with great spirit on both sides. The large number of Macedonians ensured a constant stream of reinforcements to keep up the fighting; but the townspeople, with the same men guarding the walls day and night, grew exhausted from wounds and sleepless nights and the ceaseless struggle. On the fourth day, when ladders were being set up all around the walls and extra pressure was being applied to the gate, the townsfolk repulsed an attack on the walls and

gathered to protect the gate by rushing forth in a sudden sally against the enemy. Since unthinking passion more than true belief in their strength impelled them, the small band of weary men was forced back by fresh troops. They turned their backs, and fleeing through the open gate, allowed the enemy in. And so the city was seized and looted; also the persons of free birth who survived the slaughter were put up for sale.

Abandoning the city, almost completely sacked and burned, Perseus moved his base to Phalanna and the following day went on to Gyrton. Learning there that Titus Minucius Rufus and Hippias, the chief magistrate of the Thessalians, had entered it with a garrison, he did not even attempt to assail it but went on his way and took Elatia and Gonnus, where his unexpected arrival had petrified the inhabitants. Both towns lie in the pass where one approaches Tempe, but Gonnus is closer, so he left it guarded with a more substantial garrison of cavalry and infantry, as well as with a triple ditch and rampart.

He himself proceeded to Sycurium and decided to await the approach of the enemy there; at the same time he told his army to forage widely in the adjacent enemy territory, for Sycurium is in the foothills of Mount Ossa. Where Ossa slopes down to the south, it commands the plains of Thessaly; Macedonia and Magnesia lie to its rear. In addition to these advantages were the very wholesome climate and the abundance of water, which lasts all year and flows from multiple surrounding springs.

55. In this same period the Roman consul was en route to Thessaly with his army. Initially his progress through Epirus was easy, but subsequently, after he had crossed into Athamania, where the terrain was rough and nearly pathless, it was only with great difficulty that he made his way to Gomphi by slow stages. Had the king drawn up his forces at the time and place of his choosing and challenged the consul while he was leading this inexperienced army of exhausted men and horses, even the Romans acknowledge that they would have suffered a major reverse.* So once the consul reached Gomphi without a fight, beyond the joy at having crossed through a dangerous pass, the Romans felt contempt for enemies who were so blind to their own best chances. The consul offered the proper sacrifice, distributed food to the soldiers, and waited for a few days to rest the animals and his men. Then he heard that the Macedonians were criss-crossing Thessaly freely and pillaging the fields of the allies. Since his troops were sufficiently rested by then, he marched to Larisa.

When he was about three miles away, he pitched camp at Tripolis, which they call Scaea, overlooking the Peneus river.

Meanwhile Eumenes arrived in Chalcis with the navy, accompanied by his brothers Attalus and Athenaeus; he had left his brother Philetaurus at Pergamum to look after the kingdom. Leaving Athenaeus at Chalcis in charge of 2,000 infantry, Eumenes took Attalus, 4,000 infantry, and 1,000 cavalry and joined the consul. The other Roman allies from all over Greece assembled there too, but most of these were so few that they have been forgotten. The people of Apollonia sent 300 cavalry and 100 infantry; from the Aetolians came the equivalent of one cavalry squadron, which was their entire mounted force; there were still at most 300 Thessalians in the Roman camp, although the hope had been for their entire cavalry; the Achaeans contributed around 1,500 of their young men, who were mostly equipped with Cretan weaponry.

56. Also during the same period, the praetor who was in charge of the fleet at Cephallania, Gaius Lucretius, instructed his brother, Marcus Lucretius, to sail with the fleet around Cape Malea to Chalcis while he himself took a trireme to the Gulf of Corinth to secure control of Boeotia. His voyage was rather slow because he was ill. When Marcus Lucretius reached Chalcis, he heard that Publius Lentulus was attacking Haliartus, so he sent a messenger to direct him, by the praetor's orders, to withdraw. The lieutenant, who had mounted the attack with Boeotian youths who were Roman sympathizers, withdrew from the walls. His abandonment of the siege created the opportunity for it to be resumed anew: in fact, Marcus Lucretius immediately invested Haliartus with troops from the fleet: 10,000 armed men as well as the 2,000 of Eumenes' men who had been left with Athenaeus. Just as they were preparing to attack, the praetor arrived from Creusa.

Around the same time, ships from the allies gathered at Chalcis: there were two Carthaginian quinqueremes, two triremes from Heraclea on the Pontus, four from Chalcedon and another four from Samos, and five quadriremes from Rhodes. The praetor sent these back to the allies since there was no fighting going on at sea. Quintus Marcius also came to Chalcis with his ships;* he had taken Phthiotic Alope and attacked so-called 'Hanging' Larisa.*

Such was the state of affairs in Boeotia while Perseus was encamped at Sycurium, as noted above. Once the crops in the immediate neighbourhood had been harvested, he sent troops to pillage the territory of Pherae. His scheme was to be able to entrap the Romans as they were drawn further and further from their camp to help the cities of their allies. When he observed that this raiding did not prompt them to move at all, he recalled his troops to camp and distributed the booty (except for the human beings) among his troops; most of it consisted of various types of livestock, and so it served for a feast.

57. Then the consul and the king held simultaneous councils of war to discuss how to commence their military operations. Confidence was high among the king's advisers because the enemy had not interfered with their pillaging of Pheraean land. Consequently they thought that the king should proceed directly to the enemy's camp without giving the Romans opportunity for further delay. The Romans, too, recognized that their hesitation shamed them in the eyes of their allies, who deeply resented the fact that the Pheraeans had not been given any assistance.

While the Romans—and Eumenes and Attalus, who were also at the meeting—were considering what to do, an alarmed messenger reported that the enemy was at hand with a large force. The council was dismissed, and the signal was immediately given to take up arms. It was decided to send out 100 cavalry and the same number of javelin-throwers (on foot) from Eumenes' forces. Around the fourth hour of the day, when Perseus was a little more than a mile from the Roman encampment, he ordered the infantry to halt. He rode out with his cavalry and skirmishers; Cotys and the leaders of the other auxiliaries accompanied him. They were less than half a mile from the Roman camp when the enemy cavalry came into view:* there were two squadrons of the cavalry, mostly Galatians commanded by Cassignatus, and about 150 light-armed Mysians and Cretans. The king paused, uncertain about the strength of the enemy. Then he dispatched from his column two Thracian squadrons, two Macedonian squadrons, and two cohorts of Cretans and Thracians. The battle proved indecisive since they were fighting with equal numbers and neither side received reinforcements. Around thirty of Eumenes' men died, including the Galatian leader Cassignatus.

At that point Perseus withdrew his forces to Sycurium; but the next day, at the same time, he moved his troops into position in the same place. Carts with water accompanied them, for the twelve-mile route had no water and a great deal of dust; and it was clear the soldiers would have had to fight in a dehydrated condition if they had engaged at the first sight of the enemy. Since the Romans made no move, having withdrawn even their outposts within their defences, the king's army also returned to camp. The royal forces followed the same procedure for several days, hoping that the Roman cavalry would attack the rear of their column as they withdrew and that, once the fight was under way, they could lure the Romans farther from their camp; at that moment, wherever they happened to be, they could easily reverse the tide of battle since they were superior in cavalry and skirmishers.

58. When this strategy failed, the king moved his camp closer to the enemy and fortified a site five miles away. Then, at dawn, Perseus drew up the line of infantry in the same place as usual and marched his entire cavalry and light-armed forces up to the camp of the enemy. The sight of the cloud of dust, both closer and thicker than before, triggered alarm in the Romans' camp. At first they did not really believe the man who spread the word, as every day previously the enemy had never appeared before the fourth hour; this time it was sunrise. Then the shouting and rushing back of many men from the gates dispelled all doubt. Total panic struck. The tribunes, prefects, and centurions rushed to the consul's quarters while the soldiers ran to their tents.

Perseus had drawn up his men less than half a mile from the outer wall, around a small hill called Callinicus.* King Cotys commanded the left wing with all his people; the cavalry squadrons alternated with the light-armed troops. The Macedonian cavalry was on the right wing, with the Cretans interspersed among their squadrons; Midon of Beroea commanded the light-armed troops, and Meno of Antigonea the cavalry and the unit as a whole. Just within the wing positions were stationed the king's cavalry and a mixed group consisting of the elite auxiliaries of several peoples: Patrocles of Antigonea and Didas, the governor of Paeonia, commanded these forces. The king was in the very middle, surrounded by the unit they call the agema and the cavalry of the Sacred Squadron.* Perseus posted the slingers and the javelin-throwers out in front of him: each division had 400 men; he put Ion of Thessalonica and Artemon, from Dolopia, in charge of them. Such was the arrangement of the king's forces.

The consul had the infantry drawn up within the outer wall, and he sent out the entire cavalry along with the light-armed troops; they were drawn up in front of the wall. The consul's brother, Gaius Licinius Crassus, commanded the right wing, comprised of the entire

Italian cavalry interspersed with skirmishers; on the left, Marcus Valerius Laevinus led the allied cavalry from Greece; the Greeks' light-armed troops occupied the centre of the line, together with special elite cavalry under Quintus Mucius. Out in front of the standards of these men 200 Gallic horsemen were drawn up, as well as 300 Cyrtii from Eumenes' auxiliaries. Four hundred Thessalian horsemen were positioned slightly beyond the left wing. King Eumenes and Attalus were stationed with their entire force at the rear, between the last row of troops and the wall.

59. When the columns were drawn up more or less in this fashion, with nearly equal numbers of cavalry and light-armed troops on each side, they rushed together. The fighting started between the slingers and javelin-throwers, who had been sent out ahead. Right at the start the Thracians, acting like wild animals released from lengthy captivity, hurled themselves with such shouting against the Italian cavalry on the right wing that they unnerved their opponents, although normally they were fearless because of their experience and aptitude for war. Wielding long spears, the Thracians at one moment attacked the infantry, at another slashed the horses' legs, and at another pierced their sides.

Charging the centre, Perseus scattered the Greeks with his first assault.* They were routed, and the enemy pressed hard on their heels. At first the Thessalian cavalry had been mere observers, held as reserves a slight distance from the left wing and apart from the fray, but they proved most useful when the battle had turned against the Romans. By gradually giving way, but maintaining formation, they joined Eumenes' auxiliaries, and together with him they provided their allies with a safe retreat between their own ranks, as the men scattered in their flight; and, as the enemy pressed forward in only loose formation, the Thessalians even had the nerve to advance and gathered up many of their men fleeing towards them. The king's men, already dispersed in the general pursuit, did not dare to join battle with the Thessalian cavalry as it approached steadily in battle order.

Just as the king, having won the cavalry battle, cried out that his triumph would have been complete if the infantry had contributed even the slightest push, his phalanx opportunely appeared. For Hippias and Leonnatus had heard that the cavalry had been victorious and on their own initiative hastily brought forward this force in order to join the daring enterprise. As the king hesitated, caught between hope and apprehension at taking such a bold step, Evander the Cretan, whose services he had relied on in the plot against Eumenes at Delphi, spotted the column of infantry advancing under its standards. He raced up to the king and strenuously advised him not to be elated by luck and risk everything on a needless throw of the dice; if, satisfied with the current success, he stopped for the day, he would have either the preconditions for an honourable peace or more allies for the war, who would flock to the winning side should he choose to fight on. The king's mind was receptive to this advice, and so, praising Evander, he ordered the standards to be reversed, the infantry to march back to camp, and the cavalry's retreat to be sounded.

60. That day the Romans lost 200 horsemen and no fewer than 2,000 infantry; around 600 were taken prisoner. On the king's side, though, twenty horsemen and forty infantrymen fell. All the victors were in high spirits as they returned to camp, but the Thracians outdid the rest with their coarse glee; they rode back singing and carrying enemy heads fixed on their spears.

Among the Romans there was not just sorrow because the battle had gone badly, but also anxiety that the enemy might make an immediate assault on the camp. Eumenes urged the consul to transfer it across the Peneus so that they could use the river for protection until the distressed soldiers' morale revived. The shame of admitting his fear galled the consul, but reason won out, and he led his forces across in the silence of the night and fortified a camp on the farther bank.

The next day the king set out to provoke his enemies into fighting. When he saw them safely encamped on the other side of the river, he acknowledged that he had in fact erred by not having pressed home the victory the day before, but that it was rather more serious to have given up overnight. For, even had he deployed none of his other men and sent out just the light-armed troops, the majority of his opponents might have been wiped out during their panic-stricken crossing of the river.

Safe in their camp, the Romans had indeed shaken off their fear for the moment; but, among the other factors, the damage to their reputation disturbed them the most. And in a meeting presided over by the consul, one by one each man blamed the Aetolians:* they had been the source of the panic and flight; the rest of the Greek allies had copied the Aetolians' fear. The five Aetolian leaders who were said to have been seen first turning their backs were sent to Rome.

The Thessalians were praised in an assembly, and their leaders were also given special gifts for their bravery.

61. The spoils from the enemy casualties were brought to the king. These he conferred as gifts: remarkable weapons to some, horses to others, slaves to certain others. There were more than 1,500 shields; the corslets and sets of body armour totalled more than 1,000; even greater was the number of helmets, swords, and missiles of every type. These gifts, which were impressive and pleasing in themselves, were amplified by the words of the king when he assembled his troops to address them:

'You have before you a war with a foregone conclusion. You routed the Roman cavalry, which was the strength of the enemy forces and which they vaunted as invincible. Their cavalry is composed of their most prominent young men, and the cavalry in turn is the nursery of their Senate: from there they choose consuls to be enrolled as "fathers"; from there they choose their generals. Just now we distributed among you spoils from these men. No less do you have victory over the legions of the infantry: escaping you by fleeing under cover of night, they filled the river with the terror of shipwrecked men as they swam all over the place. Crossing the Peneus will be easier for us, when we are pursuing defeated men, than it was for them in their fear. As soon as we reach the other side, we will assail their camp, which we would have taken today had they not fled. And if they wish to challenge us in combat, you may expect the same outcome from an infantry contest as in the cavalry battle.'

His victorious forces, hot-blooded, their shoulders draped with the spoils of their slaughtered opponents, drank in his approval of them, and based their expectations of the future on what had transpired. And the infantry, especially those in the Macedonian phalanxes, fired by their comrades' glory, desired to serve their king and to win for themselves equal glory from the enemy. The assembly was dismissed, and the next day the king went to Mopselus and set up camp there.* This is a knoll that rises up before Tempe, and it is about halfway from Larisa for one travelling to Gonnus.

62. The Romans stayed along the bank of the Peneus, but transferred their camp to a more secure location. They were joined there by the Numidian Misacenes, who came with 1,000 cavalry, the same number of infantry, and twenty-two elephants.

In this period the king held a meeting about the general state of affairs. Since the overconfidence born of his success had subsided, some of his friends dared to recommend that he take advantage of his good luck to seek favourable peace-terms, rather than let unwarranted expectations lead him into irreversible misfortune. They said that it was characteristic of the wise man, whose success was well earned, to set a limit on it and not to put too much trust in the sunny skies of momentary good fortune. The king should send men to the consul to renew the treaty with the same terms on which his father Philip had accepted peace from Titus Quinctius Flamininus, after the latter's victory. There was no more splendid way to end a war than with such a memorable battle, and no firmer assurance of lasting peace could be given than one that could make the Romans, weakened by their loss, more inclined to come to terms. But if the Romans, with their innate stubbornness, should then reject fair terms, gods and men alike would be witnesses to both Perseus' restraint and the Romans' bottomless arrogance. The king's mind was never disposed to reject such advice and so, since this position met with the approval of the majority, it was adopted.

The envoys sent to the consul were heard out in a fully attended meeting. They asked for peace, guaranteeing in return that Perseus would make as large a financial contribution as his father Philip had promised and that he would cede as soon as possible those cities, fields, and places that his father had. Such was the envoys' offer. During the consultation that took place after their departure, Roman resolve prevailed. In those days it was their practice to maintain a positive outlook in adversity and to contain their joy when conditions turned favourable. They decided to answer that peace would be granted if the king gave the Senate the unconditional right to decide every matter concerning the king and all of Macedonia.

When the envoys brought this response, the Romans' characteristic stubbornness stunned those unfamiliar with it, and most people rejected any further discussion of peace, saying that the men who had scorned their offer would soon be begging for it. The very same arrogance, however, unnerved Perseus, on the grounds that it must come from total confidence in their power. He increased the amount of money, as if he could buy peace, and he persisted in trying to sway the consul's mind. But the consul did not deviate from the original answer, and the king despaired of peace. Returning to Sycurium, where he had started out, he prepared to chance the fortunes of war again.

63. As word of the cavalry battle spread through Greece,* the direction of popular sentiment became manifest. Not just supporters

of Macedonia, but the large number who were indebted to the Romans
for considerable favours—and some too who had encountered Perseus'
might and arrogance—rejoiced to hear the news; they had no other
reason than that vulgar enthusiasm for favouring a puny underdog
that the common herd indeed adopts at sporting events.

Meanwhile, in Boeotia the praetor Lucretius was vigorously pros-
ecuting the siege of Haliartus. The besieged party, who had no outside
help and expected none (other than the youth of Coronea, who had
slipped within the walls at the beginning of the siege), nevertheless
resisted, though more by willpower than by actual strength. They
made frequent attacks on the siege-works; and when a battering ram
was moved into position, they crushed it to the ground, now with
huge rocks and now with a leaden weight; and any place they failed
to prevent it from smashing the wall, they built an emergency
fortification at the break, hastily piling up pieces of masonry left over
from the destruction.

As the siege-works were not advancing the assault rapidly enough,
the praetor ordered ladders to be distributed amongst the maniples
so that he could mount a comprehensive attack on the walls by encircling them. He calculated that his numbers would suffice for this
purpose since it was neither important nor possible to attack the section of the city ringed by swampland. He himself marched 2,000
select troops up to the section where two turrets and what was left of
the wall that had been between them had collapsed. His intention
was to attempt to cross the ruins so that while the townsfolk made a
counter-assault on him, whatever other part of the wall was left
defenceless could be taken by the men with their ladders. The townspeople vigorously prepared themselves to repel his assault. They
heaped bundles of dry brushwood in the ruin-strewn area; and
standing there with burning torches, they threatened to ignite the
barrier so that a fiery barricade between them and the enemy would
allow them time to interpose an inner wall. Chance interfered with
their effort: suddenly rain pounded down so heavily that it made
lighting anything difficult and extinguished what was already burning. And so it was that a passage opened up through the smoking,
scattered brushwood and, with everyone focused on the defence of
that one place, the walls too were taken from the ladders in many
locations simultaneously. In the immediate chaos of the city's defeat,
the elderly and the young who happened to be in the way were cut

down at random; the armed men fled together to the citadel. But the next day they surrendered and were sold into slavery, for no hope remained. There were in fact about 2,500 of them. The adornments of the city, statues, paintings, and any kind of valuable booty, were taken down to the ships; the city was razed to the ground.

From there the army marched to Thebes, where it was admitted without resistance. The praetor entrusted the city to the exiles and those belonging to the Roman faction; he auctioned the property of men from the other faction and that of supporters of the king and the Macedonians. After these actions in Boeotia, the praetor returned to the sea and the fleet.

64. During this activity in Boeotia, Perseus spent several days encamped at Sycurium. Then he heard that the Romans were hastily seizing crops reaped from fields round about, that the soldiers were then husking the ears in front of their tents so that the grain could be ground more pure, and that they had made great heaps of straw throughout the camp. This struck Perseus as the perfect chance to start a fire, and so he ordered torches, pine wood, and flammable projectiles of tow smeared with pitch to be made ready. He set out in the middle of the night so that his approach at dawn might go unnoticed. But the outposts were seized in vain: the uproar and tumult of their men roused the others, and the signal to take up arms was given immediately. The soldiers took their positions simultaneously along the wall and at the gates. Any hope of an assault was lost. Perseus immediately counter-marched his battle line and ordered the equipment carts to go first and then the infantry, preceded by their standards. He himself remained with the cavalry and the light-armed troops to bring up the rear; his thought was—and this is what happened—that the enemy would try to pick off the end of the column. The light-armed troops were involved in a skirmish, mostly with individuals making sallies; the cavalry and infantry returned to camp without any trouble.

After harvesting the crops in that area, the Romans moved their camp to Crannon, where the fields lay untouched.* They felt secure having their base there, both because of the remote location and because of the lack of water along the route between Sycurium and Crannon. Early one morning, however, the king's cavalry and light-armed troops unexpectedly appeared on the hills overlooking the camp and caused widespread panic. These forces had set out from Sycurium at noon the day before; at daybreak they had left the column of infantry on the nearest plain. Perseus waited on the hill-side for a little, thinking that the Romans' cavalry might be lured into battle. When they did not come out, he sent a horseman to order the infantry to withdraw to Sycurium, and he followed shortly after-wards. The Roman cavalry pursued them at a slight distance in order to be able at any point to attack stragglers or anyone who fell out of formation; but once the Romans perceived Perseus' forces retreating in an orderly fashion, remaining in formation rank by rank, they too returned to camp.

65. And so the king, vexed at the length of the journey, moved his camp to Mopselus; and the Romans, having harvested the crops of Crannon, moved on to the land around Phalanna. When the king learned from a deserter that the Romans were criss-crossing the fields there freely, without any armed protection, and were cutting down crops, he set out with <. . .> cavalry and 2,000 Thracians and Cretans. Travelling in loose formation they made as much speed as possible and caught up with the unsuspecting Romans. Nearly 1,000 carts with their teams, most fully laden, were seized along with about 600 men. The king delegated the protection of the booty and the task of bringing it back to camp to 300 Cretans. He himself regrouped the cavalry, which was engaged in widespread slaughter, and together with the infantry advanced on the nearest outpost, assuming that not much of a fight would be required to overpower it.

Lucius Pompeius was the military tribune in charge. He withdrew his troops, who had been shaken by the enemy's sudden approach, to a nearby hill and prepared to use the location to defend himself since he was ill-matched in numbers and strength. He gathered the sol-diers into a circle there so that they could protect themselves from arrows and javelins by interlocking their shields. Perseus surrounded the hill with his soldiers, ordering some of them to try to assail it on all sides and to engage in hand-to-hand combat, and directing others to launch missiles from farther away.

Extreme terror engulfed the Romans, for packed together they could not repel those who were struggling up the hill, and whenever they broke ranks for a sally, they exposed themselves to darts and arrows. The cestrosphondene in particular inflicted heavy damage. It was a new type of weapon, invented for that war. A jagged projec-tile, the length of two hands, was attached to a shaft that was half a forearm long and as thick as a finger; three thin fir-wood ridges were twisted around it, as with arrows; the sling had in the middle two thongs of unequal length; when the slinger balanced a projectile in it and swung it by the strap with great torque, the projectile was discharged and shot out like a missile.*

When some of the Romans had been wounded by this and every other kind of missile and in their state of exhaustion they could scarcely hold their weapons, the king pressed them to surrender, offered pledges of good faith, and at times held out rewards. He could not sway the resolution of one single person, and then unexpectedly a gleam of hope shone forth when they had consigned themselves to death. For when those of the foragers who escaped reported to the consul that the outpost was completely surrounded, he was concerned by the danger to so many citizens—there were about 800 of them and all Romans—and set out from camp with the cavalry and the light-armed troops, joined by the new auxiliaries, that is, the Numidian infantry, cavalry, and elephants; and he ordered the military tribunes to follow with the legions. He led the way to the hill with the light-armed troops of the auxiliaries, backed up by his skirmishers. At the consul's side were Eumenes, Attalus, and the Numidian prince Misacenes.

66. At the first sight of their comrades' standards, the beleaguered Romans, who had indeed been on the edge of despair, experienced renewed confidence. Perseus should have been content in the first place with his fortuitous success (the capture and killing of some of the foragers) and should not have wasted his time trying to take the outpost; alternatively, having made some sort of assault on it, he should have escaped while he could, once he knew that he did not have enough manpower with him. Instead, carried away by his success, he himself awaited the enemy's approach and hastily sent some men to summon the phalanx. This force would have arrived too late for the circumstances and in a rush, and while still in complete disarray from its hasty approach, would have found itself facing troops that were organized and marshalled for combat.

The consul was the first to arrive and immediately joined battle. At first the Macedonians fought back. They were unevenly matched in every aspect; they had already lost 300 infantry and twenty-four cavalrymen from the elite wing known as the Sacred Squadron; even its commander, Antimachus, was one of the victims. Then they tried to retreat, but the escape route was practically more chaotic than the battle itself. The phalanx that had been summoned by the terrified messenger was marching on the double when it came to a standstill, blocked at a narrow spot first by the column of captives and then by the wagons laden with grain. There was great confusion on both sides. No one would wait for the column of captives to be led out of the way somehow or other, but the troops toppled the carts down the hill—for there was no other way to clear a passage—and whipped the mules to the point where they attacked the crowd. Scarcely had the soldiers extracted themselves from the disorder of the column of captives when they ran into the king's battle column and his defeated cavalry. Then, moreover, the outcry from those directing the phalanx to retreat caused a panic bordering on total collapse: if their enemies had dared to enter the pass and pursue them further, they could have inflicted a crushing defeat. But the consul rescued the garrison from the hilltop and, content with the modest success, led his forces back to camp.

According to some sources, there was a major battle on that occasion: the enemy lost 8,000 men, including the king's generals Sopater and Antipater; about 2,800 were taken alive; and twenty-seven standards were seized. Nor did the Romans escape without loss: over 4,300 of the consul's army died, and five standards were taken from the allied left wing.

67. That day reinvigorated the Romans and demoralized Perseus. Having spent a few days at Mopselus, mostly seeing to the burial of the men he had lost, he left a sufficiently strong garrison at Gonnus and retreated to Macedonia. He instructed someone named Timotheus, one of his commanders whom he left with a small troop at Phila, to try to win over Magnesia from close at hand. Back at Pella, Perseus sent his troops into their winter quarters and went to Thessalonica with Cotys. There was a story circulating there that a Thracian prince named Autlesbis and Corragus, one of Eumenes' commanders, had invaded Cotys' territory and taken over the region known as Marene. Accordingly Perseus, thinking that he should let Cotys defend his own kingdom, sent him on his way with generous gifts; he gave Cotys' cavalry 200 talents, or half a year's wage, although he had initially agreed to pay them for a year's service.

Once the consul heard that Perseus had left, he moved his camp to Gonnus to see whether he could take over the town. Situated in the very gateway to Tempe, the town provides Macedonia with an extremely secure barrier and offers the Macedonians an unobstructed descent into Thessaly. Given the impregnability of the location and its strong garrison, the consul abandoned the enterprise. Redirecting his route into Perrhaebia he took Malloea with a single assault and destroyed it; then he recovered Tripolis as well as the rest of Perrhaebia and returned to Larisa.

From there he sent Eumenes and Attalus home and distributed Misacenes and the Numidians into winter quarters in the nearest Thessalian cities. He also spread some of his troops around Thessaly so that they could have comfortable winter quarters and provide protection for the cities. He dispatched his subordinate Quintus Mucius with 2,000 men to occupy Ambracia, and he dismissed all the allies from the Greek communities except for the Achaeans. He himself took part of the army to Phthiotic Achaea where he razed Pteleum* to the ground (deserted after the townspeople had fled) and accepted the voluntary surrender of Antronae from its inhabitants. Then he moved his army to Larisa. The city itself had been abandoned; the entire population had retreated to the citadel. This he prepared to attack. The Macedonian troops installed by the king were terrified and left first; once they had been abandoned, the townspeople immediately gave themselves up. Just as the consul was debating whether to attack Demetrias or to investigate the situation in Boeotia first, the Thebans, harassed by the Coronaei, asked him to come to Boeotia. In response to their appeals and because Boeotia was a better place to winter than Magnesia, he marched his army there.

BOOK FORTY-THREE

1. During the same summer that these events were happening in Thessaly, the consul sent <. . .> as his lieutenant to Illyricum to attack two wealthy towns. This commander overpowered Ceremia and forced it to submit. Then he returned everything to the proper owner, intending to foster a belief in his clemency and thereby win over the inhabitants of Carnus, which was fortified. When he failed either to drive the Carni into surrendering or to take their city by siege, he looted Ceremia, previously left untouched, so that his army would derive some benefit from the exhausting labour of the two sieges.

The other consul, Gaius Cassius, accomplished nothing of note in Gaul, the province that he had been allotted; he then made a fruitless attempt to lead his legions through Illyricum into Macedonia. Word that the consul had embarked on this journey reached the Senate through envoys from Aquileia. They were complaining that their colony was young, insecure, and not yet sufficiently fortified against the hostile peoples of the Istrians and the Illyrians. The envoys begged the Senate to have some regard for its defence. When asked whether they wished to have the task entrusted to the consul Gaius Cassius, the envoys answered that Cassius had pressed troops into service at Aquileia and departed for Macedonia via Illyricum.

At first this seemed unbelievable, and the senators all assumed that the consul was making war on the Carni or perhaps the Istrians. The Aquileienses replied that they neither knew nor dared to assert anything more than that thirty days' worth of food had been given to the soldiers and that guides who knew the routes from Italy to Macedonia had been sought out and taken along. The Senate was outraged that the consul had been so bold as to abandon his own province, cross into another's, lead an army by an unfamiliar, treacherous route amongst foreign peoples, and leave the way into Italy open to so many peoples.* In a full session they decreed that Gaius Sulpicius, the praetor, should name three envoys from the Senate to set out from Rome that very day and to track down Gaius Cassius as quickly as possible, wherever he might be. They were to communicate to him that he was not to attack anybody except those the Senate had voted he should wage war on. The men who went as envoys were Marcus Cornelius Cethegus,

Marcus Fulvius, and Publius Marcius Rex. For the time being, anxiety about the consul and his army postponed concern about fortifying Aquileia.

2. Next some representatives from several peoples of the two Spanish provinces were brought before the Senate. They complained about the greed and arrogance of Roman officials; on bended knee they begged the Senate not to let Rome's own allies be robbed and persecuted more scandalously than its enemies. The ambassadors bewailed other outrages too, and it was indeed clear that their property had been seized. As a result, Lucius Canuleius, the praetor who had drawn Spain as his lot, was charged with appointing five assessors of senatorial rank for each man from whom the Spaniards were demanding restitution; in addition, Canuleius was to give the Spaniards the power to choose whichever patrons they wished to act as their advocates. The representatives were summoned to the Curia where the Senate's decree was read aloud, and they were directed to name their advocates. Four were named: Marcus Porcius Cato, Publius Cornelius Scipio (the son of Gnaeus), Lucius Aemilius Paullus, and Gaius Sulpicius Galus.*

The assessors began with Marcus Titinius, who had been the praetor in Nearer Spain during the consulship of Aulus Manlius and Marcus Junius.* Twice they deferred judgement on the defendant; on the third occasion they found him innocent. Then a difference of opinion arose between the representatives from the two provinces: the people from Nearer Spain wanted Marcus Cato and Publius Scipio as their advocates while those from Farther Spain wanted Lucius Paullus and Sulpicius Galus. Publius Furius Philo was brought up before the assessors by the people of Nearer Spain and Marcus Matienus by those from Farther Spain. Furius had been a praetor three years earlier, in the consulship of Spurius Postumius and Quintus Mucius,* and Matienus had held the office two years before, during the consulship of Lucius Postumius and Marcus Popillius.* They were charged with very grave crimes, and their cases were deferred. When the trial began anew, the defence offered on their behalf was that they had gone into exile. Furius went to Praeneste for his exile and Matienus to Tibur.

There was a rumour that the advocates were precluding accusations against well-known and powerful men. The praetor Canuleius compounded this suspicion by discontinuing the proceedings and turning to conducting the draft; he then abruptly departed for his province before more men could be harassed by the Spaniards. Although the events of the past were thus obliterated by silence, the Senate issued a decree on behalf of the Spaniards for the future. By its terms no Roman magistrate was to assess the value of grain for purposes of taxation, or to compel Spaniards to sell their one-twentieth quotas at a price of his choice; and local governors were not to be installed in Spanish towns to exact money.*

3. There was yet another delegation from Spain, from a completely new class of men. They explained that they were sons of Roman soldiers and Spanish women, who were not officially entitled to marriages recognized by Roman law,* and that there were more than 4,000 of them. They asked to be given a town where they could live. The Senate decided that these men should submit their names to Lucius Canuleius; they should also give him the names of any freedmen they might have. It was agreed that a colony should be established at Carteia by the ocean; current residents of Carteia who preferred to remain there could enrol in the colony and be assigned land. This was to be a Latin colony* and to be known as a freedmen's colony.

In this same period there arrived from Africa both Prince Gulussa, the son of Masinissa, acting as his father's emissary, and some Carthaginians.* Gulussa was given an audience with the Senate first. He outlined his father's contributions to the Macedonian war, and he pledged that Masinissa would provide anything else they cared to demand, as the Roman people deserved. He also cautioned the conscript fathers to beware of trickery from the Carthaginians: they had made plans for assembling a very large fleet, ostensibly for the Romans and against the Macedonians; but once the fleet was finished and marshalled for battle, the Carthaginians would be able to choose their own friends and foes. <. . .>

[There is now a very large gap in the manuscript: approximately three-fifths of Book 43 is lost, covering the rest of the year 171 and the first part of 170. At the beginning of the missing section must have been the rest of the Senate's audience with Gulussa and the Carthaginians. The lost pages end with an account of an uprising in Spain (where the narrative resumes in chap. 4). Some of the material in between can be reconstructed from various sources, including the *Periocha* for Book 43. This notes that Publius Licinius Crassus attacked and abused several Greek cities, as did Lucius Hortensius, the praetor in charge of the fleet; it also mentions Perseus' victorious

campaigns over the Thracians, the Dardani, and the Illyrians (referred
to in chap. 19 below). Other sources specify Perseus' victories over the
Romans: a cavalry action against Licinius (now a proconsul) near
Larisa, a raid against the Roman fleet at Oreus, the defeat of Aulus
Hostilius Mancinus, the consul for Macedonia in 170, at Elimea, and
the latter's refusal of a direct challenge from Perseus. An apparently
major episode not included in the *Periocha* but discussed by Polybius
(27.16) and Diodorus (30.5a) was a nearly successful attempt by two
men from Epirus to kidnap Hostilius and deliver him to Perseus.
Livy almost certainly recounted this episode, but to judge from what
remains of Book 43, the *Periocha* probably accurately reflects an
emphasis on Perseus' successes and the Romans' abuse of their
Greek allies, such as the sacking of Coronea and Abdera. (The latter
episode receives attention in chap. 4.)

Luce plausibly suggests that Livy devoted Book 43 to Roman fail-
ures (*Livy*, 120). Obviously Book 43 is the focal point of the pentad,
and since Book 42 ends with Roman successes and Book 44 begins
with a renewed sense of Roman purpose and competence, making
the central book the nadir of the Romans' fortunes against Perseus
would give a strong shape to the pentad.

The narrative now abruptly resumes at the very end of the quelling
of the revolt in Spain. According to the *Periocha*, the rebellion collapsed when the leader, one Olonicus, was killed. The text indicates
that there were two leaders and that the Romans displayed their
heads (presumably to prove that they were dead and perhaps to
terrify their followers into submission). The rebels then rushed to
make amends.]

4. <...> The Romans entered the camp, flourishing their opponents' heads and inspiring such fear that the camp could have been
taken if the infantry had been brought up immediately. Even so,
there was widespread flight, and some people thought that messengers should be sent to beg for peace. Several cities surrendered as
soon as they heard the news. They exonerated themselves, casting
blame instead on the madness of the two men who had, of their own
accord, offered themselves for punishment. The praetor pardoned
these peoples and set out for the other cities. Because everyone was
complying with his orders, the Roman forces remained inactive
during the praetor's travels through territory that had recently been
engulfed in the flames of wide-scale revolt, but now lay tamed.

The praetor's mild methods, by which he had subdued the most aggressive people without shedding a drop of blood, pleased the people and the Senate all the more because Licinius, the consul, and Lucretius, the praetor, had conducted the war in Greece with excessive cruelty and greed. In Lucretius' absence, the tribunes of the plebs launched vicious attacks on him in constant public meetings, although the defence was offered on his behalf that he was away on public business. In those days, however, even Rome's environs were so unknown that he was actually then on his own estate at Antium,* spending his war-booty on establishing a route for water from the Loracina river to Antium. He is reputed to have contracted this job out for 130,000 *asses*; he also adorned a shrine of Aesculapius with paintings from the booty.

The resentment and shame attached to Lucretius were diverted to his successor Hortensius by representatives from Abdera. In front of the Curia they wept and complained that their town had been stormed and then looted by Hortensius; the explanation for the city's destruction was that when he demanded 100,000 *denarii* and 50,000 measures of wheat, they had asked for time to send envoys about this matter to Rome and the consul Hostilius. Scarcely had they approached the consul when they heard that the town had been stormed, the leading citizens beheaded, and everyone else sold at public auction. These events seemed outrageous to the senators, and they issued the same decree* covering the people of Abdera as they had for the Coronaei the year before. They also ordered the praetor Quintus Maenius to make an announcement about these matters in a public meeting, and two envoys, Gaius Sempronius Blaesus and Sextus Julius Caesar, were sent to liberate the people of Abdera. The same men were charged with informing the consul Hostilius and the praetor Hortensius that the Senate considered the war undertaken against the Abderites unjust and judged it right that all those forced into slavery should be sought out and liberated.

5. Complaints about Gaius Cassius were brought before the Senate at the same time. He had been consul the year before and was currently serving as a military tribune with Aulus Hostilius in Macedonia. It was representatives from Cincibilus, a king of the Gauls, who came. His brother delivered the speech in the Senate, complaining that Gaius Cassius had devastated the fields of people dwelling in the Alps who were Roman allies, and then had hauled away to slavery several thousand people.

At the same time representatives came from the Carni and the Istrians and the Iapydes. They said that Cassius had demanded guides from them to show him the way as he led his army to Macedonia; he had left them peaceably, as if he were going to wage a different war. Then, they said, he had turned around in the middle of his journey and scoured their fields as if he was at war with them; murder, looting, and arson were committed here, there, and everywhere; nor did they yet know why the consul regarded them as enemies.

The Senate gave as its reply both to the Gauls' absent leader and to these peoples that it had not known that the behaviour of which they complained would occur, nor did the Senate consider it acceptable if it had; at the same time, without a hearing, it was unjust to condemn a man of consular status in his absence when he was away on public business; when Gaius Cassius returned from Macedonia, should they then wish to accuse him in person, the situation would be investigated and the Senate would see to it that he gave satisfaction.* In addition to giving this reply, the Senate resolved to send ambassadors to the local communities, two to the princeling on the far side of the Alps and three to the peoples mentioned, to make a public declaration of the Senate's position. The Senate decided that gifts of 2,000 *asses* each should be sent to the representatives; for the two princeling brothers, there were special gifts: two torques, fashioned from five pounds of gold, and five silver dishes weighing twenty pounds, and two horses elaborately decked out and attended by stable boys, equestrian weaponry, and military cloaks; and there was clothing for their attendants, free and slave alike. That is what was sent. Upon the Gauls' request, they were also allowed to buy ten horses and to take them out of Italy. The ambassadors sent with the Gauls across the Alps were Gaius Laelius and Marcus Aemilius Lepidus; Gnaeus Sicinius, Publius Cornelius Blasio, and Titus Memmius went to the other peoples.

6. Embassies from many Greek and Asian cities converged on Rome simultaneously. The Athenians were granted the first hearing. They explained that they had sent whatever ships and soldiers they had to the consul Publius Licinius and the praetor Gaius Lucretius; the latter two, making no use of the manpower, had demanded 100,000 measures of grain from them and, the Athenians said, they had collected it so as not to fail in their duties, despite the fact that the land they cultivated was so infertile that they fed their own farmers

with grain purchased abroad; and they were still prepared to supply whatever else was demanded from them.

The Milesians, without reference to their previous contributions, promised that they stood ready to supply whatever the Senate wished to ask for the war. The people of Alabanda officially noted the fact that they had erected a temple of the City of Rome and instituted annual games in honour of that divinity;* further, that they had brought a golden crown weighing fifty pounds, to be deposited on the Capitol as a gift to Jupiter Optimus Maximus; there were also 300 cavalry shields which they would deliver once they had been told to whom these should be given. The people of Alabanda sought permission to place their gift on the Capitol and to offer sacrifices. The people of Lampsacus made the same request, having brought a crown of eighty pounds and having noted the fact that they had severed their ties with Perseus after the Roman army had entered Macedonia, although they had been subjects of Perseus and of Philip before him; in return for this, and because they had furnished all manner of supplies for the Roman generals, they asked only that they be admitted into an official friendship with the Roman people, and that if there were peace with Perseus, there would be a special provision to shield them from falling under his control again.

The other embassies received cordial answers; and Quintus Maenius, the praetor, was ordered to enrol the Lampsaceni in the register of allies. Gifts of 2,000 *asses* were distributed to each embassy. The group from Alabanda was directed to take the shields back with them to the consul Aulus Hostilius in Macedonia.

Also at this time the Carthaginians' representatives and Masinissa's came from Africa again. The Carthaginians declared that they had brought down to the sea 1,000,000 measures of wheat and 500,000 of barley in order to convey it wherever the Senate should decide; they knew that this performance of their duty was less than the Roman people deserved and less than their own willingness to contribute, but that often on other occasions, during periods of plenty for both peoples, they had fulfilled the obligations of grateful and faithful allies. Masinissa's envoys, too, promised the same amount of wheat, as well as 1,200 cavalry and twelve elephants; and if there were any other need, the Senate had only to command: the king would provide it as readily as he had furnished what he had promised of his own volition. Thanks were conveyed to the Carthaginians and the king, and the envoys were asked to transport the promised supplies to the consul Hostilius in Macedonia. Gifts of 2,000 *asses* each were sent to the envoys.

7. Envoys from Crete reported that they had sent to Macedonia the number of archers the consul Publius Licinius had asked for. When questioned, however, they did not deny that more archers were fighting with Perseus than with the Romans. They were told that if the Cretans were well and truly committed to having a stronger alliance with the Romans than with Perseus, the Roman Senate would in turn respond to them as it did to reliable allies. In the meantime, the envoys should report to their people that the Senate wished the Cretans to see to it that the soldiers in the garrisons of King Perseus were recalled at the very first opportunity.

After the Cretans had been dismissed with this answer, the Chalcidians were called in. The very entrance of the delegation was moving. Their leader, Micythio, was lame and was carried on a litter. It instantly seemed that his business with the Senate was of dire necessity: either he did not think he should seek to be excused on the grounds of his health, despite his affliction; or his request had been denied.* Micythio prefaced his remarks by saying that the only spark of life left to him was the power of speech to deplore the misfortunes of his country. He proceeded to recount the favours his city had done for Roman commanders and troops, both in the past and in the war with Perseus. He then explained first how Gaius Lucretius, the Roman praetor, had treated his people with arrogance, cruelty, and greed. Next he told them that Lucius Hortensius' conduct was even worse at that very minute. While the Chalcidians believed that rather than forsake their alliance they should endure anything—even worse treatment than what they had experienced—at the same time they believed that where Lucretius and Hortensius were concerned, it would have been safer to shut the gates in their faces rather than allow them into the city. The cities that had excluded Lucretius and Hortensius—Emathia, Amphipolis, Maronea, and Aenus—were intact; but in the case of Chalcis, the shrines had been stripped of their ornaments, and Gaius Lucretius had the fruits carried to Antium by his temple-robbing vessels; free persons had been pressed into slavery; the wealth of allies of the Roman people had been and was being stolen on a daily basis. Following the practice instituted by Gaius Lucretius, Hortensius also billeted sailors in Chalcidian towns both winter and summer, and their homes were filled with a rabble of seamen; these men, who had no scruples about what they said or did, were coming and going freely amongst the Chalcidians themselves and their wives and children.

8. The Senate decided to summon Lucretius so he could make his case in person and defend himself. But far more was said once he was present than he had been accused of in his absence, and his accusers were joined by two very influential and powerful men, the tribunes of the plebs Manius Juventius Thalna and Gnaeus Aufidius. Not just lambasting him in the Senate, they even dragged him out into a public meeting, covered him with reproaches, and set a date for his trial.

At the Senate's direction, the praetor Quintus Maenius responded to the Chalcidians that the Senate knew the truth of what they said about their meritorious conduct towards the Roman people both before and during the current war, and that this conduct was valued as it deserved to be. As for the previous actions of Gaius Lucretius and the current behaviour of Lucius Hortensius of which they complained—how could anyone think that these actions and this behaviour occurred at the Senate's will, anyone, that is, who knew that the Roman people waged war against Perseus, and before him against his father Philip, for the freedom of Greece,* and not so that their allies and friends should suffer at the hands of Roman magistrates? He said that they would communicate in writing to the praetor, Lucius Hortensius, that the behaviour the Chalcidians objected to was unacceptable to the Senate; if any free men had been enslaved, he was to see to it that they be sought out at the very first opportunity and restored to liberty; moreover, that the Senate judged it right that except for the captains, no sailors should be quartered in civilian homes. This was written to Hortensius at the Senate's direction.

Gifts of 2,000 *asses* each were given to the envoys, and conveyances were hired at public expense to take Micythio comfortably to Brundisium. When the day came for Gaius Lucretius' trial, the tribunes prosecuted him before the people and set a fine of 1,000,000 *asses*. When the assembly was held, all thirty-five tribes voted to condemn him.

9. Nothing worthy of record happened in Liguria that year: the enemy did not take up arms, and the consul did not lead his legions into the field. Once he had assured himself sufficiently about peace for the year, the consul sent the soldiers of the two Roman legions home—within sixty days of his entering the province. Then, having

settled the forces of the Latin and Italian allies into winter quarters at Luna and Pisa early on, he himself with the cavalry toured most of the towns in the province of Gaul.

Although Macedonia was the only scene of outright conflict, there were nevertheless suspicions about Gentius, the Illyrian king. Consequently the Senate decided that eight ships should be fitted out and sent from Brundisium to Gaius Furius, the junior officer at Issa who was in charge of the island with a force of two ships. Two thousand soldiers were embarked on these eight ships. The praetor Marcus Raecius conscripted the men, by senatorial decree, from the part of Italy lying opposite Illyricum. At the same time the consul Hostilius sent Appius Claudius into Illyricum with 4,000 infantry to protect the people dwelling on its borders. As the latter was not content with the manpower he had brought with him, he petitioned for assistance from allies and armed an additional force of about 8,000 men of various races. Once he had traversed the entire region he settled at the Dassaretian town of Lychnidus.

10. Not far from there lay Uscana,* which bordered Perseus' dominions. It had 10,000 citizens and a small garrison of Cretans for protection. Messengers repeatedly came from there in secret to Claudius, saying that if he moved his forces closer, there would be those who were ready to hand over the town. And, they added, it was worth the effort: the booty was enough to satisfy not just himself and his personal friends but the soldiers too. The expectations stirred by greed so blinded Appius' mind that he did not detain any of those who approached him, he did not require hostages as a guarantee against any act of treachery, he did not send anyone to reconnoitre, and he did not obtain an oath of good faith. He simply arranged a date, set out from Lychnidus, and encamped about twelve miles from the city to which he was marching. He advanced from his camp about the fourth watch,* leaving approximately 1,000 men to guard the camp. Disorganized, spread out in a long column, dispersed and scattered by the nocturnal journey, his forces made their way to the city. Their carelessness increased once they saw not a single armed man on the walls. But as soon as they were within missile range, simultaneous attacks were launched from two gates; and at the cry of those mounting the attack, an enormous cacophony arose from the walls as the women shrieked and bronze clanged on all sides, and an unorganized crowd, together with a rabble of slaves, screamed

and shouted. The vocal intimidation coming at them from every direction was so effective that the Romans could not withstand even the first wave of the onslaught. As a result, more died fleeing than fighting: barely 2,000 men escaped with their leader to the camp. The added distance to the camp afforded the enemy on their heels more opportunity to hunt down the exhausted Romans. Appius did not remain in the camp long enough even to regroup his men from their scattered flight, though this would have afforded safety to those wandering in the fields; instead he led the survivors of the debacle straight back to Lychnidus.

11. Word of this episode and of other failed operations in Macedonia reached Rome through one Sextus Digitius, a military tribune who had gone to the city to offer sacrifices. These developments filled the fathers with the fear that they might suffer some greater disgrace. They dispatched Marcus Fulvius Flaccus and Marcus Caninius Rebilus as envoys to Macedonia; they were to discover what was going on and report back. In addition, the consul Aulus Atilius was to announce an assembly for the consular elections so that they could take place in January, and he himself was to come to the city at the very first opportunity. Meanwhile, the praetor Marcus Raecius was charged with issuing a decree to summon all senators from around Italy back to Rome, unless they were absent on public business; those who were in Rome were not to go more than a mile from the city.

These measures were taken in accordance with the senatorial orders. The consular elections took place on the twenty-sixth of January. The men elected as consuls were Quintus Marcius Philippus, for the second time, and Gnaeus Servilius Caepio. Two days later the praetors were chosen: Gaius Decimius, Marcus Claudius Marcellus, Gaius Sulpicius Galus, Gaius Marcius Figulus, Servius Cornelius Lentulus, and Publius Fonteius Capito. In addition to the two urban praetorships, four areas of responsibility were decreed for the incoming praetors: Spain, Sardinia, Sicily, and the fleet.

The Senate's envoys returned from Macedonia at the very end of February. They reported on Perseus' successful undertakings of that summer and the degree to which Rome's allies were in the grip of fear, now that the king had brought so many cities back under his control. Moreover, the consul's army lacked its full complement because of leaves of absence; they had been granted freely, out of the desire to curry political favour. The consul held the military tribunes responsible for this state of affairs; they in turn cast the blame on him. The envoys, in reporting that the casualties were mostly emergency conscripts from the area and not of Italian stock, minimized the disgrace caused by Claudius' rashness. The incoming consuls were directed to bring the matter of Macedonia to the Senate for discussion as soon as they had entered their magistracies. Italy and Macedonia were designated as their provinces.

There was an intercalation that year: an additional month was inserted the third day after the Terminalia.* Three priests died during the year. Lucius Flamininus, the augur, died <. . .>.* Two pontiffs, Lucius Furius Philus and Gaius Livius Salinator, passed away. The pontiffs appointed Titus Manlius Torquatus to Furius' place, and Marcus Servilius to that of Livius.

12. At the beginning of the following year, when the new consuls introduced discussion of the provinces, it was agreed that at the very first opportunity they should either settle between themselves the responsibility for Macedonia and Italy or draw lots. It was decided to establish what supplementary forces the circumstances called for in each province before the drawing of the lots, while the outcome was unknown; this way personal influence would have no weight. In the case of Macedonia the decision was for 6,000 Roman infantry, 6,000 of the Latin and Italian allies, 250 Roman cavalry, and 300 allied cavalry; the old soldiers were to be discharged so that in each Roman legion there would not be more than the 6,000 infantry and 300 cavalry. In the case of the second consul, no definite limit was set as to the number of Roman citizens he could enrol as reinforcements: the only limit was that he should conscript two legions, each of which was to have 5,200 infantry and 300 cavalry. The number of Latins assigned to the second consul was higher than for his colleague: 10,000 infantry and 600 cavalry. Moreover, four legions were to be conscripted, to be deployed if need arose. The consuls were not permitted to appoint the military tribunes for these legions; the people elected them. From the Latin and Italian allies 16,000 infantry and 1,000 cavalry were called up. It was agreed that this army should simply be at the ready so that it could go anywhere circumstance might demand. Macedonia was the greatest source of concern. For the fleet, the order was that 1,000 sailors, Roman citizens from the order of freedmen, and 500 from Italy should be enlisted; an equal

number was to be enlisted from Sicily; and the consul who obtained Macedonia as his province was charged with the responsibility of transporting these men there, wherever the fleet happened to be.

The reinforcements for the army in Spain were set at 3,000 Roman infantry and 300 cavalry. The number of soldiers in the legions there was also limited to 5,200 infantry and 300 cavalry; and the praetor who obtained Spain was ordered to call up 4,000 infantry and 300 cavalry from the allies.

13. I am not unaware that the heedlessness underlying the wide-spread modern refusal to believe that gods issue portents also causes prodigies no longer to be announced in public or included in the historical record. Nevertheless, as I write about bygone affairs, my mind in some way takes on an antique cast, and a certain spirit of religious respect prevents me from regarding as unworthy of recording in my history matters that the deeply sagacious men of old deemed meritorious of public attention.* At Anagnia, two prodigies were announced that year: a comet was seen in the sky, and a heifer spoke; she was being maintained at public expense. During the very same days the sky at Minturnae had glowed with the appearance of something on fire. At Reate there was a shower of stones. The statue of Apollo on the citadel at Cumae shed tears for three days and three nights. Within the city of Rome, two temple attendants reported prodigies: one said that in the temple of Fortuna a crested snake was seen by quite a number of people; the second reported that in the shrine of Fortuna Primigenia on the Quirinal two different prodigies occurred: a palm tree bloomed in the forecourt, and there was a shower of blood during daylight hours. Two prodigies were not taken up: one because it took place in a private location (Titus Marcius Figulus declared that a palm tree bloomed in his *impluvium**), and the other because it happened on foreign territory (it was said that at Fregellae in the house of a Lucius Atreius a spear, which he had bought for his son's military service, had been on fire for over two hours one day, but had emerged completely unscorched). The decemvirs consulted their books for the public prodigies. They decreed the gods to whom the consuls should sacrifice forty full-grown animals; further, they announced that there should be a supplication, all the magistrates should sacrifice full-grown animals at all the sacred couches, and the people should wear wreaths.* Everything was done in accordance with the decemvirs' dictates.

14. Then the elections for choosing the censors were announced. Leading citizens contended for the office: Gaius Valerius Laevinus, Lucius Postumius Albinus, Publius Mucius Scaevola, Marcus Junius Brutus, Gaius Claudius Pulcher, and Tiberius Sempronius Gracchus. The Roman people elected the last two as their censors.*

Because of the Macedonian war there was more anxiety about the conduct of the draft than at other times. In a meeting of the Senate the consuls consequently blamed the plebs, because even the younger men* were not responding to the call. The praetors Gaius Sulpicius and Marcus Claudius argued against the consuls in defence of the plebs, saying that the draft did not pose a challenge for consuls in general, but only for politically ambitious ones; such consuls would not make anyone become a soldier against his will. So that the conscript fathers could see for themselves that this was the case, with the Senate's approval the praetors would carry out the draft themselves, although the weight of their magisterial power and their authority were less.

The task was entrusted to the praetors, with great willingness on the part of the fathers, but not without insult to the consuls. The censors lent their aid to the undertaking by issuing the following decree in a public meeting: while conducting the census, they would add to the oath shared by all citizens sworn answers to these questions: 'Are you less than forty-six years old?'; and 'Have you registered for the draft in accordance with the edict of the censors Gaius Claudius and Tiberius Sempronius?'; and 'If you are not drafted, will you continue to register for the draft, as long as conscription may occur while these men remain in office?' Further, since the story was circulating that many men in the Macedonian legions were on leave indefinitely because the commanders were trying to garner popularity, the censors decreed that soldiers who enlisted in the consulship of Publius Aelius and Gaius Popillius* or subsequent consuls and who were in Italy should return to their province within thirty days after registering with the censors, and that the names of those men who were still under the authority of their father or grandfather* should be submitted to the censors. The censors said that they would investigate the reasons behind each discharge from military service; where premature dismissals seemed to them based on favouritism, they would order the men to continue to serve. When this decree and the censors' declaration had been disseminated throughout the town centres and gathering places, such a crowd of men under forty-six converged on Rome that the unusual crush was a burden to the city.

15. In addition to the conscription of men designated to be sent out as reinforcements, four legions were enlisted by the praetor Gaius Sulpicius, and the draft was completed within eleven days. Then the consuls drew lots for their provinces. The praetors had drawn theirs earlier to ensure the administration of justice: the urban praetorship had fallen to Gaius Sulpicius, and Gaius Decimius was in charge of legal affairs involving foreigners; Marcus Claudius Marcellus drew Spain, Servius Cornelius Lentulus Sicily, Publius Fonteius Capito Sardinia, and Gaius Marcius Figulus the fleet. Of the consuls, Gnaeus Servilius obtained Italy and Quintus Marcius Macedonia. Marcius left as soon as the Latin Festival was over.

Caepio* then referred to the Senate the question of which two of the new legions he should take with him to Gaul. The senators decreed that the praetors Gaius Sulpicius and Marcus Claudius should give to the consul the legions that seemed best to them out of those they had conscripted. The consul endured his subordination to the praetors' judgement with ill-grace. He dismissed the Senate and, standing at the tribunal of the praetors, he demanded that they give him two legions in accordance with the Senate's decree. The praetors followed the consul's judgement in making the selection.

The censors then revised the roll of the Senate. Marcus Aemilius Lepidus was named *princeps senatus** for a third census period. Seven men were expelled from the Senate. In reviewing the census of the people, the censors learned from the lists how many soldiers from Macedonia had deserted their posts; these they compelled to return to their province. The censors studied the reasons for the leaves of the men who had been discharged, and where the discharge appeared not to have been earned, they forced the soldier to swear to the following: 'Do you solemnly swear that you will return to the province of Macedonia, in accordance with the decree of the censors Gaius Claudius and Tiberius Sempronius, inasmuch as you are able to do so in good faith?'

16. The censors were especially harsh and severe in reviewing the equestrians.* They stripped many men of their horses. This action antagonized the equestrian order. And then the censors fuelled the flames of resentment with an edict, in which they decreed that no one who had contracted to collect public taxes or undertake public works in the censorship of Quintus Fulvius and Aulus Postumius could attend the auction at which they would take bids on these contracts;

nor could such a man be a partner or an associate in a transaction at the auction. Despite repeated complaints, the established tax-collectors could not persuade the Senate to rein in censorial power. Finally they won over Publius Rutilius, a tribune of the plebs, to promote their cause; he was angry at the censors because of a personal dispute. The censors had ordered a client of his, a freedman, to demolish a house-wall along the Sacred Way, opposite the public shrines, because it had been built up against public property. As a private citizen he had appealed to the tribunes. When no one besides Rutilius intervened, the censors sent men to confiscate property as surety, and at a public meeting they fined him. This had been the origin of the dispute.

When the established contractors had recourse to the tribune, without warning and all on his own he promulgated a motion to treat as void the contracts for all taxes and public works that Gaius Claudius and Tiberius Sempronius* had let; these were to be bid on again so that everyone, without distinction, would have the right to buy up and undertake them. The tribune of the plebs set a date for a meeting of the assembly to discuss the motion. When the day came and the censors appeared to speak against it, there was silence as long as Gracchus was speaking; but Claudius was drowned out by shouting and ordered the herald to obtain him a hearing. When silence had been imposed, Rutilius protested that in calling for silence Claudius had taken over his meeting and thus demeaned his authority. With that, Rutilius left the Capitoline (which was where the assembly was meeting).

The following day Rutilius provoked a massive disturbance. He began by declaring Tiberius Gracchus' property forfeit to the gods since Tiberius too had demeaned his authority by not complying when Rutilius intervened on behalf of the man who appealed to him over the fine and the impounding of property as security. Rutilius charged Gaius Claudius with having taken over the public meeting. Further, Rutilius announced that he considered both censors guilty of treason, and he asked the urban praetor, Gaius Sulpicius, to set a date for their impeachment. The censors offered no resistance to having judgement passed on them by the people at the very first opportunity. The twenty-third and twenty-fourth of September were set as the dates for the treason trial. The censors proceeded directly to the Hall of Liberty. There they sealed the public records and closed their office and dismissed the public slaves, declaring that they would conduct no public business before the people had passed judgement on them.

Claudius' trial took place first. At the point when eight out of the twelve equestrian centuries, as well as many other centuries of the first class, had voted against the censor, the leading citizens publicly removed their golden rings and put on mourning robes in order to go around the plebs as suppliants.* But Tiberius Gracchus is said to have done the most to alter opinion; for, when the plebs cried out on all sides that there was no danger to Gracchus, he swore a solemn oath that if his colleague were convicted, he would accompany him into exile without awaiting the outcome of his own trial. Just the same, Claudius was nearly cheated of his hopes: his conviction failed by only eight centuries. Once Claudius had been absolved, the tribune of the plebs declined to proceed with the charge against Gracchus.

17. The same year representatives from Aquileia made a formal request to have the number of colonists increased; 1,500 households were enrolled by senatorial decree. The committee of three sent out to see to their settlement consisted of Titus Annius Luscus, Publius Decius Subolo, and Marcus Cornelius Cethegus.

Also that year the envoys who had been sent to Greece, Gaius Popillius and Gnaeus Octavius, first announced at Thebes and then circulated around the cities of the Peloponnese the Senate's decree that no one should supply Roman magistrates with anything for the war except what the Senate had previously determined. The decree had the further effect of inspiring confidence that, in the future, people would be relieved of the burdens that were draining them dry as commander after commander made demand after demand.

The council of the Achaeans met with the envoys at Aegium. The exchange was pleasant on both sides; the Romans left these utterly reliable people with the highest of expectations for future relations. They then crossed over to Aetolia. Matters there had not yet reached open revolt, but there was an all-pervasive sense of mistrust and accusations piled upon counter-accusations. For these reasons the envoys demanded hostages but did not impose a resolution on the situation before they went on to Acarnania. The Acarnanians met with the envoys at Thyrreum. There was factional strife there too: certain leading men made a formal request that garrisons be introduced into their towns, in response to the insane impulse of some men to align their people with Macedonia; another group objected that allied cities at peace should not receive the same demeaning treatment customarily dealt out to captured enemy cities. This latter petition seemed reasonable to the envoys. They returned to Hostilius, the proconsul at Larisa, since he was the one who had sent them out. He kept Octavius with him and sent Popillius with about 1,000 men to Ambracia for the winter.

18. At the beginning of the winter Perseus did not dare to venture beyond the borders of Macedonia, out of fear that the Romans would invade his kingdom somewhere if it were left empty; but around the solstice, when the depth of the snow makes the mountains impassable from the Thessalian side, he thought he saw a chance to crush the hopes and spirits of his neighbours such that they would pose no threat while he was occupied with the Roman war. Cotys ensured peace from Thrace, and Cephalus, with his recent abrupt defection from the Romans, did the same from Epirus; Perseus' own recent war had just brought the Dardani securely under control. He could see that only the section of Macedonia adjacent to Illyricum was at risk. The Illyrians were indeed restless and offered a way in for the Romans. If, however, he subdued the closest Illyrians, King Gentius too, who had been wavering for a long time already, could be won over. Perseus accordingly set out and went to Stuberra with 10,000 infantrymen (some of whom were phalanx troops), 2,000 light-armed troops, and 500 cavalry.

Once there, he procured many days' worth of supplies, and directed the siege machinery to be brought along behind him; three days later he pitched camp at Uscana, which is the largest city in the territory of the Penestae. Before resorting to force, however, he sent men ahead to test the attitudes first of the garrison's leaders and then of the townsfolk. This garrison consisted of Romans and a corps of Illyrian youth. Once Perseus learned from his men's report that no one was disposed to peace, he started his offensive and attempted to besiege the city. The Macedonians attacked relentlessly, night and day, with one wave of soldiers succeeding another, some tackling the walls with ladders, others assailing the gate with torches. The city's defenders nonetheless sustained the onslaught, hoping that in their exposed position the Macedonians could not endure the winter's force for very long and that the respite from the Roman war would not be such as to allow them to linger. But the defenders' defiance crumpled when they observed sheds being brought up to shield the siege-workers and towers being erected. For aside from the fact that they could not match their opponents' manpower, they had no reserves of food or any supplies on hand (as happens with an unexpected siege). There was consequently no hope of resisting. Gaius Carvilius of Spoletium and Gaius Afranius were sent from the Roman garrison to petition Perseus, preferably to allow them to depart with their weapons and personal property and then, failing that, at least to guarantee their lives and freedom. The king's promises were more generous than his behaviour: after he had directed the Romans to leave the city with their weapons, he first stripped them of these. Upon their departure, the troop of Illyrians, 500 in all, and the people of Uscana surrendered themselves and the city.

19. Perseus left an occupying force there and marched the whole herd of captives, which was nearly as numerous as his army, to Stuberra. Except for the officers, Perseus distributed the approximately 400 Romans among the citizenry for safekeeping and sold the population of Uscana and the Illyrians. He then marched his army back to the land of the Penestae in order to establish control over Oaeneum. The location of this town is generally a good one, and in particular there is a pass there to the Labeatae, Gentius' kingdom. As Perseus was passing a heavily manned stronghold, known as Draudacum, one of the men familiar with the region said that there was no point in taking Oaeneum unless he controlled Draudacum too, for the latter was better situated in all respects. The moment Perseus approached with his army, everyone surrendered. Puffed up by this unexpectedly swift capitulation, and observing how much fear his battle column inspired, Perseus took control of eleven more strongholds also by intimidation. In a few cases actual force was required; the rest surrendered voluntarily. Perseus also captured 1,500 Roman soldiers who had been posted in these garrisons. In negotiating with them Perseus derived great benefit from Carvilius of Spoletium's assertions that the Macedonian had not treated the Romans cruelly.

When Perseus reached Oaeneum, it could not be taken without a full-scale assault. Its strength lay in having rather more men of military age than the other places, in the fortified walls of the town, and in being enclosed on one side by a river, known as the Artatus, and on the other by a mountain which was very high and difficult of access. These factors gave the townspeople some hope of resisting.

Perseus invested the town and began constructing a ramp on the upper side of the city; its height would bring him up over the city walls. While this was being done, there were frequent skirmishes. The townsfolk defended their walls and impeded the enemy's projects with regular sallies. In these they suffered many casualties while the survivors were weak from struggling round the clock and from their wounds.

As soon as the ramp reached the city wall, a royal troop, known as 'the Conquerors',* went across while an attack was launched against the city from ladders set up simultaneously at multiple locations. All the adult males were slaughtered; the women and children were kept under guard; the rest of the plunder went to the army. Returning triumphantly to Stuberra, Perseus sent Pleuratus, an Illyrian who was living in exile with him, and Adaeus, a Macedonian from Beroea, as envoys to Gentius. Perseus instructed them to recount his accomplishments against the Romans and Dardani during that summer and winter; they were also to report his recent accomplishments during his winter expedition in Illyricum; and they were to exhort Gentius to join in an alliance with him and the Macedonians.

20. The envoys crossed the summit of Mount Scordus and the wastelands of Illyricum, which the Macedonians had intentionally stripped bare to deprive the Dardani of an easy approach into Illyricum or Macedonia, and finally, after great effort, reached Scodra. King Gentius was at Lissus. The envoys were summoned there, and he listened to them in a receptive way as they recounted what they had been charged to impart. But the reply they brought back was equivocal: Gentius by no means lacked the will to make war on the Romans, but he was greatly lacking in the financial resources to do so as he wished. The messengers reported this response to Perseus at Stuberra just when he was engaged in selling the captives from Illyricum. The same messengers were immediately dispatched again, accompanied by a certain Glaucias from the corps of bodyguards, but without any mention of money, the sole means that could impel the impoverished barbarian to fight. Perseus then pillaged Ancyra and marched his army back into the territory of the Penestae. He reinforced the garrisons at Uscana and all the strongholds around it that he had captured, and then returned to Macedonia.

21. A Roman lieutenant, Lucius Coelius, had oversight of Illyricum. He had not dared to enter the area when Perseus was there. After the latter's departure he at last attempted to take back Uscana in the land of the Penestae. The Macedonian garrison there inflicted multiple injuries on his men and repulsed him. Coelius marched his forces back to Lychnidus. A few days later he sent a man of Fregellae, Marcus Trebellius, with a fairly powerful force to the Penestae to collect hostages from those towns that had maintained their allegiance faithfully. Coelius directed Trebellius then to proceed to the Parthini, who had also pledged to give hostages. Trebellius encountered no resistance from either people in exacting hostages. The cavalrymen of the Penestae were sent to Apollonia, while those of the Parthini went to Dyrrachium, better known to the Greeks of those days as Epidamnus.

Appius Claudius, wishing to erase the ignominy he had incurred in Illyricum, started to besiege Phanote, a fortress in Epirus. In addition to his Roman forces he brought Chaonian and Thesprotian auxiliaries, for a total of roughly 6,000 men. But it was not worth the effort: a man named Cleuas whom Perseus had left there was defending the fortress with a strong garrison.

Perseus himself proceeded to Elimea, where he conducted a *lustrum* of the army. He then marched to Stratus at the invitation of the Epirotae. At the time, Stratus was the most powerful city in Aetolia; it was situated above the Ambracian Gulf near the Inachus river. Perseus started out with 10,000 infantry and 300 cavalry; the equestrian force was somewhat reduced because of the narrowness and roughness of the roads. When on the third day he reached Mount Citium, he crossed it with difficulty because of the depth of the snow, and he could scarcely find a place to camp. He continued on, more because it was impossible to stay than because there was anything tolerable about either the route or the weather. After great difficulty, especially for the pack animals, Perseus encamped the next day at a temple of Jupiter Nicaeus, as he is called. Then, after a massive march, he rested for <. . .> days* at the Aratthus river, impeded by the height of the water. In this span of time a bridge was finished. He marched his forces across and after a day's journey met Archidamus, the Aetolian leader who was offering to betray Stratus to him.

22. That day he pitched camp on the edge of Aetolian territory; two days after that he reached Stratus where he set up camp next to the Inachus river. Expecting the Aetolians to pour out of every gate and entrust themselves to him, he discovered instead that the gates

were barred and that on the very night of his arrival a Roman garrison, led by their officer Gaius Popillius, had been admitted. While
Archidamus was there, the city leaders had been impelled by his
influence to invite the king; but after Archidamus' departure, they
were less active and gave an opposing faction the chance to call in
Popillius from Ambracia with his 1,000 infantry. Dinarchus too, the
commander of the Aetolian cavalry, came at the same time with 600
infantry and <. . .> cavalry. It was common knowledge that he had
set off for Stratus as if to join Perseus, but that as circumstances
changed, so too did his purpose; thus he had attached himself to the
Romans, his intended adversaries.

Popillius was no less cautious than he had to be, surrounded by such
fickle minds. He kept the keys to the gates and the defence of the walls
under his own control from the start; and he moved Dinarchus and his
Aetolians, along with the fighting force of Stratus, into the citadel,
under the pretext that they were its garrison. Perseus attempted to
negotiate from the hills overlooking the upper part of the city, but when
he observed that the occupants were standing firm and even fending
him off with long-distance missiles, he established his camp five miles
from the city across the Petitarus river. There he convened a council of
war. Archidamus and the Epirotae deserters wanted to stay, but the
leading Macedonians thought they should not contend with the least
hospitable part of the year, when they had no supplies on hand and, as
the besiegers, would suffer deprivation before the people they were
besieging, especially since the enemy's winter quarters were not far
away. Perseus was frightened and moved his camp to Aperantia.
Archidamus had great influence and status among the Aperanti, and for
that reason Perseus received universal welcome. Archidamus himself
was given command over their fortress, with a troop of 800 soldiers.

23. Perseus' return to Macedonia involved just as much trouble for
the pack animals and his men as the outward journey had. The report
of his march on Stratus, however, dislodged Appius from the siege of
Phanote. Cleuas, with a band of energetic young men, pursued Appius
along the almost impassable foothills of the mountains where he killed
about 1,000 and captured about 200 from Appius' heavily encumbered
column. After traversing the mountainous passes, Appius set up a base
for a few days on the plain they call Meleon.

Meanwhile, Cleuas was joined by Philostratus, who had a band
of Epirotae with him, and crossed to the territory of Antigonea.

The Macedonians set out to pillage; Philostratus established himself with his cohort in a hidden location and lay in wait. Then troops charged out of Antigonea against the scattered pillagers. Chasing headlong after the fleeing Macedonians, the Antigonean troops hurled themselves into the valley occupied by the enemy. About 1,000 Antigonenses were killed there, and about 100 were taken prisoner. After this completely successful enterprise, Cleuas and Philostratus moved their camp close to Appius' base to prevent the Roman army from attacking their allies.

As Appius was spending his time there to no purpose, he dismissed the Chaonian and Thesprotian contingents as well as the rest of the Epirotae and retreated with the Italian soldiers to Illyricum. He dispersed his men into winter quarters among the allied cities of the Parthini and returned to Rome to offer sacrifices.

Perseus recalled 1,000 infantry and 200 cavalry from the land of the Penestae and sent them to Cassandrea to serve as a garrison. The messengers came back from Gentius bearing the same report. Perseus did not stop trying to win him over, sending one embassy after the other, for it was clear what a bulwark he would provide. At the same time, the Macedonian king could not bring himself to expend his capital for a cause of the greatest import in every respect.

BOOK FORTY-FOUR

1. As the winter during which these events transpired began to turn to spring, the consul Quintus Marcius Philippus left Rome and proceeded to Brundisium with 5,000 men to transport as reinforcements for the legions. The former consul, Marcus Popillius, and some younger men of equivalent nobility accompanied the consul to serve as military tribunes for the Macedonian legions. Gaius Marcius Figulus, the praetor to whom the fleet had been allotted, went to Brundisium at this time too. They left Italy together, reaching Corcyra the following day and Actium, the port of Acarnania, the day after that. From there, the consul disembarked at Ambracia and proceeded overland to Thessaly, and the praetor continued by sea past Cape Leucate into the Gulf of Corinth. He left his ships at Creusa, and then he too pushed on by land, through the middle of Boeotia, to the fleet at Chalcis (the journey being a single day's march for someone lightly equipped).*

At the time, Aulus Hostilius was encamped in Thessaly near Palaepharsalus. Although he had had no success in combat to speak of, he had transformed the army, redirecting it from unbridled licence to strict military discipline, and he had treated the allies honourably and protected them from any kind of maltreatment.* When he heard of his successor's approach, Hostilius carefully inspected his arsenal, men, and horses and then went with the troops in parade order to meet the consul en route. The initial meeting was appropriate to each man's personal dignity as well as to that of the Roman name. The two leaders stayed on excellent terms throughout the campaign, with the proconsul remaining attached to the army.

After a few days the consul delivered an address to the soldiers. Starting with Perseus' murder of his brother and his murderous intentions towards his father, Marcius went on to cite Perseus' acquisition of his kingdom by criminal means, the poisonings and the slaughter, the abominably thuggish attack on Eumenes, the wrongs done to the Roman people, and the plundering of allied cities in contravention of the treaty. Perseus, Marcius said, would learn from the outcome of his enterprises how very abhorrent all these acts were to the gods too; for the gods smiled on dutifulness and constancy,* the attributes that raised the Roman people to such heights. Marcius then compared the might of the Roman people, already encompassing the known world, with that of the Macedonians, and the army of the one with the army of the other: how much greater, he asked, were the resources of Philip or Antiochus, which had been smashed by forces no greater?

2. By talking in this fashion, Marcius ignited the troops' enthusiasm. He then turned to consultations about strategy. The praetor, too, Gaius Marcius, had arrived from Chalcis, after collecting the fleet. There was general agreement to waste no more time tarrying in Thessaly, but to break camp immediately and march onward into Macedonia; the praetor would meanwhile be responsible for a simultaneous attack along the enemy's coastline. The praetor was sent on his way. The soldiers were ordered to bring with them provisions for a month. Nine days after taking charge of the army, Marcius had the troops on the move. After advancing for a day, he summoned guides for the various routes and asked them to explain to his war council which way each of them would take.* Marcius then dismissed the guides and asked his advisers which route they considered the best. Some preferred to go via Pythium, others through the Cambunian Mountains, which Hostilius had used the year before during his consulship, and yet others past Lake Ascuris. The routes overlapped to some extent, and so deliberation over the matter was postponed until the time came when they would make camp close to where the ways diverged. Marcius then marched into Perrhaebia and established a base between Azorus and Doliche* to reconsider which route to take.

Perseus, meanwhile, decided to occupy all the passes since he knew the enemy was on the move but could not anticipate which road he would take. He sent 10,000 light-armed troops under Asclepiodotus to the ridge of the Cambunian Mountains, which the Macedonians call Volustana. Hippias was ordered to hold the pass near the fortification overlooking Lake Ascuris—the place is called Lapathus—with a force of 12,000 Macedonians. Perseus at first stationed himself with the remaining troops around Dium.* Subsequently the king gave the impression of being so deficient in strategic thinking as to be completely senseless, hurrying back and forth along the coast, together with unarmed cavalry, now to Heracleum and now to Phila, before returning to Dium by the same route.*

3. At this point the consul made up his mind to march through the pass near Otolobus where one of Perseus' generals had established

his camp.* Marcius nonetheless decided to send 4,000 men in advance to seize advantageous positions. Marcus Claudius and Quintus Marcius, the consul's son, were put in charge of this troop. The main body of the army followed directly after. But the road was so steep, rough, and rocky that in two days the advance party, despite being lightly equipped, covered scarcely fifteen miles before making camp. The place they occupied is called Dierus. The next day they progressed seven miles further. After occupying a hill not far from their adversary's camp, they sent word back to the consul that they had reached the enemy and were entrenched in a place that was safe and advantageously situated in all respects; accordingly, he should push on to join them with all speed.

The consul was concerned about the difficulty of the route he had embarked on and about the fate of the scant number of men he had sent ahead, right into the enemy's stronghold, but the arrival of the messenger at Lake Ascuris filled him with confidence. The forces were reunited and made camp on the slopes of the occupied hill where the lie of the land was most suitable. The lofty summit commanded a view far and wide; under their eyes lay not just the enemy's camp, which was a little more than a mile off, but the entire region, to Dium, Phila, and the coast. In this setting, the soldiers' spirits were stirred now that they were gazing upon the heart of the war and all the king's forces and enemy territory from so close at hand. Consequently they eagerly urged the consul to lead them directly to the enemy's camp; he gave them instead a day's rest from the demands of the march. The following day the consul left part of his forces to guard the camp and advanced upon the enemy.

4. Hippias had recently been sent by the king to guard the pass. From the moment he saw the Roman camp on the hillside, he had his men mentally ready for combat, and at the consul's approach he went out to meet him. The Romans had marched forth stripped for action. Their opponents were light-armed troops, precisely the kind of force most likely to provoke a fight. Accordingly, the moment they met they let fly with their weapons; and in the reckless assault, although few lives were lost on either side, a considerable number of wounds were inflicted by both parties. The following day tempers were already hot, and the men would have flung themselves into the fray even more aggressively and with even more numbers if there had been enough room to assume battle formation; but the narrow, tapered spine of the mountain was scarcely wide enough for three columns of soldiers. And so, with only a few fighting, the rest of the crowd, especially those in full body armour, stood apart from the battle and watched. The light-armed troops were actually able to run ahead through the curves of the ridge and engage their counterparts on the flanks, regardless of the unevenness or the flatness of the terrain. More were wounded than killed that day, and nightfall broke up the fighting.

On the third day the Roman general did not know what to do: he could neither remain on the barren ridge nor retreat without shame, and even danger, should the enemy attack from the heights during a withdrawal. Marcius had no option but to counteract the boldness of his enterprise by compounding it, a course of action which does sometimes prove wise in the end.* Indeed the situation had reached the point where if his opponent had been similar to the Macedonian kings of old, the consul might have suffered a calamitous defeat. But although the king was roaming the shore near Dium with the cavalry and could practically hear the shouting and din of the combatants twelve miles off, he did not strengthen his forces by replacing exhausted soldiers with fresh ones, nor did he himself, which was of the greatest importance, join the battle. The Roman commander, by contrast, though he was over sixty years old and corpulent of form, threw himself tirelessly into all military duties. He commendably persisted to the end in what he had boldly undertaken.* Leaving Popillius to guard the ridge, he sent out an advance party to clear a path and crossed into uncharted wilderness. He asked Attalus and Misacenes to use the auxiliary forces of their peoples to provide protection for the men who were opening up a path through the mountainous terrain; he himself sent the cavalry and the carts to the front and brought up the rear of the column with the legionaries.

5. The Romans' struggles as they descended and the damage to the pack animals and baggage defy description. They had advanced scarcely four miles, when nothing seemed more desirable than to retrace their steps—if they could have. As for the battle column, the trouble caused by the elephants was almost as severe as an enemy assault. When these animals reached the pathless part, they shook off their handlers and provoked great fear, especially among the horses, by their fearsome trumpeting. But then a means of leading the elephants down was devised. The pitch along the slope was measured,

and two long, strong poles were fixed into the ground below, separated from each other by not much more than the width of an elephant; then a beam was laid lengthwise across the poles, and thirty-foot-long planks were bound to it to make a platform, which was covered with dirt. A similar platform was then set up a little farther down, and then a third, and a whole series of them where the cliffs were sheer. An elephant would advance from solid ground onto a platform; before he reached the end, the poles were severed, and the platform gave way, forcing the elephant to slide gently onto the beginning of the next one. Some elephants slid upright, while others went down resting on their haunches. When the level surface of the next platform caught them, they were carried by a similar collapsing of the lower one until they reached the more horizontal terrain of the valley floor.*

The Romans advanced just over seven miles that day, but they accomplished only a fraction of the journey on their feet. For the most part they made their way forward jolting and bumping, rolling themselves, their weapons, and the rest of their gear downwards. Not even their leader, who was responsible for the journey, denied that the entire army could have been wiped out by a small band. They reached a moderate-sized plateau at night. Although they had unexpectedly at least found level ground where they could halt, they had little opportunity to see how unsafe the enclosed nature of the place made it. The following day they had to wait in the hollows of the valley for Popillius and the troops left with him. This latter group, too, although at no point in danger of enemy attack, was tormented by the rough terrain as if by hostile forces. On the third day the forces were united and marched through the pass known to the locals as Callipeuce. Then on the fourth day, the route was equally pathless, but the Romans were more skilled because of their experience and more hopeful because the enemy had not shown himself anywhere and because they were approaching the sea. The Romans pitched camp when they reached level ground between Heracleum and Libethrum. Most of the camp lay in the foothills; elsewhere they enclosed a section of the plain with a palisade for the cavalry to occupy.

6. It is said that the king was taking a bath when word arrived that the enemy was nearby.* Terrified at the news he leapt from the bathtub and rushed out, shouting that he had been beaten without a fight. Thereupon, turning in fright from one cowardly order or command to another, Perseus summoned two of his courtiers, one to go to Pella

to throw into the sea the money that had been stored at Phacus, and the other to go to Thessaly to burn the shipyards; he recalled Asclepiodotus and Hippias and their garrisons from the fortresses and left all the approaches open to attack. Perseus himself seized all the golden statues at Dium, to save them from becoming enemy plunder, and compelled the inhabitants of that area to move to Pydna. Thus what might have been viewed as rashness on the part of the consul— to advance beyond the point where he could retreat without the enemy's compliance—the king transformed into a rather shrewd piece of boldness. For the Romans had two passes through which they could escape from their position: one through Tempe into Thessaly, and the other past Dium and into Macedonia.* Both of these were held by the king's garrisons. And so, if the king had maintained a cool head for a few days and endured the first appearance of imminent danger, there would have been no retreat for the Romans through Tempe into Thessaly, and no route would have opened up for the conveyance of their supplies.

For the vale of Tempe is not easy to traverse even without the threat of attack. In addition to the five-mile defile where the track is narrow for a laden pack animal, the cliffs on both sides are so sheer that it is almost impossible to look down without feeling your head spin; the sound and the depth of the Peneus river as it rushes through the middle of the valley are terrifying. This area, so inhospitable by its very nature, was held by four royal garrisons in separate locations. The first was by the entrance at Gonnus, the second in Condylum, an impregnable fort, the third by Lapathus (which they call Charax), the fourth directly on the path, right in the middle where the vale is most narrow, and easily guarded by even ten men.

If the Romans' access to supplies had been cut off, together with the line of retreat through Tempe, they would have had to withdraw by the mountains they had come over. But while they had been able to accomplish this by stealth, they could not do it in plain view with the enemy controlling the overlooking peaks. Further, their familiarity with the challenge would have eradicated all hope. Given the rashness of the undertaking, no other course remained but to escape past Dium into Macedonia, through the heart of the enemy. If the gods had not stolen the king's wits,* this too would have been enormously difficult. The foothills of Mount Olympus leave little less than a mile of land before the sea, and half of it is covered by the mouth of the Baphyrus river, which overflows extensively; in addition, part of the plain is occupied by the temple of Jupiter and the town. What little remains could have been closed off with a moderate ditch and rampart, and there was such a supply of rocks and trees to hand that even a full-scale wall could have been erected and towers raised. But the king's mind was so clouded by the sudden alarm that he could see none of this. All the fortifications were stripped and left vulnerable to attack, and the king fled to Pydna.

7. The consul saw a great deal of both protection and reason for hope in his opponent's idiocy and inertia. Marcius sent a messenger to Spurius Lucretius at Larisa and directed him to occupy the fortresses around Tempe that the enemy had abandoned; and he sent Popillius ahead to investigate the routes around Dium. Upon learning that there were no obstacles anywhere in the vicinity, Marcius advanced to Dium in two days. He ordered the camp to be set up right next to the temple to forestall any violation of its sacred area.* He then entered the city, which was small, but beautified with public spaces and numerous statues, as well as being extremely well fortified. He could scarcely believe that one kind of trap or another did not lurk in amongst such great works, abandoned for no reason.

After devoting a day to general reconnaissance, he moved camp. Confident that there would be enough food in Pieria,* the consul advanced that day to a river called Mitys. The following day he went on to Agassae, where he established control of the city, which the inhabitants surrendered to him. Then, in order to win over the minds of the rest of the Macedonians, he contented himself with hostages and promised the residents that he was leaving the city to them without a garrison and that they would live free from taxation and under their own laws. From there he advanced a day's journey and pitched camp at the River Ascordus. Thereupon, perceiving that the farther he went from Thessaly, the greater the paucity of all resources, he returned to Dium. Not a doubt remained in anyone's mind as to what he would have suffered if he had been cut off from Thessaly, since there was no safe way to proceed far beyond it.*

Perseus gathered all his soldiers and commanders together and berated those in charge of the garrisons, especially Asclepiodotus and Hippias, saying that they had handed over the gates of Macedonia to the Romans. No one, however, could have been accused of this more justly than he himself.

As for the consul, initially the sight of the fleet offshore gave him hope that the ships were bringing provisions (for grain was extraordinarily expensive and in extremely short supply*), but he heard from the men already in the harbour that the supply ships had been left behind at Magnesia. At that point he was uncertain what to do—to such an extent did he have to contend simply with the difficulty of his situation, even without any pressure from the enemy to aggravate it. By great good fortune a letter from Spurius Lucretius arrived, with the news that he had control of all the fortresses overlooking Tempe and around Phila and that they had found stores of grain in them, as well as of other useful supplies.

8. Overjoyed by this communication, the consul marched from Dium to Phila, intending to strengthen the garrison there and simultaneously to distribute food to the men, since transporting it was a slow business. This journey generated rather unfavourable talk. Some men said that he had retreated from the enemy out of fear, since a battle would have been inevitable if he remained in Pieria; others said that he did not understand war—and the way that fortune introduces new elements every day—but, as if circumstances waited on his convenience, he had let slip from his hands a situation that could not soon recur. Moreover, the consul's abandonment of Dium finally awoke in the enemy the realization that he must recover what previously he had criminally lost.

For when Perseus heard of the consul's departure, he returned to Dium and restored what the Romans had left strewn about and ruined; he replaced the battlements knocked down from the walls and strengthened the entire circuit of the walls. He then encamped five miles from the city, on the near bank of the River Elpeus, intending to use the river itself, which is extremely difficult to cross, for protection. Flowing from a ravine on Mount Olympus, it is a mere trickle in the summer, but in the winter, the same river, rushing with rainwater, swirls over the boulders in whirlpools, and down below, spitting into the sea the soil it has dug out, it makes deep chasms, hollowing out the middle of the riverbed and leaving steep cliffs on both sides. Perseus, confident that the enemy's route was sufficiently cut off by this river, intended to wait out the rest of the summer.

Meanwhile the consul sent Popillius from Phila to Heracleum with 2,000 armed men. Heracleum is approximately five miles from Phila, situated halfway between Dium and Tempe on a cliff overlooking the river. **9.** Before advancing troops against the walls, Popillius sent men to urge the leading citizens and magistrates to test the constancy and mercy of Rome rather than its might. This advice had no effect since the king's campfires could be seen burning from his base on the Elpeus.

The Romans began the siege by land and sea (the fleet, anchored offshore, was brought into action) using arms, siege-works, and machines.* Also some of the Roman youths took the lowest part of the walls by adapting a circus trick for military use. It was the custom in those days, before the current extravagance of filling the circus with every manner of beast had been introduced, to seek out different kinds of spectacles, for a single four-horse chariot race and one race with bareback riders combined occupied the arena for scarcely an hour. Among the other displays, approximately sixty youths in full armour would be brought in—sometimes more at more elaborate games. Their entrance was a simulation, partly of an army on the move, but partly also of a style more sophisticated than military, and closer to the gladiatorial use of arms. After demonstrating other manoeuvres, they formed a square; and linking their shields over their heads, they created a sloping *testudo*,* similar to the roof of a building, with the first row of men upright, the second crouched, the third and fourth lower still, and the last kneeling. Thereupon, starting about fifty feet apart, two armed men rushed together and made threatening moves against each other. After climbing from the bottom to the top of the *testudo*, they pretended at times to be defending themselves at its edges, and at times they came to grips in the middle, leaping about as if on solid ground.

A *testudo* similar to this one moved forward to the lowest part of the wall. When the soldiers standing on it were right up against the wall, they were level with the defenders atop it. The Romans drove these back, and then two units clambered across into the city. This *testudo* was different in one respect: the men in front and along the sides did not raise their shields over their heads and thereby expose their bodies, but positioned the shields to protect themselves, as if for combat. Consequently the spears hurled from the wall did not injure the Romans as they approached, and those thrown at the *testudo* fell harmlessly to the ground, like rain off a slippery roof.

After the capture of Heracleum the consul moved his camp there as if he were in fact about to proceed to Dium, and from there, after

dislodging Perseus, to Pieria. But Marcius was already making preparations for winter. He ordered the construction of roads to convey
supplies from Thessaly, the selection of places suitable for the stor-
age of grain, and the building of temporary quarters to house the
people delivering supplies.

10. When Perseus finally recovered his nerve after the attack of
fear he had experienced, he began to wish that his orders had not
been carried out, since in his panic he had commanded that his treasure at Pella be thrown into the sea and the shipyard at Thessalonica
be burnt. Andronicus, the man who had been sent to Thessalonica,
had stalled, leaving time for Perseus to regret the order, which was
exactly what happened. At Pella, Nicias was less cautious and threw
into the sea the part of the royal treasury that had been at Phacus. It
looked, however, as if he could correct his mistake, because practically all of the treasure was recovered by divers. The king was so
mortified by his panic that he ordered the divers to be secretly put
to death; then Andronicus and Nicias were dispatched the same way
to eliminate any witness to the king's half-witted orders.

Meanwhile Gaius Marcius* sailed from Heracleum to Thessalonica.
He landed troops at several points along the shore and pillaged
widely. The people who made sallies from Thessalonica were reduced
to a state of terror by a series of Roman victories and driven back
within the walls. But when Marcius threatened the city itself, the
inhabitants activated every artillery machine at their disposal. The
rocks fired from these struck not just the Romans who were ranging
about and rashly approaching the walls, but even those aboard the
ships. So Marcius recalled the men to the ships, gave up the assault,
and went on to Aenea. This city is about fifteen miles away, situated
opposite Pydna in fertile land. The Romans ravaged the edges of its
territory and then, sailing along the coast, reached Antigonea.

They disembarked there. At first they plundered the fields unsys-
tematically and brought back some booty to the ships. But as they
were wandering to and fro, they were set upon by a Macedonian
troop composed of both cavalry and infantry. The Romans fled in disarray and were chased back to the sea, with the Macedonians killing
about 500 of them and capturing at least as many. When the Roman
soldiers were prevented from retreating safely to the ships, equally in
despair for their safety and shamed, they finally regained their
strength of mind out of dire necessity. The battle resumed on the

shore, and the men aboard the fleet came to the rescue. Nearly 200 Macedonians were killed there and the same number taken prisoner.

The fleet sailed from Antigonea to the territory of Pallene where a party disembarked to raid. This area was within the lands of Cassandrea;* it was by far the most fertile part of all the coastline they had sailed past. King Eumenes,* who had come from Elaea, with twenty decked vessels* joined them there, as did five of the same type, sent by King Prusias.

11. This addition to the resources at his disposal gave the praetor the ambition of besieging Cassandrea. This city was founded by King Cassander right on the narrow strip of land linking the territory of Pallene to the rest of Macedonia; the city is bounded by the Gulf of Torone on one side and that of Macedonia on the other. The peninsula on which Cassandrea lies rises high and extends into the sea as far as lofty Mount Athos does; in the direction of the territory of Magnesia the peninsula has two capes of unequal length: Posideum is the name of the bigger, and the smaller is called Canastraeum.

The siege was undertaken from two directions. The Roman praetor constructed fortifications at a place called Clitae, including a palisade to blockade the road from the Gulf of Macedonia to the Gulf of Torone. On the other side there is an inland channel, where Eumenes made his assault. For the Romans, filling in the defensive trench recently begun by Perseus involved a great deal of labour. Not seeing any piles of dirt there, the praetor asked where the excavated earth had gone. Archways were pointed out to him.* These had been constructed with a single layer of bricks and did not have the same thickness as the original wall. This gave the praetor the idea of creating a route into the city by digging through the wall; and he thought that he could avoid detection if he used ladders to mount an attack on the walls in another quarter of the city: the ensuing panic would divert the city's defenders from protecting his point of attack.

The defensive forces of Cassandrea included the young men of the town (by no means a despicable group), 800 Agrianes, and 2,000 Illyrians, Penestae, whom Pleuratus had sent; these were both martial peoples. They were guarding the walls even as the Romans who were doing their best to tunnel through them penetrated the walls of the arches and rendered the city open to attack. And if the men who broke through had been armed, they would have taken the city on the spot. When it was announced to the soldiers that the work was complete, in their eagerness they suddenly let out a great cry of joy, expecting that they would burst into the city at multiple points.

12. At first their adversaries were astonished by the sudden cheering and what it could mean. When Pytho and Philippus, the commanders of the garrison, learned that the city was exposed, it struck them that whoever attacked first would have the benefit of the labour that had been performed. They sallied forth with a powerful band of Agrianes and Illyrians. The Romans were still gathering from various sectors and being summoned for the invasion of the city. Disorderly and disorganized, they were put to flight and pursued to the trench. They were driven into it in a headlong rush and ended up in a heap. Roughly 600 men were killed on the spot, and nearly all those who were trapped between the wall and the trench were wounded.

The reverse the praetor met with in this attempt thus made him less energetic about his other plans. Eumenes was meeting with no more success in his two-pronged attack by land and sea. So they agreed to strengthen the watch posts to foreclose the possibility of a garrison from Macedonia entering the city and, since direct force had failed, to assail the walls with siege-works. While they were arranging these matters, ten of Perseus' galleys were dispatched from Thessalonica with select Gallic auxiliaries. These ships spotted the enemy's fleet standing out to sea and so, in single file, they entered the city under cover of darkness, hugging the shore as closely as possible.

Word of this new garrison forced the Romans and Eumenes to abandon the siege. They sailed round the peninsula and headed for Torone. They tried to attack it too, but when they found it defended by a powerful force, they gave up on the enterprise and set out for Demetrias.* As they approached, they could see that the walls were swarming with armed men, so they sailed past and landed at Iolcus, intending to seize crops from there and then to attack Demetrias too.

13. In the midst of all this, to avoid simply idling time away in enemy territory, the consul sent Marcus Popillius with 5,000 soldiers to attack the city of Meliboea. Commanding a strategic position over Demetrias, Meliboea is situated in the foothills of Mount Ossa where it borders on Thessaly. At first the enemy's approach struck fear into the hearts of the locals but then, regaining their presence of mind after the sudden alarm, they took up arms and ran to the gates and the city walls where they anticipated the attack, instantly erasing the hope that the city would fall at the first assault.* And so preparations

were made for a siege, and the Romans began to construct the machinery for the assault.

When Perseus heard that Meliboea was under siege from the consul's army and that the fleet was anchored off Iolcus in preparation for an assault on Demetrias, he sent one of his generals, a certain Euphranor, with 2,000 select troops to Meliboea. Perseus told Euphranor that, assuming he first dislodged the Romans from Meliboea, he was to enter Demetrias unobserved, before the Romans could move their base from Iolcus to the city. And when Euphranor unexpectedly appeared in a place overlooking them, the terrified attackers of Meliboea abandoned operations, setting fire to the siege-works. And so the Romans withdrew from Meliboea.

Once Euphranor had successfully raised the siege of the one city, he immediately marched to Demetrias. His arrival that night inspired the inhabitants with confidence that they could protect the city walls and fend off the foragers in their fields. They made sallies against the men who were out foraging, and inflicted some injuries. The praetor and Eumenes nonetheless made a circuit of the walls and considered the city's position, in particular whether they could try to take it, either by siege-works or by brute force. There was a story in circulation that terms for an alliance between Eumenes and Perseus were being discussed by a Cretan, Cydas, and Antimachus, the leading magistrate of Demetrias. In any case, the Romans and Eumenes unquestionably did withdraw from the city.* Eumenes sailed to the consul, congratulated him on having invaded Macedonia successfully, and returned to Pergamum, in his own kingdom. Marcius Figulus, the praetor, sent part of the fleet into winter quarters at Sciathus and sailed with the rest to Oreus, on Euboea. He considered it the most suitable city from which to send provisions to the forces in Macedonia and Thessaly.

Historians tell completely different stories about King Eumenes.* If you trust Valerius Antias, his version is as follows. Eumenes lent no assistance with his fleet to the praetor, although the latter had written to him again and again to bring aid; nor did Eumenes go back to Asia on good terms with the consul, but indignant because he had not been permitted to encamp with the Romans and, furthermore, that Eumenes could not be persuaded by the consul even to leave behind the Galatian cavalry he had brought with him. It was rather Eumenes' brother Attalus who remained with the consul, showing pure, consistent loyalty and being of outstanding usefulness in the war.

14. While the war in Macedonia continued, ambassadors came to Rome from a leader of the Transalpine Gauls. His name is reported to be Balanus; which tribe he was from is not on record. The ambassadors promised assistance in the war against Macedonia. The Senate officially acknowledged its gratitude and sent as gifts a torque made from two pounds of gold, drinking cups made from four pounds of gold, a fully equipped warhorse, and a set of cavalry weapons. After the Gauls, Pamphylian ambassadors brought into the Curia a golden crown fashioned from 20,000 *philippei*.* At their request, they were given permission to deposit this gift in the temple of Jupiter Optimus Maximus and to offer sacrifice on the Capitol. The ambassadors received a favourable reply when they sought to renew their alliance with Rome, and they were sent gifts of 2,000 *asses* each.

Next, audiences were given to envoys from King Prusias and slightly later from the Rhodians.* The two delegations spoke in extremely different ways about the same subject: the restoration of peace with King Perseus. Prusias' envoys had more of a plea than a demand to convey. He avowed that up to that point he had stood by the Romans and he would do so as long as the war lasted; nevertheless, when envoys from Perseus had approached him about ending the war with the Romans, he promised them that he would plead their case with the Senate; if the senators could convince themselves to give up their anger, he asked them whether they could feel gratitude towards him for the restoration of peace. That was what Prusias' envoys had to say.

The Rhodian party began by arrogantly recollecting their good deeds on behalf of the Roman people and practically took credit for most of its success, particularly in the war against Antiochus. They added that they had formed a friendship with King Perseus while the Romans and the Macedonians were at peace; that they had reluctantly broken it off, though no action had been taken against them, because the Romans had decided to draw the Rhodians into joining them in war. For the third year they were experiencing many inconveniences from the war, with the sea closed to trade; their island had limited resources, and maritime traffic supported their people. Since they could no longer tolerate the current state of affairs, they had sent other envoys to Perseus in Macedonia to announce that it was the

Rhodians' view that he should conclude a peace with the Romans; and that they themselves had been sent to Rome to make the same announcement. Should either party oppose an end to the war, the Rhodians would consider what steps they would take against the offenders.

I feel certain that to this day this statement can be neither read nor heard without provoking indignation. Thus one can only estimate the reaction of the fathers when they heard it.

15. According to Claudius, there was no reply at all, except that a senatorial proclamation was read out, whereby the Roman people decreed the liberation of the Carians and the Lycians* and the immediate dispatch of letters to both peoples so they would know this had been declared; and that when the leader of the embassy heard this, he collapsed—although just a moment before the grandeur of his eloquence nearly exceeded the capacity of the Curia. Other sources report this answer: that the Roman people had been informed at the beginning of the war, on good authority, that the Rhodians had entered into secret talks with King Perseus against the Republic; that if there had been any doubt previously, it had been transformed into certainty only a little while before on the testimony of their own envoys; deceit generally exposes itself, even if it starts somewhat cautiously. So now the Rhodians were controlling decisions about war and peace the world over? Now the Romans were to take up and lay down their weapons at a nod from the Rhodians? Now the Rhodians, not the gods, were considered the guardians of treaties? Was it indeed so? Unless the Romans complied and hauled their armies back from Macedonia, the Rhodians would see how to respond? The Rhodians knew exactly what they would see. The Roman people, once they had defeated Perseus, as they expected to do any day, would see that each city involved in the war received its proper reward.

A gift of 2,000 *asses* was nonetheless sent to each member of the delegation; it was refused.

16. Next, a report from the consul Quintus Marcius was read out, recounting how he had crossed the pass into Macedonia: there he had accumulated supplies from various places for the winter, and he had received 20,000 bushels of wheat and 10,000 of barley from the Epirotae; compensation for this food should be entrusted to their representatives at Rome; clothing for the soldiers should be sent from Rome; he needed about 200 horses, particularly Numidian ones,

since he could not obtain them there. The Senate decreed that everything should be carried out in accordance with the consul's report. The praetor, Gaius Sulpicius, put out to bid the transport of 6,000 togas, 300 tunics, and 200 horses to Macedonia, to be delivered as the consul saw fit, and he paid the Epirotae representatives for the grain.

The praetor also brought before the Senate Onesimus, a Macedonian noble, the son of Pytho. He had consistently urged peace on the king and had advised him to practise regularly, if not always, the habit his father Philip had formed and observed to his last breath, namely reading at least twice daily the treaty he had made with the Romans. Once Onesimus had failed to dissuade Perseus from going to war, he began to excuse himself, for one reason or another, from being involved in activities that he did not approve of; finally, when he found himself under suspicion and occasionally charged with treason, he deserted to the Romans and made himself very useful to the consul. When Onesimus was brought before the Senate and had made a formal report of his activities, the Senate directed that he be enrolled in the register of allies, that accommodation and official entertainment be arranged for him at public expense, that he be granted 120 acres of Tarentine territory belonging to the Roman people, and that a house in Tarentum be purchased for him. The praetor Gaius Decimius was charged with taking care of these matters.

On the thirteenth of December the censors conducted their review more strictly than in the past. Many men lost their equestrian status, including Publius Rutilius, the man who had attacked the censors ferociously in his capacity as tribune of the plebs.* He was removed from his tribe and made an *aerarius*. By senatorial decree, half the tax-revenue of that year had been allotted by the quaestors to the censors for public works. With his share of the funds, Tiberius Sempronius purchased for the state the home of Publius Africanus* behind the 'Old Shops' in the direction of the statue of Vortumnus,* and also the butcher shops and adjoining cookshops; he also saw to the construction of a basilica, which was afterwards called the Basilica Sempronia.

17. The year was already drawing to a close. Especially because of anxiety over the Macedonian war, people were discussing which men to elect as consuls for that year, to end the war at long last. The Senate consequently decreed that Gnaeus Servilius should come back at the very first opportunity to hold the elections. The praetor

Sulpicius sent the Senate's decree in writing to the consul and, a few days later, read out the reply; in it the consul announced a premature date for the elections and said that he would return to Rome before that day. The consul indeed made all haste, and the elections were conducted on the day he had named. The men elected as consuls were Lucius Aemilius Paullus, for the second time (in the fourteenth year after he had held the office for the first time), and Gaius Licinius Crassus. The next day the praetors were chosen: Gnaeus Baebius Tamphilus, Lucius Anicius Gallus, Gnaeus Octavius, Publius Fonteius Balbus, Marcus Aebutius Helva, and Gaius Papirius Carbo.

Anxiety over the Macedonian war acted as a goad, causing everything to be done earlier than usual. Thus it was agreed that the incoming magistrates should immediately draw lots for the provinces, so that when it was known which consul was assigned by lot to Macedonia and which praetor to the fleet, they could already be considering and preparing what was needed for the war, and they could consult with the Senate should anything necessitate doing so. The Senate further decided that once these men took up their duties, the Latin Festival should take place at the very first opportunity that was compatible with the dictates of religion; this way nothing would detain the consul who was to go to Macedonia. After these decisions were made, Italy and Macedonia were designated as the consular provinces, and the fleet, Spain, Sicily, and Sardinia, in addition to the two positions involving jurisdiction at Rome, were designated as the praetors' areas of responsibility. Between the consuls, Macedonia fell to Aemilius and Italy to Licinius. Among the praetors, Gnaeus Baebius drew urban jurisdiction, and Lucius Anicius the peregrine jurisdiction (and anything else that the Senate should adjudge him); Gnaeus Octavius was allotted the fleet, Publius Fonteius Spain, Marcus Aebutius Sicily, and Gaius Papirius Sardinia.

18. It was immediately apparent to everyone that Lucius Aemilius intended to prosecute the war with vigour. Apart from the fact that he was an energetic man in other respects, day and night he thought of nothing except what pertained directly to this particular war. First of all, he requested that the Senate send a commission to Macedonia to inspect the army and the fleet and to make a full report of the facts concerning the need for ground and naval forces; further, the commissioners were to investigate, as much as they could, the king's forces, as well as what territory was in Roman hands and what was

under the enemy's control; whether the Romans were encamped in a ravine or had completed the traversal of the mountain passes and reached level ground; which allies seemed faithful to us,* which ones seemed to be wavering and leaving their loyalty contingent on the outcome, and which ones seemed definitely antagonistic; how extensively supplies were stockpiled, and from where they could be transported, by both land and sea; what had been accomplished that summer on land and at sea. Once these matters had been thoroughly investigated, Paullus said, it would be possible to make firm plans for the future. The Senate charged the consul Gnaeus Servilius with the responsibility of selecting three men, subject to Lucius Aemilius' approval, to go to Macedonia. The commissioners, Gnaeus Domitius Ahenobarbus, Aulus Licinius Nerva, and Lucius Baebius, set out two days later.

At the end of the year it was announced that there had been two meteor showers, one in Roman territory and one in Veientine territory. The nine-day ritual was performed twice. The priests Publius Quinctilius Varus, the *flamen Martialis*, and Marcus Claudius Marcellus, a decemvir, died that year. The latter was succeeded by Gnaeus Octavius. And although luxury was already on the rise, it was observed that at the public games of Publius Cornelius Scipio Nasica and Publius Lentulus, the curule aediles, there were contests involving sixty-three panthers and forty bears and elephants.

19. The following year, the consulship of Lucius Aemilius Paullus and Gaius Licinius began on the fifteenth of March, and the fathers were particularly eager to know exactly what business would be brought before them by the consul who had Macedonia as his province. Paullus said he had nothing to bring before the Senate since the commissioners had not yet returned. They were, however, at Brundisium already, despite having been driven back to Dyrrachium twice; he would soon learn from them what it was essential to know first, and then he would bring it before the Senate; this would be within a few days. Paullus said also that he had set the twelfth of April* as the date for the Latin Festival so that nothing would delay his departure. With the Senate's approval, he and Gnaeus Octavius would both leave as soon as the sacrifice had been properly performed. In his absence it would be the responsibility of his colleague Gaius Licinius to prepare and dispatch anything the campaign might require. Meanwhile, foreign embassies could be received.

The Alexandrian ambassadors from King Ptolemy and Queen Cleopatra were the first to be called in. They entered the Curia and prostrated themselves, with beards and hair untrimmed, and clutching olive branches.* Their speech was even more pitiful than their appearance. King Antiochus of Syria, the one who had been a prisoner of state at Rome, was using the noble pretext of restoring the elder Ptolemy to make war on Ptolemy's younger brother, who currently controlled Alexandria. Antiochus had won a naval battle at Pelusium and then, with makeshift engineering, erected a bridge over the Nile and crossed it. He now had Alexandria itself in a state of terror, besieged by his army, and he appeared to be close to achieving mastery over a very wealthy kingdom. The ambassadors, lamenting these matters, beseeched the Senate to bring aid to their kingdom and to their rulers, who were friends and allies of the Roman empire. Such were the favours the Roman people had done Antiochus, such was their authority among all rulers and peoples, that if they should send envoys with a proclamation that the Senate was not pleased to see war between its royal allies, Antiochus would immediately withdraw his army from the walls of Alexandria and march back to Syria. If the Senate should hesitate to act in this way, Ptolemy and Cleopatra would soon come to Rome, exiles from their kingdom. An element of shame would attach itself to the Roman people for having rendered no aid at a crisis-point in their fortunes.

The fathers were moved by the pleas of the Alexandrians and sent Gaius Popillius Laenas, Gaius Decimius, and Gaius Hostilius as their envoys to end the war between the kings. The envoys were directed to approach first Antiochus and then Ptolemy and to announce that, if they did not stop fighting, the Romans would no longer regard whichever party was responsible as either a friend or an ally. **20.** These envoys set out, together with the Alexandrian delegation, within three days.

Just then the commissioners returned from Macedonia on the final day of the Quinquatrus;* they had been awaited so eagerly that the consuls would have summoned the Senate immediately, except that it was evening. The Senate met the following day and heard from the commissioners. They reported that the marching of the army into Macedonia through pathless and mountainous terrain had been more dangerous than advantageous. The army had reached Pieria, which Perseus controlled. The Romans and Macedonians were encamped at such close quarters that the Elpeus river alone separated them. The king was not offering battle while our side did not have enough strength to force an engagement.* Furthermore, winter had proved an additional obstacle to action. The army was idle and being maintained with difficulty, and the soldiers did not have more than six days of supplies. The Macedonian troops were reputed to number 30,000. If Appius Claudius' force at Lychnidus had been sufficiently strong, it would have been possible to divide the king's attention with war on two fronts: as it was, Appius, along with as much of a garrison as he had, would be in very grave danger, unless either a full army were sent to him immediately, or his men were marched out of there. The commissioners further reported that they had gone from the infantry camp to the fleet, where they had learned that some of the sailors had succumbed to disease and that others, especially the Sicilians, had gone home; the fleet was accordingly short-handed. The men who were there had not been paid and lacked clothing. Eumenes and his navy had come and gone without explanation, as if the ships were just borne on the wind. The king's intentions clearly could not be relied upon, but while everything having to do with Eumenes was uncertain, Attalus' resolute constancy was remarkable.*

21. After the envoys' report, Lucius Aemilius said that he was officially bringing the question of the war before the Senate. The Senate decreed that the consuls and the people should each select an equal number of tribunes for the eight legions; it was agreed, however, that only those who had held office were eligible for selection that year. Further, Lucius Aemilius could then choose from all of them the military tribunes he wanted for the two legions in Macedonia; and that as soon as the Latin Festival had been celebrated, he and Gnaeus Octavius, the praetor assigned to the navy, should set out for their area of responsibility. The Senate decided too that they should be accompanied by Lucius Anicius, the praetor responsible for overseeing the law as it applied to foreigners; it was agreed that he should succeed Appius Claudius at Lychnidus with Illyricum as his province.

Responsibility for the draft was placed on the consul Gaius Licinius. His instructions were to enlist 7,000 Roman citizens and 200 cavalry; to call up 7,000 infantry and 400 cavalry from the Latin and Italian allies; and to write to Gnaeus Servilius, who had Gaul as his province, to conscript 600 cavalry. Licinius was told to send this army to his colleague in Macedonia at the very first opportunity.

There were to be no more than two legions in the province; but they were to be brought up to full strength so that they would have 6,000 infantry and 300 cavalry; the remaining infantry and cavalry were to be posted in garrisons. Men who were not fit for service were to be discharged. In addition, 10,000 infantrymen and 800 cavalrymen were to be called up from the allies; these would provide reinforcements for Anicius, beyond the two legions he was instructed to take to Macedonia; these legions each had 5,200 infantry and 300 cavalry. For the fleet, 5,000 sailors were called up also. The consul Licinius was instructed to govern his province with two legions; he was to supplement that force with 10,000 infantry and 600 cavalry from the allies.

22. After the Senate's decrees, the consul Lucius Aemilius went from the Curia to a public meeting where he delivered a speech along the following lines:

'Roman citizens, I have the impression that since Macedonia became my province by lot I have been congratulated more than when I was elected consul or on the day I entered office. And the only explanation seems to be that you supposed that I can terminate, in a fashion suitable to the dignity of the Roman people, the war with Macedonia, which has dragged on for too long. I hope that the gods too have looked with favour upon what has fallen to me by lot, and that they will be by my side as the campaign proceeds. As far as those matters are concerned, I can make predictions about some and form hopes for others. But this I dare to assert confidently: I will strive with all my might not to disappoint the expectations you have formed of me. The Senate has determined what is required for the war; and since it wishes me to embark without delay and since I am ready to do so, my colleague, Gaius Licinius, an outstanding man, will undertake the preparations as assiduously as if he were going to conduct the campaign himself.

'As for you, believe what I write to the Senate and to you; do not let your credulity nourish rumours for which no one will take responsibility.* For indeed I have noticed that what generally happens in war is particularly common in this one: no one so despises an idle tale that his thinking is not impaired by it. In every conversation, even— would you believe?—at dinner parties, there are men who can march the army into Macedonia, who know where camps should be established, which places should be occupied by garrisons, when and by which pass Macedonia should be invaded, where to situate granaries, where there are sea and land routes for transporting food, when it is time to engage in close combat, and when it is better to refrain from action. These men do not just decide what should be done; whenever something is done differently from the way they determined it should be, they launch accusations against the consul, as if in a public trial. This behaviour constitutes a significant impediment for those who are conducting the campaign, nor can all men maintain such resolution and constancy of purpose in the face of rumour as Quintus Fabius did.* He chose to let his power be reduced by the foolishness of the people, putting responsible leadership before a favourable reputation.

'I am not, citizens of Rome, a man who believes that generals should not take advice; on the contrary, I consider a man who does everything on his own initiative not wise but arrogant. What, then, is the right way to proceed? Commanders should first take advice from thoughtful men who are true experts in military matters and who have been schooled by experience. Secondly, commanders should take advice from those who are participating in the campaign; they can size up the lie of the land, the enemy, and the suitability of the occasions that arise; and they share the danger, just like the crew of a ship. And so if anyone believes that he can show me what is best for the state in this war that I am about to wage, he should not deny the commonwealth his services; he should accompany me to Macedonia. I personally will put at his disposal a ship, a horse, a tent, provisions, and even a travelling allowance. But if anyone finds doing this too much trouble and prefers the leisure of city life to the toil and grind of the army, let him not steer the ship from the shore. The city provides its own generous supply of material for conversations; let him confine his garrulity to them; he may rest assured that we will be happy with our councils of war.'

The Latin Festival followed this public meeting; it took place on the thirty-first of March. When the sacrifice had been properly performed on the mountain, both the consul and the praetor, Gnaeus Octavius, set out directly from there for Macedonia. The story has been passed down that a larger crowd than usual accompanied the consul to honour him, and that men predicted with nearly unqualified confidence that the end of the Macedonian war was at hand and the consul would soon return in a brilliant triumph.

23. Such was the state of affairs in Italy. Meanwhile, because Perseus would have to part with some of his wealth, he could not bring

himself to finish what he had started: namely, to gain the allegiance of Gentius, the king of the Illyrians.* But once Perseus saw that the Romans had entered the pass* and that the crisis-point of the war was at hand, he calculated that this step could not be postponed any longer. Hippias acted as his agent, and Perseus agreed to pay 300 talents of silver, on the condition that there was a reciprocal exchange of hostages.* He sent Pantauchus, from among his most trusted friends, to complete the arrangements. Pantauchus met the Illyrian king at Meteon in the territory of Labeatis and accepted Gentius' oath of fidelity and his hostages there. Gentius sent as his representative a man named Olympio to claim Perseus' oath and hostages. He was accompanied by men sent to collect the money. At the instigation of Pantauchus, Parmenio and Morcus were designated to go with the Macedonians as envoys to Rhodes. These men were accordingly instructed to set out for Rhodes only after the exchange of oaths, hostages, and money.* By invoking the names of the two kings together, the embassy would be able to rouse the Rhodians to enter the war against the Romans. An alliance with this city, at that time renowned above all others for naval power, would strip the Romans of any hope by land or by sea.

As the Illyrians approached, Perseus left his camp on the Elpeus river and went to meet them at Dium with his entire cavalry. There Perseus and the Illyrians, surrounded by his cavalry, ratified the agreement. The Macedonian king wished his men to be present at the sealing of the treaty with Gentius because he thought that the transaction would go some way towards improving their morale. The hostages were exchanged in full view of everyone, and some men were sent to the royal treasury at Pella to receive the money while the men who were going to Rhodes with the Illyrian envoys were ordered to embark at Thessalonica. Metrodorus was there; he had recently arrived from Rhodes.* With the authorization of Dinon and Polyaratus, who were leading men of that city, he gave his word that the Rhodians were ready for war. He was made head of the joint embassy with the Illyrians.

24. Also at this time, Eumenes and Antiochus were sent the same request, which the current climate made it possible to suggest. A free city and a king were—so the argument went—inimical to each other by nature. The Roman people were taking on kings one by one and, what was truly dishonourable, fighting them with the resources of other kings. Perseus' father had been crushed with the help of Attalus; Antiochus had been attacked with the help of Eumenes and, to some extent, even that of Perseus' own father, Philip; now Eumenes and Prusias were both taking up arms against him. If the kingdom of Macedonia succumbed, Asia, which the Romans had already partly appropriated under the pretence of liberating cities, would be next, and then Syria. Already there was greater regard for Prusias than for Eumenes;* already Antiochus was being kept away from Egypt, a prize of war. Perseus told Eumenes and Antiochus that after they reflected upon these facts, they should persuade the Romans to make peace with him or, if the Romans persisted in their wrongful war, consider the Romans an enemy common to all kings. The request was sent openly to Antiochus.* A messenger was dispatched to Eumenes under the pretext of redeeming prisoners of war; in actuality, certain more covert matters were under way. These burdened Eumenes, already the object of hatred and suspicion among the Romans, with even more weighty and false accusations. For he was considered a traitor and practically an enemy at the same time that the two kings were entrapped in a rivalry of trickery and greed.*

Cydas* was a Cretan and one of Eumenes' intimates. He had first had discussions at Amphipolis with a certain Chimarus, a country man of his who was fighting on Perseus' side. Subsequently Cydas had held talks at Demetrias, under the very walls of the city, once with a certain Menecrates, and then again with Antimachus; both men were generals of Perseus. Herophon, too, the man who was sent on this occasion, had twice before undertaken similar ambassadorial missions to Eumenes. The conversations were in confidence, and the embassies were certainly viewed with suspicion, but it was not known what had happened or what had been arranged between the kings. The situation, however, was as follows.

25. Eumenes did not want Perseus to win the war, nor did he intend to assist him in it. The reason was not so much the hostility between their fathers as that it had been exacerbated by the hatred Eumenes and Perseus had for each other. The rivalry between kings is such that Eumenes could not endure the prospect of Perseus acquiring as much wealth and glory as awaited him if the Romans were defeated. Further, Eumenes saw that from the beginning of the conflict Perseus had pursued the possibility of peace by every means and that each day the threat drew closer, the less his thoughts or

actions were directed to anything else; the Romans too, both the Senate and the generals, were not averse to ending such an inconvenient, troublesome war since it was dragging on longer than they had expected. Thus had Eumenes analysed the disposition of both sides. He preferred to sell his services to make peace, which he thought might come about on its own through the weariness of the stronger party and the fear of the weaker party. And so he was bargaining for remuneration, at one time for not helping the Romans in the war by land or sea, at another for achieving peace with them: for 1,000 talents he would stay out of the war; for 1,500 he would negotiate the peace. Eumenes indicated that under either scenario he was prepared to pledge his word and supply hostages.

Driven by fear, Perseus was entirely ready to begin the transaction and proceeded without delay in the receiving of hostages. It had been agreed that once he had received them, they should be sent to Crete. But when it came to talk of money, there Perseus hesitated. He said that cash, at least the first sum, was shameful and debasing between kings of such important names, and even more so for the recipient than the giver; out of hope for peace with Rome he would not refuse the outlay, but he would deliver the money when everything was over; in the meantime he would deposit it in a temple on Samothrace. Since this island was within Perseus' domain, Eumenes saw that the money might just as well be at Pella. He tried to get some part of the money immediately. Ultimately, the kings' mutual efforts to ensnare one another were in vain and generated nothing but disrepute.*

26. Nor was this all that Perseus' avarice sabotaged. If he had paid out the money, Eumenes could have achieved a peace for Perseus, which the Macedonian king should have purchased even at the cost of part of his kingdom, or if Eumenes double-crossed Perseus, the Macedonian could have exposed his enemy, caught with bribe in hand, and thereby made the Romans justifiably antagonistic towards him. Out of avarice, however, Perseus had already lost first the alliance arranged with Gentius and then the massive help offered by Gallic auxiliaries, who had streamed down through Illyricum.* Ten thousand cavalry were coming, and an equal number of infantry, who matched the stride of the horses and, if riders fell off, these men rode the vacated steeds into battle. The horsemen had been promised ten gold pieces upon arrival; the infantry were to receive five apiece;

and their leader 1,000. As the Gauls approached, Perseus set out from his camp at the Elpeus to meet them with half of his forces. He started announcing to the villages and towns along the way that they should ready supplies so that there would be abundant grain, wine, and livestock. He himself brought horses and military decorations and cloaks as a gift for the Gauls' leaders, and a small portion of gold to divide among a few of them, believing that the majority could be lured on by hope. Perseus proceeded to the city of Almana and pitched camp on the bank of the Axius river. The army of Gauls had encamped around Desudaba in Maedica, awaiting the money that had been promised. Perseus sent Antigonus, one of his courtiers, there. Antigonus' directions were to order the Gallic band to move their camp to Bylazora, a place in Paeonia, while the leaders were to gather together and come to Perseus. (The Gauls were seventy-five miles from the Axius river and Perseus' camp.)

Antigonus conveyed these instructions to them and went on to describe how copiously stocked their route would be, all at the king's instructions; he recounted too the gifts of clothing, silver, and horses with which the king would receive the leaders who came to him. The Gauls replied that they would know well enough about these matters when they were face-to-face with the king; they asked about the ready cash that they had stipulated, and specifically whether Antigonus had brought with him the gold to be divided among the individual soldiers and cavalrymen. When this question went unanswered, their king, Clondicus, said: 'Then return to your king and tell him that the Gauls will not move one step further until they have received the gold and the hostages.'

When this message was relayed to the king, he summoned his council. It became obvious what everyone was going to urge on him, and the king, a better guardian of his money than his kingdom, began to discourse on the treachery and savagery of Gauls, as revealed in the disasters that many had suffered; it was dangerous to allow such a multitude into Macedonia in case their allies became more burdensome to them than their enemies the Romans. Five thousand cavalry would suffice—enough to use in the war but not a multitude to occasion any fear.

27. It was clear to everybody that Perseus feared for nothing but the money, but since no one dared to offer an argument even though the king was consulting them, Antigonus was sent back to report that

the king could use the services of 5,000 cavalry only and would not detain the remainder of the multitude. When the barbarians heard this, there were cries of outrage from the rest of them because they had been roused from their homes for no reason. Clondicus asked again whether he could pay the 5,000 men the agreed amount. He saw that double-dealing was going to be mixed in with this as well. The duplicitous messenger was left alone (a fate he could scarcely have hoped for), and the Gauls returned to the Danube, pillaging the part of Thrace that was along their route.

If the Gallic band had entered Thessaly through the Perrhaebian pass while the king was passively encamped at the Elpeus across from the Romans, the Gauls could have stripped and ravaged the fields, thereby eliminating the Romans' expectation of getting any supplies from there; and the Gauls could also have demolished even cities while Perseus had the Romans pinned at the Elpeus and therefore unable to bring relief to the allied cities. The Romans would have had to give some thought to themselves too since they would not have been able to remain if Thessaly were lost—it was the source of the army's food—but neither would they have been able to advance, with the Macedonian camp opposite them.

By dismissing this source of aid, Perseus considerably lowered the morale of the Macedonians, who had pinned their hopes on the Gauls. The same avarice alienated King Gentius from Perseus. Perseus had counted out the 300 talents at Pella for Gentius' representatives, and he allowed them to seal the money. Then he sent ten talents to Pantauchus and told him that these should be given to the king right away. Perseus instructed his men who were transporting the remaining money, which had been sealed with the sign of the Illyrians, to convey it in short stages; then, when they reached the border of Macedonia, they should halt there and await messengers from him. Once Gentius had received the tiny fraction of the money, Pantauchus kept on urging him to provoke the Romans with a hostile action. Gentius imprisoned their envoys, Marcus Perperna and Lucius Petillius, who happened to have come to him in that period.* Upon receipt of this news, Perseus thought that necessity had now driven Gentius into war with the Romans anyway, and he sent a man to recall the person who was transporting the money.* It was as if Perseus' every action was designed to preserve as much booty as possible for the Romans after his defeat.

Herophon returned from Eumenes; his covert activities remained a secret. The Macedonians' story had been that his business had to do with prisoners of war and, to avoid suspicion, Eumenes assured the consul on this point.

28. Perseus was disappointed after Herophon's return from Eumenes, but he sent his naval commanders, Antenor and Callippus, to Tenedos with forty galleys, accompanied by five cutters.* From Tenedos, they were supposed to protect the ships which, spread throughout the Cyclades, were on their way to Macedonia with grain. The fleet was launched at Cassandrea and went initially to the harbours under Mount Athos; then it proceeded across to Tenedos by a calm sea. The Rhodians' light galleys and their commander Eudamus were anchored in the harbour. The Macedonian fleet did not attack, but even gave a friendly greeting before sending them on their way. It was then learned that on the other side of the island fifty Macedonian cargo-vessels were blockaded by Eumenes' warships, which were anchored at the mouth of the harbour. These were commanded by Damius. Antenor promptly sailed around the island,* scared off the enemy ships, and dispatched the cargo-vessels to Macedonia with an escort of ten galleys; once they had escorted the cargo-vessels to Macedonia safely, the galleys were to return to Tenedos. They returned nine days later to the fleet which by that time was anchored at Sigeum.*

From there, the Macedonians crossed to Subota, an island situated between Elaea and Chios. By chance, the day after the fleet reached Subota, thirty-five ships of the type known as horse-transports departed from Elaea with Galatian cavalrymen and their riders en route to Phanae, a cape on the island of Chios; they would be able to cross from there to Macedonia. These were being sent to Attalus by Eumenes. When Antenor was given a signal from a look-out post that the ships were well out to sea, he left Subota between the cape of Erythrae and Chios, where the strait is at its most narrow, and approached them. Nothing was harder for Eumenes' commanders to believe than that a Macedonian fleet was at large in those waters: it was Romans; it was Attalus, or some ships sent back by Attalus on their way to Pergamum from the Romans' camp. The commanders were terror-stricken when the shape of the approaching galleys became unmistakable and the rapid motion of the oars and the prows directed at them made it obvious that they were under enemy attack.

There was no hope of resisting, given the cumbersome build of their ships and Galatians' minimal tolerance for the sea. Some of them, who were closer to the encircling shoreline, swam to Erythrae; others set sail for Chios and ran the ships aground. They abandoned the horses there and sought the city in scattered flight. The galleys, however, disembarked soldiers closer to the city, where it was easier to land. The Macedonians caught up with some of the Galatians as they fled along the road and killed them there; they slaughtered some others in front of the gate where they had been locked out. (The Chians had closed the gate since they did not know the identity of either the fugitives or the pursuers.) Roughly 800 Galatians died, and 200 were taken alive. Some of the horses drowned as the ships were wrecked. The Macedonians slit the hamstrings of others on the shore. Antenor ordered the same ten galleys that he had sent before to transport twenty especially fine horses and the prisoners to Thessalonica and to rejoin the fleet at the very first opportunity; he said that he would wait for them at Phanae. The main fleet stayed at Chios for three days or so. From there they went on to Phanae. The galleys returned more swiftly than expected, and the fleet set sail, crossing the Aegean to Delos.

29. In the course of this activity, the Roman ambassadors Gaius Popillius, Gaius Decimius, and Gaius Hostilius left Chalcis in three quinqueremes. When they reached Delos, they found the forty Macedonian galleys and five quinqueremes of King Eumenes there. The holiness of the shrine and the island protected them from one another.* Thus Romans and Macedonians and Eumenes' sailors mingled and strolled about the shrine, the sacredness of the place affording them a truce.

When Antenor, Perseus' commander, received a signal from watchtowers that some cargo-vessels were passing by out at sea, he went in pursuit with some of the galleys and sent others around the Cyclades. He was trying to sink or pillage every ship except those that were headed for Macedonia. Popillius rushed to help the vessels he could, with his or Eumenes' ships. The Macedonians, however, escaped notice by sailing off at night, mostly in groups of two or three ships.

Around this time the Macedonian and Illyrian delegations reached Rhodes together. Their authority was enhanced by the attacks of the galleys that were cruising throughout the Cyclades and the Aegean, by the formation of an alliance between King Perseus and

King Gentius, and by the story that the Gauls were on the way with large numbers of infantry and cavalry. And since the Rhodians had grown in confidence under the influence of Dinon and Polyaratus, who were on Perseus' side, a favourable response was given to the kings.* Further, the Rhodians had it openly decreed that they would force an end to the war with their own authority, and thus the kings too should resign themselves to accepting peace.

30. It was now the beginning of spring, and the new generals arrived at their area of command: the consul Aemilius in Macedonia, Octavius to the fleet at Oreus, and Anicius in Illyricum, where he was to conduct the campaign against Gentius.* Gentius' father was Pleuratus, who had been king of the Illyrians; his mother was Eurydice. He had two brothers: Plator, the son of Pleuratus and Eurydice, and Caravantius, Eurydice's son. Because the father of Caravantius was of humble origin, Gentius was not so suspicious of him, but to secure his throne he executed Plator and his two companions, Ettritus and Epicadus, both enterprising men. The story was that Gentius was jealous of his brother's engagement to Etleua, a daughter of Monunius, a prince of the Dardani, on the grounds that Plator was gaining that people's loyalty by the marriage. Gentius' marriage to the young woman after Plator was killed made this seem extremely likely. Once he no longer had his brother to fear, Gentius started to become oppressive towards his people. Immoderate consumption of wine aggravated the innate violence of his disposition.

Nonetheless, as was mentioned before, Gentius was impelled into the Roman war. He assembled all his forces at Lissus. They totalled 15,000. He sent his brother from there with 1,000 infantry and 150 cavalry to terrorize or force the Cavii into submission. Gentius himself marched the five miles from Lissus to the city of Bassania. They were Roman allies and so, although heralds were sent in first to test their sentiments, they preferred to undergo a siege rather than to surrender. The town of Durnium in Cavian territory openly welcomed Caravantius upon his arrival; Caravandis, another city, shut him out. He raided the fields extensively, but some soldiers out foraging were killed by a band of farmers.

At this point Appius Claudius, who had enlisted auxiliaries from the Bullini and the Apollonites and Dyrrachini, left his winter quarters and pitched camp near the Genusus river. Appius had heard about the alliance between Gentius and Perseus. He was enraged by

Gentius' outrageous violation of the envoys and intended to wage all-out war against him. The praetor Anicius was in Apollonia when he heard about the events in Illyricum. He sent a message on ahead to Appius, telling him to await him at the Genusus; Anicius himself reached the camp two days later. Anicius supplemented his existing complement of auxiliaries with 2,000 infantry and 200 cavalry chosen from the youth of the Parthini (Epicadus commanded the former and Algalsus the latter) and prepared to lead them into Illyricum. His main objective was to raise the siege of Bassania.

Word that galleys were ravaging the coastline delayed his invasion. There were eighty of these vessels, and at the suggestion of Pantauchus, they were sent by Gentius to ravage the territories of Dyrrachium and Apollonia. Then the fleet <. . .>

[The next page is lost. In his summary of Anicius' campaign, the Greek historian Appian indicates that the praetor defeated Gentius' navy before turning to the war on land (*Illyrian Wars*, 9). The text resumes with the rest of Livy's account of the ground campaign before he turns to the battle of Pydna.]

<. . .> They surrendered.

31. Then in turn the cities of this region did the same; the Roman praetor's clemency towards all and his fairness increased their inclination to do so.

Anicius went on from there to Scodra, which was the key to the campaign, not just because Gentius had adopted it as the citadel, so to speak, of his entire kingdom, but also because it is by far the most fortified place the people of Labeatis had and it is difficult to reach. Two rivers gird it: the Clausal flows from the side of the city that faces east, and the Barbanna, which arises in Lake Labeatis, flows from the western side. There is a confluence of these two rivers where they merge with the River Drilo; this last flows down from Mount Scordus; it is fed by many other streams and runs into the Adriatic. Mount Scordus, which is by far the highest peak in the area, dominates Dardania to the east, Macedonia to the south, and Illyricum to the west.

Even though Scodra's location serves as a natural fortification for it, and the entire Illyrian people and the king himself were guarding the city, the Roman praetor still expected that since the initial stages had turned out well, good fortune would continue from the beginning through the entire operation and that sudden terror would win the day. He drew up his forces in battle order and approached the walls. If the Illyrian soldiers had shut the gates, spread themselves out, and defended the walls and the towers at the gates, they would have driven the Romans empty-handed from the walls. Instead, they charged out of the gate and joined battle on level ground with greater spirit than they sustained it. They were forced back and crowded together in flight. The deaths of over 200 men at the very entrance of the gate inspired so much fear that Gentius instantly sent Teuticus and Bellus, leaders of his people, to speak with the praetor. Through them he asked for a truce so that he could consider his position. He was granted three days.

Since the Roman camp was scarcely half a mile from the city, the king boarded a ship and sailed up the Barbanna river to Lake Labeatis as if he were seeking a secluded place for a council of war. It became apparent, however, that he was motivated by the false hope that his brother Caravantius was approaching with large numbers of troops dragooned from the area where he had been sent. This rumour evaporated, and three days later Gentius took the same ship back downstream to Scodra. He had sent messengers on ahead to seek an opportunity for him to speak with the praetor. Gentius was given the chance to do so and went to the camp.

He started his speech by castigating his own stupidity; at the end he burst into begging and crying, collapsed at the praetor's knees, and surrendered to him. Gentius was first told to take heart and then invited to dinner. He returned to his own people in the city, and later that day, when he had dined honourably with the praetor, the Illyrian was handed over to the military tribune Gaius Cassius for safekeeping. This was the condition to which the king was reduced because he had taken ten talents—scarcely a gladiator's wage—from another king.

32. As soon as Scodra fell, Anicius' very first instruction was that the envoys Petillius and Perperna be sought out and brought to him. Their rank was restored, and Anicius immediately sent Perperna to round up the king's courtiers and relatives. Perperna went to Meteon, a city of the Labeates, and brought back to the camp at Scodra Gentius' wife Etleua, their two sons Scerdilaedus and Pleuratus, and his brother Caravantius. Anicius had ended the Illyrian conflict within a month. He sent Perperna to Rome to announce the victory. Then a few days later he sent Gentius himself, together with his mother, his wife and children, his brother, and other leading Illyrians.

This war is unique in having ended before word reached Rome that it had begun.*

In the days while these events were transpiring, Perseus was in a state of great terror on account of the simultaneous advance of the new consul Aemilius who, he heard, was approaching with great menace, and of Octavius, the praetor. For Perseus was equally fearful about the Roman fleet and the danger to the coast. Eumenes and Athenagoras were in charge at Thessalonica, together with a small garrison of 2,000 peltasts. Perseus sent his commander Androcles there, under orders to maintain a camp close to the dockyards themselves. He sent 1,000 cavalrymen and Creon of Antigonea to Aenea to safeguard the coast so that they could instantly bring help to the country folk, anywhere along the shore where they heard that enemy ships had landed. Five thousand Macedonian troops were dispatched to the garrison for Pythium and Petra; their leaders were Histiaeus, Theogenes, and Midon. Once these men had left, Perseus advanced to defend the bank of the Elpeus river, since the channel had dried up and the river could be forded. In order to have as many men as possible at his disposal for this task, he compelled the women from the neighbouring cities to bring food to the camp; the soldiers were ordered to fetch wood from the surrounding forests kindly <. . .>

[The next two pages are missing. When the text resumes, Livy is narrating the preliminary stages of Paullus' campaign at Pydna, and the rest of Book 44 is devoted to Aemilius Paullus' successful campaign in Macedonia. At several points, unfortunately, other lost pages mean that important parts of the story are left out. The fullest surviving narrative is found in Plutarch's biography of Paullus. Plutarch had access to all of Polybius as well as to first-hand accounts written by Publius Scipio Nasica, one of Paullus' officers, and someone named Posidonius, also a participant in the battle. Plutarch's biography is helpful because it adds to our understanding of the campaign and offers multiple perspectives on individual aspects of it.

The manuscript resumes with the infinitive of a word meaning 'carry' or 'bring'. Aemilius Paullus has recently assumed command over the troops in Macedonia and is directing a search for water.]

33. <. . .> In the end he ordered the water-carriers to follow him to the sea, which was less than 300 paces away, and to dig here and there at short intervals along the shore. The expectation that the mountains had water hidden within them that seeped down to the

sea and mingled with the seawater was created by their great height and strengthened by the apparent absence of any streams issuing from them. Scarcely had the top layer of sand been removed when springs—muddy and shallow at first—began to spurt and then to gush with clear and plentiful water, like a gift from the gods. This episode also had the effect of considerably enhancing the general's image and authority among the soldiers.

The soldiers were thereupon ordered to prepare their weapons for use. Meanwhile, Lucius Aemilius went with the tribunes and the senior centurions to reconnoitre places to ford the river, where armed men could easily descend and where the ascent on the far bank was the least steep. Once he had investigated these thoroughly, he attended to the following matters also.

First he saw to it that when the army was on the march, everything would happen in an orderly and controlled fashion at the general's slightest indication. When a command is given to everyone simultaneously, but not everyone hears it clearly, the order is received in garbled form and some men exceed what is called for while others fall short of it; at that point, there are conflicting cries everywhere, and the enemy knows what is afoot before one's own men do. For this reason it seemed sensible for the military tribunes to issue orders to each legion's centurion privately; and then from him, for each centurion to tell the next, in order of rank, what action was required, whether the command was passed from the front ranks to those at the very back, or from the rearmost to the front line.

Also in a departure from previous practice, Aemilius forbade the sentries to carry shields while on guard duty; for a sentry does not enter combat, where he needs weaponry, but his job is to keep watch so that when he detects the approach of the enemy, he can withdraw and rouse others to arms. Sentries stand around with their helmet on and with their shield propped up before them; then, when they become drowsy, they lean on their spears; their heads rest on the rim of the shield, and they are asleep on their feet. As a result, the glare from their weapons makes the sentries visible at a great distance to the enemy while they themselves notice nothing in advance.

Paullus altered the existing procedure for outposts also. The soldiers used to stand at arms for the whole day, and cavalrymen had bridled horses with them. When this happened on summer days with the sun burning down relentlessly, well-rested enemy forces often attacked the troops on guard duty and their horses when they were worn out from so many hours of heat and inactivity, and even a few could inflict damage on many. In response to this situation, Aemilius ordered some men to be withdrawn at midday from the morning watch and others to take over for the afternoon watch; in this way it would never be possible for fresh hostile troops to attack exhausted men.

34. Paullus called an assembly of the army and announced how he wanted these matters to be carried out. He then added a speech resembling his public address at Rome. In the army, the commander alone considers in advance and decides what needs to be done, sometimes on his own responsibility, sometimes with people whom he summons for consultation; people who are not so summoned should not throw their advice around, whether openly or in private. A soldier has these three responsibilities: to keep his body as strong and nimble as possible, to have his equipment ready for action, and to maintain provisions in case of unexpected orders; he should know that everything else pertaining to him is the concern of the immortal gods and his commander. No good comes from an army where the soldiers offer their opinions and the commander changes his mind according to the rumours of the crowd. As for himself, he would see to it that he provided them with the opportunity for success in battle, as was the obligation of the commander; they should not ask what was going to happen; when the signal was given, then they should devote themselves to their military duty.

The consul dismissed the meeting with these precepts. Everyone, even the veterans, admitted that that day they had learned for the first time the right way of running a military operation, as if they were raw recruits. Nor did they restrict to mere words their appreciation for what they had heard from the consul; the effect on their actions was immediately visible as well. Shortly thereafter you could not see anyone at rest throughout the camp: some men were sharpening their swords; others were polishing their helmets, including the cheek-pieces; yet others were burnishing their breastplates while some put on their body armour and were testing the agility of their limbs with it on; still others were brandishing their spears while some were wielding their swords and testing the edge. One could easily see that the moment they were given the opportunity to meet the enemy in battle, they would finish the war, whether the end were an outstanding victory or a death worthy of commemoration.

Perseus too noticed that, with the arrival of the consul and the advent of spring, all was noise and motion amongst his enemies, as if they were engaged in a brand-new war, that they had left Phila and encamped on the opposite bank, that their leader kept moving about, sometimes to inspect Perseus' fortifications—no doubt in search of places to ford the river—and sometimes <. . .>

[The next page is lost. The missing text must have included the announcement of Gentius' defeat. Chap. 35 begins with the Roman and Macedonian reactions to the news, which was apparently brought from Scodra by Perseus' agent Pantauchus; the extant sources do not include an explanation either of his escape from Illyricum or of the people who accompanied him.]

35. The same news that gave the Romans confidence inspired no small fear in the Macedonians and their king. Indeed at first he attempted to suppress and keep secret any report of the matter by sending men to prevent Pantauchus, who was on his way from there, from approaching the camp. But in fact some boys had already been seen by their relatives as they were being led along amongst the Illyrian hostages.* Further, the more carefully the events were concealed, the more easily they slipped out through the garrulity of the king's underlings.*

At almost the same time, the Rhodian envoys reached the Roman camp, with the same directive about peace that had roused the wrath of the fathers at Rome. The military council listened to them even less receptively. Some of the Romans thought that the envoys should be thrown into chains while others were ready to drive them from the camp right then and there, without an answer; but the consul said that he would give them his answer after fifteen days.

Meanwhile, he began to discuss strategy for the campaign, as a way of showing how little weight the Rhodian peacemakers carried with him. Some men, the youngest in particular, favoured making an assault across the bank of the Elpeus and the fortifications. They argued that if they packed themselves together and formed a single unit, the Macedonians would not be able to resist: the year before, the Macedonians had been expelled from just as many out-posts, and those had been rather higher and more fortified and occu-pied by strong garrisons.* Others preferred that Octavius sail to Thessalonica with the fleet and distract the king's forces with raids along the coast: if a second front opened up behind Perseus, he would turn around to protect the interior of his kingdom and be forced to leave the crossing-points at the Elpeus partly exposed.

It seemed to Paullus that neither nature nor the defensive works allowed passage over the riverbank; and aside from the fact that artillery machines were set up everywhere, he had heard that the Macedonians deployed their missiles very skilfully and with highly accurate force. The general's thoughts were turned in an entirely different direction. He dismissed the council and summoned two Perrhaebian traders, Coenus and Menophilus, men whose trust-worthiness and shrewdness were already known to him. He asked them in private what sort of routes there were into Perrhaebia. They replied that there were places that were not difficult but that these were controlled by the king's garrisons. Paullus took hope: if he attacked by night with a powerful force before his opponents realized it, the garrisons could be overthrown; for in the darkness, where a target cannot be seen at a distance, javelins and arrows and other missiles are useless; it would be a hand-to-hand fight with swords in a tangled mass of people; with his sword a Roman soldier was victorious.

Paullus planned to use Coenus and Menophilus as guides. He summoned the praetor, Octavius, explained the plan of action, and directed Octavius to sail with the fleet to Heracleum and to have ten days of cooked rations for 1,000 men. Paullus sent Publius Scipio Nasica and his own son, Quintus Fabius Maximus,* to Heracleum with 5,000 select troops, as if they were going to join the fleet and pil-lage the coastline of central Macedonia, as had been discussed in the meeting. To prevent anything from delaying these forces, they were told in secret that rations were ready for them with the fleet. The guides for the journey were then ordered to divide the march in such a way that the Roman forces would be able to attack Pythium in the fourth watch of the third day.

At dawn on the following day, Paullus engaged the enemy's pick-ets in the middle of the riverbed to prevent the king from noticing other developments. On both sides light-armed troops were doing the fighting; in such an irregular riverbed it was not possible to fight with heavier infantry. Both banks sloped down about three-tenths of a mile into the riverbed; the space in the middle, which the current had hollowed out differently in different places, was little more than a mile wide. While spectators from both sides watched from their ramparts—the king and the Macedonian forces and the consul with his troops—the fight took place right in the middle. The royal auxiliaries fought more successfully at a distance with their missiles; in hand-to-hand combat the Romans were steadier and more protected, whether with lightweight shields or the Ligurian type.*

Around midday the consul ordered the retreat to be sounded for his men. The fighting consequently broke off for that day, with considerable casualties on both sides. As the sun rose the following day, tempers were already running high from the conflict, and battle was joined even more aggressively. The Romans, however, suffered a great many injuries: some were inflicted by the men in the actual combat, but many more by a crowd that was standing ranged along the fortifications and using every type of projectile, particularly rocks. When the Romans neared the enemy's side of the river, the missiles from the artillery machines reached even the rear ranks. There were far more casualties that day, and the consul withdrew his men a little later. On the third day he refrained from battle and went down to the lowest part of the camp, as if he were going to attempt to cross the branch of the Macedonian fortifications that sloped down to the sea.

Perseus, what was before his eyes < . . . >

[After this beginning, now unintelligible, the rest of the sentence is lost. The next four pages are missing. Plutarch (*Aemilius Paullus* 15 and 16) describes Scipio Nasica's invasion through Perrhaebia. The Romans succeeded in overthrowing Perseus' garrison in the pass, so Paullus' diversionary tactics at the Elpeus worked. According to Plutarch, a Cretan deserter alerted Perseus about the force that was outflanking him. The Macedonian king was compelled to retreat to avoid being surrounded, and Paullus crossed the Elpeus and joined the advance party. Presumably Livy covered these events in the missing pages. The manuscript resumes at the point where Paullus and the main body of the army arrive at Pydna.]

36. < . . . > The time of the year was after the summer solstice;* the time of day was already close to noon; the journey had been made amidst much dust and the increasing warmth of the sun. Fatigue and thirst were already setting in, and it was soon apparent that both would intensify in the midday heat. Paullus therefore decided not to pit his tired troops against fresh and rested opponents; the soldiers, however, were so eager for combat whatever the conditions that the consul needed no less skill outwitting his own men than his opponent.* Since not all of them were in formation yet, he pressed the military tribunes to hurry the men to fall in. He made the rounds of the ranks personally and raised the soldiers' appetite for battle with inspirational talk. Thereupon at first they called eagerly for the signal for action; then, as the heat increased, their faces grew less lively and their voices lost energy; some men even stood resting on their shields and supported by their spears. Then at last Paullus publicly ordered the senior centurions to have the front of the camp marked off and the baggage put down. When the soldiers realized what was happening, some openly rejoiced because Paullus had not forced them to fight when they were exhausted from the toil of marching in the blazing heat.

By contrast, the junior officers and foreign leaders, including Attalus, who were accompanying Paullus all approved as long as they believed that the consul was going to fight; not even to them had he revealed that he was stalling. Then, at the sudden change in plan, they fell silent, except for Nasica. He alone dared to advise the consul not to let slip between his fingers an enemy who had toyed with previous commanders by fleeing from a confrontation; Nasica feared that the king might slip away by night; he would have to be pursued, with maximum effort and danger, into the most remote parts of Macedonia, and the summer would pass, as it had for previous generals, in wandering through the byways and ravines of the Macedonian mountains. Nasica said that he strongly urged Paullus to attack while he had the king on an open plain and, since an opportunity to defeat him was presenting itself, not to lose it.

The consul was by no means offended by the frank advice of such an upstanding young man. He said: 'I once had the same attitude which you now have, Nasica, and you will come to have the one I now do. From much experience in war I have learned when it is right to fight and when it is right to refrain from fighting. There is no profit in explaining to you now as you stand lined up for battle the reasons why it is better not to have engaged today. Seek answers another time; for now be satisfied with the authority of a veteran commander.' The youth held his tongue: he accepted that the consul must perceive some obstacles to battle that were not apparent to him.

37. When Paullus saw that the camp had been marked out and the baggage arranged in its place, he extracted first the *triarii* from the

rear of the column, and then the *principes*; in the meantime the *hastati* stayed at the front of the line in case the enemy so much as stirred; Paullus drew these troops off last, starting from the right wing and removing the soldiers of the individual units little by little. In this fashion the infantry was withdrawn without commotion, while the cavalry and the light-armed troops stood in front of the battle line, facing the enemy. The cavalry were not recalled from their post until the outer line of the rampart and the ditch were complete. Although the king would have been ready to fight without holding back that day, he was also content to have his troops know that their adversary had been responsible for postponing the battle, and he led them back to camp.

After the Romans had fortified their camp, Gaius Sulpicius Galus, a military tribune of the second legion who had been a praetor the year before, obtained the consul's permission and summoned the soldiers to an assembly. He announced to them that that night there would be an eclipse of the moon from the second to the fourth hour* and that accordingly no one should treat it as a portent. Because in the natural order of things eclipses fall at definite times, it was possible to know about them in advance and predict them. After all, the soldiers were never awestruck that the moon is sometimes full and sometimes wanes to a tiny crescent; neither should they take it as a prodigy even when the moon was covered by the shadow of the earth and disappeared. When the lunar eclipse occurred at the time announced on the night before the fourth of September, Galus' knowledge seemed practically divine to the Roman soldiers. The Macedonians, meanwhile, regarded the eclipse as a bad omen, signalling the fall of their kingdom and the ruination of their people. So did their prophets, and wailing and shouting filled the Macedonian camp until the light of the moon re-emerged.

On the following day both armies had become so hot for battle that certain individuals on each side criticized the king and the consul respectively for retreating without a fight. The king was quick to justify himself: in part, his opponent had publicly refused to fight and been the first to march his troops back to camp; further, the Roman general had halted in a place where the phalanx, which just slightly uneven terrain renders useless, could not advance. As for the consul, beyond the fact that the previous day he had apparently failed to take advantage of the chance to fight and given the enemy the opportunity to slip away by night if he wished, Paullus seemed then also to be wasting time, under the guise of offering libations; but the signal to fight should have been raised and he should have gone into battle at dawn. Finally, at the third hour, when Paullus had carried out the ritual correctly, he called an assembly. And then in the meeting the consul seemed to some men to be filling the time for action with conversation and inopportune consultations. In response to such talk, the consul delivered an oration along the following lines:

38. 'Out of all of you who wanted to fight yesterday, Publius Nasica alone, that outstanding young man, revealed his thoughts to me. That same young man subsequently held his tongue, as a way of appearing to have come to share my opinion. To certain other individuals it seemed better to criticize their commander behind his back, rather than advising him in person. To you, Publius Nasica, and also whoever, more surreptitiously, felt as you did, I will not refuse to render an account for having postponed the battle, for I am so far from regretting yesterday's rest that I believe I saved the army with my strategy. Should any of you think it is unreasonable for me to hold this opinion, come, if you wish, review with me how many factors favoured our enemy and were disadvantageous to us.

'So, first of all, I feel certain that each of you knew in advance how outnumbered we are, and that you observed it yesterday as you gazed upon the troops marshalled for battle. From our limited numbers, a quarter of our troops had been left behind to guard our equipment; and you know that it is by no means the most cowardly troops who are left to protect the baggage. But suppose all of us had been available; do we, I ask you, consider this a trivial matter: that with the blessing of the gods, today, or tomorrow at the latest, if it seems right, we will go forth in formation from the camp where we stayed last night? Is there no difference here at all? On the one hand, you could order the soldiers to take up their weapons, not when the exertion of marching that day or of fortifying the camp has exhausted them, but when they are reinvigorated and renewed in their tents; and you could lead them out in formation when they are full of strength and in top physical and mental condition. On the other hand, you could send our men out when they are exhausted from a long march and worn down by their loads, when they are dripping with sweat and their throats are aching with thirst, when their eyes and ears are choked with dust, when the midday sun is burning down, and meanwhile the enemy is fresh and rested and brings to battle strength that is not drained from some earlier task. By your faith in the gods, what man thus matched, no matter how weak or unwarlike, would not defeat the bravest man? And what about the fact that our opponents had lined up for battle with the utmost leisure, that they had rallied their spirits, that they all stood in order, rank by rank, while at the same time we would have had to scurry to marshal ourselves and would have had to enter the fray in total disorder?

39. '"But, by Hercules," you object, "although we would have had a confused and disorganized battle column, our camp would have been fortified, our water supply provided for, a safe route to it posted with sentries, and the area thoroughly scouted." Or, do you think that, having nothing but the empty field in which we were fighting, we should have battled it out as homeless vagabonds with no base to return to even if we were victorious?

'Your ancestors considered a fortified camp an army's haven in all eventualities: from a fortified camp they marched out to battle; and when they had been tossed about by the storm of the battle, there they could find shelter. For that reason, once they had enclosed a camp with fortifications, they reinforced it with a strong garrison, too: for a man who had been deprived of his camp, even if he had fought successfully in the line, was considered to have lost. A camp is shelter for the victor and sanctuary for the defeated. How many armies have been driven behind their ramparts when their military fortunes were low and then, in their own time, maybe only a moment later, made a sudden attack and driven back their triumphant foes? The camp is the soldier's second homeland: for each soldier the rampart stands as a city wall, and his tent is his home and household god.

'Your counter-objection to these difficulties and complications of fighting is the following: what if the enemy had slipped away during the intervening night? How much effort would have had to be expended in again chasing him deep within the recesses of Macedonia? For myself, however, I am certain that he would not have waited and he would not have brought up his troops in battle order if he had intended to retreat from here. How much easier it was for him to leave when we were farther away than now, when we are breathing down his neck and he cannot escape our notice whether he leaves by day or by night? What, in turn, is more desirable for us than

to attack, from the rear and in an open plain, men who have abandoned their fortifications and left in disarray, after we attempted to
assail their camp when it was protected by the high bank of the river
and surrounded in addition by a rampart and an array of towers for
firing missiles? These were the reasons for having postponed the
battle from yesterday to today. Yes, I too want to fight; and therefore,
since the way to the enemy was blocked by the Elpeus river, I opened
a new route, by using another pass and overpowering the enemy's
garrisons, and I will not stop until I have fought to the finish.'

40. Silence followed the speech: some men had been won over to
Paullus' point of view while others feared giving offence needlessly,
in a matter where what had transpired was in any case past recall.
And yet neither the king nor the consul himself wished to fight that
particular day, either. The king was reluctant, because this time he
would not be attacking the Romans when they were worn out from
marching as they had been the day before, scrambling to draw up
their column, and scarcely arrayed for battle; the consul, because
wood and fodder had not been brought into the new camp and a large
force had left the camp to seek these from the surrounding area.

Without the volition of either commander, Fortune, which is
more powerful than the designs of man, precipitated the battle.*
There was a river, not especially big, lying closer to the camp of the
enemy. Both the Romans and the Macedonians were drawing their
water from it, and there were guards posted on both banks so that
they could do so safely. On the Roman side there were two cohorts,
one of the Marrucini, one of the Paeligni, and two squadrons of
Samnite cavalry, commanded by Marcus Sergius Silus, a junior
officer. Another force was stationed in front of the camp; it was
under the junior officer Gaius Cluvius and comprised three cohorts,
one from Firmum, one from the Vestini, one from Cremona, as well
as two squadrons of cavalry, one from Placentia, one from Aesernia.
Since neither the Romans nor the Macedonians went on the
offensive, it was peaceful at the river. Around the ninth hour, a mule
escaped from its handlers and fled towards the far bank.* As three
soldiers chased it through water that was nearly knee-deep, two
Thracians dragged the mule from midstream to their side of the
river. One of them was killed, and the Romans retrieved the mule and
brought it safely back to the picket of their comrades. The garrison of
Thracians on the enemy bank was 800 strong. At first a few of these,

outraged that one of their own had been cut down right before their eyes, crossed the river to pursue the killers; then more men followed, and finally all of them, together with the garrison <. . .>

[Two pages are lost here. The missing material presumably dealt with the opening stages of the fighting. Plutarch provides a vivid description (*Aemilius Paullus* 18–20).]

41. <. . .> Paullus* directed the battle. The dignity of his office, the reputation of the man, and above all his age commanded admiration; more than sixty years old,* nonetheless he was constantly performing the duties of young men, in undertaking an exceptional share of labour and danger.

One legion occupied a gap lying between the peltasts and the phalanxes* and penetrated the enemy line. With the peltasts to their rear, the Roman legionaries faced the heavy infantry; these were known as the 'Bronze Shields'.* Lucius Albinus, a former consul, was ordered to advance the second legion against the 'White Shield' phalanx; this troop was in the centre of the enemy line. On the right wing, where the battle had broken out at the river, Paullus brought up the elephants and the allied units. That was where the Macedonians' flight began. For just as men's new schemes generally amount to words alone and evaporate without achieving anything when the time comes not to expound on them but to translate them into action, so were the 'elephant-fighters' useless—a mere name.* The Latin and Italian allies followed the elephants' charge and drove back the left wing of the Macedonians. In the centre, the second legion was sent against the phalanx and forced it to scatter.

The clearest reason for the victory was the fact that the battles were numerous and widespread. At first these disrupted the phalanx, and it faltered; then they broke it into pieces even though, when its bristling spears are densely packed and trained on the enemy, the force of a phalanx is irresistible.* If by advancing in separate units you force men in a phalanx to rotate their spears, which are cumbersome because of their length and weight, the men become entangled in a confused mass. Moreover, if some sudden commotion arises at the rear or on a flank, the soldiers are thrown into disarray, as if collapsing. Thus it happened on this occasion that the Macedonians were forced to advance with their column disrupted in many places towards the Romans, who were approaching in separate detachments. The Romans inserted units into whatever spaces opened up.

If they had made a full frontal assault as a single column against a marshalled phalanx, as the Paeligni did at the beginning of the conflict when they recklessly joined battle with the peltasts, they would have impaled themselves on the spears and they would not have been able to withstand the closely packed battle line.

42. But although the troops of the infantry were being slaughtered everywhere, except for those who abandoned their weapons and fled, the cavalry left the battle virtually unscathed. The king himself led the flight. He was even then on his way to Pella from Pydna, accompanied by the Sacred Squadrons of the cavalry; Cotys and the cavalry of the Odrysae followed directly after. The remaining Macedonian squadrons also rode off with their ranks intact since the infantry column lay in the path of the enemy; the killing of these men, which detained the victors, had made them forget to pursue the cavalry. The slaughter of the phalanx, from the front, from the flanks, from the rear, went on for a long time. Eventually those who had escaped the enemy's hands fled unarmed to the sea. Some of them even plunged into the water, and holding out their hands to those aboard the fleet, begged for their lives like suppliants. When they saw rowing boats hastily approaching from all around the ships, they assumed that these were coming to collect them and take them prisoner rather than kill them; they went out deeper, and some of them actually swam. But then, when they were viciously cut down from the boats, those who could turned and swam back to land, only to encounter another, more gruesome fate; for as they emerged from the water, the elephants, who had been herded down to the shore by their handlers, bore down on the men, trampling and crushing them.

There is ready agreement that in that one battle a greater number of Macedonians fell at Roman hands than on any other occasion: around 20,000 men were killed. About 6,000 men, who had abandoned the battle for Pydna, came under Roman power alive, and 5,000 fugitives were taken captive as they fled. There were fewer than a hundred casualties among the victors, and by far the majority of them were Paeligni.* The number of wounded was somewhat higher. But if the fighting had begun earlier, such that enough of the day would have remained for the winners to mount a pursuit, the slaughter would have been total. As it was, the onset of nightfall concealed the fugitives and made the Romans disinclined to give chase in unfamiliar territory.

43. Perseus fled towards the forest of Pieria, taking an army road; he was accompanied by a large column of cavalry and his innermost circle. When they reached the forest, where paths diverged in many different directions, it was close to nightfall, and he turned off from the road with a handful of his most trusted companions. Abandoned by their leaders, some of the cavalry slipped away by various routes to their own towns; a few in fact reached Pella even more quickly than Perseus since they took the direct route, which is easy to traverse. The king had no rest until nearly midnight because of losing the way and the various difficulties of his route. Euctus and Eulaeus,* who were in charge of Pella, and the Royal Pages* were waiting for Perseus in the palace. By contrast, none of his courtiers who had survived the battle by one circumstance or another and reached Pella came to him, although they were summoned repeatedly. He had only three companions in the flight: Evander the Cretan, Neon the Boeotian, and Archidamus the Aetolian. During the fourth watch Perseus made his escape with these men, fearful that those who refused to come to him might soon try something bolder. Just 500 Cretans followed him. Perseus was making for Amphipolis, but he had left Pella at night, hurrying to cross the Axius river before dawn, because he thought that the difficulty of crossing it would put an end to the Romans' pursuit of him.

44. Although the consul had returned to his camp the victor, anxiety about his younger son troubled him and prevented him from feeling unalloyed happiness. This son was Publius Scipio, the one later also called Africanus, after he had destroyed Carthage; he was the child by birth of the consul Paullus, and became the grandson of Scipio Africanus by adoption. At the time he was in his seventeenth year, and his youth only added to the anxiety. He had been carried off in a crowd to another area while engaged in unrestrained pursuit of the enemy. When he returned a great deal later, then at last the consul experienced the joy of such a great victory since his son was back safe.

Once word of the battle had reached Amphipolis, the women rushed to the temple of Diana (whom they call Tauropolos) to implore her aid.* Diodorus, the man in charge of the city, was afraid that the Thracians—there was a garrison of 2,000 of them—would plunder the city amidst the upheaval. In the middle of the forum he accepted delivery of a letter from a man he had had, as a trick, dress up as a courier. The missive said that the Roman fleet had landed at Emathia, that the fields nearby were being raided, and that the commanders of Emathia were begging him to send the garrison against the plunderers. Diodorus read the message out loud and urged the Thracians to go and protect the coast of Emathia: they could take many lives and seize much booty from the Romans, who were widely scattered in the fields. At the same time Diodorus played down word of the defeat, saying that if it were true, one new refugee after another would have been pouring in. Using this pretext to send the Thracians on their mission, he watched until they were on the far side of the Strymon and instantly locked the city gates.

45. Perseus reached Amphipolis two days after the battle. From there, he sent spokesmen with a herald's staff to Paullus. Meanwhile, Hippias, Midon, and Pantauchus, the king's most important courtiers, left Beroea where they had fled after the battle and of their own accord surrendered to the Romans in the presence of the consul. Others, too, were stricken with fear and prepared to do the same in turn.

The consul sent his son, Quintus Fabius, Lucius Lentulus, and Quintus Metellus to Rome with dispatches to announce the victory. He granted the spoils from the enemy dead to the infantry and the plunder of the surrounding land to the cavalry, though the latter were not to be absent from camp for more than two nights. Paullus himself relocated the camp closer to the sea, at Pydna. First Beroea, then Thessalonica and Pella, and then in turn practically all Macedonia surrendered, within two days. The people of Pydna, who were the closest, had not yet sent ambassadors; the combination of the general populace, which was a hotchpotch of many peoples, and the mass of fugitives that had been driven together from the battle prevented the city from deliberating and reaching agreement; the gates were not just locked but actually walled up. Midon and Pantauchus were sent to negotiate with Solon, who was in charge of the city, under its walls. He oversaw the dismissal of the mass of soldiers. The town then surrendered and was given to the army for looting.

Perseus appealed to the Bisaltae, his single hope of assistance. After the embassy to them had proved useless, Perseus, accompanied by his son Philip, proceeded to hold an assembly. His purpose was to offer words of encouragement and fortify the minds of both the Amphipolitani themselves and of the cavalry and infantry who had followed him or been transported there in their flight. But several times, as he began to speak, he choked on his tears, and since he was unable to deliver the speech, he explained to Evander the Cretan what he wanted to be said to the crowd and stepped down from the podium. While the crowd had groaned and wept at the spectacle of the king and his heartrending tears, it reacted contemptuously to Evander's speech. Some men from the middle of the pack even dared to shout back at him: 'Go away! There are not many of us left; don't make us die for your sake.' Their hostility silenced Evander.

The king retired to his house, had his money and his gold and silver stowed in the galleys moored in the Strymon, and went down to the river himself. The Thracians were afraid to entrust themselves to the ships and slipped away to their homes. So did the rest of the crowd of a military character. The Cretans tagged along in hope of cash, and since they were more likely to take offence than to feel grateful when it was distributed, fifty talents were left on the bank for them to snatch. After the scramble, they boarded the ships in disorder: they caused one overly encumbered ship to sink at the mouth of the river. The king and his party reached Galepsus that day; they arrived at Samothrace, their intended destination, the following day. It is said that nearly 2,000 talents were transported there.

46. Paullus sent out men to take charge of all the cities that had surrendered; the men were supposed to make sure that no harm came to the defeated side while peace was in its infancy. He kept the king's heralds with him and, not knowing that Perseus had fled, sent Publius Nasica to Amphipolis with a small band of infantry and cavalry; Nasica's mission was to lay waste to Sintice and to block all the king's initiatives.

At this time Meliboea was taken and sacked by Gnaeus Octavius. At Aeginium, which he sent his lieutenant Gnaeus Anicius to attack, 200 men died when a sally was launched from the town: the inhabitants had not known about Perseus' defeat.

The consul left Pydna with the entire army and reached Pella the next day. Once he had encamped a mile from the city, he remained there for several days while examining all aspects of the city's position; he saw that it had been chosen as the king's capital with good reason. It was located on a rise facing south-west. Swamplands of impenetrable depth surround it in summer and winter alike; these are formed by overflow from rivers. In the swampland, where it comes closest to the city, the stronghold of Phacus rises like an island;*

it sits on earthworks built with tremendous labour. The earthworks support a wall and are not damaged by the damp of the surrounding marsh. From a distance the island appears to be joined to the city wall, but it is set off by a moat, and linked by a bridge. Thus Phacus offers no approach for anyone attacking from the outside; and if the king were to imprison anyone, there would be no means of escape apart from the bridge, which can be guarded with the greatest of ease. Such was the location of the king's treasure. At that time, however, nothing was found there, except for the 300 talents that had been en route to Gentius but then kept at Pella instead.

During these days, when the Romans were based at Pella, numerous deputations (from Thessaly in particular) came to offer congratulations and were granted audiences. Then when a message was received that Perseus had crossed to Samothrace, the consul left Pella and reached Amphipolis after a four-day march. The fact that the entire population turned out to meet him revealed to anyone that not from a good or just king <. . .>

[There is a brief gap in the text before the beginning of Book 45.]

BOOK FORTY-FIVE

1. Carrying word of the victory, Quintus Fabius, Lucius Lentulus, and Quintus Metellus hurried to Rome with as much speed as they could muster. They found, however, that their joyous news had been anticipated. Three days after the battle with the king, games were taking place in the Circus when suddenly whispering spread through every section of spectators that there had been fighting in Macedonia and that the king had been defeated; the hum of talk grew louder; finally shouting and clapping arose, as if there had been a definite announcement of victory. The magistrates were amazed and sought the sources of the spontaneous joy; but when none materialized, the happiness at the apparent certainty evaporated, though the favourable omen remained in people's minds. After this was confirmed by genuine reports when Fabius, Lentulus, and Metellus arrived, people rejoiced not just in the actual victory, but also in its presentiment in their minds.*

A different version told about the Circus crowd's happiness has an equal appearance of truth.* On the sixteenth of September, which was the second day of the Roman games, just as the consul Gaius Licinius was ascending the platform to start the chariot race, a courier claiming to have come from Macedonia is said to have handed him a document wreathed in laurel. The consul started the race and mounted a chariot. As he rode back through the Circus towards the stands, he waved the laurelled message at the crowd. Once they had seen it, the people forgot all about the entertainment and ran down into the middle of the Circus.

The consul summoned the Senate there* and, once the document had been read out, with the Senate's permission, Licinius announced to the people in front of the stands that his colleague Lucius Aemilius had fought a pitched battle with King Perseus; the Macedonian army had been slaughtered and put to flight; the king had fled with a few men; and all the Macedonian cities had come under the control of the Roman people. At the sound of this announcement, shouting and deafening applause broke out. The games were abandoned, and most men brought the happy news home to their wives and children. That was twelve days after the battle in Macedonia.

2. The next day the Senate convened in the Curia. Public prayers were voted, and there was a senatorial decree that the consul should discharge the men who had taken the oath of loyalty,* except for the soldiers and sailors; discussion concerning the dismissal of these forces should be taken up after the arrival of Lucius Aemilius Paullus' envoys, the ones who had sent the courier on ahead.

On the twenty-fifth of September the envoys entered the city about the second hour of the day. They made their way to the Forum, followed by a huge crowd of those who met them all along the way and accompanied them. The Senate happened to be in the Curia; the consul brought the envoys in. They were detained there only as long as it took to recount the extent of the king's forces, both infantry and cavalry; how many thousands of these had been killed or captured; how few Romans had died amongst such slaughter of the enemy; how few Macedonians had fled with the king; that he was believed to be making his way to Samothrace; that the fleet was ready for pursuit and that he could not escape by land or by sea. Shortly afterwards the envoys were taken to a public meeting where they recounted the same information.

Rejoicing began anew when the consul proclaimed that all sacred buildings would be open, and each person left the meeting to thank the gods for himself. Throughout the city the temples of the immortal gods were filled with a great throng of men and women alike. The Senate was called back into the Curia and decreed public prayers at all the sacred couches for five days in observance of the consul Lucius Aemilius' outstanding accomplishments. The Senate also ordered sacrifices with full-grown victims. It was agreed that the ships anchored in the Tiber, ready and prepared to be sent to Macedonia should the situation seem to demand it, were to be towed to shore and placed in the dockyards; the crews were to be discharged with a year's pay, together with all those who had sworn the oath of loyalty before the consul; as for the troops at Corcyra, Brundisium, the Adriatic, and in the territory of Larinum—for the army had been stationed in all these locations so that Gaius Licinius would be able to bring help to his colleague should the situation demand it—all these troops were to be discharged. At a general meeting, a public offering of prayers for the people was announced, beginning on the eleventh of October and lasting for the four subsequent days.

3. Two envoys from Illyricum, Gaius Licinius Nerva and Publius Decius, announced that the Illyrian army had been defeated, that

King Gentius had been taken captive, and that Illyricum was under the control of the Roman people.* The Senate voted three days of public prayer for these deeds, accomplished under the leadership and auspices of the praetor Lucius Anicius. The consul announced that these would be on the tenth, eleventh, and twelfth of November.

Some sources report* that the Rhodian envoys had not yet been sent away and that after the announcement of the victory they were summoned before the Senate in derision, so to speak, for their stupid arrogance. In the meeting their leader, Agepolis, spoke as follows. They were sent by the Rhodians as ambassadors to make peace between the Romans and Perseus because this war was burdensome and grievous for all the Greeks, and expensive and disadvantageous for the Romans themselves. The good fortune of the Roman people had served the ambassadors well, since in ending the war by other means it had afforded them the opportunity of congratulating the Romans on an outstanding victory. That was what the Rhodian had to say.

The Senate's reply was as follows. The Rhodians had sent this embassy, not out of concern for what was advantageous for the Greeks or costly for the Roman people, but on behalf of Perseus. For if their feigned concern had been real, then the ambassadors should have been sent when Perseus had led his army into Thessaly and for two years was besieging some Greek cities while terrorizing others with the threat of armed force; but at that time there had been not a word about peace from the Rhodians. After they had heard that the Romans had surmounted the passes and crossed into Macedonia and that Perseus was pinned down and trapped, then the Rhodians had sent their embassy, with no other object than to rescue Perseus from imminent peril. The ambassadors were sent away with this as their answer.

4. In this same period also Marcus Marcellus returned from his province of Spain, where he had taken the famous city of Marcolica, and he deposited in the treasury ten pounds of gold and silver to the sum of a million sesterces.

After Paullus Aemilius, as was noted above,* encamped at Sirae in Odomantian territory, a letter from Perseus* was delivered by three messengers, men of humble status. When he looked at it, Paullus is said himself to have wept over the human condition: just a little while earlier Perseus, not satisfied with his kingdom of Macedonia, had attacked the Dardani and the Illyrians; he had called on the aid of the Bastarnae; and now, having lost his army, bereft of his kingdom, driven to a tiny island, a suppliant at an altar, he was protected not by his own resources, but by respect for religion. But after Paullus read the salutation, 'Greetings, from King Perseus to Paullus the consul', the stupidity of the king, who was blind to his own condition, banished all compassion. And so, even though the entreaty in the rest of the missive was in no way regal, the embassy was still sent away without a word or any written communication. Perseus understood that a defeated man must forget his title; and so a fresh letter was sent under the heading of his personal name, and it succeeded in achieving his request that some men be sent to him with whom he could discuss his circumstances and the state of his affairs. Three envoys were dispatched: Publius Lentulus, Aulus Postumius Albinus, and Aulus Antonius. The embassy accomplished nothing: Perseus clung tenaciously to his royal title, and Paullus insisted that Perseus was to entrust himself and everything under his control to the fidelity and clemency of the Roman people.

5. In the meantime Gnaeus Octavius' fleet sailed to Samothrace. His arrival inspired fear, and alternating between threats and promises, he too attempted to induce Perseus to hand himself over. Something, whether born of chance or design, came to his assistance in the endeavour. When Lucius Atilius, a distinguished young man, observed that the people of Samothrace were assembled in a public meeting, he asked their magistrates to allow him to address a few words to the people. Permission was granted, and he said, 'My Samothracian hosts, are we right or wrong in believing that this island is sacred and that all of it is holy ground, not to be violated?' When everyone acknowledged the reputed sacredness, he said, 'Why then, has a murderer polluted it? Why has a murderer profaned it with the blood of King Eumenes? And when the opening formula of all sacred rituals excludes from them those whose hands are not pure, why will you allow your shrines to be contaminated by the presence of a brigand stained with blood?'

The story that Evander had nearly assassinated Eumenes at Delphi was well known in all the Greek cities. Thus, aside from the fact that the Samothracians saw that they themselves, the entire island, and the shrine were in the hands of the Romans, they also thought that being reproached for these matters was not unjust. They sent Theondas, who was their chief magistrate—their term is 'king'—to Perseus to report that Evander the Cretan was charged with murder; further, that they had judicial proceedings, instituted in traditional fashion, for those who were said to have brought polluted hands within the sacred boundaries of the shrine; if Evander believed that he was being charged with a capital offence of which he was innocent, he should come to argue his case; if he did not dare to entrust himself to the court, he should free the temple of pollution and give thought to his situation. Perseus called Evander aside and advised him by no means to submit to a trial: both the charge and his unpopularity put him at a disadvantage. (As for Perseus, he had succumbed to the fear that if Evander were found guilty, he would expose Perseus as the mastermind behind the unspeakable crime.) What then, asked Perseus, remained for Evander but to die bravely?

Evander did not resist openly, but after saying that he preferred death by poison to death by the sword, he secretly prepared to flee. When this was reported to the king, he feared that he might divert the Samothracians' anger onto himself if he appeared to have rescued the defendant from punishment; Perseus ordered Evander to be killed. The murder was rashly carried out. Not a moment later it occurred to Perseus that he had undoubtedly taken upon himself the stain that had been on Evander: Eumenes had been wounded by Evander at Delphi; Evander himself had been killed by Perseus at Samothrace; in sum, the two most sacred shrines in the world had been desecrated with human blood by his sole agency. Perseus forestalled an accusation in this matter by bribing Theondas with cash to report to his people that Evander had taken his own life.

6. But by committing such a crime against his one remaining friend, who had been tested by countless misfortunes and then betrayed by Perseus because he had not betrayed Perseus, the king alienated everyone else. One by one they deserted to the Romans. Left almost entirely alone, Perseus was forced to devise a plan for his escape. In the end he asked a Cretan, Oroandes, who knew the shores of Thrace because he had traded in the area, to take him aboard and transport him to Cotys. Demetrium is a port on a certain headland of Samothrace. Oroandes' galley was moored there. At sunset Perseus' necessities were carried down to it; as much money as could be secretly carried down was brought as well. In the middle of the night the king himself and three men who knew about the escape went out by the back door of the house and into the garden next to his bedchamber; from there,

they cleared the wall with difficulty and went down to the sea. Oroandes had waited only until the money was carried aboard before slipping from his anchorage in the twilight and heading out to sea en route for Crete. After the discovery that the ship was not in the port, Perseus wandered for some time along the shore. Finally, fearing the break of day, which was already approaching, and not daring to return to his lodgings, he concealed himself in a hidden nook on a side of the temple.

Among the Macedonians, the sons of the leading men who were chosen to serve the king were called the 'Royal Pages'. This troop had followed the king in his flight and did not desert him even at that stage. But then, by order of Gnaeus Octavius, a herald made the proclamation that if the Royal Pages and other Macedonians on Samothrace came over to the Romans, they would retain their personal safety and liberty as well as all their possessions, both what they had with them and what they had left behind in Macedonia. This announcement led everyone to desert, and they gave their names to the military tribune Gaius Postumius. A man of Thessalonica, Ion, surrendered to Octavius the king's younger sons also. No one remained with Perseus except for Philip, his oldest son. Then Perseus surrendered himself and his son to Octavius. He blamed fortune and the gods whose shrine he was in because they had offered no aid to him as a suppliant.

Perseus was directed to be placed aboard the praetor's ship; his remaining money was brought there too. The navy immediately returned to Amphipolis. From there Octavius sent the king to the consul's camp, with a message dispatched in advance so Paullus would know that Perseus was in custody and being brought to him.

7. Paullus considered this a second victory, as indeed it was, and slaughtered sacrificial animals at the news. He also summoned his council and read out the praetor's message, before sending Quintus Aelius Tubero* to meet the king; everyone else he asked to remain in constant attendance at his headquarters. No other spectacle, on no other occasion, drew such a crowd. In their fathers' time, King Syphax* had been taken prisoner and brought into the Roman camp. Aside from the fact that neither his reputation nor that of his family was worthy of comparison, at the time he had been an accessory in the Punic war, just as Gentius was in the Macedonian one. It was Perseus who was the centrepiece of the war; nor did just his reputation and that of his father and grandfather, his relatives by blood and birth, distinguish him; but the aura of Philip and Alexander the Great,

who had made Macedonia the foremost empire in the world, shone about him.

Perseus entered the camp wrapped in a dark cloak. Except for his son Philip, he had no other attendant from among his associates: such a companion in Perseus' downfall would have rendered him more pathetic. The crowd of those rushing to the spectacle prevented him from proceeding until the consul sent lictors to clear a path for him to Paullus' headquarters. The consul rose, ordered the others to stay in their seats, advanced slightly forwards, and stretched out his right hand to the king as Perseus entered. When Perseus fell at his feet, Paullus raised him up and did not allow him to grasp Paullus' knees. The consul brought Perseus into the tent and directed him to sit opposite the men who had been summoned to the council.

8. Paullus asked first what wrong had driven Perseus to undertake a war against the Roman people with such aggression as to bring himself and his kingdom to the brink of destruction. Everyone awaited his response as Perseus silently wept for a long time, staring at the ground. The consul spoke again: 'If you had inherited your kingdom as a young man, I would indeed be less amazed that you did not know how valuable a friend and how dangerous an enemy the Roman people are; but as it is, since you had taken part in the war that your father fought against us, and you remembered the subsequent peace, which we observed with the greatest fidelity towards him, what was your reason for preferring war over peace, with men whose force-fulness in war and fidelity in peace were thoroughly familiar to you?'

When Perseus responded to neither questioning nor censure, Paullus said, 'Well, however matters turned out in this fashion, whether by human weakness or chance or necessity, take heart. The downfall of many a king and many peoples has made the mercy of the Roman people well known; it offers you not just hope, but nearly certain confidence for your safety.'

That was what he said in Greek* to Perseus. Then he said in Latin to his own men, 'You are witnessing a signal example of the mutability of human affairs. I address this to you in particular, young men. Perseus' case shows that one in favourable circumstances should not formulate arrogant and aggressive designs against anyone, nor trust in current good fortune, since it is uncertain what the day's end will bring. He alone will be a real man whose spirits are neither carried away by the winds of success nor broken by adversity.'

Paullus dismissed the council and entrusted Quintus Aelius with looking after the king. That same day Perseus was invited to dine with the consul, and he was treated with every other mark of respect possible for one caught in such a situation. The army was then sent into winter quarters.* 9. Amphipolis took in the majority of the forces while nearby cities accepted the rest.

This was the end of the war between the Romans and Perseus, after four years of uninterrupted conflict. It was also the end of a kingdom famous throughout most of Europe and all of Asia. The Macedonians counted Perseus as their twentieth king starting from Caranus, who was the first to rule. Perseus inherited the kingdom in the consulship of Quintus Fulvius and Lucius Manlius; he was recognized as king by the Senate in the consulship of Marcus Junius and Aulus Manlius;* he reigned for eleven years. The Macedonians were almost entirely unknown until Philip, son of Amyntas; from that time and through his agency, they started to expand, but remained within the confines of Europe, taking over all of Greece and part of Thrace and Illyricum. Next, the Macedonians overflowed into Asia, and in the thirteen years of Alexander's reign, they first subdued everything that had constituted the Persian empire and its nearly limitless expanse; from there they traversed Arabia and India, where the Red Sea encircles the farthest limits of land. That was the acme of the Macedonians' rule and reputation in the world. Then, with the death of Alexander, Macedonia was broken into multiple kingdoms as each man fought for his share of its wealth. Even with its power crippled, it lasted 150 years from the highest peak of its fortunes to its ultimate demise.*

10. After word of the Roman victory reached Asia, Antenor,* who was stationed with a fleet of galleys at Phanae, sailed from there to Cassandrea. When Gaius Popillius,* who was at Delos with a force protecting ships en route to Macedonia, heard that a decisive battle had been fought in Macedonia and that the enemy galleys had abandoned their position, he sent Attalus' fleet home and continued his voyage to Egypt to carry out the ambassadorial mission he had undertaken: to be able to intercept Antiochus before he reached the walls of Alexandria.

The Roman envoys were sailing along the coast of Asia and reached Loryma, which is a harbour a little more than twenty miles from Rhodes, situated directly opposite the city of Rhodes itself. The leaders of the Rhodians came out to meet the Romans and begged them to anchor at Rhodes, for the story of the victory had already been reported to them too. They said that it was important for the reputation and safety of their city that the Roman envoys learn everything that had happened and was happening in Rhodes and bring back to Rome reports of what they themselves ascertained, not the gossip that was circulating. Although the Romans refused for a long time, the Rhodians prevailed on them to submit to a brief delay in their trip for the well-being of an allied city. When the Romans arrived in Rhodes, again the same leaders of the city by begging constrained them to attend a public meeting.

The arrival of the envoys increased rather than diminished the fear in the city. For Popillius reviewed their communal and individual hostile words and deeds during the war. A man of harsh temperament, he intensified the enormity of what he said with his fierce expression and accusatorial tone. The result was that since Popillius had no basis for a personal grudge against their city, the Rhodians inferred from the harshness of that one Roman senator what was likely to be the disposition of the entire Senate towards them. The speech of Gaius Decimius was more moderate: he said that in the case of most of what Gaius Popillius had noted, the blame rested not with the people but with a few populist troublemakers; that these men, who put their tongues up for sale, had secured the passing of decrees full of flattery of Perseus, and they had sent embassies that always induced as much regret as shame among the Rhodians; all these matters, however, would redound on the wrongdoers' own heads, if the people agreed. Decimius was listened to with general assent, as much because he was relieving the general population of guilt as because he had directed the blame onto the parties responsible.

And so when the leaders of the Rhodians responded to the Romans, the speech of those who tried in any way possible to refute Popillius' accusations was by no means as pleasing as that of those who agreed with Decimius about making the guilty parties atone for their wrongdoing. There was therefore an immediate decree: a capital sentence* for those convicted of having done or said anything on behalf of Perseus and against the Romans. Some of these people had left the city upon the Romans' arrival; others committed suicide.

The envoys spent no more than five days in Rhodes before departing for Alexandria. But the Rhodians were no less vigorous on that account in administering justice as set out by the decree made while the Romans were still there. Decimius' mildness had as much to do with their persistence in carrying it out as did Popillius' severity.

11. Meanwhile, Antiochus had besieged the walls of Alexandria in vain, and then had abandoned the city and taken over the rest of Egypt.* He left the older Ptolemy at Memphis. Ostensibly, Antiochus was attempting to win the kingdom for Ptolemy with his own resources. In fact, Antiochus withdrew his army into Syria with the aim of attacking the victor in short order. Ptolemy was not unaware of Antiochus' intention. As long as he had his younger brother terrified by the threat of a siege, he estimated that he could return to Alexandria, provided that his sister lent her support and his brother's friends offered no opposition. Ptolemy did not stop sending, primarily to his sister and secondly to his brother and his brother's friends, until he secured peace with them. The fact that Antiochus had retained a garrison at Pelusium while handing over the rest of Egypt to Ptolemy had made Ptolemy suspicious of him. Antiochus manifestly controlled the gateway to Egypt and could march his army back in whenever he wanted. It was also clear that the outcome of an internecine struggle between the brothers would be a victor exhausted by the combat and no match for Antiochus.

The younger Ptolemy and his advisers accepted and concurred with these prudent observations from the older Ptolemy; their sister contributed the most to his case, not just with her advice, but with entreaties too. Consequently, since all the parties were in agreement, a peace was concluded, and the older Ptolemy was accepted back into Alexandria. Not even the general population was opposed; it had been weakened by the shortage of all supplies during the war—not just in the siege, but also after it had been abandoned, since nothing was brought in from the Egyptian countryside.

If Antiochus had brought his army into Egypt to reinstate Ptolemy— which was the specious pretext he used when exchanging embassies and communications with all the Greek and Asian cities—in all consistency he would have been delighted at these developments; but he was so resentful that he prepared a campaign against both brothers that was far more vicious and aggressive than what had previously been intended for just the one. He immediately sent his fleet to Cyprus. At the beginning of spring he himself entered Coele Syria with his army, en route for Egypt. Near Rhinocolura, envoys from

Ptolemy brought his thanks to Antiochus for restoring him to his ancestral kingdom. The envoys asked too that Antiochus safeguard his act of generosity and state what he wanted to happen rather than transforming himself from friend to enemy and launching an invasion. Antiochus answered that he would not recall the fleet nor withdraw his troops unless all of Cyprus and Pelusium and the territory surrounding the Pelusian mouth of the Nile were surrendered to him; he established a deadline for receiving an answer about compliance with his demands.

12. After the date granted for the truce passed, Antiochus' commanders sailed from the mouth of the Nile at Pelusium, while he himself marched through the Arabian desert and was received even by the inhabitants of Memphis, as well as by the rest of the Egyptians (some willingly and some out of intimidation). Antiochus made his way to Alexandria by easy stages. He crossed the river at Eleusis, a place four miles outside Alexandria. The Roman envoys intercepted him there. As they approached, Antiochus greeted them, and then he held out his right hand to Popillius. Popillius gave him the tablet containing the Senate's decree and ordered him first of all to read it. Antiochus read it through and said that he would summon his friends and consider with them his course of action. Popillius, in keeping with his harsh temperament, drew a circle around Antiochus with a rod he was holding and said, 'Before you step out of this circle, give me an answer to take back to the Senate.' Stunned at so aggressive a command Antiochus hesitated for a moment before saying, 'I will do as the Senate decrees.'* At that point Popillius offered his right hand to the king as if to an ally and a friend.

So Antiochus evacuated Egypt by the day prescribed and the harmony between the brothers Ptolemy, who had only just concluded a peace, was strengthened under the authority of the Roman envoys. Afterwards they sailed for Cyprus. From there they sent Antiochus' navy home, which had already defeated the Egyptian fleet in battle. This embassy was famous throughout the world because Egypt, which was already in Antiochus' grasp, had been emphatically taken away from him and their ancestral kingdom had been restored to the Ptolemaic family.

Of the two consuls that year, the magistracy of one, with its distinguished victory, was as famous as the other's was obscure, since he had no opportunity to accomplish anything. When Licinius initially set a date for his legions to assemble, he entered the shrine without having taken the auspices.* When the matter was referred to the augurs, they decreed that the date had been set by a faulty religious procedure. The consul went to Gaul and established camp around Campi Macri near Mounts Sicimina and Papinus. He spent the winter in the same area with the Latin and Italian allies; the Roman legions had remained at Rome because the date for the army to assemble had been set by a faulty religious procedure.

The praetors, too, went to their provinces, except for Gaius Papirius Carbo, who had been allotted Sardinia. The fathers decided that he should oversee the law between Romans and foreigners at Rome, for he had been allotted this responsibility too.

13. Popillius and the embassy that had been sent to Antiochus returned to Rome. He reported that the disputes between the kings had been resolved and that Antiochus' army had been withdrawn from Egypt to Syria.

Ambassadors from the kings themselves came next. Antiochus' ambassadors said that for the king a peace that had pleased the Senate seemed more desirable than any victory and that he had obeyed the commands of the Roman envoys just as he would an order from the gods. Then the ambassadors offered their congratulations on the Romans' victory; the king would have lent his assistance to it if any had been enjoined. The ambassadors from Ptolemy offered thanks in the name of the king and Cleopatra together, saying that they owed more to the Senate and Roman people than to their own parents, more even than to the immortal gods; through the Senate and Roman people they had been liberated from the most grievous of sieges and they had been restored to their ancestral kingdom when it was nearly lost to them.

The Senate replied that Antiochus had acted well and properly in obeying the envoys and that this was pleasing to the Senate and Roman people. The response to the rulers of Egypt, Ptolemy and Cleopatra, was that if anything good or beneficial had befallen them because of the Senate, then the Senate rejoiced greatly, and it would see to it that they always considered that the greatest bulwark of their kingdom lay in the fidelity of the Roman people. The praetor Gaius Papirius was assigned to ensure that the customary gifts were sent to the ambassadors. Then letters arrived from Macedonia that doubled the joy over the victory: King Perseus was under the consul's control.

The embassies were sent home. There was then a dispute between representatives from Pisa and Luna.* The Pisani were complaining that they were being driven off their land by Roman colonists; the Lunenses were asserting that the land under dispute had been assigned to them by a three-man land commission. The Senate sent out a team of five men to investigate and establish the boundaries: Quintus Fabius Buteo, Publius Cornelius Blasio, Tiberius Sempronius Musca, Lucius Naevius Balbus, and Gaius Appuleius Saturninus.

A joint delegation from the brothers Eumenes, Attalus, and Athenaeus came to offer congratulations on the victory. And when Masgaba, a son of King Masinissa, disembarked at Puteoli, the quaestor Lucius Manlius, who had been sent to meet him, was on hand with a supply of ready cash to escort Masgaba to Rome at public expense. The Carthaginian was granted an audience with the Senate immediately upon his arrival. There the young man spoke in such a way that his style of expression rendered all the more pleasing the substance of what he had to say, which was already pleasing in itself. He enumerated how many infantrymen and cavalry, how many elephants, and how much grain his father had sent to Macedonia in the four-year period. He said that two matters had caused Masinissa shame: one was that the Senate had requested through envoys and not simply ordered supplies that were essential for the war; the other was that the Senate had sent him money for the grain. Masgaba said that Masinissa remembered that he held a kingdom that had been created, increased, and expanded by the Roman people; he was content to be entitled to use the kingdom, and he knew that the true legal ownership and right to it belonged to the people who conferred it on him;* thus with perfect justice the Romans could take, not request, things from him; nor, since they were the givers, should they buy from him fruits produced by the land there that were of use to them. Whatever the Roman people did not need was and would be enough for Masinissa. Masgaba said that after he had left with these instructions from his father, horsemen had followed after him to report the defeat of Macedonia, and they had directed him to offer congratulations to the Senate, and to communicate that this was a matter of such great joy to his father that he wished to come to Rome to sacrifice to Jupiter Optimus Maximus on the Capitol and to offer thanks. Masgaba was to seek permission from the Senate for Masinissa to be allowed to do this, unless it was a nuisance in some way.

14. The reply given to the prince was that his father Masinissa acted as became a good and generous man, thereby adding value and honour to the services owed by him. On the one hand, he had aided the Roman people in the Punic war with good and faithful service; on the other, he had acquired his kingdom with the support of the Roman people; although these matters balanced each other out, subsequently Masinissa had performed his duty in one war after another against three kings. Truly, it was not surprising that such a king took pleasure in the victory of the Roman people, a king who had completely fused his fortune and that of his kingdom with Roman concerns. Let him give thanks to the gods for the victory at his own altars; his son could do this for him at Rome; Masgaba had also offered sufficient thanks in his own name and that of his father. The Senate judged that it was not in the interests of the commonwealth of the Roman people for Masinissa himself to leave his kingdom and go out of Africa, quite apart from the fact that it was of no advantage to him.

When Masgaba asked that Hanno, the son of Hamilcar, a hostage, in place of <. . .>.* By decree of the Senate, a quaestor was directed to spend one hundred pounds of silver on gifts for Masgaba, to accompany him to Puteoli, to cover all his expenses as long as he was in Italy, and to hire two ships to convey him and his companions to Africa; further, garments were given to all his attendants, free and slave alike.

Along similar lines, shortly afterwards a letter from Misacenes, another son of Masinissa, was delivered: after Perseus was defeated, Misacenes had been sent by Lucius Paullus to Africa with his cavalry; during the voyage the fleet had been broken apart in the Adriatic, and he had been transported to Brundisium sick and with three ships. The quaestor Lucius Stertinius was dispatched to him at Brundisium with gifts equal to those that had been conferred on his brother at Rome; Stertinius was ordered to see to his accommodation <. . .>

[The loss of a page here leaves this episode incomplete. According to Valerius Maximus, the praetor arranged for Misacenes' care, lodging, expenses in Brundisium, and transport home, as well as conveying the Senate's gifts to him (5.1.1d). All this could probably be inferred. The more serious consequence of the lost text is that when the manuscript resumes, Livy is describing the activities of the censors elected for 169. They are involved in the technical and complex business of assigning former slaves to voting districts.

Because the beginning of Livy's account of the censorship is lost and the first sentence is incomplete, the situation, its history, and its resolution are not entirely clear.]

15. <. . .> Freedmen had been enrolled in the four urban tribes,* with two exceptions: those men who had a son over five years of age were to be counted where they had been in the previous census; and those men who had rural land or lands worth more than 30,000 *sesterces* were given the right to be registered in the rural tribes, as had previously been the case for them. Once this arrangement had been made, Claudius said that, without the permission of the people, a censor could not withhold the franchise from any man, still less an entire class of people; and that even if a censor could remove a man from a voting district, which amounted to ordering him to change his voting district, a censor could not then remove him from all thirty-five voting districts, which was in effect to strip away his citizenship and personal freedom: that is, to determine not where a man was registered, but to exclude him from registration altogether. The two censors entered into a dispute over these matters. It finally came down to their choosing one of the four urban tribes, by lot, openly, in the Hall of Liberty; the censors were to assign to that tribe all those who had been slaves. The Esquilina was chosen by lot.* Tiberius Gracchus announced the decision that all freedmen would be registered in it. Because of this affair, the censors were held in great esteem by the Senate, and official thanks were voted to Sempronius, for having persisted in a noble undertaking, and to Claudius, for having not obstructed it.

The censors removed more men from the Senate and ordered more men of equestrian status to sell their horses than the previous censors had.* All these men were then removed from their tribe and their order and made *aerarii*; nor was anyone demoted by one censor only to have his public disgrace erased by the other. The censors requested that their term of office be extended for eighteen months so that they could, following established custom, enforce the completion of repairs to public buildings and certify the quality of work that had been contracted out. The tribune Gnaeus Tremellius interposed his veto because he had not been selected for the Senate.

That same year—five years after he swore an oath to do so—Gaius Cicereius dedicated the temple of Moneta on the Alban Mount. Lucius Postumius Albinus was inaugurated as *flamen Martialis* that year.

16. The consuls, Quintus Aelius and Marcus Junius, referred the assignment of provinces to the Senate. The fathers decided that Spain should again constitute two provinces; it had been just one during the Macedonian war. The same men, Lucius Paullus and Lucius Anicius, were to remain in charge of Macedonia and Illyricum until, in accordance with the advice of the commissioners, they had settled those states, which had been thrown into confusion by the war and needed to be organized into a new political order in the place of monarchy. Pisa and Gaul were assigned to the consuls, with two legions each of 5,200 infantry and 400 cavalry. The lot for the praetors fell out as follows: Quintus Cassius drew urban jurisdiction, and Manius Juventius Thalna jurisdiction involving foreigners; Tiberius Claudius Nero drew Sicily; Gnaeus Fulvius drew Nearer Spain, and Gaius Licinius Nerva Farther Spain. Sardinia had fallen to Aulus Manlius Torquatus, but he was unable to go to his province because a senatorial decree kept him back to preside over investigations into capital crimes.

Then the Senate was consulted about the prodigies that had been announced. The temple of the Penates on the Velia had been struck by lightning, as were two city gates and part of the wall at Minervium. At Anagnia there had been a shower of dirt, and at Lanuvium a comet had been spotted in the heavens; and in publicly held land at Calatia a Roman citizen, Marcus Valerius, announced that blood had oozed from his hearth for three days and two nights. Because of this last one in particular the decemvirs were directed to consult the books: they decreed a one-day supplication for the people, and they sacrificed fifty goats in the Forum. There was a supplication at all the sacred couches on another day for the other prodigies, and there was a sacrifice with full-sized victims, and the city underwent a *lustrum*. In other matters concerning the honour of the immortal gods, the Senate decreed that, since public enemies had been defeated, and Kings Perseus and Gentius, along with Macedonia and Illyricum, were under Roman control, at all the sacred couches there should be offerings equivalent to the ones that had been given in the consulship of Appius Claudius and Marcus Sempronius for the defeat of King Antiochus; the praetors Quintus Cassius and Manius Juventius were to take responsibility for making such offerings.

17. The fathers then chose the commissioners on whose advice Lucius Paullus and Lucius Anicius would settle the affairs of Macedonia and Illyricum: there were ten commissioners for Macedonia and five for Illyricum. The most distinguished men were named for Macedonia: Aulus Postumius Luscus and Gaius Claudius, who were both former censors, <Quintus Fabius Labeo, . . .>, and Gaius Licinius Crassus, Paullus' colleague in the consulship; his command had been extended, and he had kept Gaul as his province. Added to these former consuls were Gnaeus Domitius Ahenobarbus, Servius Cornelius Sulla, Lucius Junius, Titus Numisius Tarquiniensis, and Aulus Terentius Varro. The men named for Illyricum were the former consul Publius Aelius Ligus, Gaius Cicereius and Gnaeus Baebius Tamphilus (Tamphilus had been a praetor the previous year and Cicereius many years earlier), Publius Terentius Tuscivicanus, and Publius Manilius. The consuls were then advised by the fathers at the very first opportunity either to decide between themselves on their provinces or to draw lots, for one of them needed to take the place in Gaul of Gaius Licinius, who had been named a commissioner. They drew lots. Marcus Junius obtained Pisa. Before he could go to the province, it was agreed that he would present to the Senate the embassies converging on Rome from all over to offer congratulations. Quintus Aelius obtained Gaul.

In addition, though it was possible to expect, given the character of the men being sent, that when the generals acted on the commissioners' advice, they would issue no decree unworthy of either the mercy or the deliberateness of the Roman people, the Senate discussed the principal matters of policy. The intended outcome was for the commissioners to be able to convey from Rome to the generals the outline of a comprehensive plan.

18. First of all, it was agreed that all the Macedonians and Illyrians should be free. In this way it would be evident to all peoples that the military might of the Roman people did not bring servitude to the free, but rather freedom to the enslaved, and it would be clear to those peoples who were free that their freedom would be preserved for them for ever under the protection of the Roman people; meanwhile, those who were living under kings would have faith that, for the time being, their rulers would comport themselves with greater moderation and justice out of regard for the Roman people, and if there were ever a war between their kings and the Roman people, the outcome would bring victory to the Romans and freedom to the subject peoples.

Further, it was agreed to abolish the leasing of the Macedonian mines, which were a vast source of revenue, as well as of the rural estates.* The leasing could not be managed without someone collecting the revenue, and where there was a revenue-collector,* either the official legal system was bypassed or the allies lost their freedom. It was agreed that the Macedonians themselves could not serve this function either: for where there was a profit for middlemen, there would always be a basis for disputes and conflict.

Finally, for fear that, if there were a federal council of the people,* an unscrupulous flatterer of the masses could draw their freedom, which was being granted to promote healthful governance, in the direction of pernicious lawlessness, it was agreed to divide Macedonia into four districts so that each could have its own council. And it was agreed to levy tribute for the Roman people that was half as much as the Macedonians had been accustomed to pay their kings. Provisions similar to these were drawn up for Illyricum. The remaining decisions were left to the generals and commissioners: in those matters, the present treatment of affairs would suggest more specific measures to them.

19. Among the many embassies from kings, states, and peoples, King Eumenes' brother Attalus in particular attracted everyone's notice and attention. Those who had fought with Attalus in the war received him much more warmly than if King Eumenes himself had come. On the surface, two honourable motives had brought Attalus: one was to offer congratulations befitting a victory to which he himself had contributed; the other was to express concern about a Galatian uprising and a defeat inflicted on Pergamum that had put the kingdom in jeopardy.

At the same time, Attalus had underlying expectations of honours and rewards from the Senate. It was unlikely that these could come his way without damage to bonds within his family. Further, certain Romans acted as evil influences and fostered Attalus' greed with hope. They said that at Rome Attalus was regarded as a friend on whom the Romans could rely, while Eumenes was seen as an ally whom neither the Romans nor Perseus could trust; for this reason it was practically impossible to determine which was easier to obtain from the Senate: what Attalus sought for himself, or what he sought to the detriment of Eumenes. Such was the degree, they said, to which the senators one and all wanted both to give him everything and deny his brother absolutely anything.

As this episode proved, Attalus was one of those men who want as much as hope could have promised, except that a wise warning from a single friend reined in, as it were, his spirits when they were exulting in good fortune. With Attalus was a doctor, Stratius. He had been sent to Rome by Eumenes who was worried about this very situation. Stratius was to spy on Attalus' behaviour and to give him faithful counsel if Attalus seemed to be deviating in his allegiance.

When Stratius arrived, Attalus' ears were already buzzing and his thinking was already agitated. Stratius approached him with timely words and reversed a condition close to collapse. He said that different kingdoms had grown by different means. Their kingdom was young and not based on age-old resources; it depended on fraternal harmony; although one brother bore the title of king and wore the crown on his head, all the brothers governed the kingdom. In truth, who did not consider Attalus, who was second in age, a king? And not just because one could see how great his current resources were, but also because it was patently obvious that he would rule any day now; such were the frailty and advanced age of Eumenes, who had no line of offspring. (In point of fact Eumenes had not yet acknowledged the son who subsequently ruled.*) What benefit was there in forcing a condition that would soon come his way of its own accord?

Further, Stratius continued, the Galatian uprising had brought new upheaval to the kingdom, and, even with unanimity and harmony among the kings, it could scarcely be fended off; if in fact an internal conflict were added to the external war, the Galatian attack could not be withstood. Stratius said that Attalus would, in order to prevent Eumenes ruling to his deathbed, achieve nothing except robbing himself of his own imminent expectation of sovereignty. If both actions—preserving the kingdom for his brother and taking it away from him—could bring renown, still the praise for having saved the kingdom would be greater since it was linked to respect for family. But since in fact the alternative was despicable and practically parricide, was there any uncertainty left to be considered? Whether he should aspire to part of the kingdom or take it all? If just a part, then both sections would be weakened and their military strength crippled, and both would immediately be vulnerable to all kinds of attack and abuse. If Attalus sought the whole kingdom, would he then command his older brother to become a private citizen or finally, an exile, to die of old age and physical frailty? Even if no mention was made of the fate of impious brothers, as handed down by myth,* the fall of Perseus seemed a remarkable example: just as if the gods had mani-fested themselves to demand punishment, he had knelt in the shrine of Samothrace and set at the feet of his victorious enemy the crown that he had stolen through fratricide. Stratius ended by saying that even the men who were goading Attalus on—and they were doing so as enemies of Eumenes rather than friends of his—even these would praise his piety and constancy if he remained loyal to his brother to the end.

20. These factors prevailed in Attalus' thinking. And so, when he was given an audience in the Senate, he offered congratulations on the victory, he recounted his services and those of his brother (if there were any*), in the war, and he described the Galatian uprising that had recently taken place and caused enormous turmoil; and he asked the Senate to send to the Galatians representatives whose authority could dissuade them from fighting. When Attalus had treated the business entrusted to him for the good of the kingdom, he asked for Aenus and Maronea for himself. Having thus disappointed the hopes of those who had believed that he would denounce his brother and seek a division of the kingdom, he walked out of the Curia. Rarely at any time has any king or private citizen been listened to with so much goodwill and approval from everybody: Attalus was lavished with every honour and gift then and there and escorted on his way when he left.*

Amongst the many embassies from Greece and Asia, the represen-tatives from Rhodes in particular caught the city's attention. For initially they appeared in white clothing, both because it was appro-priate for men offering congratulations, and because if they had worn dark clothing, they might have created the appearance of mourning Perseus' fall. Then, as they were standing in the Comitium, the consul Marcus Junius asked the fathers whether or not they would provide the Rhodian representatives with room and board and an opportunity to address the Senate. The senators judged that no law of hospitality had to be observed towards the Rhodians. The consul exited the Curia, and when the Rhodians said that they had come to offer congratulations on the victory and to exonerate their city of the accusations made against it and asked that they be granted a meeting with the Senate, the consul declared that the Romans were accustomed both generally to treat their friends and allies with kindness and hospitality, and in particular to grant audiences with the Senate; in this war the Rhodians had not earned the right to be considered friends and allies.

Upon hearing this, the Rhodians all prostrated themselves. They called upon the consul and the others present not to deem it fair for new and false accusations to overshadow the Rhodians' long record of service, to which they themselves could attest. They then donned dark clothing and went around to the homes of the leading men, begging and crying, calling on them to investigate the case before issuing a condemnation.

21. Manius Juventius Thalna was the praetor responsible for overseeing the law between citizens and foreigners. He was inciting the people against the Rhodians, and he had promulgated a motion that war be declared on the Rhodians and that the people choose for the war one magistrate from those elected for the year and dispatch him with the fleet. (He was hoping that he would be the one.) The tribunes of the plebs Marcus Antonius and Marcus Pomponius opposed his proposal.

But both the praetor and the tribunes had set a new and bad precedent when they embarked on this matter. The praetor was at fault because he did not consult the Senate or inform the consuls before bringing on his own initiative a motion as to whether the people wished and commanded war to be declared on Rhodes; always in the past the Senate was consulted beforehand about a war and then, with authorization from the fathers, a motion was brought to the people. The tribunes of the plebs were at fault because the practice was for no one to veto a law before private citizens had the opportunity to speak for or against it; this way it had frequently happened that men who did not state in advance that they would exercise their veto did so, because they discovered flaws in the law from those who spoke against it; and men who had come to intercede refrained from doing so because they were won over by weighty testimony from those who spoke for the law. Then the praetor and the tribunes entered into a rivalry of over-hasty actions. The tribunes, by interposing their veto ahead of time, matched the praetor's hastiness <. . .> the arrival of the general <. . .>

[This sentence is incomplete because the next page is missing. Livy must have moved from narrating the dispute between the praetor and the tribunes to introducing the debate over the Rhodians' fate. According to Polybius, one of the tribunes forcibly removed the praetor from the speaker's platform (30.4). The manuscript resumes with Astymedes' speech in defence of his city-state.]

22. '. . . is. Whether or not we were at fault has yet to be determined; but we are already suffering all manner of punishments and disgrace. On the occasions when the Carthaginians had been vanquished and after Philip and Antiochus had been defeated, we came to Rome, and we went from our state accommodation to the Curia to congratulate you, conscript fathers, and from the Curia to the Capitol, bearing gifts for your gods. This time we come from a squalid inn, where we were barely admitted, even for cash, and we have been ordered to remain outside the city walls, practically as if we were enemies; in this filthy condition we enter the Roman Curia, we, the Rhodians, to whom you recently gave Lycia and Caria as provinces, and to whom you gave the most distinguished prizes and honours. Meanwhile, so we hear, you order the Macedonians and Illyrians to be free on the grounds that they were enslaved before they fought against you. We do not envy the good fortune of anyone; rather, we recognize the clemency of the Roman people. But are you about to transform the Rhodians, who did nothing more than remain neutral in this war, from friends to enemies?

'Certainly you are the very same Romans who affirm that your wars are successful because they are just; and you pride yourselves not so much on their outcome, because you are victorious, as on their origins, since you never enter into them without reason. The siege of Messana in Sicily rendered the Carthaginians your foes;* the siege of Athens, the attempt to enslave Greece, and money and soldiers sent to Hannibal made Philip your enemy.* Further, in the case of Antiochus, he was summoned by your enemies the Aetolians, and he crossed with his fleet from Asia to Greece; when he had taken possession of Demetrias, Chalcis, and the pass at Thermopylae, he attempted to dislodge you from control of your empire.* When your allies were besieged by Perseus, or when princes and leaders of states or peoples were killed, you had a justification for the war. If we are about to perish, what, I ask, will be the ostensible motive for our destruction?

'I am not yet distinguishing the situation of our city from that of our fellow citizens Polyaratus and Dinon, or from that of those men whom we brought to surrender to you. Suppose all of us Rhodians are equally guilty, what is our offence in this war? That we favoured Perseus' side, and we stood by the king and against you on this occasion, just as in the wars against Antiochus and Philip we stood with you and against the kings? Ask Gaius Livius and Lucius Aemilius Regillus, who commanded your fleets in Asia, just how we are accustomed to help our allies and how vigorously we go to war. Your ships never fought without us. We fought with our own navy once at Samos and again off Pamphylia against Hannibal when he was the commander. That victory is so much the more glorious for us because although at Samos we had lost the better part of our navy and the flower of our youth in a defeat, we were not frightened even by so great a disaster, but we dared to face the royal fleet again as it approached from Syria.* I have mentioned these events not to boast— for we are hardly in the position for that—but to remind you just how the Rhodians are accustomed to help their allies.

23. 'After Philip and Antiochus were defeated, we received very generous rewards from you. If the good fortune which now is yours— by the kindness of the gods and your courage—had been Perseus', and if we had gone to Macedonia to seek rewards before the victorious king, what, I ask, would we say? That he received help from us in the form of money or grain? In the form of land or naval forces? What garrison had we held? Where had we fought, either under his generals or by ourselves? If he should ask where our army or where our navy had been within his strongholds, what would we say?

'Perhaps we would be defending ourselves before him as the victor, just as we are now in front of you. For by sending representatives about peace to you and Perseus, we had gained favour from neither of you and indeed had incurred blame and the danger of harm from one of you. Admittedly, Perseus might rightly object, as you, conscript fathers, cannot, that at the beginning of the war we had sent envoys to you to promise you what was needed for the war— that we would be prepared for anything, with ships and weapons and our young men, just as in previous wars. It is your fault that we did not provide them: for whatever reason at the time, you scorned our help. Thus we neither did anything of a hostile nature, nor did we fall short in any duty of good allies; instead, we were prevented by you from fulfilling the promise.

'You may say, "What then? Was nothing said or done in your city, O Rhodians, that you would regret and that might justifiably offend the Roman people?" On this point I am not now about to defend what happened—I am not so insane as that—but I will separate the accusation against the community from the culpability of private individuals. Every city contains wicked citizens from time to time and an ignorant populace all the time. I have heard that even among you there have been those who operated by flattering the populace, and that the plebeians occasionally seceded from you, and that the Republic was not under your control.* If this could happen in this city, which is so well ordered, can anyone wonder that there were those among us who sought the king's friendship and misled our populace with their advice? But these men did not prevail beyond making us lapse in our duty.

'I will not pass over what is the most serious accusation against our city in this war: we sent representatives about peace simultaneously to you and to Perseus. This ill-fated plan was rendered utterly foolish by a madman of a spokesman, as we subsequently heard. It is generally understood that he talked in the same manner as did Gaius Popillius, the Roman envoy, whom you sent to dissuade the kings Antiochus and Ptolemy from going to war. But even so, whether this behaviour should be termed arrogance or stupidity, it was the same for both you and Perseus.

'The ways of cities are just like the ways of individuals: that is, some peoples are irascible, some daring, some timid, and others are more susceptible to wine or sex. The Athenian people have a reputation for being swift and bold beyond their strength in their enterprises; the reputation of the Lacedaemonians is to delay and to embark reluctantly on matters where they have total confidence.* Further, I would not deny that the entire region of Asia produces greater weakness of character, and that our manner of speaking is inflated* because we imagine that we are better than neighbouring communities, and this supposed superiority is based not on our resources but on honours and indications of esteem from you.

'Truly, that embassy was castigated sufficiently on the occasion when it was dismissed with such a stern response from you. If the shame did not register enough at the time, then certainly our pathetic, suppliant embassy should be penitence great enough for an embassy even more presumptuous than the previous one was. Irascible men hate arrogance, especially of a verbal sort; wise men laugh at it, especially if it is directed by the weaker against the stronger. No one ever

deemed it worthy of capital punishment. Now there was real danger—
that the Rhodians had contempt for the Romans! Some men curse
even the gods in very abusive language, but we do not hear of anyone
struck by lightning for that reason.

24. 'What then remains for us to justify, if we did not commit any
hostile act, and if excessively puffed-up speech deserved to offend
your ears, but not to destroy our city? I hear as you talk amongst
yourselves, conscript fathers, that you are, so to speak, calculating
the damages for our unexpressed inclination (that we favoured the
king and wanted him to win). Consequently, some of you think we
should be punished by force. Others of you believe that that was
indeed what we wanted, but that it is not a reason to punish us by
force; no city's customs or statutes provide that someone suffers capital punishment for wishing his enemy to die but doing nothing to
bring it about.

'We are indeed grateful to those who excuse us from punishment
but not responsibility. We set the following terms for ourselves: if all
of us wanted what we are accused of—and we are not distinguishing
wish from action—let us all be punished; if some of our leaders sided
with the king and others with you, I do not seek that the king's
partisans escape unscathed because we sided with you; I beg instead
that we do not die because of them. The city of Rhodes regards them
no more favourably than you do; and most of them have either fled
or committed suicide because they knew this; others have been
condemned by us and will be placed under your power, conscript
fathers.

'As for the rest of us Rhodians, for this war we deserve no thanks,
but equally no retribution. Let our accumulated previous good deeds
compensate for the current lapse of duty. Through the years, you
have waged war with three kings; do not let the fact that we fell short
in this one war count more against us than the fact that we fought for
you in two of them. Treat Philip, Antiochus, and Perseus as three
votes: two acquit us; is the remaining one, being open to question, to
count more? If those monarchs were to pass judgement on us, we
would be condemned. But you, conscript fathers, are judging whether
or not Rhodes should be completely obliterated from the face of the
earth; it is not war you are deliberating about, conscript fathers, since
although you can attack us, you cannot fight us, given that no Rhodian
would take up arms against you.

'If you persevere in your wrath, we will ask you for time to take this mournful delegation home. All free citizens, as many Rhodian men and women as there are, will take ship with all our money, and leaving behind our household gods, public and private alike, we will come to Rome; we will heap up all our gold and silver, whether public or privately owned, in the Comitium and in the entryway to your Curia; and we will entrust our bodies and those of our wives and children to your power, prepared to suffer here whatever will have to be suffered; let our city be destroyed and burnt down far from our eyes. You Romans have the power to judge that the Rhodians are your enemies. We too, however, have our own judgement on ourselves: that we will never consider ourselves your enemies, nor will we commit any hostile action, even if we are subject to every punishment.'

25. After a speech along these lines they all prostrated themselves again, and they waved olive branches in supplication and sought forgiveness; finally they were made to stand, and they went out of the Curia.

The senators were then asked for their opinion. The men most opposed to the Rhodians were the consuls, praetors, and lieutenants who had conducted the war in Macedonia. Marcus Porcius Cato gave the greatest support to the Rhodians' case; although a man of harsh temperament,* on that occasion he conducted himself as a moderate and merciful senator. I will not include a reproduction of that master of words by recording what he said; his speech survives as written, included in the fifth book of his *Origines*.* The answer given to the Rhodians was such as neither to turn them into enemies nor to perpetuate their status as allies.

Philocrates and Astymedes were the leaders of the delegation. It was decided that part of the delegation should deliver a report to Rhodes with Philocrates while part should remain at Rome with Astymedes to ascertain what was happening and to keep their people informed. For the moment the Romans ordered the Rhodian people to withdraw their governors from Lycia and Caria by a fixed deadline. Though by itself this announcement would have been grim, it delighted the Rhodians since it reduced their fear of a greater evil: they had feared war. Accordingly, they immediately voted a crown of 20,000 gold pieces. They sent Theaedetus, the commander of the fleet, on this embassy; they wished an alliance with the Romans to be requested in such a way that there would be no decree of the people concerning it and nothing committed to writing, because unless they succeeded the rejection would compound their disgrace. The commander of the fleet alone was constitutionally empowered to act on this matter without the passage of any motion. The Rhodians had been in a position of friendship for so many years, but they had never bound themselves to the Romans by a treaty of alliance.* The only reason for this was to leave open the kings' hope of Rhodian aid should they need it, and the Rhodians' own accrual of benefits from the kings' good graces and wealth. But at this time an alliance seemed especially worth seeking, not because it would make the Rhodians safer from others—for they did not fear anyone besides the Romans—but because it would make the Romans themselves less suspicious of the Rhodians.

In the same period* the Caunii revolted from the Rhodians, and the Mylassenses occupied the cities of the Euromenses. The Rhodians' spirits had not been so devastated that they did not recognize that they would be limited to the shores of their small island and its unproductive land (which could not by any means feed the population of such a big city) if the Romans took away Lycia and Caria, and if the remaining places either revolted and gained their freedom or were taken over by their neighbours. The Rhodians therefore quickly dispatched their soldiery, who forced the Caunii to submit to Rhodian rule, although the former had taken in the Cibyratae as allies. In a battle around Orthosia the Rhodians defeated the Mylassenses and the Alabandenses, who had also come to acquire the province of the Euromenses and combined forces with the Mylassenses.

26. While those events were transpiring there and the others in Macedonia and Rome, in Illyricum Lucius Anicius had captured King Gentius, as was said before. He established a garrison at Scodra, which had been the royal seat, and put Gabinius in charge of it, and he left Gaius Licinius in charge of the strategic cities of Rhizon and Olcinium. Once these men were installed in Illyricum, Anicius went to Epirus with the rest of the army. Phanote was the first place there to put itself in his hands, and the entire populace raced out to meet him waving banners of surrender.

He established a garrison there and crossed into Molossis. After recovering all the towns except for Passaron, Tecmon, Phylace, and Horreum, he marched first to Passaron. The city's leaders were Antinous and Theodotus, and they were known both for their goodwill towards Perseus and for their hatred of the Romans; they were also responsible for making the entire people defect from the Romans. Aware that the wrongdoing was theirs and bereft of any hope for a pardon, they locked the gates of the city so that they and their fatherland would be destroyed together. They exhorted the populace to prefer death to slavery. No one dared to speak against these exceptionally powerful men. Finally, when his considerable fear of the Romans surpassed his dread of his own leaders, a certain Theodotus, himself a well-born young man, said, 'What madness drives you, you who make a city the accessory to the wrongdoing of two men? Of course I have often heard talk of men who sought to die for their fatherland; but these men are the first ever known who think it right that their fatherland die for them. Why do we not instead open the gates and accept the rule that the entire world has accepted?' Since the populace sided with him when he expressed this view, Antinous and Theodotus rushed against the first enemy outpost and, there exposing themselves, were wounded and died. The city surrendered to the Romans. Tecmon was barricaded out of a similar stubbornness on the part of its leader, Cephalus; he was killed, and Anicius accepted the town's surrender. Neither Phylace nor Horreum withstood an assault.

After pacifying Epirus, Anicius distributed his forces into winter quarters in strategically located cities. He then returned to Illyricum. At Scodra, where the five commissioners had come from Rome, Anicius convened a meeting of leaders whom he had summoned from throughout the province. At the congress he announced from his tribunal that, in accordance with the opinion of his advisers, the Senate and the Roman people ordered that the Illyrians should be free;* and that he himself would withdraw the garrisons from all towns, citadels, and forts; the people of Issa, the Taulantii, the Pirustae of the Dassaretii, and the people of Rhizon and Olcinium would be not just free, but exempt from tribute, since they had defected to the Romans while Gentius was still in power. Anicius said that he was granting the Daorsi exemption from taxes too because they had abandoned Caravantius and joined the Romans with their weapons. The taxes placed on the people of Scodra, the Dassarenses, the Selepitani, and the rest of the Illyrians would be half what they had paid the king.

Anicius then divided Illyricum into three parts: one from everything that is above Dyrrachium, the second comprising all the Labeatae, and the third being the inhabitants of Acruvium, Rhizon, Olcinium, and their neighbours. Once this charter for Illyricum had been made public, Anicius returned to winter quarters at Passaron in Epirus.

27. While these events were transpiring in Illyricum and before the arrival of the ten commissioners, Paullus sent his son Quintus Maximus, who had already come back from Rome, to loot Aeginium and Agassae. Agassae was a target because the people had defected back to Perseus after they had surrendered the city to the consul Marcius and, in addition, sought a Roman alliance. The Aeginienses' crime was recent: giving no credence to the story of the Romans' victory, they had savagely attacked some soldiers who came to their city. Paullus also sent Lucius Postumius to loot the city of the Aenii because they had persisted in a state of war more obstinately than the neighbouring communities.

The season of the year was nearly autumn, and Paullus decided to use the early part of it to travel around Greece and to visit places where rumour enhances reputation and what the eyes discern falls short of what the ears have heard. He left Gaius Sulpicius Galus in charge of the camp and set out with a small troop. His son Scipio and Athenaeus, the brother of King Eumenes, escorted him as he journeyed through Thessaly to Delphi, the famous oracle. There, after he had sacrificed to Apollo, he gave instructions that the unfinished column bases in the forecourt, on which statues of King Perseus were to have been put, should be used for victory statues of himself instead.*

He went to the shrine of Jupiter Trophonius at Lebadia too; there, when he had seen the mouth of the pit through which those consulting the oracle descend to ask questions of the gods, he sacrificed to Jupiter and to Hercynna, whose shrine is there.* He went down to Chalcis, to the sight of the Euripus and the island of Euboea,* which is linked to the mainland by a bridge. From Chalcis he crossed to Aulis, three miles away, the harbour that is famous as the erstwhile mooring of Agamemnon's fleet of a thousand ships, and the temple of Diana, where that king of kings achieved passage to Troy for his ships by bringing his daughter to the altar as an offering.*

From there, Paullus went on to Oropus in Attica, where the ancient prophet is worshipped as a god* and his old shrine is pleasantly encircled by springs and streams. Next was Athens, which of course is filled with age-old fame and still has much to see: the acropolis, the harbour, the walls linking Piraeus to the city,* the shipyards, the statues of great generals, the images of gods and men that are noteworthy for every kind of medium and artistic technique.

28. After sacrificing in the city to Minerva, protectress of the acropolis, Paullus departed and reached Corinth on the next day. At that time, before its destruction,* it was a splendid city. Also the citadel and the Isthmus constituted sights in themselves; the citadel is within the walls, way up high on a massive elevation and teeming with springs; with its narrow passage the Isthmus separates two neighbouring seas, to the east and to the west. From Corinth, Paullus went to the famous cities of Sicyon and Argos, and then Epidaurus, which was not, of course, their equal in wealth, but is well known for the famous temple of Aesculapius. This is about five miles from the city; at that time it was rich in gifts that the sick had dedicated to the god as recompense for beneficial treatments; but now it is rich in traces of the gifts, which have been forcibly removed. Next Paullus went to Lacedaemon, memorable not for the magnificence of its structures but for its educational system and its institutions.* From there, Paullus travelled by way of Megalopolis up to Olympia. There, after he saw other sights worth seeing, gazing at the statue of Jupiter, he was moved as if the god were present.* And so he ordered a greater sacrifice than usual to be prepared, just as if he were about to offer sacrifice on the Capitol.

In order not to trouble the allies with fear of anything, Paullus travelled through Greece in such a way as to avoid enquiring into what anyone might have experienced in the war with Perseus, whether personally or in an official capacity. Then he returned to Demetrias. Along the way a troop of Aetolians in mourning approached him. He was taken aback and asked what was going on. He was told that Lyciscus and Tisippus had had 550 leading citizens killed; the Aetolian senate had been surrounded by Roman soldiers who were sent by the garrison's commander, Aulus Baebius; other men were driven into exile; and the property of those who had been killed and of the exiles had been appropriated. Paullus directed the men who were being accused to assemble at Amphipolis. He himself met Gnaeus Octavius at Demetrias. After word arrived that the ten commissioners had crossed the sea already, Paullus set everything else aside and went to them at Apollonia.

When Perseus took advantage of overly lax custody and went from Amphipolis to meet Paullus there (a day's journey), Paullus spoke with him in a friendly fashion. But once Paullus reached the camp at Amphipolis, it is reported that he gave Gaius Sulpicius a severe lecture, first because he had allowed Perseus to roam so far away from him throughout the province, and second because he had indulged the soldiers to such a degree that he allowed them to strip tiles from the city walls to cover their quarters for the winter; Paullus ordered the tiles to be returned and the exposed areas to be repaired.* And he handed Perseus and his older son Philip over to Aulus Postumius and sent them into custody. Perseus' daughter and younger son were summoned from Samothrace to Amphipolis, where Paullus maintained them with all generosity and care.

29. The day arrived that Paullus had set for ten leaders from every community to be present in Amphipolis and for all documents, wherever they had been deposited, and royal treasure to be gathered together. Paullus sat at a tribunal with the ten commissioners, surrounded by the entire throng of Macedonians. Although they were accustomed to monarchic power, nevertheless they were unnerved by this new form of it, made manifest by the tribunal, the clearing of a path for Paullus, the herald, Paullus' approach, the summons: all these, which could terrify even allies, let alone defeated enemies, were unfamiliar to their eyes and ears.

When the herald had established silence, Paullus announced in Latin what he and the Senate had decided, in accordance with the opinion of his advisers. Gnaeus Octavius, the praetor—for he was there too—translated Paullus' words into Greek and repeated them.* First of all, Paullus and the Senate ordered that the Macedonians should be free, keeping the same cities and fields, following their own laws, and electing annual magistrates; they were to pay the Roman people half the tribute they had paid the kings.

Next, Macedonia was to be divided into four regions. One of them, the first section, would be the land between the Strymon and Nessus rivers; this part would be supplemented by what Perseus had held across the Nessus to the east: the villages, forts, and towns, except for Aenus, Maronea, and Abdera; and in addition, territory on the near side of the Strymon, lying to the west: namely all of Bisaltia, along with what they call Heraclea Sintice. The second region would be the land enclosed by the Strymon to the east, except for Heraclea Sintice and the Bisaltae, and ending on the west at the Axius river; the Paeones who live near the Axius river in the region to its east were included too. The third region was to consist of what the Axius encircles on the east and the Peneus on the west; the northern border was constituted by Mount Bermium; added to this part was the section of Paeonia where it extends to the west along the Axius river; Edessa and Beroea also were assigned to this same part. The fourth region was to be across the spine of Mount Bermium, bordered on one side by Illyricum and by Epirus on another. Paullus established the regions' capitals, where their assemblies would be: Amphipolis for the first region, Thessalonica for the second, Pella for the third, and Pelagonia* for the fourth. Paullus directed that in those locations the assemblies of each region would convene, the money would be collected, and the magistrates would be selected.

Then he announced that he and the Senate had agreed that there would be no marriage or trade in lands or buildings with anyone across the borders of one's own region. Nor were the gold and silver mines to be worked, but copper and iron mines could be. The rent placed on those working the mines was half what they had paid to the king. Paullus also forbade the use of imported salt.

When the Dardani asked to have Paeonia back, on the grounds that it had been theirs and bordered their territory, Paullus announced that he was conferring freedom on everybody who had been under Perseus' sway. But, after denying the Dardani Paeonia, he allowed them to import salt; he decreed that the third region would bring salt to Stobi in Paeonia, and he set the price. He forbade the Macedonians themselves to cut timber for a fleet or to allow others to cut it. He permitted the regions that lay next to barbarians—in other words, all but the third region—to have armed garrisons on their outer borders.

30. The announcement of these matters on the first day of the meeting produced mixed reactions. The unexpected granting of freedom raised the Macedonians' spirits, as did the reduction in annual taxes; but with the regional division of commerce, Macedonia seemed mangled, like an animal whose mutually interdependent limbs have been wrenched apart. The Macedonians, too, did not realize how large Macedonia was, how easy it was to divide in such a way that each part was self-sustaining. The first region has the Bisaltae, the bravest of men, who live on the far side of the Nessus river and around the Strymon; and it has also many special types of crops, and mines, and the advantageous location of Amphipolis, which acts as a barrier and blocks all approaches to Macedonia from

the east. The second region has the busiest cities, Thessalonica and
Cassandrea, in addition to Pallene, which is fertile and productive land;
the ports too—at Torone and Mount Athos, at Aenea and Acanthus,
some strategically facing Thessaly and Euboea and others the
Hellespont—offer maritime resources. The third region has the well-
known cities of Edessa, Beroea, and Pella, and the warlike tribe of the
Bottiaei, and many Gauls and Illyrians, who are dedicated farmers.
The Eordaei, the Lyncestae, and the Pelagones inhabit the fourth
region; Atintania is linked to these, as are Tymphaea and Elimiotis.
This entire region is very cold, tough to cultivate, and harsh; the
farmers have characters to match the land. Their barbarian neighbours also make them more aggressive, sometimes challenging them
in war and sometimes sharing customs with them in peace. By thus
dividing Macedonia and separating the assets of the parts, Paullus
revealed how great it was as a whole.

31. After this charter for Macedonia had been announced and
Paullus had promised that he would provide laws also, the Aetolians
were called in.* During the inquiry, the point at issue was not so
much whether one faction or the other had committed or received
any injury; it was rather which faction had sided with the Romans
and which with the king. Those who had committed the murders
were absolved from guilt; equally, for those who had been driven out,
their exile was considered justified, as were the deaths of the men
who had been killed. Aulus Baebius alone was condemned, because
he had supplied Roman soldiers to facilitate the slaughter.

Among all the states and peoples of Greece, this outcome in the
case of the Aetolians inflated to an intolerable degree of arrogance the
minds of those who had been on the Roman side, while those who
had been brushed with any hint of a suspicion of favouring the king
were left crushed at their feet. There were three kinds of leaders in
the cities. Two types, by fawning on either the Romans' might or the
kings' friendship, had oppressed their cities and amassed private fortunes for themselves. The middle group opposed both parties and
guarded liberty and the laws; the more affection there was for these
men among their own people, the less influence they had among
outsiders.

At the time the partisans of the Romans had been elevated by the
latter's success and monopolized the magistracies and the embassies.
When these men arrived from the Peloponnese, Boeotia, and other

Greek leagues, they filled the ears of the ten commissioners. They said that not only were there those who out of vanity had openly boasted of themselves as being guest-friends and intimates of Perseus, but that far more had sided with the king secretly; that under the pretext of protecting freedom, these men had organized everything in their leagues to the detriment of the Romans; and that these peoples would not remain loyal unless the will of the opposition was broken and the authority of those who looked to nothing but Roman rule was nourished and strengthened.

Based on the names submitted by these men, Paullus wrote and summoned men from Aetolia, Acarnania, Epirus, and Boeotia to follow him to Rome to plead their case. Two of the ten commissioners, Gaius Claudius and Gnaeus Domitius, went to Achaea to summon men with their own edict. This was done for two reasons: one was that the commissioners believed that the Achaeans had more confidence and spirit to disobey, and perhaps even that Callicrates and the rest of the accusers and informers would be endangered;* the other reason they issued the summons in person was that in the king's records the commissioners had found letters from the leaders of the other peoples; but in the case of Achaea the charge was unsubstantiated since none of their letters had been found.

After the Aetolians were dismissed, the people of Acarnania were called in. Nothing was changed in their case except that Leucas was removed from their league.

Then, by enquiring widely who either officially or privately had sided with the king, the commissioners extended their investigation into Asia too. And they sent Labeo to destroy Antissa on the island of Lesbos and to bring the inhabitants to Methymna, because when Antenor, the king's admiral, was sailing around Lesbos with his galleys, they had aided him, sheltering him in their harbour and giving him provisions. Two important men were beheaded, Andronicus, son of Andronicus, an Aetolian, because he had followed his father and taken up arms against the Romans, and Neon the Theban, who had led his people to form the alliance with Perseus.

32. After the delay caused by these investigations into outside matters, a council of Macedonians was summoned for a second time. There was an announcement that, as far as the constitution of Macedonia was concerned, senators should be chosen. (The Macedonians call them 'synhedri'.) The state was to be run in

accordance with their advice. Next were read the names of the Macedonian leaders who, along with their children over fifteen, were chosen to proceed ahead to Italy. Although this initially looked barbaric, it soon became apparent to the Macedonian populace that it was done for the sake of their freedom. For the men named were the friends and courtiers of the king, generals in the army, commanders of fleets and garrisons, men accustomed to serve the king humbly and to give arrogant orders to everyone else; some were extremely wealthy while others did not have the same resources but were equally lavish in their spending; all of them ate and dressed on a royal scale; none of them had civic spirit or tolerated laws or equal access to freedom. Accordingly, all who had been in any royal office, even those who had served as envoys, were ordered to leave Macedonia and to go to Italy: anyone who disobeyed the order was threatened with death. Paullus conferred laws on Macedonia with so much care that he seemed to be conferring them not on defeated enemies but on well-deserving allies, and the laws were ones that stood the test of time, which alone has the force to emend laws.

After these weighty matters, Paullus put on an entertainment with great pomp at Amphipolis. There had been extensive preparations in advance; men had been sent to the communities of Asia and the kings to announce it; as Paullus himself was travelling around the cities of Greece, he had given formal notice of it to the leaders. A multitude of performers, practitioners of every kind of theatrical craft, athletes, and horses of the purest stock came together from all over the world, as did delegations with sacrificial animals. And whatever else usually happens at major games in Greece for the sake of gods and men was done in such a way that the crowd admired not just Paullus' lavishness, but his expertise in putting on spectacles, which at that time the Romans did without any finesse. Further, feasts were prepared for the delegations with the same opulence and care. People kept on repeating Paullus' own dictum that the man who knows how to organize a feast and put on games is the same man who knows how to win a battle.

33. After the entertainment concluded and bronze shields were hung on the ships, the remaining weapons, all kinds, were piled in a great heap. Paullus invoked Mars, Minerva, and Mother Lua, as well as the rest of the gods to whom it is right and lawful to dedicate enemy spoils, and he himself placed a torch under the pile and lit it;

thereupon each of the military tribunes, who were standing around it, threw a torch into the fire.

In that gathering of Europe and Asia, with a mass of people drawn together from every region, partly to offer thanks and partly to see the show, and amidst so many naval and ground forces, there was such a remarkable abundance of supplies and grain was so cheap that the general gave gifts, mostly of that sort, to individuals, cities, and whole tribes, not just for the immediate occasion, but also for them to take home.

The spectacle that the crowd had come for was no more the drama or contests among men or chariot races than it was the spoils of Macedonia. Everything was put on display: sculptures and paintings and tapestries and vases, which were made in the palace with great care, from gold, silver, bronze, and ivory, not just to produce an impression as it was with the sorts of things crammed into the palace at Alexandria—but for permanent use. The items were loaded on the fleet and entrusted to Gnaeus Octavius to take back to Rome.

Paullus sent the delegations away in a gracious fashion. Then he crossed the Strymon and encamped a mile outside Amphipolis. He went on from there and reached Pella four days later. Once he had passed that city, he spent two days at the place they call Pelium. He sent Publius Nasica and his son Quintus Maximus with part of his forces to loot the Illyrians who had helped Perseus in the war; they were instructed to meet him at Oricum. Paullus himself set out for Epirus and reached Passaron fourteen days later.

34. Anicius' camp was not very far away. Paullus sent him a letter alerting him not to disrupt what was going on: the Senate had granted to Paullus' troops the booty from the cities of Epirus that had defected to Perseus. After Paullus sent centurions to each city to announce that they had come to remove the garrisons so that the Epirotae might be free just as the Macedonians were, he summoned ten leading citizens from each city. After he had announced to these men that their gold and silver should be brought out in public, he sent detachments of troops to all the cities. The groups going to the more distant ones left before those going to the closer ones so that they could reach all the cities on the same day. The tribunes and the centurions had received orders about what to do. Early in the morning all the gold and silver was collected; at the fourth hour an order was given to the soldiers to sack the cities. There was so much

plunder* that 400 *denarii* were distributed to each cavalryman and 200 to each infantryman, and 150,000 people were seized. Then the walls of the pillaged cities were destroyed; there were about seventy of them. All the booty was sold, and then the proceeds were paid out to the soldiers.

Paullus travelled down to the sea at Oricum thinking, wrongly, that the feelings of the soldiers had been satisfied. They were outraged that they had no share of the royal plunder, as if they had not fought in Macedonia at all. When Paullus found at Oricum the forces that he had sent with Scipio Nasica and his son Maximus, he put his army on the ships and crossed to Italy. And a few days later, when Anicius had completed a meeting with the rest of the Epirotae and Acarnanians, he ordered the leaders whose cases he had reserved for senatorial investigation to follow him to Italy. After waiting for the ships used by the troops that had been in Macedonia, he himself crossed to Italy.

While these events were taking place in Macedonia and Epirus, the envoys who had been sent with Attalus to terminate the war between the Galatians and King Eumenes reached Asia. A truce had been made for the winter. The Galatians had gone back to their homes, and the king had retreated to winter quarters in Pergamum. He was gravely ill. The beginning of spring brought the Galatians out of their homes, and they had already reached Synnada by the time Eumenes had assembled his army at Sardis from all over. When the Romans spoke to the Galatians' leader, Solouettius, at Synnada, Attalus came too, but it was agreed that he would not enter the Galatians' camp, in order to avoid a quarrel and the flaring of tempers. After Publius Licinius, the former consul, spoke with the chieftain of the Galatians, he reported that his appeal had made Solouettius more hostile. Thus, it seemed an extraordinary paradox that while between the very wealthy kings, Antiochus and Ptolemy, mere words from Roman envoys had been so powerful that they effected an immediate peace, they had absolutely no effect on the Galatians.

35. The first to be taken off to Rome under guard were the captured kings Perseus and Gentius, with their children. The mass of other prisoners went next, and then a herd of Macedonians who had been given notice to go to Rome; Greek leaders were included too. For, if in their own states, they had received a summons, and further, anyone reputed to be at a royal court was sent for by letter. A few

days later Paullus himself travelled up the Tiber to the city, in a royal ship of enormous size, powered by sixteen banks of rowers, and adorned with Macedonian spoils, not just splendid weaponry, but even royal tapestries. The riverbanks were packed with crowds that poured forth to meet him. Anicius and Octavius arrived with their fleets a few days later. The Senate voted a triumph for all three of them. The praetor Quintus Cassius was instructed to arrange with the tribunes of the plebs to bring before the plebs a motion, backed by the Senate, authorizing the three generals to retain their *imperium* on the day they entered the city in triumph.

Mediocrity is exempt from spite, which generally takes aim at the lofty. There was no debate about the triumph for either Anicius or Octavius, though they would have blushed to compare themselves to Paullus. He, however, was assailed by malicious carping behind his back. He had handled the soldiers with old-fashioned discipline; he had distributed booty to them more parsimoniously than they had expected from such enormous royal riches (though they would have left nothing for him to deposit in the public treasury if he had indulged their greed). All the soldiers who served in Macedonia were enraged at the commander and were not about to give any attention to attending the assembly when the law was to be presented.* But Servius Sulpicius Galba, who had been a military tribune of the second legion in Macedonia and was privately hostile to the general, kept on canvassing and causing unrest throughout the soldiers of his own legion until he had goaded them into turning out in large numbers for the vote. He told them to take revenge on their domineering and mean-spirited general by rejecting the motion that was being brought about his triumph. Galba told them that the urban plebs would follow the judgement of the soldiers. Paullus had not been able to give them money; the soldiers were able to give him honour. But he should not expect the fruits of gratitude where he had not earned them.

36. The men were thus in an excited condition when the tribune of the plebs Tiberius Sempronius brought the motion on the Capitoline. And when the time came for private citizens to speak about the law, no one at all came forward to urge passing it, as if there were little dispute about the matter. Suddenly, Servius Galba came forward and demanded of the tribunes that, since it was already the eighth hour of the day and he did not have enough time to show why they

should not vote a triumph for Lucius Aemilius, they should postpone the matter until the following day and take it up in the morning: he needed an entire day to argue his case. When the tribunes
directed him to talk that day if he wished to say anything, he dragged
the matter out by talking into the night, recollecting and reminding
them of the harsh exaction of their duties as soldiers. He said that
more work and more danger had been imposed on them than the task
had called for; conversely, when it came to rewards and recognitions,
everything had been reduced; and if this sort of leader were successful, military service would be excessively harsh and burdensome
while the troops were fighting, and it would lack remuneration and
esteem once they had won. The Macedonian soldiers were better off
than the Romans. If the Roman soldiers turned up in large numbers
the following day to reject the law, men of influence would understand that not everything was up to the general, but some things lay
in the hands of the soldiers.

Egged on by these words, the soldiers thronged the Capitoline the
following day in such numbers that there was no space for anyone
else to enter to cast a vote. When the first tribes called in voted
against the proposal, the city's leading men charged the Capitoline,
shouting that it was a shameful deed to deprive of his triumph
Lucius Paullus, the winner of so great a war, and that generals were
being abandoned to be at the mercy of their soldiers' unruly behaviour and greed. Even as it was, all too often the currying of favour led
to mistaken decisions; what if the soldiers became the masters and
were placed over the generals? The leading citizens then all heaped
reproaches on Galba.

When the commotion finally subsided, Marcus Servilius, who had
been a consul* and a master of the horse, asked the tribunes to repeat
the process from the beginning and to give him an opportunity to
address the people. The tribunes stepped aside to confer. They were
won over by the influence of the leading citizens and began to repeat
the process from the beginning. The tribunes announced that they
would call the same tribes back in once Marcus Servilius and other
private individuals who wished to speak had done so.

37. Then Servilius spoke: 'Roman citizens, if it were impossible to
calculate by any other means how outstanding a commander Lucius
Aemilius is, this one point would be enough: although he had in his
camp such seditious and unreliable soldiers and such a well-born,

such a reckless enemy, one so adept at stirring up a crowd with words, he did not have any rebellion in the army. The very same strict authority that they now despise restrained them then. Thus, handled with old-fashioned discipline, they neither said nor did anything mutinous.

'Truly, if by bringing charges in the matter of Lucius Paullus, Servius Galba wished to shed his apprenticeship and to put his eloquence on display,* he should not have obstructed Paullus' triumph which, if nothing else, the Senate had judged to be deserved. Instead, on the day after Paullus' triumph had been celebrated, when Galba could look upon him as a private citizen, he should have instituted criminal proceedings against him and called him to account in a court of law. Or a little later, when Galba himself had taken up his first magistracy, he could have brought his enemy to trial and charged Paullus before the people. In this way Lucius Paullus would have both a reward for good conduct, namely a triumph for a superbly run campaign, and punishment, if he had done anything unworthy of his glory, old or new. But of course, since Galba was not able to cite any crime or any impropriety, he wished to carp at Paullus' laudable attributes. Yesterday he requested a whole day to bring his accusation against Lucius Paullus; he consumed four hours, as much of the day as remained, with talk. What defendant was ever so guilty that that much time could not suffice to reveal the shortcomings of his life? And within that time, what did Servius Galba bring up against Lucius Paullus that Paullus would want to deny if he were arguing in his own defence?

'Let someone create for me, for just a moment, two assemblies, one of soldiers from the Macedonian campaign, and another, uncontaminated one, of the entire Roman people, with its judgement less impaired by partisanship and prejudice. First, let the defendant be tried before the civilian, togate assembly. What would you say, Servius Galba, before full Roman citizens? That entire speech of yours would have been truncated: "you manned your posts too strictly and intently; watches were inspected more harshly and rigorously than before; you did more labour than before, since the commander himself went around and supervised; on one and the same day you both marched and from marching went forth into battle; he did not allow you to rest even when you had won; he led you immediately in pursuit of the enemy;* although he could make you wealthy by sharing out the plunder, he intends to have the royal treasure carried in the triumph and deposited in the public treasury."

'Although these matters provide some sort of stimulus to prod the spirits of the soldiers, who think their unruly behaviour and greed were insufficiently pandered to, they would have carried no weight at all among the Roman people. Those who do not remember earlier events that they heard about from their parents—what defeats were suffered because of the personal ambition of commanders, what victories were achieved because of strict authority—can certainly recall what a difference there was between the master of the horse Marcus Minucius and the dictator Quintus Fabius Maximus in the most recent Punic war.* Thus it would have been apparent that the accuser had been in no position to open his mouth, and the defence of Paullus would have been superfluous.

'Let us cross over to the other assembly. Now I imagine myself about to address you, not as Roman citizens, but as soldiers—if this appellation at least is able to rouse your sense of shame and to provoke some embarrassment for treating your commander with disrespect. 38. For my part, I have a different way of thinking when I imagine myself speaking before the army, than I did shortly before when my oration was directed at the urban plebs. Tell me, soldiers, what are you saying? Apart from Perseus, is there anyone in Rome who does not want there to be a triumph over Macedonia, and would you not tear such a man to bits with the very hands you used to defeat the Macedonians? A man who prevents you from entering the city in triumph would have prevented you from conquering if he could have.

'You are in error, soldiers, if you think that the triumph is an honour solely for the commander and not also for the soldiers and for the entire Roman people. Nor is the reputation of Paullus alone at stake. Many men, moreover, who did not obtain a triumph from the Senate have held one on the Alban Mount. No one can deprive Lucius Paullus of the honour of having ended the Macedonian war any more than he could deprive Gaius Lutatius of having ended the First Punic War, or Publius Cornelius the Second Punic War, or those who triumphed after them; nor will a triumph make Lucius Paullus any greater or lesser a commander. Far more at risk here is the reputation of the soldiers, of the entire Roman people: chiefly that it not have a name for spitefulness and a churlish attitude towards any outstanding citizen, and thereby appear to imitate the Athenian people, who make accusations against their leading men out of spite.* Sufficient wrong was inflicted on Camillus by your forefathers; their outrageous treatment of him, however, took place before he rescued our city from the Gauls.* Sufficient wrong was recently inflicted on Publius Africanus by you yourselves: we should blush that the house and home of the conqueror of Africa were in Liternum, and that it is Liternum where his grave is to be seen.* Lucius Paullus should equal these men in his glory; your behaviour should not be equally insulting. First then let our notoriety be erased; it is shameful among other peoples, but ruinous for us. For in a city that is grudging and hostile to good men, who would want to resemble either Africanus or Paullus?

'If no disgrace were involved and it were solely a question of glory, what triumph, I ask you, does not share its glory with the name of Rome? Are so many triumphs over the Gauls, so many triumphs over the Spanish, so many triumphs over the Carthaginians said to be for just the commanders themselves or for the Roman people? For just as the triumphs were conducted not simply over Pyrrhus and not simply over Hannibal, but over the Epirotae and the Carthaginians, so too, not Manius Curius and Publius Cornelius alone, but the Romans triumphed. Assuredly, the occasion belongs to the soldiers, who wear laurel themselves, and each man who has been decorated stands out with his awards; they call upon Triumphus by name, and they sing praises of themselves and their commander as they process through the city. If ever soldiers are not brought home from a province for a triumph, they complain; and yet even then, they believe that they triumph, though absent, because the victory was won by their hands. If anyone should ask you, soldiers, why you were brought back to Italy and not immediately discharged when your duty was done; if anyone should ask you why you have come to Rome in full numbers troop by troop, why you linger here and do not go your separate ways home, what answer could you give other than that you wish to be seen in a triumph? Certainly as the winners you ought to have wished to be on display.

39. 'In the recent past, triumphs have been celebrated over Perseus' father Philip and Antiochus; both kings still held their thrones when the triumphs over them occurred. Is there to be no triumph over Perseus, who has been taken captive and brought to the city with his children? But if, when Lucius Anicius and Gnaeus Octavius, decked out in gold and purple, are ascending the Capitol in a chariot,

Lucius Paullus, just one private citizen in a crowd of togate citizens, should ask them from his inferior position, "Lucius Anicius, Gnaeus Octavius, do you think that you are more deserving of a triumph than I am?", they would probably yield the chariot to him and themselves hand over their insignia in shame. And you, Roman citizens, do you prefer to have Gentius led in a triumphal procession rather than Perseus, and do you prefer the triumph to be for an accessory to the war rather than the war itself? The legions from Illyricum, in laurel, will enter the city, and so will the sailors; will the Macedonian legions watch other triumphs while their own has been voted down? Further, what will happen to such prime plunder and the spoils of such a profitable victory? Where on earth will so many thousands of weapons, stripped from the bodies of our enemies, be tucked away? Or will they be sent back to Macedonia? Where will they go, the sculptures of gold and marble and ivory, the paintings and the tapestries, so much engraved silver, so much gold, so vast a royal treasure? Or will they be carried off to the public treasury at night, as if they were stolen goods?

'What then? Where will the greatest sight of all, a captive king of the highest birth and the most extensive wealth, be displayed to the people who are his conquerors? Most of us remember what crowds turned out when King Syphax, an accessory in the Second Punic War, was captured. Are King Perseus, the captive, and his sons Philip and Alexander, such great names, to be hidden from the city's gaze? All eyes yearn to see Lucius Paullus, consul twice, conqueror of Greece, entering the city in a chariot. We made him consul for this very purpose, to end a war that to our deep shame had dragged on for four years. When Paullus drew the lot for the province and when he set out for it, we anticipated his victory and triumph in our minds, and we preordained them for him;* now that he has been victorious, are we going to deny him the triumph?

'And are we not going to be cheating the gods of the honour, as well as Paullus? For a triumph is owed not simply to mortals, but to the gods too. Your ancestors began and ended every great enterprise with the gods. When a consul or a praetor sets forth for his province and a war, with his lictors dressed in military cloaks, he pronounces vows on the Capitol; once he has brought that war to a close, he returns as a victor to the Capitol in a triumphal procession, bringing well-deserved gifts from the Roman people to those same gods to whom he pronounced vows. By no means the smallest part of a triumph are the sacrificial victims that lead the way; they make it clear to the gods that the commander returns expressing his gratitude for the successful outcome of the public business. As for all those animals that the consul dedicated to be led in the triumph—are you going to sacrifice them at some other time under someone else's direction? And what about the Senate's feast, which takes place not in a private location nor on secular public land, but on the Capitol: whether this is prepared for human pleasure or to honour the gods, will you disrupt it on the authority of Servius Galba? Will the gates be closed against a triumph for Lucius Aemilius? Will Perseus, king of the Macedonians, and his children and the rest of the mass of prisoners, together with the spoils of Macedonia, be left in the Flaminian Circus? Will Lucius Paullus go to his house from the city gate a private citizen, as if he were returning from the countryside?

'And you, centurion, soldier, heed what the Senate has decreed about your general Paullus, not the stories fabricated by Servius Galba; and heed my words, not his. He has learned nothing except how to talk, and to do so abusively and spitefully. I have challenged and fought an enemy twenty-three times; in all cases it was I who carried off the spoils from hand-to-hand combat; I have a body marked by honourable scars, all incurred with my face to the enemy.' It is said that he then removed his garment, and he detailed in which war which wounds were received. As he was showing these, parts of the body that ought to be concealed were accidentally revealed, and his swollen testicles provoked laughter in those closest to him.* 'This condition too, at which you laugh,' he said, 'I have from sitting on a horse day and night, and it causes me no more shame or regret than my scars do since it never prevented me from serving my country well at home or abroad. An old soldier, I have shown my old body, often injured by the sword, to young soldiers; let Galba lay bare his smooth and shining body.

'Tribunes, if it seems right to you, summon the tribes to vote again; soldiers, to you I <. . .>'

[The rest of Servilius' speech is missing because the next page is lost, but these words suggest that he was nearly finished. Presumably the missing text included the vote in favour of Paullus' triumph, and the beginning of the actual procession. Exceptionally, Paullus' triumph lasted three days. Accounts survive in many sources.

Both Diodorus (31.8) and Plutarch (*Aemilius Paullus* 32–4) give lengthy, itemized (though not identical) descriptions. The text of Livy resumes with estimates of the campaign's material gains. Regardless of the figures disputed here, the war against the Macedonians was so profitable that Roman citizens did not pay personal taxes again for over 120 years.]

40. <. . .> Valerius Antias reports that 120,000,000 sesterces was the total value of all the gold and silver that had been seized and was brought in; certainly a much higher total than this is reached from the number of wagons and from the weight of the silver and gold as he records them individually. Sources report that the same amount again was either spent in the previous war or lost in Perseus' flight when he was headed for Samothrace. Thus it is all the more amazing that so much money had been amassed in the thirty years since Philip's war with the Romans, partly from the income of the mines and partly from other taxes. Consequently, while Philip was very poor, Perseus was on the contrary extremely rich when he began to wage war against the Romans.

Finally Paullus himself came in a chariot, displaying the utmost grandeur not just in the dignity of his bearing but in his very age; behind the chariot and amongst the other noble youths were his two sons, Quintus Maximus and Publius Scipio; then came the cavalry, squadron by squadron, and the infantry, troop by troop, each in their own century. The infantry were given 100 *denarii* each; centurions received twice as much; and cavalry three times as much. People think that as much again would have been given to the infantry, and that others would have been rewarded proportionally, if they had voted the honour for Paullus in the first place or if they had shouted their approval eagerly when the amount was announced.*

As Perseus was led in chains through the city of his enemies before the victorious general's chariot, he was not the only lesson in human misfortune during those days; Paullus the victor, gleaming in gold and purple, was one too. For when he had given away two of his sons in adoption, he had kept two at home as the sole heirs to his name, the ancestral religious rites, and his household; the younger of these two was scarcely twelve and died five days before the triumph, and the older, who was fourteen, died three days after it. They should have been wearing the *toga praetexta* and riding in the chariot with their father, fixing their minds on similar triumphs for themselves.

A few days later, the tribune of the plebs Marcus Antonius held a
public meeting. When Paullus described his accomplishments
according to the convention of other commanders, his speech was
memorable and worthy of a leading citizen of Rome.

41. 'Although I think you know both the good fortune with which
I guided the state and the two thunderbolts that have struck my
home during these days, Roman citizens, since both my triumph and
the funerals of my sons have been on display before you, still I beg that
you permit me a few words to compare my own condition with the
public good fortune; I shall do so in the appropriate frame of mind.

'After leaving Italy—I set sail from Brundisium at sunrise—I
reached Corcyra with all my ships at the ninth hour of the day. On
the fifth day after that I sacrificed to Apollo at Delphi on my own
behalf and for your armies and navies. From Delphi I reached the
camp on the fifth day. Once I had taken charge of the army, I changed
certain matters that were significant impediments to victory. Since
the enemy's camp was impregnable and the king could not be compelled to fight, I advanced through his garrisons, traversing the pass
at Petra, and defeated him in a battle near Pydna. I brought
Macedonia under the control of the Roman people. And the war that
for four years my three predecessors as consul conducted in such a
way that they always passed it to their successor in a worse state,
I ended in fifteen days. I met with the fruits, so to speak, of one success after another: all the Macedonian cities surrendered, the royal
treasure passed into my hands, the king himself—as if the gods were
turning him over—was captured with his children in the shrine of
the Samothracians.

'Fortune seemed already only too generous to me, and consequently
not to be trusted. I began to fear the dangers of the sea in carrying off
so much of the king's fortune to Italy and transporting the victorious
army. Once everything and everybody arrived in Italy with winds
favourable to the fleet, there was nothing left for me to pray for.
I wished that since Fortune customarily reverses its course from any
pinnacle, the change would fall on my household rather than the
state. And so, because my triumph, like a mockery of human experience, occurred between the two funerals of my sons, I hope that
the public fortune is satisfied with such a marked tragedy for me.
And although Perseus and I are now looked on as especially notable
examples of the lot of mortals, he as a captive saw his children led as

captives before him, and yet nonetheless has them safe, but I, who triumphed over him, went from the funeral of one son to my triumphal chariot and, returning from the Capitol, arrived as my other son was on the brink of death; nor from such a line of children does any single one remain to bear the name Lucius Aemilius Paullus. The Cornelian and Fabian families have two of my sons, given away in adoption as if from an enormous store of children; no Paullus remains in my house except for this old man. But your good luck and the public good fortune console my household for this calamity.'

42. These words, spoken with so much fortitude, overwhelmed the hearts of those listening more than if he had used his speech as a pathetic lament for his childlessness.

On the first of December Gnaeus Octavius held a naval triumph over King Perseus. It was a triumph without prisoners and without spoils. Octavius gave seventy-five *denarii* apiece to the sailors, double that to the pilots of the ships, and four times as much to the captains.

Afterwards there was a meeting of the Senate. The fathers judged that Quintus Cassius should take King Perseus with his son Alexander to Alba for safekeeping;* and that, depriving Perseus of nothing, Cassius should allow him to have companions, money, silver, and gear in general. Bithys, the son of the Thracian king Cotys, was sent to Carseoli for safekeeping with the hostages.* It was agreed that the rest of the captives who had been led in the triumph were to be put in prison.

A few days after this business was conducted, representatives came from King Cotys of Thrace; they brought money to redeem his son and the other hostages. When the representatives were brought before the Senate, in their speech they put forward this exact point as proof that Cotys had not helped Perseus in the war of his own free will, but because he was forced to give hostages; Cotys' representatives asked that the fathers allow the hostages to be redeemed for whatever amount the fathers should decide on. By authority of the Senate, the answer was given that the Roman people were mindful of the friendship that had existed between them and Cotys, his ancestors, and the Thracian people; that surrendering hostages was the charge, not a defence against the charge, for the Thracian people had no need to fear Perseus even when he was inactive, and still less so when he was occupied by war with the Romans. Just the same, although Cotys had put Perseus' goodwill above the friendship of the

Roman people, they would give greater weight to what befitted the dignity of the Roman people than what could possibly be owed to Cotys, and his son and the hostages would be returned to him. The Roman people's acts of generosity came at no charge; they preferred to leave repayment in the minds of the recipients than to demand it on the spot.

Three envoys—Titus Quinctius Flamininus, Gaius Licinius Nerva, and Marcus Caninius Rebilus—were chosen to escort the hostages back to Thrace; and gifts of 2,000 *asses* each were given to the Thracians. Bithys and the rest of the hostages were summoned from Carseoli and sent to his father with the envoys.

The royal ships that had been taken from the Macedonians were on a scale never seen before; they were hauled into the Campus Martius.

43. While the memory of the Macedonian triumph was still fresh in men's minds, and practically right before their eyes, Lucius Anicius held his triumph over King Gentius and the Illyrians on the festival of Quirinus.* Everything about the triumph struck people as similar but not equal: the commander himself was of lower rank, both Anicius in comparison with the high birth of Aemilius, and the constitutional power of a praetor as compared with that of a consul; nor could Gentius be matched with Perseus, or the Illyrians with the Macedonians, or the spoils with the spoils, or the cash with the cash, or the donatives with the donatives. Even though the recent triumph thus outshone Anicius', still it was apparent to the onlookers that it was by no means contemptible in and of itself. Anicius had defeated the Illyrians within a matter of days; they were ferocious on land and sea and had confidence in the terrain and their fortifications. Anicius had captured their king and his entire family. In the triumph he carried many military standards and other spoils, the contents of the royal household, twenty-seven pounds of gold, <. . .> of silver, 13,000 *denarii*, and 120,000 Illyrian silver pieces. King Gentius and his wife and children were led before Anicius' chariot, as well as the king's brother Caravantius, and some highborn Illyrians. From the plunder Anicius gave forty-five *denarii* to each soldier, twice that to each centurion, and three times as much to the cavalry; he gave the same amounts to the Latin and Italian allies as he gave to Roman citizens, and he gave the sailors as much as he gave the soldiers. A more jubilant army followed along in this triumph, and the leader himself was lauded with many songs.

According to Antias, 20,000,000 sesterces were realized from the booty, beyond the gold and silver that was deposited in the treasury. But since it was not clear from where this sum could be realized, I have put down the source rather than just the information itself. By order of the Senate, King Gentius, his wife, his children, and his brother were taken to Spoletium for custody, and the rest of the captives were thrown into jail at Rome. When the Spoletini refused custody, the royals were brought to Iguvium. The rest of the plunder from Illyricum was 220 galleys. These had been taken from King Gentius. By order of the Senate Quintus Cassius distributed them to the people of Corcyra, Apollonia, and Dyrrachium.

44. That year the consuls merely ravaged Ligurian land since the enemy never led its forces out. The consuls accomplished nothing worthy of record and returned to Rome to elect their successors. On the first day for elections they presided over the election of Marcus Claudius Marcellus and Gaius Sulpicius Galus as the consuls; then on the next day they presided over the election of Lucius Julius, Lucius Appuleius Saturninus, Aulus Licinius Nerva, Publius Rutilius Calvus, Publius Quinctilius Varus, and Marcus Fonteius as the praetors. The provinces designated for these praetors were the two in the city, the two Spains, Sicily, and Sardinia.

There was an intercalation that year: the first day of the intercalary period was inserted the day after the Terminalia. The augur Gaius Claudius died that year; the augurs selected Titus Quinctius Flamininus in his place. The *flamen Quirinalis*, Quintus Fabius Pictor, also died.

That year King Prusias came to Rome with his son Nicomedes. Prusias entered the city with a large retinue and made his way from the city gate to the Forum and the tribunal of the praetor Quintus Cassius. People rushed up from all over. Prusias said that he had come to pay his respects to the gods who watched over the city of Rome, to the Senate, and to the Roman people, and to offer his congratulations because they had defeated the kings Perseus and Gentius, and they had expanded their empire by bringing the Macedonians and the Illyrians under their dominion. When the praetor said that he could grant an audience with the Senate that very day if Prusias wished, the king asked for a period of two days to see the temples of the gods, the city, his friends, and his guest-friends. The quaestor Lucius Cornelius Scipio was assigned to escort him around; the same

man had been sent to Capua to meet Prusias; a house was also rented
to provide Prusias and his companions with warm hospitality.

On the third day Prusias came to the Senate. He offered congratulations on the victory; he summarized his own good deeds in the war;
he requested permission to fulfil a vow of ten adult animals on the
Capitol at Rome and one for Fortuna at Praeneste; these vows were for
the Roman people's victory. Prusias asked also that his alliance with
them be renewed and that he be given the land that had been captured from King Antiochus, which the Roman people had not
assigned to anyone and Galatians were occupying. Last, he entrusted
his son Nicomedes to the Senate.

Prusias had the benefit of support from all the men who had been
generals in the Macedonian war. Thus in regard to every other
matter, what he was seeking was granted to him. As for the land,
however, the response was that commissioners would be sent to look
into the matter; if there had been any land belonging to the Roman
people that was not already assigned to somebody, they would consider Prusias most worthy of this gift; but if it appeared that the land
had not belonged to Antiochus, and therefore had not become the
property of the Roman people, or if it appeared that the land was
given to the Galatians, then Prusias must forgive them if the Roman
people did not wish to give anything to him at the cost of wronging
someone else; nor could a gift be pleasing even to the recipient when
he knew that the donor could take it away whenever he wanted to.
The senators accepted responsibility for Prusias' son Nicomedes.
They said that Ptolemy, king of Egypt, was proof of how much care
the Roman people took in watching over the sons of allied kings.*

Prusias was dismissed with this answer. Gifts totalling <. . .> sesterces and silver dishes weighing fifty pounds were ordered to be
given to him. The senators decreed also that gifts equal to the total
given to Masgaba,* son of King Masinissa, should be given to
Nicomedes, son of the king, The Senate further decreed that the animals and other items pertaining to sacrifice should be furnished for
the king at public expense, just as for Roman magistrates, whether he
wished to sacrifice at Rome or at Praeneste; additionally, that twenty
warships from the fleet at Brundisium should be assigned to him for
his use; until the king had travelled down to the fleet that had been
given to him, Lucius Cornelius Scipio was to stay by his side and
cover expenses for him and his companions until he had embarked.

They say that the king was overwhelmed with happiness at the Roman people's benevolence towards him, that he would not allow the gifts to be acquired for himself, but directed his son to accept what the Roman people were giving him. That is what our authors say about Prusias.

Polybius records that this king did not deserve the dignity of such a title, that he wore the cap of freedom, that his head was shaved, that he was accustomed to approach envoys, and that he referred to himself as a freedman of the Roman people; this was the reason he wore the emblems of that social rank; further, in Rome, when he entered the Curia, he had prostrated himself and kissed the threshold, and that he had addressed the Senate as his saviours, and that he had said other things that did not so much honour his listeners as degrade him.* He stayed around Rome no more than thirty days before returning to his kingdom.

And the war going on in Asia between Eumenes and the Galatians . . .

[The last few words of Book 45 are not entirely legible. Further down on the page is the heading for Book 46.]

THE *PERIOCHAE*

BOOK 1 (753–710 BCE)

1a.* The arrival of Aeneas in Italy and his activities. The reign of Ascanius at Alba and the reigns of the Silvii in turn. Mars' sexual intercourse with Numitor's daughter; the birth of Romulus and Remus. The slaughtering of Amullius. The founding of the city by Romulus. The selection of the Senate. War with the Sabines. Presentation of the *spolia opima** to Jupiter Feretrius. The division of the people into tribes. Defeat of the Fidenates and the Veientes. Apotheosis of Romulus.

Numa Pompilius instituted sacred rites. The closing of the door of the temple of Janus.

Tullus Hostilius plundered the Albans. The battle of the triplets. The punishment of Mettius Fufetius. Tullus killed by lightning.

Ancus Marcius subdued the Latins, founded Ostia.

Tarquinius Priscus defeated the Latins, constructed the Circus, subdued neighbouring peoples, constructed walls and drains.

Servius Tullius' head gave off flames. Servius Tullius subdued the Veientes and divided the people into classes; he dedicated a temple to Diana.

Tarquinius Superbus usurped the monarchy by killing Tullius. The crime of Tullia against her father. The killing of Turnus Herdonius by Tarquinius. War with the Volsci. The looting of Gabii through the deception of Sextus Tarquinius. The beginning of the Capitol. The altars of Termo and Juventas could not be moved. Lucretia killed herself. The expulsion of Superbus. The monarchy lasted 255 years.

1b. Ancus Marcius* allotted the Aventine Mount to the defeated Latins, extended the borders, and established the colony of Ostia. He revived ceremonies that Numa had instituted.

It is said that, for the sake of testing the expertise of the augur Attus Navius, Ancus consulted him as to whether what Ancus was thinking could be made to happen; when Attus said that it could, Ancus ordered him to split a whetstone with a razor, and this was immediately done by Attus.

He ruled for twenty-four years. During his reign, Lucumo, son of Demaratus of Corinth, came to Rome from the Etruscan city of Tarquinii, and Ancus counted him as a friend; Lucumo began to use Tarquinius Priscus as his name; after Ancus' death Tarquinius took over the monarchy. He elevated one hundred men to join the fathers, he subjugated the Latins, he put on games in the Circus, he increased the centuries of the *equites*, he encircled the city with a wall, and he constructed drains. He was killed by the sons of Ancus when he had ruled for thirty-eight years.

Servius Tullius succeeded him. He was the child of a high-born slave-woman from Corniculum, and it has been said that when he was still a baby in his cradle his head gave off flames. He conducted the first census and ritually closed the *lustrum*; in it 80,000 are said to have been registered. He extended the *pomerium*, he added the Quirinal, Viminal, and Esquiline Hills to the city, and together with the Latins he built a temple to Diana on the Aventine. He was killed by Lucius Tarquinius, the son of Priscus, at the instigation of Tullius' own daughter, Tullia; he had ruled for forty-four years.

After him, Lucius Tarquinius Superbus usurped the monarchy, without a directive from either the fathers or the people. He kept armed men around him for his own protection. He waged war against the Volsci, and from the spoils he erected a temple to Jupiter on the Capitol. By a trick he brought Gabii under his control. His sons went to Delphi, and when they asked which of them would be the ruler of Rome, the response was that he who first kissed his mother would be the ruler. While the sons interpreted this answer otherwise, Junius Brutus, who had come with them, pretended that he slipped, and he kissed the earth. The outcome vindicated this action of his. For when Tarquinius Superbus had incurred the hatred of all against him by his domineering conduct, finally his son Sextus forcibly overcame Lucretia's chastity at night, and she summoned her father Tricipitinus and her husband Collatinus to her, called upon them to witness that her death should not be unavenged, and stabbed herself to death. Tarquinius was driven out, mostly by the efforts of Brutus, after twenty-five years of ruling. Then the first consuls were created: Lucius Junius Brutus and Lucius Tarquinius Collatinus.

BOOK 2 (509–468 BCE)

Brutus bound the Roman people by oath to allow no one to rule as a king at Rome in the future. He forced his colleague Tarquinius Collatinus, who was under suspicion because of his familial relationship to the Tarquinii, to abdicate his consulship and leave the city. Brutus ordered the royal property to be seized as plunder, and he dedicated the land to Mars; this was called the Campus Martius. Well-born young men, including Brutus' own sons and those of his brother, had conspired to restore the kings, and so Brutus had them beheaded. Brutus conferred freedom on the slave informant, whose name was Vindicius; the *vindicta** was named after him. When Brutus had marched out the army against the royal family, which had invaded with troops drawn from the Veientes and Tarquinienses, he fought with Arruns, the son of Superbus, and they both died. The married women mourned him for a year.

The consul Publius Valerius brought before the people a law about the right to appeal. The Capitol was dedicated. Although Porsenna, king of Clusium, reached the Janiculum during a campaign he had undertaken for the Tarquinii, he was prevented from crossing the Tiber by the courage of Horatius Cocles. This man, while others were chopping down the Sublician bridge, held off the Etruscans on his own, and when the bridge had been broken apart, he plunged into the river in full armour and swam across to his own men. Another example of courage was added in the person of Mucius. When he had penetrated the enemy's camp to kill Porsenna, he murdered Porsenna's secretary, whom he had thought to be the king. Mucius was apprehended, and he placed his hand on the altar where there had been a sacrifice and let it burn, saying that there were 300 men just like him. Compelled by admiration for these men, Porsenna sought peace-terms and abandoned the war once he had received hostages. One of them, a young woman named Cloelia, tricked her guards and swam across the Tiber to her own people. When Cloelia was restored to Porsenna, she was respectfully sent back by him and rewarded with an equestrian statue.

The dictator Aulus Postumius fought successfully against Tarquinius Superbus when he mounted an offensive with an army of Latins.

Appius Claudius deserted to Rome from the Sabines. For this reason, the Claudian tribe was added, and the number of tribes increased so that there were twenty-one. When the plebeians seceded to the Sacred Mount for the sake of men who had been enslaved for debt, they were recalled from their rebellion by the counsel of Menenius Agrippa. When this same Agrippa died, he was buried at public expense because of his poverty. Five tribunes of the plebs were created. Corioli, a city of the Volsci, was captured by the courage and efforts of Gnaeus Marcius, who was called Coriolanus for this reason. When Titus Latinius, a man of the plebeians, was warned by a supernatural manifestation that he should make a report to the Senate about certain religious matters and he failed to do so, his son died, and his feet became paralysed. After he had been brought to the Senate in a litter and had revealed those same matters, he recovered the use of his feet, and he returned home. When Gnaeus Marcius Coriolanus, who had been driven into exile, had become a leader of the Volsci and had brought an enemy army against the city, first ambassadors and then priests were sent to him and beseeched him, in vain, not to make war on his fatherland; his mother Veturia and his wife Volumnia successfully requested him to retreat.

An agrarian law was proposed for the first time. Spurius Cassius, a former consul, was prosecuted and executed for the crime of aiming at monarchy. The Vestal Opillia was buried alive for sexual impurity. When the neighbouring Veientes were not so much threatening as troublesome, the Fabian family demanded responsibility to conduct the war and dispatched 306 armed men for this purpose; all but one were killed at the Cremera by the enemy. When a battle against the Volsci went badly because of the troops' defiant attitude, the consul Appius Claudius had one out of every ten soldiers beaten to death. The book also contains fighting against the Volsci and the Hernici and the Veientes as well as internal conflicts between the fathers and the plebs.

BOOK 3 (467–446 BCE)

There were uprisings over agrarian legislation. The Capitol was occupied by exiles and slaves; they were killed, and it was taken back. The census was conducted twice. In the earlier five-year period the citizens totalled 108,714, excluding orphans and widows; in the subsequent one, they totalled 117,219.

When a battle against the Aequi went badly, Lucius Quinctius Cincinnatus was made dictator and summoned to conduct the war although he was immersed in agricultural work in the country. He sent his defeated foes beneath the yoke.

The number of tribunes of the plebs was increased, such that there were ten in the thirty-sixth year after the first tribunes of the plebs. In the three hundred and second year after Rome was founded,* Athenian laws were sought out by envoys and brought back, and ten men were appointed instead of consuls, without any other magistrates, to organize and enact these, and just as power was transferred from the kings to the consuls, so it was passed from the consuls to the decemvirate. Ten tables of laws were published, and the men had conducted themselves with restraint in their office; for this reason it had been agreed that the same magistracy should exist again for a second year. After they had added two tables to the ten, when they had committed many lawless deeds, they refused to resign the magistracy and held on to it for a third year, until Appius Claudius' lust brought an end to their despised power. He had fallen in love with the virgin Virginia. He sent a man to claim her as his slave and left her father Virginius with no recourse. Virginius snatched a knife from a nearby shop and killed his daughter since there was no other way to prevent her from coming under the control of a man who would force sex upon her. The plebeians were roused by this instance of such enormous injustice. They occupied the Aventine Mount and forced the decemvirate to abdicate the magistracy. Of the ten, Appius Claudius especially had earned punishment and was thrown into jail; the rest were driven into exile.

The book contains also successful campaigning against the Sabines and the Volsci and a dishonourable ruling rendered by the Roman people. When they were chosen to adjudicate between the Ardeates and the Aricini about territory that was under dispute, they assigned it to themselves.

BOOK 4 (445–404 BCE)

The law concerning intermarriage between patricians and plebeians was carried by the tribunes after fierce argument with the patricians, who opposed it. The tribunes <. . .> of the plebs.

For some years the affairs of the Roman people were administered at home and abroad by this type of magistrate.* Also then for the first time censors were created. The land that had been taken away from the Ardeates by the ruling of the people was restored to them after colonists had been sent there.

When the Roman people were struggling with famine, the Roman equestrian Spurius Maelius liberally bestowed grain on the people at his own expense, and because of this action the plebeians were won over to him. When he sought monarchic power, he was killed by Gaius Servilius Ahala, the master of the horse, under an order from the dictator Quintus Cincinnatus;* the man who denounced him, Lucius Minucius, was rewarded with a gilded cow. Roman ambassadors were killed by the Fidenates; because they had died for the Republic, statues of them were erected on the Rostra.

Cossus Cornelius, a military tribune, killed Tolumnius, the king of the Veientes, and brought back the second set of *spolia opima*. The dictator Mamercus Aemilius limited the office of censor, which previously lasted five years, to the period of a year and six months. For this reason he was blacklisted by the censors. Fidenae was brought under control, and colonists were sent there. When the Fidenates killed them and revolted, they were defeated by the dictator Mamercus Aemilius, and Fidenae was captured.

A conspiracy of slaves was suppressed. The military tribune Postumius was killed by the army because of his cruelty. The soldiers were paid from the treasury for the first time. The book contains also campaigns against the Volsci and the Fidenates and the Falisci.

BOOK 5 (430–390 BCE)

During the siege of Veii quarters were built for the soldiers. Since this was an innovation, it roused the indignation of the tribunes of the plebs, who complained that the plebeians were being given no respite from military service, not even in winter. Then for the first time the *equites* began to serve with their own horses. When the Alban Lake flooded, a seer was captured from the enemy to interpret the event. The dictator Furius Camillus took Veii after it had been under siege for ten years; he transferred the statue of Juno to Rome; and he sent a tenth of the spoils to Delphi for Apollo. As military tribune, the same man besieged the Falisci, and when the children of the enemy were handed over to him, he returned them to their parents. The Falisci immediately surrendered, and Camillus achieved victory over them through justice.

When Gaius Julius, one of the censors, died, Marcus Cornelius was installed in his place. But this was never done again since Rome was captured by the Gauls in that *lustrum*.

Furius Camillus went into exile when a trial date was set for him by the tribune of the plebs Lucius Apuleius. When the Gallic Senones besieged Clusium and envoys were sent by the Senate to arrange a peace between them and the Clusini, the envoys fought against the Senones, standing in the Clusini's battle column. This action antagonized the Senones, and they set out for the city with a hostile force. After putting the Romans to flight at the Allia, the Gauls captured the city, except for the Capitol, where the Roman youth had betaken themselves; the older men seated themselves in the entry-ways of their homes, each with the insignia of the highest office he had held, and were killed.

At the moment when the Gauls had climbed to the top along the back side of the Capitol, they were betrayed by the honking of geese, and they were forced back down, especially through the efforts of Marcus Manlius. Subsequently, when the Romans were forced by near-starvation to come down from there to give 1,000 pounds of gold and with this sum to purchase an end to the siege, Furius Camillus, who had been created dictator in his absence, arrived with an army at the very moment of the parley about the peace-terms. He drove the Gauls out of the city after six months and slaughtered them. When there was talk that the Romans should move to Veii because Rome had been burned and ruined, Camillus was responsible for the rejection of the plan. The omen of a remark heard from a centurion also influenced the people; after he had entered the Forum, he had said to his troops: 'Halt, soldiers; this is the best place for us to stay.'

The temple of Jupiter Capitolinus was built because, before the city was taken, an utterance that the Gauls were coming had been heard.

BOOK 6 (389–367 BCE)

The book contains successful campaigns against the Volsci and the Aequi and the Praenestini. Four tribes were added: the Stellatina, the Tromentina, the Sabatina, the Arniensis. When Marcus Manlius, who had defended the Capitol from the Gauls, freed men bound by debt and released men in debt-bondage, he was condemned on the charge of seeking monarchic power and thrown from the Rock.* To mark his disgrace, the Senate passed a decree that the name 'Marcus' should not be given to anyone in the Manlian family.

Gaius Licinius and Lucius Sextius, tribunes of the plebs, promulgated a law allowing consuls, who were created from amongst the fathers, to come from the plebeians. Although the fathers opposed this law with fierce argument, after the same tribunes of the plebs had been the only magistrates for five years, they got it passed; and Lucius Sextius was made the first consul from the plebs. Another law was passed too, preventing anyone from possessing more than 500 *iugera* of land.

BOOK 7 (366–342 BCE)

Two new magistracies were added: the praetorship and the curule aedileship. The city laboured under a plague, and the death of Furius Camillus gave it a special significance. When a cure and an end were sought through new religious rituals, drama was introduced then for the first time.

When Marcus Pomponius, the tribune of the plebs, had set a trial date for Lucius Manlius because he had conducted the draft harshly and because his son Titus Manlius had been exiled to the country without any charge, the same young man, the one whose rural exile was grounds for accusing his father, entered the bedroom of the tribune, drew a sword, and forced the tribune to swear at the young man's dictation that he would not pursue the charge. Then all valuables were dropped into a very deep chasm in the city of Rome. Curtius, armed and astride his horse, hurled himself into it, and it filled up. Titus Manlius, the young man who had saved his father from tribunician persecution, entered into single combat against a Gaul who was challenging anyone from the ranks of Roman soldiers. Titus killed the Gaul and stripped a golden torque from him. From then on he wore it, and thus he was called Torquatus. Two tribes were added: the Pomptina and the Publilia. Because he possessed more than 500 *iugera* of land, Licinius Stolo was condemned under the law he had had passed. A military tribune, Marcus Valerius, killed a Gaul who had challenged him, while a crow perched on his helmet and tormented his opponent with its claws and beak. From this episode Marcus Valerius took the name of Corvus,* and the following year, when he was twenty-three, he was made consul for his courage. A friendship was formed with the Carthaginians. When the Campanians were hard-pressed in a war with the Samnites, they asked the Senate for help against them. When the Campanians did not obtain it, they gave their city and land to the Roman people. For this reason it was agreed to defend these, which had become the property of the Roman people, against the Samnites. When the army had been led by the consul Aulus Cornelius into grave danger in an unfavourable location, it was saved by the efforts of a military tribune, Publius Decius Mus. He occupied a hill above the ridge where the Samnites had encamped and gave the consul the opportunity to move to more favourable ground; when Decius himself was surrounded by the enemy, he broke through their ranks. When Roman soldiers who had been left in a garrison in Capua had conspired to occupy the city and their plan had been uncovered, they had defected from the Roman people out of fear of punishment. They were brought back to the fatherland by the dictator Marcus Valerius Corvus, who had recalled them from their madness with his counsel. The book contains also successful campaigns against the Hernici and the Gauls and the Tiburtes and the Privernates and the Tarquinienses and the Samnites and the Volsci.

BOOK 8 (341–322 BCE)

When the Latins defected with the Campanians and sent ambassadors to the Senate, they set as their condition that if the Romans wished to have peace, they should choose one of the two consuls from the Latins. When this message had been delivered, their praetor Annius fell from the Capitol in such a way that he died. Then the consul Titus Manlius, because his son fought the Latins against his orders, had him beheaded, even though his son had fought successfully. While the Romans were struggling in a battle, Publius Decius, at the time consul with Manlius, devoted himself* on behalf of the army; he spurred his horse and rode right into the thick of the enemy. He was killed, and with his death saved victory for the Romans. The Latins surrendered. When Titus Manlius returned to the city, none of the young men came out to greet him. The Vestal Minucia was condemned for sexual impurity. After the defeat of the Ausones and the capture of their city, the colony of Cales and also the colony of Fregellae were founded.

A large number of married women were caught using poison; most of them immediately drank their own potions and died. A law against poisoning was then passed for the first time. Citizenship was conferred on the Privernates after a war was fought against them and they were defeated. The people of Naples were defeated by war and a siege, and they surrendered. Quintus Publilius, who had conducted the siege, was the first both to have his *imperium* extended and to be voted a triumph as a proconsul.

The plebeians were liberated from debt because of the lust of their creditor Lucius Papirius, who had wished to rape Gaius Publilius, his own debtor.

When the dictator Lucius Papirius Cursor returned to the city from the army to take the auspices anew, his master of horse Quintus Fabius was tempted by a favourable opportunity for an attack and fought successfully against the Samnites, in contravention of Papirius' instructions. For this reason, when the dictator seemed about to exact punishment from the master of horse, Fabius fled to Rome and, when his case was meeting with little success, he was rescued by appeals from the people. The book also contains successful campaigning against the Samnites.

BOOK 9 (321–304 BCE)

The consuls Titus Veturius and Spurius Postumius led the army into a narrow space at the Caudine Forks. Since there was no hope of escape, they made a treaty with the Samnites and gave 600 Roman *equites* as hostages and led the army out on the condition that they were all sent beneath the yoke. At the urging of the consul, Spurius Postumius, who pushed in the Senate the view that the communal promise would be kept by the surrender of the individuals who were responsible for striking so shameful a treaty, these same men, together with the two tribunes of the plebs and all who had acted as surety for the treaty, were handed over. When these men were handed over to the Samnites, the Samnites refused them. Shortly afterwards, the Samnites were routed by Papirius Cursor and sent beneath the yoke, the 600 Roman *equites* who had been hostages were recovered, and the disgrace of the earlier dishonour was erased.

Two tribes were added: the Oufentina and the Falerna. Colonies were established at Suessa and Pontia. The censor Appius Claudius constructed an aqueduct, paved the road that was named the Appian Way, and selected the sons of freedmen for the Senate. Accordingly, since that order seemed debased by unworthy men, the following year the consuls oversaw the selection of the Senate in the way it had been done before the most recent censors.

The book contains also successful campaigning against the Apuli and the Etruscans and the Umbrians and the Marsi and the Paeligni and the Aequi, and the Samnites, with whom the treaty was renewed. The clerk Gnaeus Flavius, the son of a freedman, was made curule aedile through the agency of the Forum claque.* When this group upset the elections and the Campus Martius and dominated them because of its extensive resources, the censor Quintus Fabius redistributed the claque into four tribes, which he designated 'urban'. This act gave him the name Fabius Maximus.

In this book the author mentions Alexander, who lived at that time, estimates the strength of the Roman people at the time, and deduces that if Alexander had crossed to Italy, he would not have achieved a victory over the Roman people as he did over those people in the East whom he had subjugated.

BOOK 10 (302–292 BCE)

Colonies were established at Sora and Alba and Carseoli. The Marsi's surrender was accepted. The college of augurs was expanded so that there were nine where previously there had been four. For the third time a law about the right of appeal was brought before the people by the consul Murena. Two tribes were added: the Aniensis and the Terentina. War was declared on the Samnites, and the fighting against them was frequently successful. When there was a battle against the Etruscans, the Umbrians, the Samnites, and the Gauls under the leadership of Publius Decius and Quintus Fabius, and the Roman army was in grave danger, Publius Decius followed the example of his father and dedicated himself on behalf of the army; by his death he gave the victory in the battle to the Roman people. Papirius Cursor routed an army of Samnites who had gone into battle bound by an oath to fight with more constancy and valour. The census was conducted; the *lustrum* was ritually closed. The number of citizens totalled 272,320.

BOOK 11 (292–284 BCE)

When the consul Fabius Gurges had fought unsuccessfully against the Samnites and the Senate was deliberating about removing him from the army, his father Fabius Maximus pleaded that this disgrace should not be inflicted on his son; and he swayed the Senate particularly because he promised that he himself would go as a lieutenant to his son, and he carried through on his promise. Aided by his advice and efforts, his son the consul defeated the Samnites and celebrated a triumph; Fabius led the Samnites' commander Gaius Pontius in the triumphal procession and then had him beheaded.

When the city was beset by a plague, envoys were sent to bring the cult statue of Aesculapius from Epidaurus to Rome; they transported a snake, which had boarded their ship and which was generally agreed to contain the god's spirit. Thus when it disembarked at the island in the Tiber, a temple to Aesculapius was established in that very location.

The former consul Lucius Postumius was convicted because he had employed the services of soldiers on his own land when he commanded the army. When the Samnites sought peace, the treaty was renewed for the fourth time. The consul Curius Dentatus slaughtered the Samnites, overcame the Sabines, who had revolted, received their submission, and triumphed twice in the same magistracy. The colonies of Castrum, Sena, and Hadria were founded. *Triumviri capitales** were elected then for the first time. The census was conducted, and the *lustrum* was ritually closed. The number of citizens totalled 272,000. Because of debt, after prolonged and severe civil unrest the plebeians finally seceded to the Janiculum; the dictator Quintus Hortensius brought them back from there; he died while holding that office. The book contains also campaigns against the Vulsinienses as well as against the Lucani, as it had been agreed to bring help to the people of Thurii against them.

BOOK 12 (284–281 BCE)

When envoys from the Romans were killed by the Gallic Senones, war was declared on the Gauls for this reason; the praetor Lucius

Caecilius together with his legions was slaughtered by them. When the Roman fleet was seized by the Tarentini and one of the *duumviri* who was commanding the fleet was killed, ambassadors were sent by the Senate to the Tarentini to complain to them about these wrongs; the ambassadors were maltreated. War was declared on the Tarentini for this reason. The Samnites defected. There was successful fighting against them and the Lucani and the Bruttii and the Etruscans in several battles by a number of leaders. Pyrrhus, king of Epirus, came to Italy to aid the Tarentini. When a Campanian legion was sent to the defence of the Rhegini with Decius Vibullius as their commander, it killed the Rhegini and took control of Rhegium.

BOOK 13 (280–278 BCE)

The consul Valerius Laevinus fought Pyrrhus with little success: the soldiers were particularly terrified by the unfamiliar spectacle of elephants. After this battle, when Pyrrhus was inspecting the corpses of the Romans who had fallen in the fray, he found them all facing the enemy. Ravaging the land, he advanced on Rome. Gaius Fabricius was sent by the Senate to him to discuss ransoming the captives; the king tried, in vain, to influence him to desert his fatherland. The captives were sent back without ransom money. Cineas was sent by Pyrrhus as an envoy to the Senate and asked that the king be admitted to the city for the sake of arranging a peace treaty. When it had been agreed to discuss this matter at a well-attended session of the Senate, Appius Claudius, who had kept himself out of public deliberations for a long time on account of an eye disease, went to the Curia and prevailed in his opinion that Pyrrhus should be denied this request.

The first plebeian censor, Gnaeus Domitius, ritually closed the *lustrum*. The number of citizens totalled 287,222. There was another battle against Pyrrhus, with no definitive outcome. The treaty with the Carthaginians was renewed for the fourth time. When a man who had deserted from Pyrrhus to Gaius Fabricius promised to administer poison to the king, he was sent back to the king with information about what he had done. The book contains also successful campaigns against the Lucani and the Bruttii, the Samnites and the Etruscans.

BOOK 14 (278–272 BCE)

Pyrrhus crossed to Sicily. When, amongst other prodigies, the statue of Jupiter on the Capitol was knocked down by lightning, the head was located by the *haruspices*. When the consul Curius Dentatus held the draft, he was the first to auction off the property of a man who had been summonsed and had not responded. He defeated Pyrrhus for the second time when the latter returned to Italy from Sicily, and he drove Pyrrhus from Italy. As censor, Fabricius removed the former consul Publius Cornelius Rufinus from the Senate because he had ten pounds of worked silver. The *lustrum* was ritually closed by the censors, and the number of citizens totalled 271,224. An alliance was formed with Ptolemy, king of Egypt. The Vestal Sextilia was convicted of sexual impurity and buried alive. The colonies of Posidonia and Cosa were founded. The Carthaginian fleet came to the aid of the Tarentini; by this act the Carthaginians violated the treaty. The book contains also successful campaigns against the Lucani, the Bruttii, and the Samnites, as well as the death of King Pyrrhus.

BOOK 15 (272–265 BCE)

The Tarentini were defeated, and a peace treaty and freedom were conferred on them. The Campanian legion that had occupied Rhegium was besieged; it surrendered and was beheaded. When the envoys from Apollonia who had been sent to the Senate were beaten up by certain youths, the young men were handed over to the people of Apollonia. The Picentes were defeated, and peace was conferred on them. Colonies were established: Ariminum in Picenum and Beneventum in Samnium. Then for the first time the Roman people began to use silver money. The Umbrians and the Sallentines were defeated, and their surrender accepted. The number of quaestors was increased so that there were eight of them.

BOOK 16 (264–261 BCE)

The origins of the Carthaginians and the foundation of their city are recorded. The Senate decided that help should be given to the

Mamertines against the Carthaginians and Hiero, king of Syracuse, although there had been a dispute about this matter between those arguing for it and those arguing against. Then for the first time Roman troops crossed the sea, and they fought several times against Hiero with success. Peace was made with him when he asked for it. The *lustrum* was ritually closed by the censors. The number of citizens totalled 382,234. Decimus Junius Brutus was the first to put on a gladiatorial contest, in honour of his deceased father. The colony of Aesernia was founded. The book contains also successful campaigns against the Carthaginians and the Vulsinii.

BOOK 17 (260–256 BCE)

The consul Gnaeus Cornelius was surrounded by the Carthaginian fleet and, lured out as if for a parley, was captured by deception. The consul Gaius Duillius fought successfully against the Carthaginian fleet, and he was the first of all Roman generals to celebrate a triumph for a naval victory. For this reason he held also a lifetime honour: when he returned from dining out, he was preceded by a pipe-player and a torch-bearer. The consul Lucius Cornelius fought with good fortune in Sardinia and Corsica against the Sardinians, the Corsicans, and Hanno, the Carthaginian general. When the consul Atilius Calatinus had rashly led his army into a place surrounded by Carthaginians, he escaped because of the bravery and efforts of the military tribune Marcus Calpurnius, who made an assault with 300 soldiers and diverted the enemy in his direction. When the fleet the Carthaginian general Hannibal was commanding was defeated, he was crucified by his own soldiers. The consul Atilius Regulus defeated the Carthaginians in a naval battle and crossed to Africa.

BOOK 18 (256–252 BCE)

In Africa, Atilius Regulus killed an unnaturally enormous serpent with significant losses to his forces, and since he had waged several battles successfully against the Carthaginians, a successor for him was not sent by the Senate while he was conducting the war well. Through a letter written to the Senate, he complained about this

very thing; in it, amongst his reasons for seeking a successor was the
fact that his little plot of land was abandoned by the men hired to
work it. Then, since Fortune sought to make Regulus a powerful
example of both good and bad fortune, the Carthaginians called on
Xanthippus, the Lacedaemonian general, and Regulus was defeated
in battle and captured. Thereupon disasters to the fleet spoiled the
campaigns, which had been going well, of all the Roman generals
both on land and at sea. Tiberius Coruncanius was the first plebeian
to be made pontifex maximus. When the censors Manius Valerius
Maximus and Publius Sempronius Sophus reviewed the Senate,
they removed sixteen men from it. They ritually closed the *lustrum*;
during it the number of citizens totalled 297,797. Regulus was sent
by the Carthaginians to the Senate to deliberate about a peace treaty
and, if he could not achieve one, about an exchange of prisoners; and
he was constrained by an oath that he would return to Carthage if
there were no agreement about the exchange of prisoners. And he
advised the Senate to refuse both demands, and he returned with his
integrity intact and died from the punishment exacted by the
Carthaginians.

BOOK 19 (251–241 BCE)

Caecilius Metellus celebrated a brilliant triumph for his successful
achievements against the Carthaginians, with thirteen enemy generals and 120 elephants in the parade. The consul Claudius Pulcher set
out against the auspices—he ordered the sacred chickens to be
drowned since they refused to eat—and fought a luckless naval battle
against the Carthaginians, and he was recalled by the Senate and
ordered to name a dictator; he named Claudius Glicia, a man of
the lowest rank, who was forced to resign his magistracy and then
watched the games in his *toga praetexta*.* Aulus Atilius Calatinus was
the first dictator to lead an army outside Italy. An exchange of prisoners was effected with the Carthaginians. The colonies of Fregenae
and Brundisium, in Sallentine territory, were founded. The *lustrum* was
ritually closed by the censors. The number of citizens totalled 241,212.
When Claudia, the sister of Publius Claudius, the one who had fought
unsuccessfully after disregarding the auspices, was returning from the
games and was being crushed by the crowd, she said, 'Would that my

brother were alive; would that he were leading the fleet again.' For this reason, a fine was imposed on her. Two praetors were created then for the first time. When the consul Aulus Postumius wished to set out to wage war, Caecilius Metellus, the pontifex maximus, kept him in the city and did not allow him to abandon the sacred rites since Postumius was also the priest of Mars. Although campaigns were successfully conducted against the Carthaginians by many leaders, the consul Gaius Lutatius won the crowning victory by defeating the Carthaginian fleet at the Aegetes Islands. The Carthaginians sought and received peace. When the temple of Vesta burned, the pontifex maximus Caecilius Metellus snatched the sacred objects from the flames. Two tribes were added: the Velina and the Quirina.

BOOK 20 (241–219 BCE)

When the Falisci revolted they were subdued in five days and surrendered. The colony of Spoletium was founded. An army was deployed against the Ligures then for the first time. When the Sardinians and the Corsicans revolted, they were subdued. The Vestal Tuccia was convicted of sexual impurity. War was declared on the Illyrians because one of the ambassadors who had been sent to them was killed; and they were subdued and surrendered. The number of praetors was increased so that there were four. The Transalpine Gauls, who had invaded Italy, were defeated. The author says that in the war the Roman people had 80,000 troops of their own and the Latin and Italian allies. Roman armies were led then for the first time across the Po, and the Gallic Insubres were routed in several battles and surrendered. The consul Marcus Claudius Marcellus killed Vertomarus, the leader of the Gallic Insubres, and brought back the *spolia opima*. The Istrians were subdued. When the Illyrians rebelled for a second time, they were reduced to subservience and surrendered. The *lustrum* was ritually closed three times by the censors. On the first occasion the number of citizens totalled 270,212. Although previously the freedmen had been spread amongst all of the tribes, they were distributed into four of them: the Esquilina, the Palatina, the Suburana, and the Collina. The censor Gaius Flaminius built the Flaminian Way and constructed the Circus Flaminius. The colonies of Placentia and Cremona were founded in the land taken from the Gauls.

BOOK 21 (221–217 BCE)

The book describes the beginning of the Second Punic War and the crossing of the Ebro river, in contravention of the treaty, by the Carthaginian general Hannibal. Saguntum, a city of allies of the Roman people, was besieged by him and taken in the eighth month. Ambassadors were sent to the Carthaginians to protest these wrongs. When the Carthaginians refused to make amends, war was declared on them. Hannibal traversed a pass in the Pyrenees, routed the Volcae, who had tried to obstruct him, proceeded through the middle of the Gauls to the Alps, and crossed them with a great deal of effort; and after he had also repulsed in several battles the mountain-dwelling Gauls in his way, he descended into Italy, and routed the Romans in a cavalry battle at the Ticinus river. In this battle, Publius Cornelius Scipio was wounded, and he was rescued by his son, the one who subsequently received the name 'Africanus'. The Roman army was routed a second time at the River Trebia, and Hannibal crossed the Apennines also, at much cost to his soldiers because of the severity of the weather. In Spain, Gnaeus Cornelius Scipio fought successfully against the Carthaginians, and Mago, the enemy's general, was captured.

BOOK 22 (217–216 BCE)

With all-night marches through swamplands Hannibal reached Etruria, though he became blind in one eye; he travelled for four days and three nights through these swamps without any rest. The consul Gaius Flaminius, who was a reckless man, set out against the auspices: the military standards that could not be lifted were dug out, and he was thrown over the head of the horse he had mounted. Encircled by Hannibal's ambush, he was slaughtered with his army at Lake Trasimene. The 6,000 men who had broken through were treacherously put in chains by Hannibal, although Adherbal had guaranteed their safety. Amidst the mourning in Rome at the announcement of the defeat, two mothers died from unexpected joy when their sons returned. Because of the disaster, a sacred spring* was vowed in accordance with the Sibylline books.

Then, when the dictator Quintus Fabius Maximus was sent out against Hannibal and refused to engage him—for fear that he would be entrusting his troops to fight losing battles against an enemy who was fierce from so many victories—and when he was impeding Hannibal's efforts just by setting himself up as an obstacle, the master of the horse, Marcus Minucius, a fierce and reckless man, accused the dictator of being lazy and fearful and brought it about that, by order of the people, his military authority was made equal to that of the dictator. The army was divided between them, and when Minucius had fought in an unfavourable location and his legions were in grave danger, Fabius Maximus intervened with his army and rescued Minucius from danger. Won over by this generous deed, Minucius joined his camp with that of Fabius and hailed him as 'father', and he ordered his troops to do the same.

After laying waste to Campania, Hannibal was surrounded by Fabius between the town of Casilinum and Mount Callicula. He tied brushwood to the horns of cattle and set it on fire, and put to flight the Roman garrison that was occupying Callicula, and thus he crossed the pass. In addition, Hannibal spared the lands of the dictator Quintus Fabius Maximus when he burned the surrounding area, in order to cast suspicion on Fabius as a traitor.

Then, when Aemilius Paullus and Terentius Varro were consuls and generals, there was a battle at Cannae against Hannibal with a disastrous outcome: 45,000 Romans, including the consul Paullus and ninety senators and thirty former consuls, praetors, and aediles were killed in the battle. Afterwards, when out of despair young nobles were planning to abandon Italy, Publius Cornelius Scipio, the military tribune who was subsequently called Africanus, with his sword drawn and over their heads as they deliberated, swore that he would consider a public enemy anyone who did not repeat his oath after him, and he brought it about that all of them were bound by oath that they would not leave Italy.

Because of the insufficiency of troops, 8,000 slaves were armed. Although there was an opportunity to ransom the prisoners of war, they were not ransomed.

The book contains also the trepidation in the city and the mourning and the campaigning in Spain, which had a more favourable outcome. Opimia and Florentia, Vestals, were convicted of sexual impurity. Varro was met along his way, and thanks were given because he had not despaired of the Republic.

BOOK 23 (216–215 BCE)

The Campanians defected to Hannibal. Mago, the messenger sent to
Carthage about the victory at Cannae, spread out in the entry hall of
their curia the golden rings stripped from the bodies of the dead; it
is said that together the rings exceeded a quarter of a bushel. After
this messenger, Hanno, a man from the Punic nobility, urged the
senate of the Carthaginians to seek peace with the Roman people, but
as the Barca faction put up vigorous resistance, he did not prevail.

The praetor Claudius Marcellus fought successfully at Nola, in a
sally made against Hannibal from the town. Casilinum was besieged
by the Carthaginians, and was so worn down by hunger that those
inside ate leather straps and animal skins torn from shields, and mice.
The people survived on nuts floated down the Volturnus river by the
Romans.

The Senate was brought up to full size with 197 men from the
equestrian order. The praetor Lucius Postumius was killed, together
with his army, by the Gauls. In Spain, Gnaeus and Publius Scipio
overcame Hasdrubal and took control of Spain. The remnants of the
army from Cannae were banished to Sicily, which they were not to
leave until the war ended. The consul Sempronius Gracchus defeated
the Campanians. Claudius Marcellus the praetor put to flight and
overcame Hannibal's army in a battle at Nola, and he was the first to
give the Romans, who were worn out by so many calamitous defeats,
greater hope for the war.

An alliance was formed between Philip, king of Macedonia, and
Hannibal. The book contains in addition the successful campaiging
in Spain by Publius and <. . .> Titus Manlius the praetor against the
Carthaginians. The general Hasdrubal and Mago and Hanno were
taken prisoner by them. Hannibal's army so indulged itself in its
winter quarters that it weakened its physical and mental strength.

BOOK 24 (215–213 BCE)

Hieronymus, king of Syracuse, whose father Hiero had been a friend
of the Roman people, defected to the Carthaginians, and because of
his savagery and arrogance he was killed by his own people. The proconsul Tiberius Sempronius Gracchus fought successfully against

the Carthaginians and their general Hanno at Beneventum, especially through the effort of the slaves, whom he directed to be freed. In Sicily, almost all of which had defected to the Carthaginians, the consul Claudius Marcellus besieged Syracuse. War was declared on Philip, king of the Macedonians, who was overwhelmed at Apollonia in a night-time attack and was frightened off and fled to Macedonia with his army almost weaponless. Marcus Valerius the praetor was dispatched to conduct this war.

The book contains also the campaigns in Spain by Publius and Gnaeus Scipio against the Carthaginians. Syphax, king of Numidia, was drawn into friendship with the Scipios. He was defeated by Masinissa, the king of the Massylians, who was fighting for the Carthaginians, and Syphax crossed over to Scipio in Spain with a large troop opposite Gades, where Africa and Spain are separated by a narrow strait. The Celtiberi too were taken into friendship. With the acquisition of these auxiliaries, then for the first time the Roman army had mercenaries as soldiers.

BOOK 25 (213–212 BCE)

Publius Cornelius Scipio, subsequently Africanus, became aedile before the requisite age. Through the help of Tarentine youths who pretended that they were going hunting at night, Hannibal seized Tarentum, except for the citadel, where the Roman garrison had fled. In accordance with the Marcian verses,* in which the defeat at Cannae had been predicted, the Apollinine Games were instituted. The consuls Quintus Fulvius and Appius Claudius fought successfully against Hanno, the general of the Carthaginians. The proconsul Tiberius Sempronius Gracchus was led by his Lucanian guest-friend into an ambush and killed by Mago. Centenius Paenula, who had served as a centurion, had asked the Senate that an army be given to him, and he promised to defeat Hannibal if he were given one; once given 8,000 troops and put in charge of them, he engaged Hannibal in battle and was slaughtered together with the army.

Capua was besieged by the consuls Quintus Fulvius and Appius Claudius. Gnaeus Fulvius the praetor suffered a reverse against Hannibal. In this battle 20,000 men were killed; Fulvius himself fled with 200 cavalry. Claudius Marcellus captured Syracuse in the third

year and acted the part of a great man. In the confusion of the conquered city, Archimedes,* who was intent on the diagrams that he
had scratched in the dirt, was killed.

In Spain, Publius and Gnaeus Scipio met a sad end to their
numerous successes; they were killed together with practically their
entire armies in the eighth year after they had entered Spain. Control
of this province would have been lost had not Lucius Marcius, a
Roman of equestrian rank, gathered up the remnants of the armies
with courage and determination, and had not two enemy camps been
captured because of an exhortation by this same man. Around 27,000
were killed, 1,800 <. . .>, and enormous booty was seized. Marcius
was given the title of general.

BOOK 26 (211–210 BCE)

Hannibal pitched camp at the third milestone from Rome overlooking the Anio. He personally, along with 2,000 cavalry, rode right
up to the Capena Gate itself so that he could investigate the layout of
the city. And although for three days in a row the entire army on
both sides descended in battle order, bad weather postponed combat;
for once Hannibal had returned to camp, the weather instantly
turned fair.

Capua was taken by the consuls Quintus Fulvius and Appius
Claudius. The leading citizens of Campania committed suicide by
taking poison. When the members of the Campania senate were
bound at the stake to be beheaded, the consul Quintus Fulvius
placed in the fold of his toga a letter sent by the Senate, in which he
was directed to exercise mercy, and ordered the law to be carried out,
and he exacted the punishment before he read the letter.

When at the elections there was a question before the people over
whom to entrust the command in Spain to, as no one was willing to
undertake it, Publius Scipio, son of the Publius who had fallen in
Spain, said that he would go, and he was sent by the vote of the
people and with universal agreement. He captured New Carthage
when he was twenty-four years old and seemed of divine origin, both
because every day since he had donned the toga he was in the
Capitoline temple and because a snake was frequently seen in his
mother's bedroom.

The book contains also campaigning in Sicily and the treaty formed with the Aetolians and the war conducted against the Acarnanians and Philip, king of Macedonia.

BOOK 27 (210–207 BCE)

Gnaeus Fulvius the proconsul, together with his army, was slaughtered by Hannibal at Herdonea. The consul Claudius Marcellus fought against Hannibal with greater success at Numistro. Hannibal retreated from there by night. Marcellus pursued him and constantly harassed Hannibal as he was retreating, until he joined battle. In the first battle Hannibal was victorious, but in the second Marcellus was. Fabius Maximus the father as consul recovered Tarentum through betrayal.

The consuls Claudius Marcellus and Titus Quinctius Crispinus left their camp to reconnoitre and were encircled in an ambush by Hannibal. Marcellus was killed; Crispinus escaped. The *lustrum* was ritually closed by the censors. The number of citizens totalled 137,108; from this figure it was apparent how many men the Roman people had lost through adverse fortune in so many battles.

In Spain, Scipio fought with Hasdrubal and Hamilcar at Baecula and defeated them. Amidst the rest of the booty was captured a royal youth of great beauty whom Scipio sent back to Masinissa, his uncle, along with gifts. When Hasdrubal had crossed the Alps with a new army in order to join up with Hannibal, he was slaughtered, along with 56,000 men, and 5,400 men were captured. The consul Marcus Livius was in charge, but the contribution of the consul Claudius Nero was no smaller since he, when he was arrayed against Hannibal, had left his camp in such a way as to deceive his enemy, set out with a handpicked group, and had surrounded Hasdrubal.

The book contains also the successful deeds of Publius Scipio in Spain and of Publius Sulpicius the praetor against Philip and the Achaeans.

BOOK 28 (207–205 BCE)

Recorded here are the successful actions in Spain of Silanus, Scipio's lieutenant, and Lucius Scipio, his brother, against the Carthaginians, and of Publius Sulpicius the proconsul, together with an ally, Attalus, king of Asia, against Philip, king of Macedonia, on behalf of the Aetolians.

When a triumph was voted to the consuls Marcus Livius and Claudius Nero, Livius, who had been campaigning in his own area of command, rode in a chariot while Nero, who had come to his colleague's area of command to aid his victory, followed on horseback, and in this style he had all the more glory and respect; for he had also done more than his colleague in the war.

Through the carelessness of a Vestal, the flame in the temple of Vesta, which she had not protected, was extinguished; she was flogged.

In Spain, Publius Scipio and the Carthaginians fought to the finish in the fourteenth year of the war—the fifth since he had gone there—and, once the enemy had been completely driven from possession of the province, Scipio recovered the Spanish territories. And, having crossed from Tarraco to Africa, to Syphax, king of the Massylians, he made a treaty with him. Hasdrubal son of Gisgo dined there with Scipio on the very same couch. Scipio put on a gladiatorial show in honour of his father and his uncle at New Carthage, using not gladiators but those who entered the competition in honour of the general or because of a challenge. In the show, brother princes fought with swords for their kingdom. When the city of Gisia was besieged, the inhabitants built up a funeral pyre, killed their children and wives over it, and hurled themselves on it. While Scipio himself was suffering from a grave illness, mutiny arose in part of the army; when he had regained his strength, he broke up the mutiny, and he forced the Spanish peoples who were rebelling to surrender. Also a friendship was formed with Masinissa, the king of the Numidians, who promised Scipio assistance if he were to cross to Africa; a friendship was formed with the people of Gades also after Mago's departure from there. (He had orders from Carthage to cross to Italy.) Scipio returned to Rome and was made consul. When he sought Africa as his area of command and Quintus Fabius Maximus spoke against him, he was given Sicily, with permission to cross to Africa if he judged this to be in the best interests of the Republic. Mago, Hamilcar's son, crossed to Italy from the smaller of the Balearic Islands, where he had spent the winter.

BOOK 29 (205–204 BCE)

Gaius Laelius was dispatched from Sicily to Africa by Scipio. He brought back vast plunder and reported to Scipio on Masinissa's instructions that the king was complaining because Scipio had not yet brought his army across to Africa. The war in Spain that Indibilis had provoked had ended with the Roman victorious; Indibilis himself was slain in battle; Mandonius was handed over by his own men when the Romans demanded it. To Mago, who was at Albingaunum in Liguria, a sizeable band of troops was sent from Africa, as well as cash, with which he was to hire auxiliaries, and he was instructed to join forces with Hannibal. Scipio crossed from Syracuse to Bruttium and took control of Locri after the Carthaginian garrison had been driven out and Hannibal had been put to flight. Peace was made with Philip.

The Idaean Mother was transported to Rome from Pessinus, a town in Phrygia, in accordance with a verse discovered in the Sibylline oracles that a foreign enemy could be driven from Italy if the Idaean Mother were transported to Rome. And indeed she was handed over to the Romans through the agency of Attalus, king of Asia. The Idaean Mother was a black stone that the locals called the mother of the gods. Publius Scipio Nasica, son of the Gnaeus who had died in Spain, received the stone; he was the man judged the best by the Senate, although he was a youth who had not yet held the quaestorship; this satisfied the response that the divinity should be received and dedicated by the best man.

The Locri sent representatives to Rome to protest the lawless behaviour of the lieutenant Pleminius, who had stolen the treasury of Proserpina and had raped their children and wives. He was brought to Rome in chains and died in prison. When a false story about the proconsul Publius Scipio, who was in Sicily, was spread in Rome, specifically that he was living a life of luxury, representatives in this matter were sent by the Senate to find out whether or not these things were true. Scipio was cleared of the disgrace and crossed to Africa with the permission of the Senate.

Syphax had married the daughter of Hasdrubal son of Gisgo and renounced the friendship that he had made with Scipio. While Masinissa, the king of the Massylians, was fighting for the Carthaginians in Spain, his father Gala had died, and Masinissa had lost the kingdom. He had often tried to take it back by war from Syphax, the king of the Numidians; he was defeated and deprived of the kingdom altogether. As an exile he joined Scipio with 200 cavalry and straight off, in the first battle with him, he killed Hanno, the son of Hamilcar, together with a sizeable band. At the approach of

Hasdrubal and Syphax, who had come with nearly 100,000 armed men, Scipio was driven back from the siege of Utica and fortified a winter encampment.

The consul Sempronius fought successfully against Hannibal in the territory of Croton. There was a notorious quarrel between the censors Marcus Livius and Claudius Nero. On the one hand, Claudius stripped his colleague of his horse because Livius had been convicted by the people and driven into exile; on the other hand, Livius stripped Claudius of his horse, because he had borne false witness against Livius and because he had not reconciled with Livius in good faith. Further, Livius made all the tribes save one into *aerarii*, because they had convicted him when he was innocent and then subsequently made him consul and censor. The *lustrum* was ritually closed by the censors. The number of citizens totalled 214,000.

BOOK 30 (203–201 BCE)

In Africa, Scipio defeated the Carthaginians and this same Syphax, king of Numidia, and Hasdrubal in several battles, with the assistance of Masinissa; he captured two enemy camps, in which 40,000 men were killed by sword and fire. He took Syphax prisoner through the agency of Gaius Laelius and Masinissa. Masinissa instantly fell in love with the captive Sophonisba, the wife of Syphax and the daughter of Hasdrubal, and he held a wedding and made her his wife; taken to task by Scipio, he sent her poison. She drank it and died. By Scipio's many victories it came about that the Carthaginians were driven to despair and summoned Hannibal to come to the aid of the public safety. So he, leaving Italy in the sixteenth year, crossed to Africa, and attempted through peace negotiations to come to terms with Scipio, and when there was no agreement about the terms of the peace, Hannibal was defeated in battle. Peace was granted to the Carthaginians when they sought it. Hannibal dragged Gisgo away with his own hands when the latter argued against peace; then, once he had apologized for his rashness, Hannibal himself spoke in favour of peace. Masinissa's kingdom was restored to him. Scipio returned to Rome and celebrated the most elaborate and glorious triumph, in which the senator Quintus Terentius Culleo followed him wearing the cap of freedom. It is uncertain whether Scipio Africanus was so named first through the army's goodwill or through popular favour. Certainly this general was the first to be made famous by the name of the people he had defeated. Mago was wounded in a conflict which he fought with the Romans in the territory of the Insubres; after envoys were sent to recall him, as he was returning to Africa, he died from the wound.

BOOK 31 (201–200 BCE)

The following reasons are reported for renewing the war against Philip, king of Macedonia, which had been broken off. At the time of the initiation rites,* two Acarnanian youths, who had not been initiated, came to Athens and entered the sanctuary of Ceres with others of their people. For this reason, on the grounds that they had committed a sin of the gravest sort, they were put to death by the Athenians. The Acarnanians were roused by the deaths of their fellow citizens and sought reinforcements from Philip to avenge them, and they attacked Athens. The Athenians sought help from the Romans a few months after peace had been conferred on the Carthaginians. Representatives from the Athenians, who were being besieged by Philip, sought help from the Senate, and the Senate voted that it should be given, but the people disagreed because the unremitting hardship of so many wars weighed heavily; but the moral authority of the fathers prevailed, and the people, too, ordered help to be brought to the allied city. This war was entrusted to the consul Publius Sulpicius, who led his army into Macedonia and fought successfully against Philip in cavalry battles. When the people of Abydus were besieged by Philip, they killed their families and themselves after the example of the Saguntines.

The praetor Lucius Furius defeated in battle the Gallic Insubres, who were rebelling, and the Carthaginian Hamilcar, who was fomenting war in that part of Italy. Hamilcar was killed in the war along with 35,000 men.

The book contains also the military operations of King Philip and the consul Sulpicius, and accounts of how both of them took cities by storm. The consul Sulpicius campaigned with the help of King Attalus and the Rhodians. Lucius Furius celebrated a triumph over the Gauls.

BOOK 32 (199–197 BCE)

Several prodigies announced from different areas are reported, including the sprouting of a laurel tree on the deck of a warship. Titus Quinctius Flamininus fought successfully against Philip in the passes of Epirus, and when Philip had been put to flight, Flamininus forced him to retreat into his own kingdom. Flamininus himself harried Thessaly, which borders Macedonia, with the Aetolians and the Athamanes as allies. In naval action, the consul's brother Lucius Quinctius Flamininus harried Euboea and the seacoast with the assistance of King Attalus and the Rhodians. A friendship was undertaken with the Achaeans. The number of praetors to be elected was increased to six. A conspiracy formed by slaves to release the Carthaginian hostages was suppressed; 2,500 men were killed. The consul Cornelius Cethegus routed the Gallic Insubres in a battle. A friendship was formed with the Lacedaemonians and their tyrant Nabis. Assaults on cities in Macedonia are also reported.

BOOK 33 (197–195 BCE)

Titus Quinctius Flamininus as proconsul conquered and defeated Philip in a decisive battle at Cynoscephalae in Thessaly. Lucius Quinctius Flamininus, the brother of the proconsul, captured the city of Leucas, which is the capital of Acarnania, and accepted the surrender of the Acarnanians. Once Greece had been liberated, peace was granted to Philip when he sought it. Because of a sudden illness, Attalus was transferred from Thebes to Pergamum; he died. The praetor Gaius Sempronius Tuditanus along with his army was slaughtered by the Celtiberi. The consuls Lucius Furius Purpurio and Claudius Marcellus subdued the Boii and the Gallic Insubres. Marcellus held a triumph. In Africa, Hannibal made a vain attempt to foment war, and for this reason he was betrayed to the Romans in a letter from the leaders of the opposing faction. The reason was fear of the Romans, who had sent envoys to the Carthaginian Senate about Hannibal. He fled to Antiochus, king of Syria, who was preparing war against the Romans.

BOOK 34 (195–193 BCE)

The *lex Oppia*, which Gaius Oppius, a tribune of the plebs, had proposed during the Punic war to curb the expenditures of married
women, was repealed after fierce argument, since Porcius Cato had
argued that the law should not be abolished. He set out for the war
in Spain, which he began at Emporiae, and he established peace in
Nearer Spain. Titus Quinctius Flamininus successfully conducted
and finished off the war against the Lacedaemonians and their tyrant,
Nabis; and having imposed on them a peace of his own design, he liberated Argos, which had been under the dominion of the tyrant.
Successful campaigning in Spain and against the Boii and the Gallic
Insubres is reported also.

Then for the first time the Senate watched theatrical shows in a section separated from the people. The censors Sextus Aelius Paetus and
Gaius Cornelius Cethegus intervened, to the indignation of the people,
to make this possible. Several colonies were founded. Marcus Porcius
Cato celebrated a triumph for Spain. Titus Quinctius Flamininus, who
had defeated Philip, king of the Macedonians, and Nabis, tyrant of
the Lacedaemonians, and had liberated all of Greece, as a consequence celebrated a triumph lasting three days. Representatives of the
Carthaginians announced that Hannibal, who had fled to Antiochus,
was preparing with him to wage war. Hannibal, moreover, had sent
Aristo of Tyre (with nothing in writing) to Carthage to stir up the
Carthaginians to fight.

BOOK 35 (193–192 BCE)

Publius Scipio Africanus was sent as an ambassador to Antiochus
at Ephesus and talked with Hannibal, who had joined Antiochus, to
lay to rest, if it were possible, the fear that Hannibal had conceived
of the Roman people. Among other matters, when Scipio asked
which general Hannibal considered to have been the greatest,
Hannibal answered Alexander, king of the Macedonians, because he
had routed numberless armies with a small band and because he had
traversed the farthest shores, which it was beyond human expectation
to see. When Scipio then asked whom Hannibal would rank second,

Hannibal said that Pyrrhus had first shown how a camp should be laid out, and further that no one had taken up positions or stationed garrisons more skilfully. When Scipio pursued the matter, asking who was third, Hannibal named himself. Scipio laughed and said, 'What, pray tell, would you say if you had defeated me?' Hannibal replied, 'In that case I then would have put myself before Alexander and before Pyrrhus and before all the rest.'*

Among other prodigies, of which there are reported to have been very many, a cow of the consul Gnaeus Domitius is reported to have said: 'Rome, take care for yourself.' Nabis, the tyrant of the Lacedaemonians, was roused to action by the Aetolians, who were inciting both Philip and Antiochus to make war on the Roman people, and he defected from the Roman people, but in the conflict waged against Philopoemen, the praetor of the Achaeans,* he was killed by the Aetolians. The Aetolians also defected from their friendship with the Roman people. When the Aetolians formed an alliance with King Antiochus of Syria, he invaded Greece and occupied many cities, including Chalcis and all of Euboea. The book contains also campaigning against the Ligures and Antiochus' preparation for war.

BOOK 36 (191 BCE)

With the assistance of King Philip, the consul Acilius Glabrio defeated Antiochus at Thermopylae and drove him out of Greece, and he also subdued the Aetolians. The consul Publius Cornelius Scipio Nasica dedicated the temple for the Mother of the Gods,* whom he had brought to the Palatine when he had been adjudged by the Senate to be the best man. The same man defeated the Gallic Boii, accepted their surrender, and celebrated a triumph over them. Also reported are successful naval battles against King Antiochus' commanders.

BOOK 37 (190–189 BCE)

The consul Lucius Cornelius Scipio, with his brother Scipio Africanus as his lieutenant (who had said that he would be his brother's lieutenant if Greece were designated Lucius' area of responsibility, when it seemed that this province was being given to

Gaius Laelius, who had much influence in the Senate), set out to conduct the war against King Antiochus; he was the first of all Roman
generals to cross into Asia. At Myonnesus, with the assistance of
the Rhodians, Regillus fought successfully against the royal fleet of
Antiochus. Africanus' son was captured by King Antiochus and sent
back to his father. Then Antiochus was defeated by Lucius Cornelius
Scipio, with the assistance of Eumenes, king of Pergamum and son of
Attalus. The peace was granted on the condition that Antiochus cede
all the territories on the near side of the Taurus Mountains. Since he
had ended the war against Antiochus, Lucius Cornelius Scipio matched
his brother in his own *cognomen* and was called Asiaticus.

The colony of Bononia was founded. The kingdom of Eumenes,
with whose assistance Antiochus had been defeated, was expanded.
Certain cities were handed over to the Rhodians, too, since they also
had helped. Aemilius Regillus, who had trounced Antiochus' generals in a naval battle, conducted a naval triumph. Manius Acilius
Glabrio triumphed over Antiochus, whom he had driven out of
Greece, and over the Aetolians.

BOOK 38 (189–187 BCE)

The consul Marcus Fulvius besieged the Ambracians in Epirus and
accepted their surrender; he subdued Cephallania; he subdued the
Aetolians and granted them peace. His colleague, the consul Gnaeus
Manlius, conquered the Galatians (the Tolostobogii and the Tectosagi
and the Trocmi), who had crossed into Asia with their leader Brennus,
as they were the only ones within the Taurus Mountains not to be sub-
missive. The origin of these people is also included, along with the way
that they came to occupy those lands which they hold. An example of
courage and sense of shame in a woman is reported also. When this
woman, who had been the wife of the king of the Galatians, was captured, she killed the centurion who forced himself on her.

The *lustrum* was ritually closed by the censors. The number of citizens totalled 258,310. A friendship was formed with Ariarathes,
king of Cappadocia. Although the ten commissioners in accordance
with whose advice Gnaeus Manlius had drawn up the treaty with
Antiochus spoke against him, Manlius argued his own case in the
Senate, and he celebrated a triumph over the Galatians.

A trial date was set for Scipio Africanus, by the tribune of the plebs Quintus Petillius according to some, and by Naevius according to others, on the charge of having defrauded the public treasury of the booty taken from Antiochus. Once the day arrived, he was summoned to the Rostra; he said, 'Roman citizens, it was on this day that I defeated the Carthaginians,' and he ascended the Capitol with the people escorting him. Thereupon, to avoid further harassment from the injustices of tribunes, he went into voluntary exile at Liternum. It is uncertain whether he died there or at Rome, for there was a monument to him in both places. Lucius Scipio Asiaticus, the brother of Africanus, was accused and convicted on the same charge of embezzlement. As he was being led in chains to jail, Tiberius Sempronius Gracchus, tribune of the plebs, who had previously been an enemy of the Scipios, intervened; and because of this act of goodness, he married Africanus' daughter. When the quaestors were sent to take official possession of Asiaticus' property, not only did not a single trace of the king's wealth turn up, but not even so much as the amount that he had been fined was realized. He refused to accept the countless funds collected by his relatives and friends; the items that were necessary for his survival were bought back.

BOOK 39 (187–183 BCE)

The consul Marcus Aemilius subdued the Ligures and built a road from Placentia to Ariminum and linked it to the Flaminian Way. The beginnings of luxurious living, imported to Rome by the army from Asia, are recorded. Those of the Ligures who lived within the Apennines were subdued. When the Bacchanalia, nocturnal Greek rites, the breeding-ground of all forms of wickedness, had reached the point of a conspiracy involving a huge mass of people, there was an investigation, and the rites were eradicated by the punishing of many people.

The censors Lucius Valerius Flaccus and Marcus Porcius Cato (a man who excelled in the arts of both peace and war) removed from the Senate Lucius Quinctius Flamininus, the brother of Titus. The reason was that when Lucius was consul and was holding Gaul as his area of command, at a dinner party, upon a request from the notorious Carthaginian gigolo Philip whom Lucius was in love with, he killed a Gaul with his own hand; alternatively, as some have passed down the story, when asked by a prostitute from Placentia, for whom he was dying of love, he had a condemned man beheaded. The speech of Marcus Cato against him survives.

Scipio died at Liternum and, just as if fortune were linking two funerals of great men to the same time, Hannibal committed suicide by taking poison when he was about to be handed over to the Romans. They had sent Titus Quinctius Flamininus to demand Hannibal from Prusias, king of Bithynia, with whom Hannibal had taken refuge when Antiochus was defeated. Philopoemen too, the leader of the Achaeans, a great man, was poisoned by the Messenians when he was captured by them in war.

The colonies of Potentia and Pisaurum and Mutina and Parma were founded. The book contains also successful campaigns against the Celtiberi and the beginnings and causes of the Macedonian war. Its origin stemmed from the fact that Philip resented the diminution of his kingdom by the Romans and the fact that he was forced to remove his garrisons from Thrace and other places.

BOOK 40 (182–179 BCE)

When Philip had commanded the sons of those upper-class men whom he had in custody to be hunted down for slaughter, Theoxena feared the king's lust on behalf of her own children, who were still boys. Holding before them swords and a cup in which there was poison, she persuaded them that they should escape imminent degradation by death, and when she had so persuaded them she committed suicide herself.

The quarrels between Perseus and Demetrius, the sons of Philip, king of Macedonia, are recorded; and how, through the deceit of his brother, Demetrius was first indicted on trumped-up charges, including an accusation of parricide and of seeking the monarchy, and finally, since he was a friend of the Roman people, he was poisoned and, upon the death of Philip, the kingdom of Macedonia passed to Perseus.

In addition, the book contains campaigns conducted with good fortune against the Ligures and in Spain against the Celtiberi by several leaders. The colony of Aquileia was founded. The books of Numa

Pompilius* were discovered by farmers on the property of Lucius Petillius, a clerk, beneath the Janiculum; these books, both Greek and Latin, were enclosed in a stone coffer. When the praetor, to whom they had been handed over, had read in them many things that subverted religion, he swore to the Senate that it was against the interests of the Republic for them to be read and preserved. By a decree of the Senate they were burned in the Comitium.

Mental anguish consumed Philip because he had been driven by false denunciations of his son Demetrius by Perseus, his other son, and he had permitted Demetrius to be poisoned, and he deliberated about punishment for Perseus and desired to leave his friend Antigonus as successor to the kingdom instead, but he died while thus deliberating. Perseus inherited the kingdom.

BOOK 41 (178–174 BCE)

The fire in the temple of Vesta went out. The proconsul Tiberius Sempronius Gracchus defeated the Celtiberi and accepted their surrender, and he established Gracchuris, a town in Spain, as a monument to his accomplishments. And the Vaccaei and the Lusitani were subdued by the proconsul Postumius Albinus. Both men held triumphs. Antiochus, son of Antiochus, given as a hostage to the Romans by his father, was sent from Rome back to the kingdom of Syria upon the death of his brother Seleucus, who had succeeded their deceased father. Apart from his religion, as a result of which Antiochus built many magnificent temples for many allies—the temple of Olympian Jupiter at Athens and of Capitoline Jupiter at Antioch—Antiochus conducted himself as the most ignoble of kings.

The *lustrum* was ritually closed by the censors. The number of citizens totalled 258,294. The tribune of the plebs Quintus Voconius Saxa proposed a law preventing anyone from instituting a woman as an heir. Marcus Cato spoke in favour of the law. His speech survives. The book contains also campaigns successfully conducted by several generals against the Ligures and the Istrians and the Sardinians and the Celtiberi as well as the beginnings of the Macedonian war that Perseus, son of Philip, was preparing. He had sent a delegation to the Carthaginians, and they received it at night. But he also solicited other Greek cities.

BOOK 42 (173–171 BCE)

The censor Quintus Fulvius Flaccus stripped the temple of Juno Lacinia of its marble roof-tiles in order to cover the temple that he was dedicating. By order of the Senate, the roof-tiles were returned. Eumenes, king of Asia, lodged a complaint in the Senate against Perseus, king of Macedonia, whose injustices against the Roman people are recorded. Because of these, war was declared on him. The consul Publius Licinius Crassus, to whom it had been entrusted, crossed into Macedonia and fought Perseus in light-armed operations and cavalry battles in Thessaly, with <. . .> result. There was a dispute between Masinissa and the Carthaginians over territory. The Senate set a date for them for arbitration. Envoys were sent to allied cities and kings to ask them to remain loyal, but the Rhodians were wavering.

The *lustrum* was ritually closed by the censors. The number of citizens totalled 267,231. The book contains also successful campaigning against the Corsicans and the Ligures.

BOOK 43 (171–169 BCE)

Some praetors were condemned because they had administered their areas of responsibility avariciously and savagely. The proconsul Publius Licinius Crassus sacked many cities in Greece and pillaged them savagely. For this reason the prisoners who had been sold into slavery by him were restored to freedom by a decree of the Senate. Similarly, many misdeeds were lawlessly committed against allies by commanders of Roman fleets. The book contains also Perseus' successful campaigns in Thrace and his defeat of the Dardani and of Illyricum, of which Gentius was the king. The uprising that had been started by Olonicus in Spain subsided when he was killed. Marcus Aemilius Lepidus was chosen as leader of the Senate by the censors.

BOOK 44 (169–168 BCE)

Quintus Marcius Philippus entered Macedonia through pathless mountainous terrain and occupied several cities. The Rhodians sent

envoys to Rome threatening to help Perseus unless the Romans joined
with him in a peace treaty and friendship. This was received with
indignation. When the war was entrusted to Lucius Aemilius Paullus,
consul (for the second time) the following year, in a public meeting
Paullus prayed that any horror looming over the Roman people be
directed against his household instead,* and he went to Macedonia
and defeated Perseus and brought all of Macedonia back under control. Before he fought, Paullus announced to the army not to marvel
when the moon was eclipsed on the following night. When Gentius
too, king of Illyricum, had rebelled, he was defeated by the praetor
Lucius Anicius and surrendered, and he was sent to Rome with his
wife and children and relatives.

Alexandrian envoys from Queen Cleopatra and King Ptolemy
came to lodge a protest against Antiochus, king of Syria, because he
was waging war on them. Although Perseus had solicited help from
Eumenes, king of Pergamum, and Gentius, king of Illyricum, because
he did not deliver the money that he had promised, he was deserted
by them.

BOOK 45 (168–167 BCE)

Perseus was taken captive by Aemilius Paullus on Samothrace. When
Antiochus, king of Syria, was besieging Ptolemy and Cleopatra, the
rulers of Egypt, and ambassadors were sent to him by the Senate to
order him to withdraw from the territory of the king, the orders were
delivered, and Antiochus said that he would consider what he should
do. One of the ambassadors, Popillius, drew a circle around the king
with a staff and ordered him to give an answer before he stepped out
of the circle. With this harshness Popillius brought it about that
Antiochus abandoned the war.

Delegations from peoples and kings offering congratulations were
admitted to the Senate; the delegation of the Rhodians, who had
sided against the Romans in the war, was excluded. On the following
day, when the question was raised whether war should be declared
on the Rhodians, their representatives urged the case of their fatherland in the Senate; they were sent away neither as allies nor as
enemies. Once Macedonia had been reorganized into a province,
Aemilius Paullus, though obstructed by his own soldiers because of

insufficient booty, and opposed by Servius Sulpicius Galba, held a triumph and led Perseus with his three children before the chariot. It was not his lot to have a triumph of complete joy as it was marked by the funerals of his two sons: the death of one of them preceded the father's triumph; that of the second followed it.

The *lustrum* was ritually closed by the censors. The number of citizens totalled 312,805. Prusias, king of Bithynia, came to Rome to offer thanks to the Senate for the victory acquired in Macedonia, and he entrusted his son Nicomedes to the Senate. The king, bursting with flattery, called himself the freedman of the Roman people.

BOOK 46 (167–160 BCE)

King Eumenes came to Rome; he had been neutral in the Macedonian war. In order to prevent his appearing to have been adjudged an enemy, if he were barred from the city, or excused of wrongdoing, if he were allowed in, a general law was passed excluding any king from entering Rome. The consul Claudius Marcellus subdued the Alpine Gauls while the consul Gaius Sulpicius Galus subdued the Ligures.

Envoys from King Prusias lodged a protest against Eumenes because he was plundering their territory, and they said that he had conspired with Antiochus against the Roman people. The Rhodians begged for an alliance, and it was formed.

The *lustrum* was ritually closed by the censors. The number of citizens totalled 337,022. The leader of the Senate was Marcus Aemilius Lepidus. Ptolemy, king of Egypt, was driven out of his kingdom by his younger brother; he was reinstated by Roman envoys dispatched to the brother.

Upon the death of Ariarathes, king of Cappadocia, his son Ariarathes inherited the throne and renewed the friendship with the Roman people through ambassadors. The book contains also campaigns with various results against the Ligures and the Corsicans and the Lusitani, as well as the unrest in Syria when Antiochus died, leaving behind his son Antiochus, who was just a boy. This boy Antiochus and his guardian Lysias were killed by Demetrius, the son of Seleucus, who <escaped> secretly from Rome because he was not set free, and Demetrius himself was installed in the monarchy.

Lucius Aemilius Paullus, who had conquered Perseus, died. His self-restraint was such that although he had transported immense wealth back from Spain and from Macedonia, scarcely enough was realized from the auction of his estate to repay the dowry of his wife. The Pomptine marshes were drained by the consul Cornelius Cethegus, to whom this area of responsibility had been assigned, and they were transformed into farmland.

BOOK 47 (160–153 BCE)

The praetor Gnaeus Tremellius was fined because he had wrongfully argued with the pontifex maximus, Marcus Aemilius Lepidus, and because the rights of religion were more powerful than those of magistrates. A law about bribery was passed. The *lustrum* was ritually closed by the censors. The number of citizens totalled 328,316. Aemilius Lepidus was selected as leader of the Senate. A treaty was struck between the brothers Ptolemy, who were at odds, providing that one would rule Egypt, and the other Cyrene. Ariarathes, king of Cappadocia, was driven from his kingdom through the plan and resources of Demetrius, king of Syria, but he was reinstated by the Senate. Men were sent by the Senate to adjudicate between Masinissa and the Carthaginians over land. The consul Gaius Marcius fought against the Dalmatae, first with little success, and then with good fortune. The reason for engaging in war with them was that they had plundered the Illyrians, who were allies of the Roman people. And the consul Cornelius Nasica subdued the Dalmatae. The consul Quintus Opimius subdued the Transalpine Ligures, who were plundering Antipolis and Nicaea, towns of the Massilians. The book contains also campaigns conducted in Spain by several generals with little success. In the five hundred and ninety-eighth year from the founding of the city* the consuls began entering their magistracy on the first of January. The reason for moving the elections was that the Spanish were rebelling. The commissioners sent to judge between the Carthaginians and Masinissa announced that they had discovered in Carthage a large supply of wood for building ships. Some praetors were accused by provinces on the charge of rapacity and were convicted.

BOOK 48 (154–150 BCE)

The *lustrum* was ritually closed by the censors. The number of citizens totalled 324,000. The seeds of the Third Punic War are recorded. When a vast army of Numidians under the leadership of Arcobarzanes, the grandson of Syphax, was said to be within Carthaginian borders, Marcus Porcius Cato urged that war be declared on the Carthaginians, who had summoned an army and were keeping it within their borders, allegedly for use against Masinissa, in reality for use against the Romans. Publius Cornelius Nasica spoke on the other side, and it was agreed that representatives should be sent to Carthage to observe what was going on. When the Carthaginian senate had been censured, since in contravention of the treaty it had both an army and wood for building ships, the representatives wished to make peace between the Carthaginians and Masinissa, since Masinissa was ceding the land over which the dispute arose. But Gisgo, Hamilcar's son and a rabble-rouser, who was in the magistracy at the time when the senate had said to the Roman representatives that it would submit itself to their judgement, so stirred up the people by urging war against the Romans that the representatives took flight to escape being attacked. When they announced this, they made the Senate, already hostile to the Carthaginians, even more so.

Marcus Porcius Cato spent as little money as possible (for he was very poor) on the funeral for his son who died during his praetorship. Andriscus, who asserted falsely with enormous insistence that he was the son of Perseus, the former king of Macedonia, was sent to Rome. Before Marcus Aemilius Lepidus, who at the time had been selected leader of the Senate by six pairs of censors, died, he instructed his sons from his deathbed that they should have him carried out on a bier spread with plain linens without purple, and that they should not spend more than one million *asses* on the rest of his funeral: that the funerals of great men were generally ennobled not by lavish cost but by the appearance of the funeral masks.* There was an investigation into poisoning. When Publilia and Licinia, highborn women, were accused of having murdered their husbands, former consuls, and the case was tried, the women gave money as surety to the praetor, and they were put to death by the formal decision of their relatives.

Gulussa, Masinissa's son, announced that conscription was going on at Carthage, that a fleet was being constructed, and that without doubt war was being prepared. When Cato urged that war be declared, Publius Cornelius Nasica spoke against doing anything rash, and it was agreed to send a commission of ten men to investigate. When the consuls Lucius Licinius Lucullus and Aulus Postumius Albinus conducted the draft strictly and did not excuse anyone out of favouritism, they were thrown in jail by the tribunes of the plebs, who had not been able to obtain an exemption for their friends.

When the Spanish war had proceeded with little success for some time and so confounded the Roman state that men could not be found who would even accept military tribunates or be willing to go as lieutenants, Publius Cornelius Aemilianus stepped forward and said that he would undertake whatever type of military activity he was directed to. By this example he roused everyone with a passion for military service. The consul Lucullus, when his predecessor Claudius Marcellus had apparently pacified all the peoples of Celtiberia, subdued the Vaccaei and the Cantabri and other peoples in Spain not previously known. In that land, Publius Cornelius Scipio Aemilianus, son of Lucius Paullus, grandson of Africanus, though by adoption, as a military tribune killed a barbarian challenger; and in the capture of the city of Intercatia he entered into still greater danger. For he was the first to cross the wall. Servius Sulpicius Galba fought unsuccessfully against the Lusitani. When the commissioners had returned from Africa with ambassadors from the Carthaginians and with Gulussa, the son of Masinissa, and said that they had discovered both an army and a fleet at Carthage, it was agreed to ask the senators individually for their opinions. With Cato and other leading senators urging that an army should immediately be transported to Africa, since Cornelius Nasica continued to say that there did not yet seem to him to be just cause for war, it was agreed to hold off from war if the Carthaginians burned their fleet and disbanded their army; otherwise the next consuls would formally open discussion of a war against Carthage.

When the theatre put out to bid by the censors was built, it was destroyed by a decree of the Senate on the proposal of Publius Cornelius Nasica on the grounds that it was useless and harmful to public morals; and for some time the people watched entertainments standing. When the Carthaginians attacked Masinissa in contravention of the treaty, they were defeated by him (he was then ninety-two years old and accustomed to chew and taste bread dry and without flavouring) and they earned in addition war from the Romans.

The unrest in Syria and the wars conducted among the kings also are recorded. During this commotion Demetrius, king of Syria, was killed.

BOOK 49 (149 BCE)

The beginning of the Third Punic War, in the six hundred and second year from the founding of the city,* which ended within five years from when it had begun. There was a dispute, with competing opinions from Marcus Porcius Cato and Scipio Nasica, of whom the first was considered the shrewdest man in the city, and the second had actually been judged the best by the Senate;* Cato argued for war and that Carthage be razed and destroyed; Nasica argued against this. It was nevertheless agreed, since the Carthaginians had ships in contravention of the treaty, since they had led their army beyond their borders, since they had taken up arms against Masinissa, ally and friend of the Roman people, and since they had not received in their city his son Gulussa, who was with the Roman representatives, that war should be declared on them.

Before any troops were loaded onto ships, representatives from Utica came to Rome surrendering themselves and all their property. This delegation, like an omen, was pleasing to the fathers, but bitter for the Carthaginians. Following an indication from the books,* games for Father Dis were held at the Tarentum,* which had been performed one hundred years earlier, during the First Punic War, in the five hundred and second year from the founding of the city.* Thirty representatives came to Rome, through whom the Carthaginians surrendered themselves. Cato's opinion prevailed, to stand by the declaration of war and for the consuls to set off for it as soon as possible.

When they crossed to Africa, they received the 300 hostages they had demanded and whatever weapons and machinery for war happened to be in Carthage. When, on the authority of the fathers, the Romans demanded that the Carthaginians build their city in a different location, at least ten miles from the sea, they forced the Carthaginians, by the sheer indignity of the matter, to go to war. The siege and assault of Carthage were begun by the consuls Lucius Marcius and Manius Manilius. During the assault, when the city walls were left unguarded in one place, two tribunes rashly smashed their way in with their cohorts and were suffering heavy casualties from the townspeople when they were extricated by Scipio. Also through his agency, a Roman fort, which the Carthaginians were in the process of capturing by night, was liberated with the help of a few of the cavalry. Further, the same man bore off particular glory for liberating the Roman camp, when the Carthaginians sallied forth from their city with all their troops in concert and assaulted it. Moreover, when one consul (the other had gone to Rome for the elections) led the army from an ineffectual siege of Carthage against Hasdrubal, who had occupied an unfavourable pass with a sizeable troop, at first Scipio urged the consul not to fight in such an unfavourable location. Then, after Scipio had been defeated by the opinions of many men, who resented both his wisdom and his courage, he too entered the pass. When, as he had predicted, the Roman army was routed and forced to flee and two cohorts were surrounded by the enemy, Scipio returned to the pass with a few squadrons of cavalry and freed the two cohorts and led them back in safety. Even Cato, a man more inclined to use his tongue for vituperation, so lavishly described Scipio's courage in the Senate that he said that the rest of those fighting in Africa flitted about like ghosts, while Scipio was actually alive; and the Roman people embraced him with such favour that at the elections the majority of tribes chose him for consul even though this was not permissible because of his age.

When the tribune of the plebs Lucius Scribonius had promulgated a motion that the Lusitani, who had entrusted themselves to the good faith of the Roman people but had been sold as slaves in Gaul by Servius Galba, should be freed, Marcus Cato urged this position most vigorously. The speech survives included in his *Annales*. Quintus Fulvius Nobilior, who had often been attacked by Cato in the Senate, responded to him by supporting Galba: Galba too, when he saw that he was being convicted, put his arms around his two sons, who were wearing the *toga praetexta*, and the son of Sulpicius Galus, whose guardian he was, and spoke so pitiably on his own behalf that the motion was defeated. Three of Galba's speeches survive: two delivered against the tribune of the plebs Libo and his motion about the Lusitani; one against Lucius Cornelius Cethegus, in which Galba confesses that the Lusitani encamped near him were killed because he determined that, following their custom, they had sacrificed a man and a horse and under the pretext of peace had intended to attack his own army.

There was a certain Andriscus, a man of the lowest rank, who represented himself as the son of King Perseus, and who, having changed his name, was called Philip. When he had secretly escaped from the city of Rome, where Demetrius, king of Syria, had sent him because of this falsehood, many men flocked to his false story as if it were true, and he gathered an army and occupied all of Macedonia, either through the cooperation of the inhabitants or by force. He had fashioned his story along these lines: born of a concubine and King Perseus, he had been sent to a certain Cretan to be raised, so some seed, as it were, of the royal family would survive the hazards of the war that Perseus was waging against the Romans. Andriscus, so he claimed, had been raised at Hydramitis until his twelfth year, believing his father to be the man by whom he was being raised, and ignorant of his own family. Then that man fell ill, and when he was almost at the end of his life he finally revealed Andriscus' origin to him and gave his false mother a document sealed with the sign of King Perseus, which she was to give to Andriscus when he reached puberty, and the strongest oaths had been added to keep the matter secret until that time. Upon his reaching adolescence, Andriscus continued, the document was given to him; in it, two hoards of treasure from his father were said to be left to him. Next, when he knew that he had been substituted but was still ignorant of his true ancestry, he said that she had disclosed the identity of Andriscus' family to him and implored him to leave that area before the matter was leaked to King Eumenes, Perseus' rival, in order to avoid being murdered. Andriscus said he had been terrified at this, but at the same time expecting some help from Demetrius in Syria he betook himself there, and that was when he had first dared to reveal openly who he was.

BOOK 50 (150–148 BCE)

When the pseudo-Philip wished to invade and occupy Thessaly, it was defended by Roman lieutenants with Achaean auxiliaries. Prusias, king of Bithynia, and a man with all and the lowest kind of vices, was killed by his son Nicomedes, with the assistance of Attalus, king of Pergamum. Prusias had a second son, who is said to have grown a single continuous piece of bone instead of the upper row of teeth. When three commissioners were sent by the Romans to make peace between Nicomedes and Prusias, since of the three one had a head stitched together with many scars, the second had gout, and the third was considered dimwitted, Marcus Porcius Cato said of this delegation that there was neither a head nor feet nor a brain. At the time Syria had a king equal to the king of the Macedonians in his family line and similar to Prusias in his sloth and sluggishness, and while he lay about in eateries and brothels, Hammonius was ruling there; through his agency all the king's friends and Queen Laodice and Antigonus, Demetrius' son, were killed.

Masinissa, king of Numidia, died at more than ninety years of age, a remarkable man. Amongst his other youthful activities that he carried on till the end, he was even of such vigorous virility that he fathered a son after he turned eighty-six. Masinissa had left his kingdom in common to three of his sons (the oldest was Micipsa, then Gulussa, then Mastanabal, who had been educated in Greek literature also) and ordered them to divide it according to the decision of Publius Scipio Aemilianus; so Scipio divided up the parts for governing. He also persuaded Phameas Hamilco, the commander of the Carthaginian cavalry, a brave man, and one whose particular talents the Carthaginians were drawing on, to defect to the Romans with his band of cavalry. Of the three representatives who had been sent to Masinissa, Marcus Claudius Marcellus was drowned at sea when a storm came up. The Carthaginians killed Hasdrubal, Masinissa's grandson, who was their praetor, and a man suspected of treachery, in their curia; this suspicion began to spread because he was a relative of Gulussa who was helping the Roman auxiliaries.

When Publius Scipio Aemilianus was a candidate for an aedileship, he was elected consul by the people. Since it was not permitted for him to be consul on account of his age, there was a fierce argument between the plebs voting for him and the fathers rejecting him for some time, until he was made exempt from the laws and created consul.

Manius Manilius encircled some cities around Carthage and took them. The false Philip in Macedonia killed the praetor Publius Juventius along with his army, but he was defeated and captured by Quintus Caecilius, and Macedonia was conquered again.

BOOK 51 (147–146 BCE)

Carthage, which has a circumference of twenty-three miles, was blockaded with great difficulty and taken in stages, first by the junior officer Mancinus, then by the consul Scipio, who had been given Africa as his province without the lot. The Carthaginians made a new harbour, since the old one had been blockaded by Scipio, and with a large fleet that was secretly assembled on short notice, fought an unsuccessful naval battle. Also, their general Hasdrubal's camp, which had been set up in a location difficult of access near the town of Nepheris, was destroyed along with its troops by Scipio, who finally captured Carthage in the seven hundredth year after it had been founded. The majority of the spoils were returned to the Sicilians, from whom they had been taken. When in the final destruction of the city Hasdrubal had surrendered himself to Scipio, his wife, who had not succeeded in the previous few days in convincing her husband that they should desert to the victor, hurled herself with her two children from the citadel into the middle of the flames of the burning city. Following the example of his father, Aemilius Paullus, who had conquered Macedonia, Scipio held games and consigned to the beasts deserters and fugitive slaves.

The following causes of the Achaean war are reported: the Roman envoys were maltreated at Corinth by the Achaeans; they had been sent to detach from the Achaean League those cities that had been under Philip's control.

BOOK 52 (148–144 BCE)

Quintus Caecilius Metellus engaged the Achaeans in battle at Thermopylae; they had help from the Boeotians and the Chalcidians. After their defeat, the Achaeans' general, Critolaus, committed suicide by taking poison. Diaeus, the chief instigator of the Achaean uprising, was made general in his place by the Achaeans, and he was defeated at the Isthmus by the consul Lucius Mummius. Once he had accepted the surrender of all of Achaea, Mummius razed Corinth by the decree of the Senate, since the abuse of the Roman envoys had occurred there. Thebes and Chalcis were destroyed too since they had been allies. Lucius Mummius conducted himself with the greatest restraint, nor did anything from the works of art and ornaments that exceptionally wealthy Corinth possessed make its way into his home. Quintus Caecilius Metellus celebrated a triumph over Andriscus, and Publius Cornelius Scipio Aemilianus over Carthage and Hasdrubal.

In Spain, Viriathus, first a shepherd turned hunter, then a hunter turned brigand, soon the general of a proper army too, occupied all of Lusitania, routed the army of the praetor Marcus Vetilius and took him captive, and after him the praetor Gaius Plautius campaigned with no greater success; this particular enemy roused so much fear that it was necessary to pursue him with a consular general and army.

In addition, unrest in Syria and wars conducted amongst the kings are recorded. When King Demetrius was killed, as was said before, Alexander, an obscure man of uncertain family, began ruling in Syria. Demetrius, the son of Demetrius, who had previously been sent to Cnidus by his father because of warfare's unpredictable fortunes, scorned Alexander's sluggishness and sloth; with the help of Ptolemy, king of Egypt, whose daughter Cleopatra he had married, Demetrius killed Alexander in combat. Ptolemy suffered a serious head wound, and during his treatment, when the doctors were trying to trepan his skull, he died. His younger brother Ptolemy, who was ruling Cyprus, succeeded to his position. Because of the cruelty and torture to which Demetrius subjected his own people, he was defeated in battle by a certain Diodotus, one of his subjects who was claiming the kingdom for the son of Alexander, who was only two years old. Demetrius fled to Seleucia.

Lucius Mummius celebrated a triumph over the Achaeans; he carried in the triumph bronze and marble statues and paintings.

BOOK 53 (143 BCE)

The consul Appius Claudius conquered the Salassi, an Alpine people. In Macedonia, a second false Philip, as well as his army, were slaughtered by the quaestor Lucius Tremellius. The proconsul Quintus Caecilius Metellus slaughtered the Celtiberi, and after several cities were captured, the majority of Lusitania was recovered by the proconsul Quintus Fabius. The senator Acilius wrote Roman history in Greek.

BOOK 54 (141–139 BCE)

In Spain, the consul Quintus Pompeius subdued the Termestini. He made a peace treaty with them and with the Numantines that was rejected by the Roman people. The *lustrum* was ritually closed by the censors. The number of citizens totalled 328,442.

When representatives of the Macedonians had come to lodge a protest about the praetor Decimus Junius Silanus, on the charge that he had taken bribes and pillaged the province, and the Senate wished to hold an inquiry into their complaints, Titus Manlius Torquatus, the father of Silanus, requested and was allowed to have the investigation entrusted to him; and the trial was held at home, and he convicted and disowned his son. And he did not even attend his son's funeral, when Silanus had committed suicide by hanging himself, but sitting at home Manlius made himself available to those who came for advice, as was his established practice.

In Spain, the proconsul Quintus Fabius ended his successful accomplishments in disgrace when he concluded a peace with Viriathus on equal terms. Through the scheming of Servilius Caepio, Viriathus was killed by traitors; and he was greatly mourned by his own army and buried with dignity, a great man and general, who fought against the Romans for fourteen years, more often than not with success.

BOOK 55 (142–136 BCE)

When the consuls Publius Cornelius Nasica, to whom the tribune of the plebs Curiatius mockingly affixed the *cognomen* Serapio,* and Decimus Junius Brutus were conducting the draft, something happened in full sight of the recruits which turned out to be a most beneficial precedent. For Gaius Matienius was charged before the tribunes of the plebs on the grounds that he had deserted from the army in Spain, and he was convicted, placed under a *furca*,* and flogged for a long time with switches, and he was sold for one *sestertius*. Since the tribunes of the plebs failed to obtain permission to acquire exemptions for the ten soldiers apiece they each wanted, they ordered the consuls to be thrown into jail.

In Spain the consul Junius Brutus gave lands and a town to those who had fought under Viriathus; it was called Valentia. Marcus Popillius, along with his army, was routed and forced to flee by the Numantines, with whom he had made a treaty that the Senate had decided not to ratify. When the consul Gaius Hostilius Mancinus was sacrificing, the sacred chickens escaped from their coop; then as he was boarding ship in order to go to Spain, a voice said: 'Mancinus, stop.' The outcome showed that these omens foretold disaster. For he was defeated by the Numantines and deprived of his camp; since there was no hope of saving his army, he made an ignominious peace agreement with the Numantines, which the Senate refused to ratify. Forty thousand Romans were defeated by 4,000 Numantines.

Decimus Junius subdued Lusitania by capturing cities all the way to the ocean, and when his soldiers refused to cross the Oblivion river, he snatched the standard from the standard-bearer, carried it across himself, and thus persuaded them that they should cross.

The son of Alexander, king of Syria, only ten years old, was killed by his guardian Diodotus, who was known as Tryphon, through a deception—by doctors who had been bribed and who lied to the people that he was succumbing to the pain of a kidney stone; they killed him when they were cutting it out.

BOOK 56 (136–134 BCE)

In Farther Spain, Decimus Junius Brutus fought successfully against the Gallaeci. The proconsul Marcus Aemilius Lepidus met with a different result campaigning against the Vaccaei and suffered a defeat similar to the Numantine one. Mancinus, in order to extricate the Romans from the religious bond of his treaty with the Numantines, given that he was responsible for the matter, surrendered himself to them; he was rejected. The *lustrum* was ritually closed by the censors. The number of citizens totalled 317,933. In Illyricum, the consul Fulvius Flaccus subdued the Vardaei. In Thrace, the praetor Marcus Cosconius fought successfully against the Scordisci. When the Numantine war dragged on, through the fault of the generals and to the public discredit, the consulship was spontaneously entrusted to Scipio Africanus by the Senate and Roman people. Although he was not permitted to accept it because of the law that prohibited anyone from being consul for a second time, he was exempted from the law, just as in his previous consulship.

When the rebellion of slaves that arose in Sicily could not be put down by praetors, it was entrusted to the consul Gaius Fulvius. Eunus, a slave and a Syrian in nationality, was the source of this war; he assembled a band of agricultural slaves, released work crews, and reached the complement of a full army. Another slave too, Cleon, assembled about 70,000 slaves, and they joined forces and waged war repeatedly against a Roman army.

BOOK 57 (133 BCE)

Scipio Africanus occupied Numantia and restored the army, corrupted by excessive freedom and luxury, to the strictest military discipline. He pruned all accoutrements of pleasure, he expelled 2,000 prostitutes from the camp, he had the troops at work every day, and he compelled them to tote seven stakes with grain for thirty days. He said to a man proceeding laboriously because of his load: 'You can stop carrying a fortification once you have learned to fortify yourself with your sword.' To another who carried his shield with insufficient skill, Scipio said that he was carrying a larger shield than was proper, but that he did not blame him since he used his shield more effectively than his sword. Any soldier Scipio apprehended out of line, he had beaten, with vines if he were a Roman, with switches if he were a foreigner. Scipio sold all the mules so that they would not do the army's carrying for it. He often fought with success against the enemy's raids. The Vaccaei were besieged; they butchered their children and wives and killed themselves. Although it was customary among other generals to conceal gifts from kings, Scipio said in front of the tribunal that he would accept the extremely lavish gifts sent to him by Antiochus, king of Syria, and he ordered the quaestor to register all these in the public accounts: Scipio said that he would use them to give rewards to courageous men. Once he had blockaded Numantia with a siege on all sides and he saw that the besieged men were worn down by hunger, he forbade the killing of men who came out to forage since he said that if there were more of them, they would consume what grain they had all the more quickly.

BOOK 58 (133 BCE)

When the tribune of the plebs Tiberius Sempronius Gracchus proposed agrarian legislation against the will of the Senate and the equestrian class – that no one was to have more than 1,000 *iugera* of

public land—he burst into such a rage that, when his colleague Marcus
Octavius defended the cause of the opposing party, Tiberius proposed
a law and repudiated Octavius' authority, and he made himself and his
brother Gaius Gracchus and his father-in-law Appius Claudius a commission of three to mete out the land. Tiberius promulgated another
agrarian law too, to expand the land available to him, so that the same
commission of three could judge what was private land and what was
public. Then, when there was less land than could be meted out without offending the plebs also (since he had roused in them the desire
to hope for an ample amount), Tiberius revealed that he intended to
promulgate a law that the money that had belonged to King Attalus
be divided among those who ought to receive land under the
Sempronian law. (Attalus, king of Pergamum, son of Eumenes, had
left the Roman people as his heir.) The Senate was deeply disturbed
by so many outrageous acts, and Titus Annius, the former consul,
above all. When he had concluded his harangue against Gracchus in
the Senate, Annius was dragged out by Gracchus to the people and
accused before the plebs, and Annius repeated his speech as a public
address against Gracchus from the Rostra. When Gracchus wished
to be elected tribune of the plebs for a second time, he was killed by
the authority of Publius Cornelius Nasica on the Capitol by the *optimates*,* after first being beaten with pieces from broken benches and,
amongst the others who had been killed in this riot, he was thrown
unburied into the river. The book contains in addition campaigning
against the slaves in Sicily with varying results.

BOOK 59 (133–129 BCE)

The Numantines were driven by hunger into butchering themselves,
stabbing one another in turn. Scipio Africanus captured the city and
razed it, and he celebrated a triumph over it in the fourteenth year
after the razing of Carthage.

In Sicily, the consul Publius Rupilius ended the war against the
slaves. Aristonicus, the son of King Eumenes, took over Asia although,
since it had been left to the Roman people in King Attalus' will, it
ought to have been free. The consul Publius Licinius Crassus, who
was also pontifex maximus—something that had never happened
before—set out from Italy against Aristonicus. Crassus was defeated

in battle and killed. The consul Marcus Perperna defeated Aristonicus and accepted his surrender.

Quintus Pompeius and Quintus Metellus, at that time the first censors both elected from the plebs, ritually closed the *lustrum*. The number of citizens totalled 318,823, excluding male and female orphans, and widows. The censor Quintus Metellus rendered the opinion that everyone should be required to take wives for the sake of producing children. His speech survives; when Augustus Caesar was discussing marriage among the orders,* he read the speech in the Senate just as if it were written for the present time. The tribune of the plebs Gaius Atinius Labeo ordered the censor Quintus Metellus, who had passed him over when selecting the Senate, to be thrown from the Rock; the rest of the tribunes of the plebs came to Metellus' aid to prevent this from happening.

When the tribune of the plebs Carbo had brought a motion that the same man be permitted to be elected tribune as many times as he wanted, Publius Africanus spoke against the motion in the most earnest of speeches, in which he said that, in his opinion, Tiberius Gracchus had been killed justifiably. Gaius Gracchus, on the other hand, spoke in favour of the motion, but Scipio prevailed.

The wars conducted between Antiochus, king of Syria, and Phraates, king of the Parthians, as well as the equally turbulent affairs of Egypt are reported. The Ptolemy with the *cognomen* Euergetes, detested among his own people for his excessive cruelty, secretly escaped to Cyprus when his palace was set on fire by the people; and when the kingdom was given by the people to his sister Cleopatra, whom he had divorced after raping and then marrying her virgin daughter, the enraged Ptolemy killed on Cyprus the son he had had by Cleopatra and sent the head and hands and feet to the boy's mother.

Internal uprisings were aroused by the commission of three men— Fulvius Flaccus and Gaius Gracchus and Gaius Papirius Carbo— elected to mete out land. When Publius Scipio Africanus opposed them, he went home a hale and hearty man, and he was found dead in his bedroom the next day. His wife Sempronia was under suspicion of having given him poison particularly since she was the sister of the Gracchi, with whom Africanus had been at odds. No investigation into his death, however, was held. After he died the unrest from the three-man commission flared higher.

At first, the consul Gaius Sempronius suffered a reverse against the Iapydae; soon, through the bravery of the Decimus Junius Brutus who had subdued Lusitania, a victory compensated for the defeat Sempronius had suffered.

BOOK 60 (126–121 BCE)

The consul Lucius Aurelius subdued the warring Sardinians. Marcus Fulvius Flaccus was the first to reduce to subservience the Transalpine Ligures by combat when he was sent to the relief of the Massilians against the Gallic Salluvii, who were raiding the Massilians' borders. The praetor Lucius Opimius accepted the surrender of the Fregellani, who had defected, and destroyed Fregellae. In Africa, a plague is said to have arisen from a huge number of locusts and subsequently from the piles of those that had been killed. A *lustrum* was performed by the censors. The number of citizens totalled 394,736.

The tribune of the plebs Gaius Gracchus, the brother of Tiberius Gracchus, was more eloquent than his brother; he proposed several dangerous laws, including a grain law such that grain be given to the plebs at a price of six and a third *asses*; second, an agrarian law that his brother also had proposed; third, a law by which he could seduce the equestrian order, at that time similar in outlook to the Senate, such that 600 of the equestrians would be enrolled in the Curia and, since in those days there were only 300 senators, the 600 equestrians would be combined with the 300 senators; that is to say that the equestrian order would have twice as much power in the Senate. And when his tribunate was extended for a second year and his agrarian laws were passed, he saw to it that multiple colonies were founded in Italy and one on the site of the ashes of Carthage, where he himself, named one of three commissioners, founded the colony.

The book contains in addition the campaigns of the consul Quintus Metellus against the Baleares, whom the Greeks call the Gymnesians* since they do not wear clothing in the summer. They are called the Baleares from the trajectory of a missile* or from Balius, Hercules' companion who was left there when Hercules sailed to Geryon. The unrest in Syria also is recorded; during it Cleopatra killed her husband Demetrius and her son Seleucus because she was enraged that Seleucus assumed the crown without her permission after she had killed his father.

BOOK 61 (123–120 BCE)

After the proconsul Gaius Sextius defeated the Salluvii people, he founded the colony of Aquae Sextiae,* so called after the abundance of water in the cold and hot springs and after his own name. The proconsul Gnaeus Domitius fought successfully against the Allobroges at the town of Vindalium. The reason for making war on them was that they had taken in the fugitive Toutomotulus, the king of the Salluvii, and rendered him every assistance, and that they had devastated the territory of the Aedui, allies of the Roman people.

After being a rabble-rousing tribune, Gaius Gracchus also occupied the Aventine together with an armed gang; the consul Lucius Opimius, in accordance with a decree from the Senate, summoned the people to arms, and drove him out; and Gracchus was killed, and along with him the former consul Fulvius Flaccus, his partner in the same madness.

The consul Quintus Fabius Maximus, grandson of Paullus, fought successfully against the Allobroges and Bituitus, king of the Arverni. One hundred and twenty thousand men from Bituitus' army were killed; when he himself went to Rome to make amends with the Senate, he was given over for safekeeping at Alba since it seemed contrary to the peace for him to be sent back to Gaul. There was a decree too that his son Congonnetiacus should be apprehended and sent to Rome. The surrender of the Allobroges was accepted. Lucius Opimius was brought to trial before the people by the tribune of the plebs Quintus Decius because he had thrown Roman citizens into jail without a trial; he was acquitted.

BOOK 62 (119–115 BCE)

The consul Quintus Marcius defeated in battle the Styni, an Alpine people. Micipsa, king of Numidia, died and left his kingdom to his three sons: Adherbal, Hiempsal, and Jugurtha, his brother's son whom he had adopted. Lucius Caecilius Metellus subdued the Dalmatae. Jugurtha made war on his brother Hiempsal. The latter was defeated and killed; Jugurtha drove Adherbal from the kingdom; he was reinstated by the Senate. The censors Lucius Caecilius Metellus and Gnaeus Domitius Ahenobarbus removed thirty-two men from the Senate. The book contains in addition the unrest in Syria and among the kings.

BOOK 63 (114–111 BCE)

In Thrace, the consul Gaius Porcius fought unsuccessfully against the Scordisci. A *lustrum* of the city was conducted by the censors. The number of citizens totalled 394,336. The Vestals Aemilia, Licinia, and Marcia were convicted of sexual impurity, and it is recorded how the sexual impurity occurred and was detected and punished. The Cimbri, a nomadic people, entered Illyricum on a plundering expedition. The consul Papirius Cursor and his army were routed by them. In Thrace, the consul Livius Drusus fought successfully against the Scordisci, a people of Gallic origin.

BOOK 64 (112–109 BCE)

Adherbal was attacked by Jugurtha, besieged in the town of Cirta, and killed by him, contrary to the Senate's ultimatum, and for this reason war was declared on Jugurtha, and when the consul Calpurnius Bestia was ordered to conduct it, he made a peace treaty with Jugurtha without orders from the people and the Senate. Jugurtha was summoned, with a public guarantee of safe conduct, in order to name the sponsors of his plans because it was said that many in the Senate had been bribed. Jugurtha came to Rome, and when he was in danger of being indicted on a capital charge because he permitted the murder of a certain chieftain, Massiva by name, who was trying to take over Jugurtha's kingdom while Jugurtha was out of favour with the Roman people, Jugurtha fled in secret, and upon leaving the city he is reported to have said, 'Rome, a city that is for sale and soon to perish, if it finds a purchaser.' The lieutenant Aulus Postumius fought unsuccessfully against Jugurtha and after the battle added an ignominious peace treaty, which the Senate decided should not be upheld.

BOOK 65 (109–107 BCE)

The consul Quintus Caecilius Metellus routed Jugurtha in two battles and laid waste to all of Numidia. The consul Marcus Junius Silanus fought without success against the Cimbri. The Senate turned down

the representatives of the Cimbri who demanded a home and lands
where they could settle. The proconsul Marcus Minucius fought successfully against the Thracians. The consul Lucius Cassius was killed
with his army on the borders of the Nitiobroges by the Gallic Tigurini,
from a district of the Helvetii, who had defected from their state. The
soldiers who had survived the slaughter made an agreement with the
enemy to give hostages and half of everything and go away in safety.

BOOK 66 (106–105 BCE)

Jugurtha was defeated by Gaius Marius in Numidia. When Jugurtha
received help from Bocchus, king of the Moors, Bocchus' forces too
were killed in the battle, and as Bocchus was reluctant to continue
any longer an inauspiciously undertaken war, Jugurtha was put in
chains by Bocchus and handed over to Marius; the contribution of
Lucius Cornelius Sulla, the quaestor of Gaius Marius, was noteworthy
in this affair.

BOOK 67 (105–102 BCE)

Marcus Aurelius Scaurus, a lieutenant to the consul, was captured by
the Cimbri after his army was routed, and when he was summoned
by them to their council, he warned them not to cross the Alps and
make for Italy because, as he said, the Romans could not be defeated;
at that he was killed by Boiorix, a hot-tempered young man.
At Arausio, the consul Gnaeus Manlius and the proconsul Quintus
Servilius Caepio were defeated in battle by these same enemies, and
their two camps also were lost. According to Valerius Antias, 80,000
soldiers were killed, as well as 40,000 servants and camp-followers.
Caepio was convicted, since the defeat had been suffered because of
his rashness, and he was the first since King Tarquinius to have his
property confiscated, and his *imperium* was terminated.

Jugurtha and his two sons were led before the chariot of Gaius
Marius when the latter triumphed over him; and Jugurtha was killed
in jail. Marius entered the Senate in his triumphal regalia, something
that no one had done before, and his consulship was extended for
several years on account of fear of the Cimbrian war. The second and

third times he was made consul in his absence; he obtained the fourth consulship by pretending that he was not seeking it. Gnaeus Domitius was made pontifex maximus by a vote of the people. The Cimbri, after ravaging everything that lay between the Rhône and the Pyrenees, crossed into Spain by a pass and there, after raiding many places, they were put to flight by the Celtiberi, and they returned to Gaul and joined forces with the Teutoni among the Veliocasses.

BOOK 68 (102–101 BCE)

The praetor Marcus Antonius pursued pirates into Cilicia. The consul Gaius Marius defended his camp, which was besieged with massive force by the Teutoni and the Ambrones. Then he wiped out these same enemies in two battles around Aquae Sextiae; in these battles 200,000 enemies are said to have been killed and 90,000 captured. In his absence, Marius was made consul for the fifth time. He postponed the triumph conferred on him until he had also defeated the Cimbri. The Cimbri drove from the Alps the proconsul Quintus Catulus, who had been blockading the Alpine passes, and put him to flight (he had left a cohort at the River Atesis, which had constructed a fort high up, and it nonetheless extricated itself by its own courage and followed the fleeing proconsul and his army); then the Cimbri crossed into Italy and were defeated in battle by the combined forces of this same Catulus and Gaius Marius. In this battle 140,000 enemy casualties and 60,000 captives are reported. Marius was welcomed by the consensus of the entire city and was content with one triumph instead of the two he had been offered. The leading men of the city, who had scorned him for some time for being a new man* who had been raised to such honours, admitted that the Republic had been saved by him.

When Publicius Malleolus killed his mother, he was the first to be sewn up in a sack and thrown into the sea. It is reported that the shields* rattled and moved before the Cimbrian war was finished. The book contains also wars conducted amongst the kings of Syria.

BOOK 69 (100 BCE)

With the assistance of Gaius Marius and by having his rival Aulus Nunnius killed by soldiers, Lucius Appuleius Saturninus became tribune of the plebs through force. He conducted the tribunate no less violently than he had pursued it, and when he had passed an agrarian law with force, he put Metellus Numidicus on trial because he had not taken the oath for it. When the latter was defended by the good citizens, he went into voluntary exile at Rhodes in order not to be the source of political strife, and there he occupied himself happily in listening to and reading great men. Thereupon Gaius Marius, who was responsible for the discord and who had bought his sixth consulship by distributing cash amongst the tribes, forbade him water and fire.* The same Appuleius Saturninus, the tribune of the plebs, killed Gaius Memmius, a candidate for the consulship, since he feared him as an opponent of his actions. When the Senate was disturbed by these doings, Gaius Marius, a man whose character and thinking always shifted and changed according to circumstance, switched to the senatorial side. Saturninus was overcome by force of arms and was killed in something like a war with the praetor Glaucia and other partners in the same madness. Quintus Caecilius Metellus was brought back from his exile with great approbation from the entire city. In Sicily, the proconsul Manius Aquillius ended the slave war that had arisen.

BOOK 70 (99–91 BCE)

When Manius Aquillius was on trial for extortion, he was unwilling to appeal to the judges himself; Marcus Antonius, who gave the peroration on his behalf, ripped Aquillius' tunic from his chest in order to reveal his scars of honour. He was acquitted beyond all doubt. Cicero is the only source for this matter. The proconsul Titus Didius fought successfully against the Celtiberi. Ptolemy, king of Egypt, who had the *cognomen* Apion, died and left the Roman people as his heir, and the Senate ordered the cities of his kingdom to be free. Ariobarzanes was reinstated in the kingdom of Cappadocia by Lucius Cornelius Sulla. Parthian envoys sent by King Arsaces came to Sulla to seek friendship with the Roman people. Since Publius Rutilius, a man of the purest innocence, had, as the lieutenant of the proconsul Gaius Mucius, protected Asia from the injustices of the tax-collectors, he was hated by the equestrian order, who controlled the courts. Condemned for extortion, he was sent into exile. The praetor Gaius Sentius fought unsuccessfully against the Thracians.

The Senate, refusing to tolerate the abuse of power by the equestrian order, began to struggle with all its might to have the courts transferred to it. Marcus Livius Drusus supported the Senate's cause; he was a tribune of the plebs who roused the plebs with pernicious hopes of handouts in order to acquire power for himself. The book contains also the unrest in Syria and among the kings.

BOOK 71 (91 BCE)

The tribune of the plebs Marcus Livius Drusus had taken up the Senate's cause and, in order to defend it with greater resources, roused the allies and the Italian peoples with the expectation of Roman citizenship. With their assistance he forced the passage of agrarian and grain laws, and he also put through a judicial law so that control of the courts would be shared equally by the senatorial and the equestrian orders. Then, when the citizenship promised to the allies could not be granted, the enraged Italian peoples began to stir up revolt. Their gatherings and plotting and the speeches of their leaders in their councils are recorded. Livius Drusus became odious even to the Senate on account of these developments, as if he were the author of the Social War* and he was killed at home by some unknown person.

BOOK 72 (91 BCE)

The Italian peoples revolted: the Picentes, the Vestini, the Marsi, the Paeligni, the Marrucini, the Samnites, the Lucani. The beginning of the war was triggered by the Picentes when the proconsul Quintus Servilius was killed in the town of Asculum together with all the Roman citizens who were in that town. The Roman people adopted military garb. Servius Galba, who was apprehended by the Lucani, was rescued from captivity through the efforts of an individual woman at whose house he was staying. The colonies of Aesernia and Alba were besieged by the Italians. Then auxiliaries from the Latins and foreign peoples were sent, and military operations and the successful storming of cities on both sides are reported.

BOOK 73

The consul Lucius Julius Caesar suffered a reverse against the Samnites. The colony of Nola came under the Samnites' control, along with the praetor Lucius Postumius, who was killed by them. Several peoples defected to the enemy. When the consul Publius Rutilius had fought with little success against the Marsi and had fallen in the battle, Gaius Marius, his lieutenant, fought a pitched battle against the enemy with a more favourable result. Servius Sulpicius routed the Paeligni in battle. When Quintus Caepio, a lieutenant of Rutilus, was surrounded and had succeeded in breaking through the enemy, and for this success his military authority was made equal to that of Gaius Marius, he became rash, he was surrounded by an ambush, his army was routed, and he was killed. The consul Lucius Julius Caesar fought successfully against the Samnites. Because of this victory military garb stopped being worn at Rome. And, since the fortunes of war waver, the colony of Aesernia with Marcus Marcellus came under the Samnites' control, but also Gaius Marius routed the Marsi in a battle in which the praetor of the Marrucini, Hierius Asinius, was killed. In Transalpine Gaul, Gaius Caelius defeated the Salluvii, who were in revolt.

BOOK 74 (89 BCE)

Gnaeus Pompeius routed the Picentes in battle <. . .> he besieged. On account of this victory, at Rome wearing of the *toga praetexta* and other insignia of magistracies was resumed. Gaius Marius fought the Marsi with no decisive result. Then for the first time freedmen began to do military service. The lieutenant Aulus Plotius defeated the Umbrians in battle while the praetor Lucius Porcius did the same to the Etruscans, when the two peoples had defected. Nicomedes was reinstated in the kingdom of Bithynia while Ariobarzanes was reinstated in that of Cappadocia. The consul Gnaeus Pompeius defeated the Marsi in a pitched battle. When the citizenry was afflicted with debt, the praetor Aulus Sempronius Asellio, because he was administering the law to the debtors' advantage, was assassinated in the Forum by money-lenders. The book contains also the incursions of the Thracians into Macedonia and their plundering expeditions.

BOOK 75 (89 BCE)

When the lieutenant Aulus Postumius Albinus was commanding the fleet, he incurred disgrace because of an accusation of treason and was killed by his own army. The lieutenant Lucius Cornelius Sulla defeated the Samnites in battle and captured two of their camps. Gnaeus Pompeius accepted the surrender of the Vestini. Although the consul Lucius Porcius campaigned successfully and routed the Marsi several times, he was killed while he was storming their camp. This event gave the victory in this battle to the enemy. Cosconius and Lucanus defeated the Samnites in a pitched battle; they killed Marius Egnatius, the enemies' leader who had the highest standing; and they received the surrender of several towns. Lucius Sulla reduced the Hirpini to subservience, routed the Samnites in many battles, and recovered some peoples; and, with a record of achievement almost unparalleled by anyone previously who had not yet held a consulship, he set out for Rome to seek the consulship.

BOOK 76 (89 BCE)

The lieutenant Aulus Gabinius campaigned successfully against the Lucani, captured many towns, and then died while besieging the enemy's camp. The lieutenant Sulpicius slaughtered the Marrucini and recovered the entire region. The proconsul Gnaeus Pompeius accepted the surrender of the Vestini and the Paeligni. The Marsi too, broken by the lieutenants Lucius Cinna and Caecilius Pius in several battles, began to seek peace. Asculum was taken by Gnaeus Pompeius. And after the Italians too had been slaughtered by the lieutenant Mamercus Aemilius, Silo Poppaedius, the leader of the Marsi and the instigator of this business, fell in battle.

Mithridates, king of Pontus, drove Ariobarzanes from his kingdom of Cappadocia and Nicomedes from his kingdom of Bithynia. The book contains also the incursions of the Thracians into Macedonia and their plundering expeditions.

BOOK 77 (88 BCE)

The tribune of the plebs Publius Sulpicius, at the instigation of Gaius Marius, promulgated pernicious laws: that exiles be recalled and the new citizens and freedmen be assigned among the tribes, and that Gaius Marius be made the commander against King Mithridates of Pontus; and when the consuls Quintus Pompeius and Lucius Sulla opposed him, Sulpicius used force on them. Then Quintus Pompeius, the son of Quintus Pompeius the consul and the son-in-law of Sulla, was killed, and the consul Lucius Sulla entered Rome with an army and battled the party of Sulpicius and Marius in the city itself and drove that party out. Twelve men from it were judged by the Senate to be enemies of the state, including Gaius Marius, father and son. When Publius Sulpicius was hiding in a certain villa, he was dragged forth on the information of his slave and killed. In order for the slave to have the reward promised to the informer, he was manumitted and, for the crime of betraying his master, he was thrown from the Rock. Gaius Marius the son crossed to Africa. When Gaius Marius the father was hiding in the swamps of Minturnae, he was dragged forth by the townspeople, and when the slave sent to kill him, a native Gaul, was so terrified by the greatness of the man that he went away, Marius was put on a boat at public expense and transported to Africa.

Lucius Sulla imposed order on the affairs of the Republic, and then founded colonies. The consul Quintus Pompeius set out to take over the army from the proconsul Gnaeus Pompeius and was killed through the latter's design. Mithridates, king of Pontus, took over Bithynia and Cappadocia, defeated the lieutenant Aquillius, and entered Phrygia, a province of the Roman people, with a vast army.

BOOK 78 (88 BCE)

Mithridates occupied Asia, and he threw the proconsul Quintus Oppius in chains and similarly his lieutenant Aquillius, and, at Mithridates' command, everyone in Asia with Roman citizenship was butchered in a single day. He attacked the city of Rhodes, which alone had remained loyal to the Roman people, and, after he was defeated in multiple naval battles, he retreated. Archelaus, the king's commander, entered Greece with an army and occupied Athens. The book contains in addition the terror of the cities and islands, with some of them drawing their communities towards Mithridates and others towards the Roman people.

BOOK 79 (87 BCE)

When Lucius Cornelius Cinna was promulgating pernicious laws by force of arms, together with six tribunes of the plebs he was driven from the city by his colleague Gnaeus Octavius; and after his *imperium* was terminated, he bribed Appius Claudius' army, took control of it, and waged war upon the city, summoning Gaius Marius and other exiles from Africa. In this war, two brothers, one from the Pompeian army, the other from Cinna's, unwittingly fought against each other, and when the victor stripped the spoils from the deceased, he recognized his brother and let out a huge wail; he built a funeral pyre for him, and he stabbed himself over the pyre and was incinerated by the same fire. And although the war could have been suppressed in the early stages, Cinna and Marius were fortified both by the deception of Gnaeus Pompeius who, in aiding both sides, strengthened Cinna and did not bring help to the affairs of the best men until they were entirely ruined, and by the torpor of the consul. They surrounded the city with four armies, of which two were given to Quintus Sertorius and Carbo. Marius captured the colony of Ostia and plundered it savagely.

BOOK 80 (87 BCE)

Citizenship was conferred on the peoples of Italy by the Senate. The Samnites, who alone took up their weapons again, joined themselves to Cinna and Marius. The lieutenant Plautius was killed, along with his army, by these men. Cinna and Marius, with Carbo and Sertorius, attacked the Janiculum, but they were put to flight by the consul Octavius and retreated. Marius captured the colonies of Antium and Aricia and Lanuvium. When the *optimates* had no hope of resisting because of the sluggishness and treachery both of their leaders and of their troops, who had been bribed and either were unwilling to fight or were deserting to the opposing side, Cinna and Marius were allowed to enter the city; they devastated it with murder and looting just as if it had been captured; and the consul Gnaeus Octavius was murdered, and all the *nobiles** of the opposing party were butchered, including Marcus Antonius, an extremely eloquent orator, and Gaius and Lucius Caesar, whose heads were placed on the Rostra. Crassus the son was killed by Fimbria's equestrians, while Crassus the father ran himself through with his sword to avoid suffering anything unworthy of his courage. And without recourse to any elections Cinna and Marius declared themselves consuls for the following year. On the very day they entered the magistracy, Marius ordered the senator Sextus Licinius to be thrown from the Rock. Having committed many crimes, Marius died on the thirteenth of January, a man of whom, if his faults were weighed alongside his virtues, it would by no means be easier to say whether he was more helpful in war or more disastrous in peace. To such a degree did he, as a soldier, save the Republic, and as a civilian, ruin it first with every kind of deception and ultimately with armed force, just as if he were an enemy.

BOOK 81 (87 BCE)

After a siege and great exertions to capture <. . .>, Lucius Sulla restored liberty and its possessions to Athens, which Archelaus, Mithridates' commander, had occupied. Magnesia, the only city in Asia that had remained loyal, was defended against Mithridates with the greatest courage. The book contains also the expeditions of the Thracians into Macedonia.

BOOK 82 (86 BCE)

Sulla defeated in battle the king's forces, which had occupied Macedonia and moved into Thessaly, and 100,000 of the enemy were killed, and also their camp was captured. When the war was subsequently revived, Sulla routed and eradicated the king's army a second time. Archelaus turned himself and the royal fleet over to Sulla. The consul Lucius Valerius Flaccus, Cinna's colleague, was sent to succeed Sulla, but because of his greed he was hated by his own army, and he was killed by his own lieutenant, Gaius Fimbria, a man of the utmost audacity; and his military authority was transferred to Fimbria. Also recorded are the cities in Asia that were captured by Mithridates, and the savage pillaging of the province, and the Thracians' incursions into Macedonia.

BOOK 83 (85–84 BCE)

In Asia, Flavius Fimbria routed several of Mithridates' commanders in battle, took the city of Pergamum, besieged the king, and was not far from capturing him. Fimbria captured and razed the city of Ilium,* which was waiting to put itself under Sulla's power, and he recovered the majority of Asia. Sulla cut the Thracians to pieces in several battles. When Lucius Cinna and Gnaeus Papirius Carbo, who had made themselves consuls for two consecutive years, were preparing for war against Sulla, Lucius Valerius Flaccus, the leader of the Senate, who gave a speech in the Senate, and those who were eager for a resolution of conflict brought it about that envoys were sent to Sulla about peace. Cinna was killed by his own army, which he was forcing against its will to board ships and set out against Sulla. Carbo administered the consulship on his own. When Sulla had crossed into Asia, he made peace with Mithridates on condition that Mithridates would retreat from the provinces of Asia, Bithynia, and Cappadocia. Fimbria was deserted by his army, which had crossed over to Sulla; Fimbria stabbed himself and, presenting his neck, got his slave to kill him.

BOOK 84 (84 BCE)

Sulla replied to the envoys that had been sent by the Senate that he would put himself in the Senate's hands if the citizens who had been expelled by Cinna and had fled to him were reinstated. Although this condition seemed reasonable to the Senate, agreement on it was prevented by Carbo and his party, to whom war seemed more advantageous. When this same Carbo wished to demand hostages from all the towns and colonies of Italy, so that he might guarantee their loyalty to him against Sulla, he was prohibited by a consensus of the Senate. The franchise was granted to new citizens by a decree of the Senate. When Quintus Metellus Pius, who had followed the faction of the *optimates*, was in Africa preparing for war, he was repulsed by the praetor Gaius Fabius, and a senatorial decree was made through the faction of Carbo and the Marian party that all armies everywhere should be disbanded. Freedmen were distributed into the thirty-five tribes. The book contains in addition the preparation for the war that was being set in motion against Sulla.

BOOK 85 (83 BCE)

Sulla crossed to Italy with his army. He sent envoys to discuss peace, and when their sanctity was violated by the consul Gaius Norbanus, Sulla defeated that same Norbanus in battle. And when Sulla was about to besiege the camp of Lucius Scipio, the other consul, with whom he had striven in every way to make peace and had not been able to, the consul's entire army, incited by soldiers dispatched by Sulla, transferred its allegiance to Sulla. Although Scipio could have been killed, he was allowed to go away. Gnaeus Pompeius,* the son of that Gnaeus Pompeius who had taken Asculum, raised an army of volunteers and went to Sulla with three legions. The entire nobility betook itself to Sulla so that by going to the camp they left the city deserted. Also recorded are the campaigns of the leaders of both sides throughout the whole of Italy.

BOOK 86 (83–82 BCE)

While Gaius Marius, the son of Gaius Marius, was made consul through force before he was twenty, in Africa Gaius Fabius was burned alive in his headquarters because of his savagery and greed. Sulla's lieutenant, Lucius Philippus, defeated and killed the praetor Quintus Antonius and occupied Sardinia. Sulla made a treaty with the Italian people so that they would not fear that he was about to take away their citizenship and the right to vote that had recently been conferred. Out of confidence that his victory was already certain, Sulla also told litigants who were approaching him to take their summonses to Rome, although the city was still in the hands of the opposing side. When the praetor Lucius Damasippus had assembled the Senate in accordance with the wishes of the consul Gaius Marius, he butchered everyone of noble birth who was in the city. Of this group the pontifex maximus Quintus Mucius Scaevola took flight and was killed in the forecourt of the temple of Vesta. The book contains in addition the renewal of the war by Lucius Murena against Mithridates in Asia.

BOOK 87 (82 BCE)

Sulla routed Gaius Marius' army and destroyed it at Sacriportus and besieged him in the town of Praeneste, and he recovered the city of Rome from the hands of his rivals. He thwarted Marius when Marius tried to escape from his confinement. The book contains in addition the campaigns conducted by Sulla's lieutenants, with the same result everywhere for his party.

BOOK 88 (82 BCE)

Sulla wiped out Carbo's army at Clusium, Faventia, and Fidentia and drove him from Italy. He achieved a decisive victory over the Samnites, who alone of the Italian peoples had not laid down their arms, near to the city of Rome outside the Colline Gate, and having regained control of the Republic, he defiled his most beautiful victory with a cruelty paralleled by no previous human being. In the Civic Villa* he butchered 8,000 men who had surrendered, he posted a proscription list,* he filled the city and all Italy with corpses, including those of all the Praenestini, whom he ordered to be slaughtered unarmed, and he murdered Marius, a man of the senatorial order, after breaking his arms and legs, cutting off his ears, and gouging out his eyes. Gaius Marius was besieged at Praeneste by Lucretius Ofella, a man of the Sullan party; when he tried to escape through a tunnel blocked by the army, he chose to die. That is to say, in the tunnel itself, when he realized that he was not able to escape, he and Telesinus, his companion in flight, drew their swords and rushed at one another; when he had killed Telesinus, the wounded Marius succeeded in having a slave kill him.

BOOK 89 (82–80 BCE)

From Cossyra, where they had put in, Marcus Brutus was sent by Gnaeus Papirius Carbo in a fishing boat to Lilybaeum to investigate whether Pompeius was already there, and when he was surrounded by ships that Pompeius had sent, Brutus braced himself against a thwart of the boat, turned the point of his sword towards himself, and threw himself on it with the weight of his body. Gnaeus Pompeius was sent to Sicily by the Senate with military authority and captured and killed Gnaeus Carbo, who died weeping like a woman. Sulla was made dictator and appeared in public with twenty-four fasces, something that no one had ever done before. He strengthened the condition of the Republic with new laws: he diminished the power of the tribunes of the plebs, and he completely took away their power of proposing legislation, he expanded the college of priests and augurs so that there were fifteen, he filled out the Senate with men from the equestrian order, he deprived the sons of people who had been proscribed of the right of seeking office, and he auctioned off their property, from which he initially seized the most. Three hundred and fifty million sesterces were realized. He ordered Quintus Lucretius Ofella, who had dared to seek the consulship against Sulla's will, to be killed in the Forum, and when the Roman people showed their indignation, he summoned a public meeting and said that he had ordered it.

In Africa, Gnaeus Pompeius defeated Gnaeus Domitius, who had been proscribed, and Hierta, king of Numidia; they were preparing a war, and Pompeius killed them. And when he was twenty-four years old and still a Roman equestrian, he celebrated a triumph for Africa, a thing which had never happened to anyone before. When Gaius Norbanus, a former consul who had been proscribed, was apprehended in the city of Rhodes, he committed suicide. When Mutilus, one of the proscribed, had covered his head and secretly approached the back door of the house of his wife, Bastia, he was not allowed in since she said that he had been proscribed. Consequently he ran himself through and spattered his wife's door with his blood. Sulla recovered Nola in Samnium. He conducted forty-seven legions into captured territory and shared it among them. He besieged Volaterrae, a town that was still in arms, and accepted its surrender. Also Mytilene in Asia, which was the only city to keep its weapons after Mithridates had been defeated, was captured and sacked.

BOOK 90 (79–77 BCE)

Sulla died, and the Senate allowed him the honour of being buried in the Campus Martius. When Marcus Lepidus attempted to rescind

Sulla's acts, he stirred up war. He was driven from Italy by his colleague Quintus Catulus and, having tried in vain to prepare war in Sicily, he died. Marcus Brutus, who had control of Cisalpine Gaul, was killed by Gnaeus Pompeius. Quintus Sertorius, who had been proscribed, started a major war in Farther Spain. The proconsul Lucius Manlius and his lieutenant Marcus Domitius were beaten in battle by the quaestor Hirtuleius. The book contains in addition the campaigns of Publius Servilius against the Cilicians.

BOOK 91 (77–75 BCE)

Gnaeus Pompeius was still a Roman equestrian when he was sent with proconsular authority against Sertorius. Sertorius captured several cities and brought many more under his control. The proconsul Appius Claudius defeated the Thracians in many battles. The proconsul Quintus Metellus cut to pieces Lucius Hirtuleius, Sertorius' quaestor, along with his army.

BOOK 92 (75 BCE)

Gnaeus Pompeius fought against Sertorius with no decisive result, one wing on each side being victorious. Quintus Metellus routed in battle Sertorius and Perperna with their two armies. Pompeius, eager to have a share of this victory, fought with little success. Then Sertorius was besieged at Clunia and, with repeated sorties, he inflicted no less damage than the besiegers. The book contains in addition campaigns undertaken by the proconsul Curio in Thrace against the Dardani and the many cruel acts of Quintus Sertorius committed against his own men; he trumped up accusations of betrayal against many of his friends and those who had been proscribed with him, and killed them.

BOOK 93 (75–74 BCE)

In Cilicia, the proconsul Publius Servilius subdued the Isauri and captured several cities of the pirates. Nicomedes, king of Bithynia, made the Roman people his heirs, and his kingdom was reorganized with the status of a province. Mithridates made a treaty with Sertorius and started a war against the Roman people. Then occurred the organization of the royal infantry and naval resources; and after the consul Marcus Aurelius Cotta occupied Bithynia, he was defeated by the king in a battle near Chalcedon; and campaigns by Pompeius and Metellus against Sertorius <. . .> he was their equal in all the arts of war and military science, <. . .> he drove them off from the siege of the town of Calagurris and forced them to make their way to different places: Metellus to Farther Spain, and Pompeius to Gaul.

BOOK 94 (74–73 BCE)

The consul Lucius Licinius Lucullus fought successfully against Mithridates in cavalry battles, and he conducted some successful operations, and he restrained his soldiers, who were demanding to fight, from mutiny. Deiotarus, the tetrarch of Galatia, cut to pieces Mithridates' commanders who were stirring up war in Phrygia. The book contains in addition the successful campaigns of Gnaeus Pompeius against Sertorius in Spain.

BOOK 95 (73 BCE)

In Thrace, the proconsul Gaius Curio subdued the Dardani. At Capua, seventy-four gladiators escaped from Lentulus' training camp; they collected a mass of slaves and men from work crews, and with Crixus and Spartacus as their leaders, they started a war and defeated the lieutenant Claudius Pulcher and the praetor Publius Varenus in battle. The proconsul Lucius Lucullus obliterated Mithridates' army through starvation and combat near the city of Cyzicus, and he drove the king from Bithynia, who was broken by various mishaps of war and shipwrecks, and forced him to flee to Pontus.

BOOK 96 (72 BCE)

The praetor Quintus Arrius defeated Crixus, a leader of the fugitives, along with 20,000 men. The consul Gnaeus Lentulus met with a reverse against Spartacus. The consul Lucius Gellius and the praetor Quintus Arrius were defeated in a pitched battle by him also. Sertorius was killed by Marcus Perperna and Marcus Antonius and other conspirators at a banquet in the eighth year of his leadership; he was a magnificent general, and one who had been the victor more often than not against two generals, Pompeius and Metellus, but in the end he was both ruthless and extravagant. Authority over his partisans passed to Marcus,* whom Gnaeus Pompeius defeated, captured, and killed, and Pompeius recovered Spain around the tenth year after the conflict had begun. The proconsul Gaius Cassius and the praetor Gnaeus Manlius met with a reverse against Spartacus, and the war was entrusted to the praetor Marcus Crassus.

BOOK 97 (72–71 BCE)

At first the praetor Marcus Crassus fought successfully against some fugitive slaves, a group composed of Gauls and Germans, killing 35,000 of his opponents and their leaders Castus and Gannicus. Then, when he fought to the finish against Spartacus he killed him and 60,000 men. The praetor Marcus Antonius undertook the war against the Cretans with little success; he ended it with his death. The proconsul Marcus Lucullus subdued the Thracians. In Pontus, Lucius Lucullus fought successfully against Mithridates, killing more than 60,000 of the enemy. Marcus Crassus and Gnaeus Pompeius were made consuls (Pompeius, a Roman equestrian, by a decree of the Senate, before he had held the quaestorship), and they restored tribunician power. The courts also were transferred to the Roman equestrians by the praetor Marcus Aurelius Cotta. Mithridates was forced by the desperation of his situation to flee to Tigranes, king of Armenia.

BOOK 98 (70–68 BCE)

A friendship with Machares, the son of Mithridates and king of Bosporus, was entered into by Lucius Lucullus. The censors Gnaeus Lentulus and Lucius Gellius conducted the census strictly and removed sixty-four men from the Senate. They ritually closed the *lustrum*, and the number of citizens totalled 900,000. In Sicily, the praetor Lucius Metellus conducted a successful campaign against the pirates. The temple of Jupiter on the Capitol, which had been destroyed by fire and rebuilt, was dedicated by Quintus Catulus. In Armenia, Lucius Lucullus routed Mithridates and Tigranes and vast forces of both kings in several battles. The proconsul Quintus Metellus was entrusted with the war against the Cretans and besieged the city of Cydonia. Gaius Triarius, a lieutenant to Lucullus, fought with little success against Mithridates. A mutiny among the soldiers prevented Lucullus from pursuing Mithridates and Tigranes and adding the last touches to the victory, for the soldiers refused to follow, specifically the two Valerian legions, who said they had completed their period of service and abandoned Lucullus.

BOOK 99 (67 BCE)

The proconsul Quintus Metellus captured Gnossus and Lyctus and Cydonia and many other cities. The tribune of the plebs Lucius Roscius proposed legislation that the first fourteen rows in the theatre should be assigned to the Roman equestrians. By a law proposed before the people, Gnaeus Pompeius was ordered to pursue the pirates who had blocked the grain-trade; within forty days he had driven them from the entire sea, and having ended the war against them in Cilicia, he accepted the surrender of the pirates and assigned them land and towns. The book contains in addition the campaigns of Quintus Metellus against the Cretans and the letters exchanged by Metellus and Gnaeus Pompeius. Quintus Metellus complains that the glory for his accomplishments had been stripped from him by Pompeius, who had sent a lieutenant of his own to Crete to accept the surrender of the cities. Pompeius gives an explanation of how he was obliged to do this.

BOOK 100 (66 BCE)

To the great indignation of the nobles, the tribune of the plebs Gaius Manilius proposed legislation that the Mithridatic war be entrusted to Pompeius. <. . .> His public speech was good. Quintus Metellus dispensed laws to the defeated Cretans for their island, which had been free until that time. Gnaeus Pompeius set out to conduct war against Mithridates and renewed the friendship with Phraates, the king of the Parthians. Pompeius defeated Mithridates in a cavalry battle. The book contains in addition the war that transpired between Phraates, king of the Parthians, and Tigranes, the king of the Armenians, and then the war between Tigranes the son and Tigranes the father.

BOOK 101 (65 BCE)

Gnaeus Pompeius defeated Mithridates in a battle at night and forced him to flee to the Bosporus. Pompeius accepted the surrender of Tigranes and took from him Syria, Phoenicia, and Cilicia while restoring the kingdom of Armenia to him. A conspiracy to kill the consuls was formed by men who had been convicted of bribery during a bid for the consulship; it was suppressed. As Gnaeus Pompeius was pursuing Mithridates, he made his way to remote and unknown peoples. He defeated in battle the Hiberi and the Albani, who were not allowing him to pass. The book contains in addition the flight of Mithridates through the lands of the Colchians and the Heniochi, as well as his actions in the Bosporus.

BOOK 102 (65–63 BCE)

Gnaeus Pompeius reorganized Pontus into a province. Pharnaces, the son of Mithridates, attacked his father. When Mithridates was blockaded in the palace by him and took poison but did not manage to die, he was killed by a Gallic soldier named Bitocus, whose assistance he had sought. Gnaeus Pompeius subdued the Jews and took their temple at Jerusalem, which had been inviolate up to that time. After Lucius Catilina had twice endured defeats in his bid for the consulship, he conspired with the praetor Lentulus and Cethegus and many others to assassinate the consuls and the Senate, burn the city, and take over the Republic, and also he had an army marshalled in Etruria. This conspiracy was rooted out by the diligence of Marcus Tullius Cicero. Catilina was driven from the city, and punishment was inflicted on the rest of the conspirators.

BOOK 103 (62–58 BCE)

Catilina and his army were cut down by the proconsul Gaius Antonius. Publius Clodius was put on trial on the charge that, dressed in women's clothes, he had infiltrated a sacred space where it was sacrilege for a man to enter, and committed adultery with <. . .>, the wife of Metellus the priest; he was acquitted. Near Solo, the praetor Gaius Pontinus subdued the Allobroges, who had revolted. Publius Clodius transferred to the plebeians. Gaius Caesar subdued the Lusitani. When he was a candidate for the consulship and trying to gain control of the Republic, a conspiracy formed among three leading citizens: Gnaeus Pompeius, Marcus Crassus, Gaius Caesar. Agrarian legislation was passed by the consul Caesar amongst fierce argument and against the opposition of the Senate and the other consul, Marcus Bibulus. The proconsul Gaius Antonius campaigned in Thrace with little success. Marcus Cicero was sent into exile by a law proposed by the tribune of the plebs Publius Clodius because Cicero had had citizens executed without a trial. Caesar left for the province of Gaul and subdued the Helvetii, a nomadic people that, seeking a home, wished to pass through Narbonensis, Caesar's province. The book contains in addition the geography of Gaul. Pompeius celebrated a triumph over <. . .> the children of Mithridates, and Tigranes, and the son of Tigranes; and he was hailed as 'the Great' by the entire assembly.

BOOK 104 (58–56 BCE)

The first part of the book contains the geography of Germany and the local customs. At the request of the Aedui and the Sequani, whose land was being occupied, Gaius Caesar led his army against the Germans who had crossed into Gaul with their leader Ariovistus; he checked with an exhortation the trepidation that arose among the soldiers out of fear of unfamiliar enemies, and he defeated the Germans in battle and drove them from Gaul. Marcus Cicero was brought back from exile by, among others, Pompeius and Titus Annius Milo, the tribune of the plebs, to the great joy of the Senate and the whole of Italy. Responsibility for the grain-supply was entrusted to Gnaeus Pompeius for a term of five years. Caesar defeated in battle the Ambiani, the Suessiones, the Viruomandui, the Atrebates, and the peoples of Belgium, of whom there were a great many, and accepted their surrender, and then he fought at great risk against the Nervii, one of these peoples, and he wiped them out, although they fought until 500 out of 60,000 remained, and three alone from a senate of 600 escaped. A law was passed about the reorganization of Cyprus into a province and the confiscation of the king's treasury; the administration of the matter was entrusted to Marcus Cato. Ptolemy, king of Egypt, left his kingdom and came to Rome because of injuries he had suffered from his own people. Gaius Caesar defeated the Veneti, a people next to the ocean, in a naval battle. The book contains in addition campaigns conducted by his lieutenants with the same good fortune.

BOOK 105 (56–55 BCE)

When the elections were obstructed by the intervention of the tribune of the plebs Gaius Cato, the Senate changed its attire.* In the competition for the praetorship Marcus Cato suffered a reverse, with Vatinius being preferred. When that same man was impeding a law, by which provinces would be given to the consuls for five-year terms (the Spanish provinces to Pompeius, Syria and the Parthian war to Crassus), he was taken away in chains by Gaius Trebonius, a tribune of the plebs and the sponsor of the law. The proconsul Aulus Gabinius escorted Ptolemy back to the kingdom of Egypt and expelled Archelaus, whom the Egyptians had adopted as their king. After defeating the Germans in Gaul, Caesar crossed the Rhine and subdued the nearest part of Germany, and then he crossed the ocean to Britain, at first with little success because of bad weather, but with greater success the second time, and having killed a great number of the enemy, he established control over part of the island.

BOOK 106 (54–53 BCE)

Julia, Caesar's daughter and Pompeius' wife, died, and the people allowed her the honour of being buried in the Campus Martius. Some of the Gallic people defected with their leader Ambiorix, king of the Eburones. Caesar's lieutenants Cotta and Titurius were trapped in an ambush by them and were killed with the army they commanded.

And when the camps of the other legions too—including the one Quintus Cicero was in charge of amongst the Treveri—were besieged and defended with great effort, the enemy was routed in battle by Caesar himself. Marcus Crassus crossed the Euphrates river intending to attack the Parthians, and he was defeated in a battle in which his son was killed too. When Crassus had withdrawn the remnants of his forces to a hill, he was called to a parley by the enemy (whose leader was Surenas) as if they intended to discuss peace. Crassus was apprehended and, in his struggle not to be subjected to anything degrading while alive, he was killed.

BOOK 107 (53–52 BCE)

When the Treveri had been defeated in Gaul, Caesar crossed into Germany for the second time and, not encountering any enemy there, he returned to Gaul and conquered the Eburones and other communities that had conspired against him, and he pursued Ambiorix as he fled. Publius Clodius, who had been killed at Bovillae on the Appian Way by Titus Annius Milo, a candidate for the consulship, was cremated in the Curia by the plebs. When there was discord among the candidates for the consulship, Hypsaeus and Scipio and Milo, who were fighting with armed force, in order to suppress this, to Gnaeus Pompeius* <...> he was made consul by the Senate for the third time, in his absence and on his own, something that never <happened>* to anyone else. An inquiry into the death of Publius Clodius was decreed, and Milo was convicted in the trial and sent into exile. A law was passed to accept Caesar's candidacy for the consulship in his absence, although Marcus Cato was opposed and spoke against it. The book contains in addition the campaigns of Gaius Caesar against the Gauls, almost all of whom revolted under the leadership of the Arvernian Vercingetorix, as well as the laborious sieges of cities, including Avaricum of the Bituriges and Gergovia of the Arverni.

BOOK 108 (52–51 BCE)

Gaius Caesar defeated the Gauls at Alesia and accepted the surrender of all the Gallic peoples that had been in arms. Gaius Cassius, quaestor to Marcus Crassus, cut to pieces the Parthians, who had crossed into Syria. In his candidacy for the consulship, Marcus Cato met with rejection as Servius Sulpicius and Marcus Marcellus were elected. Gaius Caesar subdued the Bellovaci together with other peoples of Gaul. The book contains in addition the disputes between the consuls about dispatching a successor to Gaius Caesar, as Marcellus argued in the Senate that Caesar should come back to seek the consulship although, in accordance with the law that had been passed, he should have kept his provinces until the period of his consulship; and it contains also the campaigns of Marcus Bibulus in Syria.

BOOK 109 (51–49 BCE)

WHICH IS THE FIRST OF THE CIVIL WAR

The causes of the civil war and its beginnings are recorded, as are the quarrels about dispatching a successor to Gaius Caesar, since he said that he would not disband his armies unless Pompeius disbanded his. And the book contains the actions of the tribune of the plebs Gaius Curio, first against Caesar, then on his behalf. When there was a decree of the Senate to dispatch a successor to Caesar, and the tribunes of the plebs Marcus Antonius and Quintus Cassius were driven from the city because they obstructed this decree of the Senate with their veto <. . .> and the Senate entrusted the consuls and Gnaeus Pompeius to see to it that the Republic suffer no harm. Gaius Caesar entered Italy with an army to pursue political enemies militarily, he took Corfinium with Lucius Domitius and Publius Lentulus, and he let them go, and he drove Gnaeus Pompeius and the rest of his party from Italy.

BOOK 110 (49 BCE)

WHICH IS THE SECOND OF THE CIVIL WAR

Gaius Caesar besieged Massilia, which had barred its gates, and left his lieutenants Gaius Trebonius and Decimus Brutus to besiege that city. He set out for Spain, accepted the surrender of Gnaeus Pompeius' lieutenants Lucius Afranius and Marcus Petreius with seven legions near Ilerda, and let them all go unharmed. Also Varro,

Pompeius' lieutenant, and his army were brought under Caesar's control. Caesar conferred citizenship on the people of Gades. The Massilians were defeated in two fights at sea and after a long siege relinquished themselves to Caesar's control. Caesar's lieutenant Gaius Antonius campaigned unsuccessfully against the Pompeians in Illyricum and was taken captive. In this conflict the Opitergini, from across the Po, were allies of Caesar. When their ship was surrounded by an enemy fleet, rather than coming under the control of their enemies, they died fighting each other. After Caesar's lieutenant in Africa, Gaius Curio, had fought successfully against Varus, a leader of the Pompeian party, he was killed with his army by Juba, king of Mauretania. Gaius Caesar crossed to Greece.

BOOK 111 (48 BCE)

WHICH IS THE THIRD OF THE CIVIL WAR

When the praetor Marcus Caelius Rufus stirred up revolt in the city by inciting the plebs with the expectation that debt would be cancelled, his magistracy was terminated, and he was driven from the city and joined forces with the exiled Milo, who had assembled an army of fugitive slaves. Both men were killed while they were preparing for war. Cleopatra, the queen of Egypt, was driven from the kingdom by her brother Ptolemy. Because of the praetor Quintus Cassius' greed and cruelty, the people of Corduba in Spain deserted Caesar's party with two of the legions of Varro. Gnaeus Pompeius was besieged at Dyrrachium by Caesar and, after he had stormed Caesar's outposts with heavy losses to the latter's side, Pompeius was freed from the siege, and the war shifted to Thessaly where he was killed in a pitched battle at Pharsalia. Cicero remained in the camp, a man born for anything rather than armed conflict. Caesar pardoned all those of the opposite side who had surrendered to the victor.

BOOK 112 (48–47 BCE)

WHICH IS THE FOURTH OF THE CIVIL WAR

The panic of the defeated party and their flight to different parts of the world are recorded. Gnaeus Pompeius had made his way to Egypt.

By the agency of his tutor Theodotus (who had more authority over him) and of Pothinus, King Ptolemy, who was Pompeius' ward, gave the order and, before Pompeius stepped ashore, he was killed aboard his ship by Achillas, to whom the deed had been delegated. Pompeius' wife Cornelia and his son Sextus Pompeius fled to Cyprus. Caesar followed three days later; when Theodotus had shown him Pompeius' head and ring, Caesar was furious and wept. He entered Alexandria, which was in turmoil, without danger. Caesar was made dictator and restored Cleopatra to her kingdom in Egypt. And at great personal risk he utterly defeated Ptolemy, who undertook the war on the advice of the same men under whose influence he had killed Pompeius. As Ptolemy was fleeing, his ship sank in the Nile. The book contains in addition the laborious journey of Marcus Cato with his legions in Africa through the desert, and the war conducted with little success by Gnaeus Domitius against Pharnaces.

BOOK 113 (47 BCE)

WHICH IS THE FIFTH OF THE CIVIL WAR

The Pompeian party built itself up in Africa, and the command of it passed to Publius Scipio as Cato, to whom a shared command was offered, ceded it. And when there were deliberations about destroying the city of Utica on account of that city's support for Caesar, Juba urged that it be destroyed; but Marcus Cato had prevented this from happening, and its protection and care were entrusted to him. In Spain, Gnaeus Pompeius, the son of Pompeius Magnus,* gathered forces of which neither Afranius nor Petreius wished to take charge, and renewed the war against Caesar. Pharnaces, son of Mithridates and king of Pontus, was defeated without any delay to the war. Revolt was stirred up at Rome by the tribune of the plebs Publius Dolabella proposing a law about the cancellation of debt; and when the plebs were in an uproar for this reason, soldiers were brought into the city by Marcus Antonius,* the master of horse; and 800 plebeians were killed. Caesar granted a discharge to those veterans who mutinied and demanded it. And when he had crossed to Africa, he fought at great risk against the forces of King Juba.

BOOK 114 (47–46 BCE)

WHICH IS THE SIXTH OF THE CIVIL WAR

In Syria, a Roman equestrian of the Pompeian party, Caecilius Bassus, provoked a war after Sextus Caesar had been abandoned by his legion (which had transferred its allegiance to Bassus) and been killed. Caesar defeated the praetor Scipio and Juba near Thapsus, and captured their camp. When Cato heard the news, he stabbed himself at Utica; and although his son intervened and he was nursed, during the ministrations Cato reopened the wound and died, in the forty-eighth year of his life. Petreius killed Juba and himself. Publius Scipio was surrounded on his ship and added a comment to his noble death. For when his enemies asked for the leader, he said, 'The leader is doing well.' Faustus and Afranius were killed. Pardon was granted to Cato's son. In Gaul, Caesar's lieutenant Brutus defeated in battle the Bellovaci, who were rebelling.

BOOK 115 (46–45 BCE)

WHICH IS THE SEVENTH OF THE CIVIL WAR

Caesar celebrated four triumphs, over Gaul, Egypt, Pontus, and Africa, and he gave a banquet and spectacles of every kind. Upon the Senate's request, he allowed the former consul Marcus Marcellus to return. Marcellus was not able to enjoy this favour from Caesar since he was killed at Athens by Gnaeus Magius, his own client.* Caesar conducted a census, in which the number of citizens totalled 150,000. And he set out for Spain against Gnaeus Pompeius. After many operations on both sides and the capture of some cities, Caesar achieved the final victory, at great risk, near the city of Munda. Gnaeus Pompeius was killed; Sextus fled.

BOOK 116 (45–44 BCE)

WHICH IS THE EIGHTH OF THE CIVIL WAR

Caesar celebrated his fifth triumph, over Spain. And a vast number of extremely high honours was voted to him by the Senate, including

that he be called 'Father of the Country' and that he be sacrosanct*
and dictator in perpetuity. Then a reason for hostility towards him
was created by these factors: that when he was sitting in front of the
temple of Venus Genetrix, he did not rise for the Senate when it
came to confer these honours; and that when his colleague Marcus
Antonius was running with the Luperci* and placed a crown on
Caesar's head, Caesar put it down on his chair; and that the authority of the tribunes of the plebs Epidius Marullus and Caesetius
Flavus was terminated when they <fostered> hostility towards him
for supposedly aiming at monarchy. For these reasons a plot was
formed against him; the leaders of it were Marcus Brutus and Gaius
Cassius and, from the Caesarian party, Decimus Brutus and Gaius
Trebonius, and Caesar was killed in the Curia of Pompeius with
twenty-three wounds. The Capitol was occupied by his killers. Then
amnesty for his murder was decreed by the Senate, and, after
hostages were taken from the children of Antonius and Lepidus, the
conspirators came down from the Capitol. According to Caesar's
will, his nephew Gaius Octavius was instituted his heir to one-half of
his estate, and he was adopted as Caesar's son. When Caesar's body
was carried into the Campus Martius, it was cremated by the plebs
in front of the Rostra. The honour of 'dictatorship in perpetuity' was
banned. Chamates, a man of the lowest kind, who claimed that he
was the son of Gaius Marius, was put to death when he stirred up a
rebellion among the credulous plebs.

BOOK 117 (44 BCE)

Gaius Octavius came to Rome from Epirus (for Caesar had sent him
there in advance, intending to wage war in Macedonia), he was
greeted by favourable omens, and he assumed the name of Caesar.*
In the confused state of affairs and the upheaval, Marcus Lepidus
appropriated the position of pontifex maximus. Further, Marcus
Antonius, as consul, was wielding power without restraint and had
forced through legislation about the redistribution of provinces, and
in addition, when Caesar asked Antonius to help him against his
uncle's assassins, Antonius subjected him to grave insults.
Consequently Caesar, in order to acquire resources for himself and
the Republic against Antonius, stirred up the veterans, who had been

settled in colonies. The fourth and the Martian legions too transferred their allegiance from Antonius to Caesar; and then because of
the savagery of Marcus Antonius, who throughout his camp was
butchering those of his own men whom he did not trust, many men
deserted to Caesar. Decimus Brutus occupied Mutina with his army
in order to block Antonius when he was making for Cisalpine Gaul.
The book contains in addition the dispersal of men of both parties to
take up their provinces, as well as preparations for war.

BOOK 118 (43 BCE)

In Greece, Marcus Brutus, under the pretext of the good of the
Republic and a war undertaken against Marcus Antonius, took control of the army that Publius Vatinius was commanding, as well as his
province. Gaius Caesar, who as a private citizen had taken up arms
for the Republic, was granted propraetorian power by the Senate,
together with consular regalia, and it was added that he be a senator.
Marcus Antonius besieged Decimus Brutus at Mutina, and the
envoys sent to him by the Senate about peace made little headway in
arranging one. The Roman people adopted military garb. In Epirus,
Marcus Brutus brought the praetor Gaius Antonius and his army
under his control.

BOOK 119 (43 BCE)

In Asia, Gaius Trebonius was killed through the deception of
Publius Dolabella. For this deed Dolabella was decreed an enemy of
the state by the Senate. When the consul Pansa had suffered a reverse
against Antonius, the consul Aulus Hirtius, arriving on the scene
with his army, routed Marcus Antonius' forces and balanced the fortunes of the two sides. Then Antonius was defeated by Hirtius and
Caesar and fled to Gaul, and he attached to himself Marcus Lepidus and
the legions that were under him there, and Antonius was decreed an
enemy of the state by the Senate, along with all those who were within
his lines. Aulus Hirtius, who had actually fallen in the enemy camp after
the victory, and Gaius Pansa, who died from a wound that he had
suffered in the battle he lost, were buried in the Campus Martius.

The Senate was insufficiently grateful to Gaius Caesar, who alone of the three leaders had survived. For although Decimus Brutus, who had been liberated from the siege of Mutina by Caesar, was voted the honour of a triumph, the Senate did not make sufficiently grateful reference to Caesar and his men. For these reasons Gaius Caesar, once good relations with Antonius had been restored through the agency of Marcus Lepidus, came to Rome with his army; those men who were hostile to him were kept out by its arrival, and so he was made consul when he was nineteen years old.

BOOK 120 (43 BCE)

As consul, Gaius Caesar proposed legislation to try the men by whose doings his father Caesar was killed; Marcus Brutus, Gaius Cassius, and Decimus Brutus were prosecuted under this law and convicted in their absence. Asinius Pollio and Munatius Plancus joined Marcus Antonius and increased his forces with their armies. And Decimus Brutus, to whom the Senate had entrusted the pursuit of Antonius, was abandoned by his legions and fled; he then fell into Antonius' power and was killed, at Antonius' command, by Capenus of the Sequani. Gaius Caesar made peace with Antonius and Lepidus on the terms that they would become a triumvirate for a five-year period to organize the Republic and that he and Lepidus and Antonius would each proscribe their personal enemies. In this proscription there were many Roman equestrians, and the names of 130 senators, including Lucius Paullus, the brother of Marcus Lepidus, and Lucius Caesar, the uncle of Antonius, and Marcus Cicero. When Cicero was killed by Popillius, a legionary, he was sixty-three years old, and moreover his head was placed with his right hand on the Rostra. The book contains in addition the campaigns of Marcus Brutus in Greece.

BOOK 121 (43 BCE)
WHICH IS SAID TO HAVE BEEN PUBLISHED AFTER
THE DEATH OF AUGUSTUS

Gaius Cassius had been entrusted by the Senate to prosecute war against Dolabella, who had been decreed an enemy of the state;

assisted by the authority of the Republic, he brought Syria under control with the three armies that were in that province, and he besieged Dolabella in the city of Laodicia and forced him to die. Also, on the order of Marcus Brutus, Gaius Antonius was captured and killed.

BOOK 122 (43 BCE)

Marcus Brutus campaigned successfully against the Thracians for a little while, and when all the overseas provinces and armies were under the control of Gaius Cassius and him, they met at Smyrna to make plans for the approaching war. By common agreement they granted a pardon to Publicola, who was in chains, at the request of his brother, Marcus Messalla.

BOOK 123 (43–42 BCE)

From Epirus, Sextus Pompeius, the son of Pompeius Magnus, collected proscribed men and fugitive slaves. He had an army, but for a long time lacked any control over any territory; he engaged in piracy before he occupied first Messana, a town in Sicily, and then the entire province; and having killed the praetor Pompeius Bithynicus, he defeated Caesar's lieutenant Quintus Salvidienus in a sea battle. Caesar and Antonius crossed to Greece with their armies to wage war on Brutus and Cassius. In Africa, Quintus Cornificius defeated in battle Titus Sextius, a leader of the Cassian faction.

BOOK 124 (42 BCE)

Gaius Caesar and Antonius fought at Philippi with mixed results against Brutus and Cassius: on both sides the right wing being victorious, and both camps being captured by those who had been victorious. But the death of Cassius made the fortune of the two sides unequal: since he had been on the wing that had been beaten back, he thought that the entire army had been routed, and he committed suicide. Then on the next day Marcus Brutus was defeated, and he ended his life by prevailing upon Straton, a companion of his flight, to plunge a sword into him. He was around forty years old, <. . .>. Among them Quintus Hortensius was killed.

BOOK 125 (41 BCE)

Leaving Antonius behind overseas (for the provinces situated in this part of the empire had passed to him), Caesar returned to Italy and distributed land to the veterans. In grave danger, he suppressed the mutiny of his army that soldiers corrupted by Fulvia, the wife of Marcus Antonius, had provoked against their own commander. The consul Lucius Antonius, the brother of Marcus Antonius, waged war against Caesar on the advice of that same Fulvia. Antonius took into his own party the people whose lands had been assigned to veterans, and after Marcus Lepidus, who had been in charge of the city with an army, had been defeated, he forced his way into the city.

BOOK 126 (41–40 BCE)

When Caesar was twenty-three, he drove Lucius Antonius, who had been blockaded in the city of Perusia and had attempted to break out several times but had been driven back, to surrender out of hunger. Caesar pardoned him and all his soldiers, destroyed Perusia, and having brought under his control all the troops of the opposing side, he finished the war without any recourse to bloodshed.

BOOK 127 (40–38 BCE)

With Labienus, a former member of the Pompeian side, as their leader, the Parthians invaded Syria, and once they had defeated Marcus Antonius' lieutenant Decidius Saxa, they occupied the entire province. When Marcus Antonius, to wage war against Caesar <. . .> his wife Fulvia <. . .> to eliminate any obstacle to harmony between the leaders, made peace with Caesar and married his sister Octavia. He revealed with his own evidence that Quintus Salvidienus had plotted evil deeds against Caesar, and Salvidienus was convicted and committed suicide. Antonius' lieutenant Publius Ventidius defeated the Parthians in battle and drove them from Syria after he had killed their leader, Labienus. Since the enemy next to Italy, Sextus Pompeius, controlled Sicily and blocked the grain-trade, Caesar and Antonius made the treaty with him that he demanded, which gave him Sicily as his province. The book contains in addition the unrest in Africa and the fighting that took place there.

BOOK 128 (38–37 BCE)

When Sextus Pompeius was again making the sea dangerous with piracy and was not providing the peace he had agreed to, Caesar out of necessity undertook a war with him and fought two naval battles with no decisive outcome. Marcus Antonius' lieutenant Publius Ventidius defeated the Parthians in battle in Syria and killed their king. The Jews were also subdued by lieutenants of Antonius. The book contains in addition the preparation for the Sicilian war.

BOOK 129 (36 BCE)

There was fighting at sea against Sextus Pompeius with varying results: of Caesar's two fleets, the one commanded by Agrippa was victorious while the one led by Caesar was destroyed and the soldiers set down on land were in great danger. Then Pompeius was defeated and fled to Sicily. Marcus Lepidus had crossed over from Africa as if he were Caesar's ally in the war he was to wage against Sextus Pompeius; when he actually attacked Caesar, he was abandoned by his army; and although his office of triumvir was terminated, he was allowed to keep his life. Marcus Agrippa was rewarded by Caesar with a naval crown, an honour that no one before him had achieved.

BOOK 130 (36 BCE)

During the time when Marcus Antonius was living a life of abandon with Cleopatra, he entered Media late and started a war against the Parthians with eighteen legions and 16,000 cavalry. When he had lost two legions, since nothing was going well, he began to retreat.

As he returned to Armenia, the Parthians immediately followed and caused great fear and greater danger to the entire army; in his flight Antonius covered 300 miles in twenty-one days. He lost approximately 8,000 men because of the weather. It was his own fault that he suffered from adverse weather in addition to the Parthian campaign he had undertaken so disastrously, since in his rush to return to Cleopatra, he refused to spend the winter in Armenia.

BOOK 131 (36–34 BCE)

Even as Sextus Pompeius entrusted himself to Marcus Antonius, he was preparing a war against him in Asia, and he was caught by Antonius' lieutenants and killed. Caesar suppressed a mutiny of the veterans that had broken out and caused great evil, and he subdued the Iapydae and the Dalmatae and the Pannonii. Antonius enticed Artavasdes, king of Armenia, with a promise of safe conduct and then ordered him to be thrown in chains. He gave the kingdom of Armenia to the son he had by Cleopatra, whom he, long since ensnared by love, had begun to regard as his wife.

BOOK 132 (34–31 BCE)

In Illyricum, Caesar subdued the Dalmatae. Because of his love for Cleopatra, by whom he had two sons, Philadelphus and Alexander, Marcus Antonius wished neither to return to Rome nor, although the term of the triumvirate had expired, to give up his power; he began to prepare to wage war on Rome and Italy, and he amassed equally great naval forces and infantry for it; and he sent a notification of divorce to Octavia, Caesar's sister. Caesar crossed to Epirus with an army. Then Caesar's naval battles and successful cavalry battles are recorded.

BOOK 133 (31–29 BCE)

Marcus Antonius was defeated at Actium by the navy and fled to Alexandria. He was besieged by Caesar, and in the depths of despair at the situation, driven above all by the false rumour that Cleopatra had been killed, he committed suicide. Caesar took control of Alexandria and, in order not to be at the dispensation of the victor, Cleopatra voluntarily took her own life. Caesar returned to Rome and celebrated three triumphs, one for Illyricum, the second for the victory of Actium, the third over Cleopatra, and he put an end to twenty-two years of civil war. Marcus Lepidus, the son of Lepidus who had been a triumvir, formed a conspiracy and fomented war against Caesar, but was caught and killed.

BOOK 134 (29–27 BCE)

After Gaius Caesar had settled matters and made a definitive arrangement for the provinces, he was given the name of Augustus too; and the month of Sextilis was named in his honour. When he <. . .> he held assizes at Narbo and conducted a census of the three Gauls that his father Caesar had conquered. War against the Bastarnae and the Moesi and other peoples by Marcus Crassus <. . .> are recorded.

BOOK 135 (28–25 BCE)

War conducted by Marcus Crassus against the Thracians and by Caesar against the Spaniards is recorded, and the Salassi, a people of the Alps, were subdued.

[There are no surviving *Periochae* for Books 136 and 137.]

BOOK 138 (15–13 BCE)

The Raeti were subdued by Tiberius Nero and Drusus, Caesar's stepsons. Agrippa, Caesar's son-in-law, died. The census was conducted by Drusus.

BOOK 139 (12 BCE)

The German communities located on the near and far sides of the Rhine are attacked by Drusus, and the uprising that had arisen in

Gaul because of the census is settled. An altar for Caesar the god was dedicated at the confluence of the Arar and the Rhône, and the Aeduan Gaius Julius Vercondaridubnus was made the priest.

BOOK 140 (13–11 BCE)

The crushing of the Thracians by Lucius Piso, and equally the subduing by Drusus of the Cherusci, the Tencteri, the Chauci, and other German peoples on the far side of the Rhine are recorded. Augustus' sister Octavia died after she had lost her son Marcellus, who was commemorated by the theatre and portico dedicated in his name.

BOOK 141 (11–10 BCE)

The war conducted by Drusus against the peoples on the far side of the Rhine is recorded. In this war Chumstinctus and Avectius, military tribunes from the Nervii, fought amongst the leaders. Drusus' brother Nero subdued the Dalmatae and the Pannonii. Peace was made with the Parthians when the standards that had been captured under Crassus and subsequently under Antonius were returned by their king.

BOOK 142 (9 BCE)

The war conducted by Drusus against the communities of the Germans across the Rhine is recorded. His horse fell on his leg, and thirty days after this happened Drusus died from the fracture. The body was transported to Rome by his brother Nero who, summoned by the news of his health, had rushed to him immediately, and the body was interred in the grave of Gaius Julius. The funeral oration was delivered by his stepfather Caesar Augustus. And at the funeral rites many honours were conferred on him.

APPENDIX

LIST OF VARIATIONS FROM THE TEUBNER TEXT

This list follows standard textual notation and is primarily designed to be used with Briscoe's Teubner. Angle brackets contain material the editor thinks should be included; square brackets contain material the editor thinks should not be included; obeli (†) indicate material that cannot be translated as is. The source for the reading adopted follows it in parentheses.

	Teubner	This translation
41.6.2	<.>	<A.> (Sigonius)
41.6.4	† postulandosque honores meritos ut diis immortalibus haberetur honos †.	postulandosque honores meritos. (Briscoe)
41.7.9	<. . .>	<caesum> (Crévier)
41.8.2	[sed ea propter belli magnitudinem prouincia consularis facta; Gracchus eam sortitur, Histriam Claudius]	*translated as is* (Fr. 1)
41.8.8	† aut hos aut illos †	aut minus hos aut plus illos (Gronovius)
41.8.10	ut <. . .> ciues Romani fiebant.	ut ciues Romani fie<rent, adopta>bant. (Voigt)
41.8.12	<. . .>.	<ne is esset>. (Walch)
41.9.11	qui nunc est <. . .>	qui nunc esset <futurusue esset> (Mommsen)
41.10.2	† id †	<esse exciu>it (Madvig)
41.11.6	† tumuli †	signum ubi (Novák)
41.14.1	† triumphus de Liguribus agebatur †	<Dum is> triumphus de Liguribus agebatur (Fr. 1)
41.17.6	<. . . senatus>	<in prouinciam profectus est . . . senatus> (Vahlen, abbreviated)
41.18.1	† murosque insuper amplexi †	muroque insuper <sunt> amplexi (Goldbacher)
41.18.8	† extra templum sortem in sitellam in templum latam foris ipse oporteret †	sorte in sitella in templum illata foris ipse <mansisset, cum templum ingredi et ipsum> oporteret (Madvig)
41.20.4	insan<ire . . .>ebant	insan<ire cred>ebant (H. J. Müller)
41.20.10	† reliquorum sui moris †	*translated as is* (Madvig)
41.21.9	<. . .>	<in locum Caepionis, . . .> (Drakenborch)
41.22.1	† ix mil. †	non. Iul. (Fr. 1)

41.22.5	† nuntios tumultuo <. . .> misit †.	nuntii tumultuosi missi. (Weissenborn)
41.22.7	† <. . .>um per quorum †	populorum per quorum fines (Madvig)
41.23.6	† manereque id decretum †	manereque id decretum <sciremus> (Weissenborn)
41.23.18	<. . .>	<decernere> (Weissenborn)
41.24.10	† dissertio †	dissolutio (Watt)
41.24.12	<. . .>	<obliterent; meministis> (Weissenborn)
41.24.16	† nostros quoque et nos segni †	<nostrorum> nostros quoque et nos regno (Weissenborn)
41.26.4	† secuti †	ut (Madvig)
41.26.5	<caesa . . .>	<caesa aut> (Fr. 1)
41.27.6	no<ta.> curriculis numerand	no<tas> curriculis numerand<is> (Rossbach)
	<. . .> dam	*not translated* (Chaplin)
	trans<. . . das>	trans<uertendas> (Jal)
41.27.9	portam in Auentinum porticum silice strauerunt, † eo publico † ab aede Veneris fecerunt	uiam in Auentinum silice strauerunt et porticum in cliuo Publicio ad aedem Veneris fecerunt (Kreyssig)
41.27.11	<. . .>	edixit (Madvig)
41.27.12	in his et clo<acas et mur>um	*not translated* (Chaplin) clo<acas faciendas et mur>um (Mommsen)
	circumducen<dum . . .>	circumducen<dum locauit> (Gast)
41.28.9	<. . .>	sociis (Sigonius)
41.28.11	† tamen †	tum (Walch)
42.3.7	† id †	et (Weissenborn)
	† loca †	<loca . . .> (Weissenborn)
42.3.8	† idem immortalium †	id eum immortalium demolientem <aedes> (Hartel)
42.5.10	† hostilibus actas animis quas †	<non minus> hostilibus actas animis <quam> quos (Madvig)
42.6.1	<. . .>	<Aegium> (H. J. Müller)
42.8.8	<. . . primo >	<quoque reddi eaque primo> (Madvig)
42.11.5	† iamiam primum †	iam pridem (Koch)
42.12.6	† ad Sidenum †	ad Dium (Pandermalis)[1]
42.13.7	† Euersam †	Euersam (V)
42.14.6	et legatio Rhodiorum † erat hac falsa iturus †	et legationis Rhodiorum <ferox> erat nec falsa <simul>aturus (Vahlen)
42.14.9	<. . . Asiae> ingratam populis	<nec> ingratam populis <Asiae> (Kreyssig)

[1] *Revue des Études Grecques*, 113 (2000), 522.

42.15.5	† a semitam paulum extantem †	ad semitam paulum exstantem (Madvig)
42.15.10	† etiam amicorum ac satellitum †	amicorum ac satellitum (Wesenberg)
42.16.9	† tacite habere id pati †	tacita habere (H. J. Müller)
42.20.1	<priore . . . M. Aemili>	<priore posita ob uictoriam M. Aemilii> (Madvig)²
42.23.6	† in socium populumque †	in<ter regem> socium populumque (Madvig)
42.23.7	† quid ipsum nullam praeterquam suae libidinis arbitrio futurum †	ipsum nullum, praeterquam suae libidinis arbitrio, <finem> facturum (Fr. 1)
42.23.10	<. . .>	<inuidiam concitarunt> (Sigonius)³
42.24.3	† unde praeterea †	unde <nihil emanasse> praeterquam (Drakenborch)
42.24.4	† Romam †	crederent (H. J. Müller)
42.25.13	† aut manent ibi †	aut manentibus <aut abeuntibus> (Madvig)
42.28.11	<. . . , alterum>	<decessisse, alterum> (Fr. 1)
42.29.2	† eius †	Persei (Drakenborch)
42.29.3	† equitumque † euentum	et euentum (Vahlen)
42.29.12	† ei ad †	*omitted* (Novák)
42.30.1	† gens †. . .† deterioribus †	<e>gens ubique <multitudo> omnis . . . deterioribus <fau>ebat (Madvig)
42.30.4	† Persea magis aurae popularis erat †	<ad> Persea magis aura popularis <i>erat (Madvig)
42.30.6	† inde †	autem (Ruperti)
42.30.9–10	<. . . portendi. patres quod bonum faustum> felixque	<finium imperii portendi. patres quod faustum> felixque (Weissenborn)
42.31.3	† de CCC equites CCLƆƆƆ. LƆƆƆ †	sedecim milia (Fr. 1)
42.32.7	† qui centuriones sed †	qui centuriones scr<ibebant> (H. J. Müller)
42.34.15	† appellationem uos †	appellatione ues<tra> (Briscoe)
42.36.7	† ettra XI †	intra (Fr. 1) quintum decimum (Drakenborch)
42.37.8	† et Macedonis Philippo bello hostes fuissent †	et Philippi bello hostes fuissent (Weissenborn)
42.39.5	† etiam †	tandem (Novák)

² This is the reading adopted in the Loeb; it is not in Briscoe's apparatus because Madvig offered it not as a conjecture but as example of what the sense requires.

³ NB *misericordiam* accidentally omitted from Briscoe's edition.

42.40.4	\<foedus . . . renouandum\>	\<foedus miseris, quod tamen ipsum tibi non fuisse renouandum\> (Sigonius)
42.40.7	† Eruam †	Euersam (Fr. 1)
42.41.2	† ea †	ne\<que\> (Vahlen)
42.41.14	† foederis †	foederatis (Fr. 1)
42.43.1	† Et dicentem et cum adsensum † Marcius auctor fuit . . . legatos . . . censuissent	Haec dicentem et cum adsensu Marcius \<audiuit et\> auctor fuit . . . etiam \<amici regis\> cum . . . censuissent (Weissenborn)
42.43.4	† conparati sunt †	con\<festim\> profecti sunt (Giarratano)
42.43.7	† decretum Thebis si †	decretum Thebis fecit (Weissenborn)
42.44.7	\<. . . nihil\>	nihil (Fr. 1)
42.46.1	\<. . . litteras . . .\>	\<ad alias ciuitates litteras scripsit et\> (Goldbacher)
42.47.3	† hae cum uenturum †	\<in\> aequum uenturos (Madvig)
42.47.5	† etiam interdum †	etiam, interdum \<locum\> (Fr. 1)
42.47.7	† regis †	*omitted* (Gruter)
42.47.9	\<. . . minus\>	\<callida minus\> (Novák)
42.49.2	† quaeritur †	geritur (Fr. 1)
42.49.9	† M. †	M'. (Gronovius)
42.50.7	† quia sic tibi †	sicubi (Fr. 1)
42.51.4	† Eulyestas †	Eulyestas (V)
42.52.5	† cuius uel quorum pars †	quorum maior (Fr. 1)
42.52.9	† septem †	\<uiginti\> septem (Dobree)
42.52.14	† hos †	his (Kreyssig)
42.53.6	ad Tripolim † uocant Azorum Pythoum et Dolichen incolentes †	ad Azorum, Pythoum et Dolichen; Tripolim uocant incolentes (Weissenborn)
42.54.4	† depul †	depul\<so impetu\> (Madvig)
42.55.10	† adque †	adhuc (Harant)
42.56.5	† cuius †	eius (Hartel)
42.56.10	\<. . .\>	\<suos in castra reuocauit\> (Madvig)
42.57.8	† quanta esset duos esse †	quanta esset uis hostium (Madvig)
42.58.10	† rationem † † Certimano †	Ionem (Fr. 1) Artemona (Madvig)
42.59.3	† tre\<. . .\> is hastas petere pedites † \<. . .\> equorumque nunc succidere crura \<. . .\>is	ingentibus gladiis Thraces petere pedites nunc, nunc succidere crura equis, (Ahrens)
42.59.7	† paruo momento, si adiuuisset, debellatum esse †	paruo momento si adiuuissent, debellatum esse \<clamar\>et, opportune (Madvig)

42.60.2	† superfixa †	\<rumpiis\> superfixa (Drakenborch)
42.61.10–11	\<. . . . contione\>	\<optabant. contione\> (Fr. 1)
42.61.11	† est eminet Larisae medius abest † G\>o\<n\>num	eminet et Larisae medius abest \<G\>o\<n\>num \<abeunti\>. (Madvig)
42.63.1	\<. . .\>	\<Persei\> (H. J. Müller)
42.63.4	\<. . . nunc\>	\<saxis ingentibus, nunc\> (Kreyssig)
42.63.6	\<. . .\>	\<corruerat\> (Madvig)
42.64.5	† et inconste †	omissa spe (Madvig)
42.65.8	† propter †	prop\<el\>lere (Madvig)
42.66.8	† quoque †	omitted (Bekker)
42.67.4	† Autlesbim †	Autlesbim (Fr. 1)
42.67.7	† res †	omitted (Briscoe)
42.67.12	† et †	et \<ad\> (Weissenborn)
43.1.1	\<. . . , . . .\>	\<gesta sunt, . . .\> (Madvig)
43.3.7	Hanc iniec\<. . .\>	not translated (Chaplin)
43.4.1	\<. . .\>tis † tantum extitit pauor †	tantum pauorem (Fr. 1)
43.6.9	† reciperentur †	redigerentur (Bos)
43.6.11	\<et Masinissae . . .\>	\<et Masinissae uenerunt: Carthaginienses\> (Rossbach)
43.6.13	† et †	\<ea\> et (H. J. Müller)
43.7.10	† compilata spoliataque sacrilegiis †	conpilata spoliaque sacrilegis (Gitlbauer)
43.10.1	finium † plerique †	finitimum imperio (Weissenborn)
43.11.3	† comitia †	comitia essent (Vahlen)
43.11.11	patres † acceperunt qui †	referentes (Gronovius)
43.14.5	\<. . .\>	\<uoluntate\> (Madvig)
43.14.6	† qua †	quoad (Harant)
43.16.8	ad † eius † rogationem	ad rogationem (Vahlen)
43.18.11	primum arma ademit \<. . .\>	primum arma ademit (V)
43.19.2	† quattuor milia †	quadringenti (Weissenborn)
43.20.2	† qui †	\<at\>qui (Hertz)
43.23.3	† Epirotarum gente †	Epirotarum gentis \<cohortem\> (Koch)
44.1.5	† iunctam †	intentam (Novák)
44.1.8	\<. . .\>.	\<mansit - summa concordia fuit\>. (Heraeus)
44.3.1	dux regius castra \<. . .\>.	dux regius castra \<habebat\>. (Hartel)
44.4.4	concursum \<. . . . . . .\> belli	\<concurrissent\> (Gronovius)
44.5.12–13	† peditum, quorum pars maior tumulos tenebat; ibi ualle †	quorum pars maior tumulos tenebat; alibi uallo (Madvig)

44.6.2	<. . . . . .>	<in mare proiiceret, Thessalonicam alterum, qui naualia incenderet, misit; Asclepiodotum et Hippiam, quique cum iis erant> (Madvig)
44.6.6	† dua intrepidus decem dies †	paucos intrepidus rex dies (Madvig)
44.8.7	† hospes et †	Perseus (Fr. 1)
44.9.10	† peruic †	protulit (Weissenborn)
44.10.10	† alia †	*omitted* (H. J. Müller)
44.11.3	† inaltus †	in altum (Fr. 1)
44.13.7	moenia <. . .> modo	<urbem ingressus tantos oppidanis aduentu suo fecit animos ut non> moenia modo (Wesenberg)
44.14.10	† inopiam insulam inopem miss . . . <ma>ritimis iuuetur colendi itaque commeatibus †	inopem insulam esse suam; maritimis uiuere incolentes commeatibus (Madvig)
44.15.1	† scirent indicatum †	<ut> scirent indicatum (Sigonius)
44.16.2	† rem p. †	*omitted* (Kreyssig)
44.17.3	consulem <. . .> . . . <. . .> in urbem uenturum	consulem <misit litterasque consulis> . . . <comitia edicebat, promittebatque se ad eum diem> in urbem uenturum (Madvig)
44.18.1	aliis	al<acer rebus in al>iis (Damsté)
44.19.9	<. . .>	<uictor> fuerat (Fr. 1)
44.19.10	† imperio †	imperio <Romano> (Zingerle)
44.20.4	† in hiemem etiam in spe † † notio militi alii † <. . .>	hiemem etiam insuper (Vahlen) in otio militem <uix> ali (Perizonius) <dierum> (Sigonius)
44.20.5	† in †	*omitted* (Fr. 1)
44.21.5	† centum †	septem (Fr. 1)
44.22.2	† conpulsus consulatus †	consul essem creatus (Kreyssig)
44.22.6	uobis <. . . ru>mores credulitate uestra alatis	<credite. ru>mores credulitate uestra <ne> alatis (Fr. 1)
44.22.10	† quae †	sunt (Fr. 1)
44.24.7	grauioribus <. . .>.	grauioribus<que> onerarunt criminibus (Goldbacher)
44.25.5	† conciliandam gratiam magis †	conciliandae gratia pacis (Hartel)
44.25.6	<quingenta talenta . . .>	<mille talenta, ut pacem pataret> (Madvig)
44.26.1	† pecuniam tutam et †	pecunia data aut (Madvig)
44.27.6	Macedonum <. . . . .>	<essent. hoc amisso auxilio Perseus animos Macedonum> (Madvig)
44.28.4	† Diamius †	Damius (Fr. 1)
44.30.4	† Metutam †	Etleuam (Briscoe)
44.30.13	Parthinorum † iuuenta †	<adsumptis> Parthinorum iuuentutis (Sigonius)

44.31.4	† Oriundi †	Driloni (Heraeus)
44.32.8	† Creantigonensis misit †	\<cum\> Creonte Antigonensi misit (Kreyssig)
44.32.11	huic \<. . .\> \<. . .\>	huic \<operi\> (Crévier) \<ligna petere\> (Crévier)
44.33.2	† euergentt †	emerger\<e cerneren\>t (Koch)
44.33.4	\<. . . , qua\>	\<processit\> qua (Madvig)
44.33.5	\<. . .\>	curauit (M. Müller)
44.34.8	† scutorum †	*omitted* (Vahlen)
44.35.5	\<alii . . .\>	alii \<legatos in uincula coniciendos censerent, alii\> (Vahlen)
44.35.7	\<. . .\>	\<agmine impetum\> (Vahlen)
44.35.18	\<hinc rege . . .\>	\<hinc rege cum Macedonum exercitu\> (Madvig)
44.36.2	† meridie aestatem magis adcesserunt tum mox adparebat †.	meridiano aestu magis accessurum utrumque mox apparebat (Weissenborn)
44.37.12	† signum propositum pugnae ad exeundum †	signo proposito pugnae exeundum (Madvig)
44.37.13	\<. . .\>	\<contra huius modi\> (Madvig)
44.39.8	† nec interdiu nec nocte abeund †	interdiu aut nocte abeundo \<potest\> (Madvig)
44.40.8	trahentes \<. . .\>,	traherent (Latinius)
44.46.3	\<. . .\>	CC (Fr. 1)
44.46.5	\<. . .\>	\<amnes. arx\> (Madvig)
45.1.6	† aliter editus †	alia traditur (Madvig)
45.1.7	\<. . .\>	tradidisse (Hertz)
45.2.2	\<. . .\>.	\<uenissent\>. (Sigonius)
45.2.3	† at urbi †	*omitted* (Hiller)
45.2.5	† quam pauci †	\<cum\> quam paucis (Kreyssig)
45.2.9	† posset resistere †	poscere uideretur (Madvig)
45.3.2	† ur Latinae dictae †	eae edictae (Madvig)
45.4.2	\<. . .\>	\<traditae ei sunt; quas cum\> (Madvig)
45.4.4	† rege Persea consuli Paullo salutem †	\<a\> rege Perseo consuli Paullo salutem (H. J. Müller)
45.5.1	\<. . .\> dum	\<ea\> dum (Hertz)
45.6.2	† que †	\<deni\>que (Harant)
45.7.2	† tunc quod †	tunc (Kreyssig)
45.7.4	pullo † amictus illo †	pullo amictus \<sa\>gulo (Heusinger)
45.7.4	nullo suorum alio comite	nullo suorum \<praeterquam Philippo filio\> comite (Novák)

45.8.4	<. . .>	<quod fuit> (Madvig)
45.10.2	† adticis †	Attali (Luterbacher)
45.10.11	† tamen †	is animus (Gronovius)
45.10.15	quam <. . .>	quam <Popili effecerat asperitas>. (H. J. Müller)
45.12.1	praeteriit <. . .> nauigantibus ostio Nili ad Pelusium <. . .> per deserta Arabiae <. . .>	praeteriit nauigantibus ostio Nili ad Pelusium <praefectis ipse> per deserta Arabiae <profectus receptusque et ab iis qui> (H. J. Müller)
45.12.13	† dum †	*omitted* (Fr. 1)
45.13.16	<. . .> quae ibi proueniant	quae ibi <utilia sibi> proueniant (Novák)
45.15.2	haberent—<. . .> censendi	haberent—<iis sicut antea factum est, in tribubus rusticis> censendi (McDonald)
45.16.3	<legionibus . . .>	<legionibus quinum milium et ducenorum> (Weissenborn)
45.17.2	† culpmi †	primi (Vahlen)
45.18.6	† commune consilium gentis esset †	<denique ne si> commune concilium gentis esset, (H. J. Müller)
45.19.15	† pro †	pro<tinus> (H. J. Müller)
45.21.8	<. . .>	<aequabant> (Wesenberg)
45.22.1	<. . .>	<ueniebamus> (Sigonius)
45.22.8	† alii †	aut (Harant)
45.24.9	una † aut dubia est ita grauior sit †	una ut dubia est, ita grauior sit? (Weissenborn)
45.24.14	possunt † teste †; est enim	potestis; est tamen (Madvig)
45.25.1	† ramosque oleae supplices iactantes †	ramosque oleae iactantes supplices <ueniam orabant> (Novák)
45.26.3	† tot omnium †	est omni (Madvig)
45.26.15	Dictam Agruonitas	Dyrrachium (Zippel) Acruuionitas (H. J. Müller)
45.27.8	† ante †	*omitted* (Gronovius)
45.27.9	<. . . . . . Oropum>	<impetrauit. inde Oropum> (Madvig)
45.27.11	<. . .>	<monumenta> (Madvig)
45.28.4	† ac silentiam †	*omitted* (Fr. 1)
45.28.6	† cum † reuertit.	cum rediret. (Weissenborn)
45.28.9	† nimis solutis cuius †	nimis soluta usus (Vahlen)
45.29.2	† noui in †	noui im<perii> (Harant)
45.29.8	† Bora †	Bermion (Hammond)

45.29.9	trans † dorsum montem †	trans dorsum montis (Hammond)
45.30.2	† interruptis ad uideri lacerata †	interrupto (Madvig)
		ita uideri lacerata <Macedonia> (Vahlen)
	† et a †	ita ut (Madvig)
45.30.4	† eneae uocant hunc †	ad Aeneam et Acanthum (Harant)
45.30.8	† uniuersostendit †	uniuersa esset, ostendit (Madvig)
45.31.8	† aptium †	aduersantium (H. J. Müller)
45.32.8	† indignato †	indixerat (Fr. 1)
45.33.8	† Paeleum †	Peleum (Madvig)
45.34.11	† ex † domo exciuit	ex domo <Gallos> exciuit (Crévier)
45.34.12	ibi Romani cum et Solouettium ducem Gallorum † Synnades adlocutus ettalus †	ibi et Romani Solouettium ducem Gallorum Synnadis allocuti, e<t A>ttalus (Fr. 1)
45.34.13	† cons. †	consularis (Heraeus)
45.35.7	† imperatori ita neglegenter †	imperatori ira<tus> neglegenter <erat> (Weissenborn)
45.36.8	† in uno †	iam nunc (Büttner)
45.37.1	<. . .>	<tum Seruilius> (Fr. 1)
45.37.2	neque <. . . neque>	neque <dixerunt seditiose quicquam neque> fecerunt (Vahlen)
45.37.10	<. . . ; ne>	<existi; ne> (Heraeus)
45.37.13	accusatorem † iscire † potuisse	<apparuisset neque> accusatorem hiscere potuisse (Vahlen)
45.38.1	quid † etiam † dicitis	quidnam dicitis (H. J. Müller)
45.38.4	quam † illi qui triumphauerant †	quam illis <qui post eos> triumphauerant (Sigonius)
45.39.11	<. . .>	<bello> (Madvig)
45.39.11–12	† bonaque pr. trans †	dona populi Romani trans<uehens> (Kreyssig)
45.39.12–13	† traducendo in triumpho uindicauit, alias alios dente mactati. quidem †	traducendas in triumpho dedicauit (Kreyssig)
		alias alio ducente mactabitis? (Hertz)
		quid enim? (Weissenborn)
45.39.13	† hominumque †	honoris <parantur et uos eas> (Weissenborn)
45.39.15	† et tu centurio, miles, quibus ab imperatore Paullo donatus decreuit potius quam Seruius Galba fabulentur audis et hoc . . . audi †	et tu centurio, miles, quid de imp. Paulo senatus decreuit potius quam <quid> Seruius Galba fabuletur audi: et hoc . . . audi (Fr. 1)
45.39.16	† per prouocatio †	prouocato (Hertz)
45.40.5	† non suffragi † honori eius fuissent	initio honori eius suffragati essent (M. Müller)

45.40.9	† dedisset †	dissereret (Madvig)
45.41.11	currum <. . .> ex Capitolio prope iam exspirantem <in>ueni;	currum <escendens, domum> ex Capitolio <altero> prope iam expirante ueni; (Hertz)
45.42.4	<. . . Bithys, filius Cotyis>	<detrahens habere sineret; Bithys, filius Cotyis> (Madvig)

EXPLANATORY NOTES

BOOK FORTY-ONE

3 *The consul*: his name is Aulus Manlius Vulso.

7 *Nero*: the *cognomen* of Tiberius Claudius. His respect for the proper attire here anticipates Gaius Claudius' disregard for such matters in the following year (see below, chap. 10).

8 *be put on trial immediately*: consuls were immune from prosecution during their term of office, but could be prosecuted for their conduct when the term expired. The basis of the tribunes' attack here is that Manlius had left Gaul, the province assigned to him, and started a war against the Istrians without the authorization of the Senate and Roman people (see below, chap. 7).

   rewards owed to them: the temple of Bellona was in an area known as the Campus Martius (Map 1) which lay outside the sacred boundary (*pomerium*) of the city. Since a general lost his *imperium* (including the right to command troops) once he brought his army into the city, the Senate would meet outside the *pomerium* to hear the report of a victorious general and to decide whether his accomplishments merited a triumph.

   Sardinia: the Romans had seized Sardinia from Carthage sixty years earlier and organized the southern part as a province. The Ilienses and Balari come from the interior of the island, which resisted Roman rule throughout the Republican period.

   in whose control . . . by Lucius Cornelius Scipio: after Alexander's conquest of the Persian empire, Lycia in Asia Minor (see Map 4) had passed into the control of various Hellenistic kingdoms. The Romans detached it from Antiochus in 189 after the battle of Magnesia and awarded it to Rhodes. Although Lucius Cornelius Scipio was the general who defeated Antiochus, in fact a ten-man commission carried out the Senate's directions in reorganizing his territory (37.55 and 38.39). The nature of Rhodian control of Lycia had been an issue ever since. (See also Polybius 21.24 and 22.5.)

9 *entrusted the Lycians with a letter*: according to Polybius, Roman ambassadors delivered this message to the Rhodians (25.4–5).

   the allies received the same as the Romans: it is impossible to give modern equivalents for ancient sums. Using Polybius (6.39), Walbank estimates that these donatives are generous; in each case they represent roughly 25 per cent of annual military pay (F. W. Walbank, *A Historical Commentary on Polybius* (Oxford, 1957–79), vol. 1, p. 722).

10 *a great number of their fellow citizens were registered at Rome*: those of Rome's allies who had the juridical status of Latins (whether or not they belonged to the original Latin League, a group of surrounding communities allied

from early in the fifth century) were entitled to move to Rome and acquire Roman citizenship by being enrolled in the census. This right appears to have been little exercised until the first half of the second century when extensive migration necessitated counteractive legislation. Livy records three occasions when Latins were forced to return home (39.3, here, and 42.10). The attraction of Fregellae for the Samnites and Paeligni was that it had Latin rights and thus more privileges than their home communities. Rome's various relationships with the other communities on the Italian peninsula were complex, but in each case the primary tie was military. The allies had to supply troops to fight in Rome's wars, and shifting populations complicated the recruitment of soldiers.

11 *to become Roman citizens*: although the text is incomplete and consequently the procedures here are unclear, the general point is that people used various legal dodges to obtain Roman citizenship. Some reference to adoption seems essential because of the wording of the Senate's decree in chap. 9. For the Latin, see Appendix.

prodigies were announced: for prodigy lists, see the section on 'Ancient Historical Writing' in the Introduction.

supplication: a public religious ceremony where the Romans made a procession around the city to each of the main temples and prayed to representations of the gods, which were set out on special couches (*pulvinaria*).

12 *Marcus Claudius and Titus Quinctius*: censors in 189. Both Livy (38.28) and Plutarch (*Flamininus* 18) comment on the liberality with which they conducted the census.

The praetor Lucius Mummius: available for this duty since his province was reassigned to Sempronius.

forbade the manumission: one way to manumit someone formally in Roman law was a collusive action where the owner, the slave, and a third party came before a magistrate; the third party asserted that the slave was free, and the owner did not deny the claim. The decree is intended to prevent the Latin allies from using this procedure to obtain Roman citizenship for themselves and their sons.

rushed precipitately to his province: normally the consuls began their term of office with a ceremony on the Capitol where they offered prayers for the public safety. Each consul had twelve attendants called lictors. Like the magistrates, the lictors had both civilian and military attire. It was considered extremely bad conduct for a consul to leave the city without following the proper procedure. A notorious case is that of Gaius Flaminius, consul in 217. Hannibal's victory over the Romans at Lake Trasimene was partially attributed to Flaminius' hasty departure from Rome (21.58 and 22.9).

14 *councils of war*: the Romans and the Ligures fought regularly during the first quarter of the second century until the Romans eventually subdued the region.

15 *fifty-one and a half iugera of land*: these are generous plots by the standards of the time, and scholars have questioned the accuracy of this passage.

their resentment: it appears that in the past the allied troops received just as much as those with Roman citizenship (see chap. 7 above). So it is not surprising that Claudius' stinginess caused bad feelings.

16 *not to have a head*: the Romans adopted from the Etruscans the practice of looking for omens in the entrails of animals. The 'head' of the liver was a swelling usually found on the right side, and its absence was considered a bad sign. During the Second Punic War the Roman general Marcellus also had to repeat a sacrifice when his first victim had a 'headless' liver (Livy 27.26 and Plutarch, *Marcellus* 29.5). In 1877 a bronze model of a sheep's liver, marked into zones and labelled, was discovered near Piacenza (south-east of Milan), where it is now in the Archaeological Museum.

the conscript fathers: standard English term for the Latin *patres conscripti* and often shortened to 'fathers' (*patres*). Both terms are used apparently interchangeably with 'members of the Senate', 'senators', and 'patricians'; and the precise meanings are a matter of scholarly debate.

sescenaris: apparently a technical religious term; since it appears here only, its precise meaning is unknown.

17 *the performance of customary rituals*: it is not certain which priesthood Licinius held or what these rites were. Some priests (e.g. the *flamen Dialis*, or priest of Jupiter who, according to the second-century CE writer Aulus Gellius (*Attic Nights* 10.15), was supposed to maintain a kind of ritual purity) were restricted in their activities; and Scipio Africanus won the command against Hannibal in 205 because his colleague in the consulship—who was the uncle of this Licinius—was pontifex maximus and had to remain in Italy to carry out his religious duties (28.44). It seems, however, that political motives may underlie the magistrates' conduct in each case; just a few years later, when Licinius is consul, the Senate upholds his right to lead the campaign in Macedonia even after his colleague points out the inconsistency (cf. 42.32).

Aquae Cumanae . . . Cumae: Aquae Cumanae has not been located but was presumably a health resort near Cumae.

20 *'Letum' would be his that day*: the Latin word *letum* means death, so Petillius' words have an ominous ring.

pullarius: the keeper of the sacred chickens. If the chickens ate greedily before a battle, their appetite was taken as a prediction of Roman success; failure to eat signified a defeat. The most famous defeat associated with disregard for this procedure is a naval battle in the First Punic War where the Roman commander, Publius Claudius, was eager to engage the enemy; informed that the sacred chickens refused to eat, he snatched them up and threw them overboard, saying, 'If they won't eat, let them drink.' The story was well known: see Cicero, *On the Nature of the Gods* 2.6, Livy, *Per.* 19, and Valerius Maximus 1.4.3.

21 *a suffect consul . . . hold the elections*: a suffect consul was one appointed part-way through the year to fill a vacancy. Because of the gap in the text it is not known what procedure was used to elect the consuls for 175.

22 *what sort of man he was*: Livy's judgement is based on the assumption that a man's behaviour should be consistent with his status. Polybius, Livy's source for this passage, gives more details about Antiochus' preference for low company and unusual gifts (see the fragments of Polybius, 26).

23 *this kind of show*: traditional Greek entertainment consisted of athletic, musical, and theatrical competitions. The Romans adopted gladiatorial games from the Etruscans in the third century BCE, and they gradually spread throughout the empire.

24 *quartan fever*: a kind of flu with a fever that recurred every fourth day. Many Roman authors mention it as a common illness.

public priests: see Glossary for these different kinds of priests.

22: the text of chap. 22 is incomplete because the edge of the manuscript page is missing. As translated here, the first two and last three sentences of the chapter are affected by the gap. See Appendix for individual problems.

the envoys returned from Africa: as noted above, the extant text does not record the sending of these envoys.

the senate: Livy has substituted the Roman equivalent (senate) for the Carthaginians' own word for their governmental council. This is his practice in general; chief magistrates and generals of other peoples are often referred to as 'praetors' though this is a Roman name for Roman magistrates.

25 *Only this people . . . and the Athenians*: the background to this animosity is lost. The Achaeans probably imposed the ban in 198 (cf. Archo's speech below); and the Athenians may have done so in 200 (Livy 31.44).

<. . .> *a letter*: at least a verb such as 'sent' is missing here.

26 *the Gauls*: Callicrates refers here to an incursion of Gauls into Asia Minor in the third century that eventually led to Roman intervention and the successful campaign of Gnaeus Manlius, consul in 189 (see 38.12–27).

28 *side with the Romans or Philip*: in the two previous wars between the Romans and the Macedonians, the Achaeans were allied with Philip. But during the second of these conflicts, the Achaeans switched allegiance; despite Archo's claim, the motivation was probably the proximity of the Roman fleet. On these events of 198, see 32.19–25.

29 *the history of the Roman people*: this sentence is typical of Livy's approach to his subject: he prefers to keep his focus on the Romans and, as Luce observes, to give a full narrative of what he chooses to record, not simply to provide a brief summary (T. J. Luce, *Livy: The Composition of his History* (Princeton, 1977), p. 208). For similar statements acknowledging the way he delimits his subject matter, see 33.20, 35.40, and 39.48.

30 *the second hour*: the Romans divided every day into twelve hours of dark (night) and twelve hours of light (day). The hours were grouped into

watches, of which there were eight altogether: two daytime watches before noon and two after, two night-time watches before midnight and two after. The length of an individual hour (and thus of the watches) shrank and expanded according to the actual amount of light and dark at any point in the year (though the difference in the Mediterranean is less extreme than for those of us who live farther from the equator). So the exact length and timing of 'the second hour' depend on when the sun rose. The emphasis here is on the brevity of the battle.

Valerius Antias: the first time we have seen Livy referring to one of his sources. The specific mention of Antias probably means that he was the only one who included the information.

Marcus Aemilius: an error. He was consul the preceding year. Livy might have mistaken the year or the consul's name; or the copyist of the manuscript might have written the wrong name.

the people of Patavium: an example of an allied community ceding internal autonomy and seeking Roman intervention. Presumably it worked to the advantage of those who sought it. Livy may have a particular interest here since he came from Patavium (modern Padua).

egg-shaped markers: they served as lap-counters; one was moved every time a lap was completed.

for enumerating . . . <. . . .>: because a page of the manuscript has a torn corner, the descriptions of the censors' additions to the Circus here and the construction projects at Pisaurum and Sinuessa in the next paragraph are based on editors' conjectures. It is not possible to reconstruct what was done on the Alban Mount. See Appendix for the Latin.

31 *the senaculum*: a place where the Senate gathered before meetings were convened in the Curia.

from the temple of Saturn . . . Curia: this route does not make sense since these buildings were not on the Capitoline; the text is probably corrupt.

but Fulvius Flaccus: Fulvius seems to have been an extremely ambitious politician: in 184 he tried to run for the praetorship while he was still an aedile (39.39), and in 179 the Senate limited his expenditure on public entertainments, generally a way of gaining popularity as is this generous building programme (40.44). His ill-fated attempt to build an unusually stupendous temple in Rome features early in Book 42.

BOOK FORTY-TWO

33 *treating it as their own*: the task assigned to Postumius reflects the Senate's awareness of a problem that manifested itself in different ways throughout Republican history: the administration of defeated territory. The Romans tended not to 'micro-manage' their conquests. One result in Italy was that large landowners could squeeze out their less prosperous neighbours. In this particular case, Capua's punishment for siding with Hannibal

in the Second Punic War had been the loss of its territory, Campania, which was then designated the property of the Roman people. The land, however, was never officially distributed, hence the disorder facing Postumius some forty years later.

33 *a grudge against the citizens of Praeneste*: Praeneste (modern Palestrina) was an old and important city in Latium, just over twenty miles south-east of Rome. It is not on the most direct route to Campania, so it looks as if Postumius went out of his way to use his magistracy to punish the Praenestini (Map 2).

no one was ever . . . in any way: probably an overstatement. There is evidence from Livy himself that Roman magistrates used their position to take advantage of people under their control. For example, he notes that when Cato the Elder, who was notorious for parsimony and moral rectitude, was praetor of Sardinia in 198, he eliminated or reduced the various expenses his predecessors had placed on that island's inhabitants (32.27). Here Livy may have in mind a distinction between allies in Italy and provincials. In any case the episode fits with the theme of abuse towards the allies that he weaves throughout Books 41–5.

on the road: this sentence refers to what is called guest-friendship, a well-established custom of reciprocal hospitality. For another example, note Perseus' guest-friend Praxo at Delphi (42.15).

34 *the ambassadors who had been sent to Aetolia and Macedonia*: see 41.25 and 27 for the former and 41.22 for the latter.

a temple for Fortuna Equestris that he had vowed: in order to ensure success in battle, Roman generals regularly sought to obtain divine favour by promising a deity a temple or sacrifices or games in the event of victory. In a battle against the Celtiberi in 180 (which Fulvius won by a cavalry manoeuvre), he swore to build a temple to Fortuna Equestris (the goddess of good luck for cavalry) and to celebrate games in honour of Jupiter Optimus Maximus (40.40). The Senate attempted to circumvent aristocratic competition by limiting the amount that could be expended on the games but apparently did not anticipate that Fulvius might lavish his attention on the temple instead (40.44).

35 *neither Pyrrhus nor Hannibal*: Pyrrhus was a king from Epirus in the early third century. He was invited by Tarentum (originally a Greek city) to Italy, to help the Tarentines combat Roman expansion. Between 280 and 275 he won three major battles against the Romans, but in each he suffered such heavy casualties, without inducing the Romans to surrender, that he is said to have commented after the second one that 'One more victory like that will cost us the war' (Plutarch, *Pyrrhus* 21). Hannibal was the Carthaginian general who invaded Italy in 218 and waged war on the Italian peninsula for fifteen years before he was forced to return to Africa and was ultimately defeated in 202. Both Pyrrhus and Hannibal pillaged southern Italy, but while Hannibal stayed away from the temple of Proserpina at Locri, Pyrrhus stole the temple treasures. A storm at sea carried them back ashore (29.28).

36 *his wife . . . . Apelles*: Livy is the only surviving source for Perseus' murder of his wife; his second marriage is mentioned at 42.12. For Apelles' involvement in Demetrius' murder, see 40.20, 54, and 55.

scorned the newly created kingdom: although Eumenes' ancestors had controlled the fortress of Pergamum since the beginning of the third century, it had become a powerful state only under his father (Attalus I). The latter consistently sided with the Romans and in 188 received a large amount of the territory that the Romans took from Antiochus after the battle of Magnesia.

The Aetolians . . . the Thessalians: very little is known or understood about these financial troubles in Aetolia and northern Greece. The Aetolians had sided with this Antiochus' father, also named Antiochus, in his war with Rome. In their treaty, they agreed to pay indemnity over six years, so the Roman peace demands may underlie the debt there. The same explanation, however, cannot hold for Perrhaebia and Thessaly. Our ignorance here results from the sources' focus on Rome.

37 *tardy payment of tribute*: apparently the rest of the indemnity Antiochus' father agreed to in 188 after being defeated by the Romans; the payments were originally scheduled to be made within twelve years. For the terms of the peace settlement (known as the treaty of Apamea), see Polybius 21.42 and Livy 38.38.

Antiochus' stay in Rome: Antiochus had been kept in Rome as a condition of the treaty of Apamea for twelve or thirteen years before a nephew took his place. His reign began in 175.

38 *a gift of 100,000 asses*: the *as* (plural *asses*) was a bronze coin. In this period the Senate regularly gave some money to each member of an embassy; unusual here are the size of the amount and the fact that it all went to Apollonius. Perhaps he was expected to share it or, as the next sentence implies, perhaps the Senate was aware of his unusual value for good relations between Rome and Antiochus (see Loeb edn., trans. E. Sage and A. C. Schlesinger (Cambridge, Mass., 1938), 310).

Corsica: the Romans seized Corsica from the Carthaginians in 259; it was administered as a province together with Sardinia. According to a historian contemporary with Livy, the Corsicans paid an annual tribute of honey, resin, and wax (Diodorus Siculus 5.13.4). Beeswax was used for candles.

39 *abuse of the crushed*: the last time Livy reported on Roman–Ligurian fighting (41.17–18), the Ligures were cast as the barbarians in their savage treatment of Roman colonists. Here the Ligures are the victims, and Livy uses some of the same vocabulary to describe the way Popillius abuses them. This reversal is typical of his willingness to criticize Romans and of the subtlety with which he constructs his narrative. A careful reader of the Latin would see that here the consul is the barbarian and the barbarians are civilized.

40 *in accordance with Gaius Claudius' decree*: see 41.8–9.

40 *The census . . . the common good*: a puzzling sentence that seems to gloss over some obvious tensions between the two men. When Livy first discusses their censorship, he focuses on public works and makes it explicit that the men diverged in their attitudes towards spending public money (41.27). Livy notes also in that initial discussion that nine men were expelled from the Senate. This is a large number, and one of the victims was Fulvius' own brother. So it is hard to believe that the censors shared their duties in complete harmony, even though Livy says here that their decisions were unanimous. As a class, *aerarii* are somewhat obscure, but the demotion is significant.

41 *most historians*: this passage is a good example of the tendency among ancient historical writers to discuss sources only when they conflict. Having indicated the discrepancy, Livy then uses the version he wants to endorse. As will become obvious from Eumenes' speech, Livy, like his source Polybius, favoured Eumenes' version of events, which represents the Roman interpretation. The charges Eumenes makes correspond to what was apparently an official litany of complaints since they appear in a contemporary inscription found at Delphi. (For the text, with translation and commentary, see R. K. Sherk, *Roman Documents from the Greek East* (Baltimore, 1969), 233–41).

43 *Abrupolis*: the leader of a Thracian tribe who apparently tried to seize the mines of Mount Pangaeus, a major source of Macedonian wealth. Traces of the story can be found in ancient sources going back to Polybius (22.18).

Arthetaurus: an otherwise unknown Illyrian leader.

44 *Eversa and Callicritus*: also otherwise unknown. In chap. 41 below, Livy has Perseus ascribe their death to a shipwreck.

45 *a curule chair and an ivory staff*: the symbols of the highest Roman magistracies.

46 *the plot*: this episode joined the rest of the charges conventionally made against Perseus and can be found in the inscription at Delphi. Scholars have argued, however, that Eumenes invented the attempt on his life from an entirely coincidental landslide. Many of the details Livy provides, including the nature of the terrain, the use of boulders as weapons, the subsequent cascading of rocks, and the disappearance of the assassins, support this interpretation. For a sceptical account of the episode, see N. G. L. Hammond and F. W. Walbank, *A History of Macedonia*, vol. 3 (Oxford, 1988; repr. 2001), p.499.

dragged across the neck of the Isthmus: in antiquity, ships could be hauled across the Isthmus on a special track. Although various attempts were made (from Periander in the sixth century BCE to Nero in the first century CE) to put in a canal, the idea was not realized until the end of the nineteenth century.

Aegina: an island in the middle of the Saronic Gulf (Map 3). At the time of these events it was under the control of Pergamum and so a safe place to take the injured Eumenes.

courting his wife with unseemly speed: Livy has chosen to give a condensed version of a story other authors found rather juicy. According to Plutarch (*Moralia* 184 B and 489 E–F), Eumenes' 'widow' Stratonice and Attalus actually married. Despite indications of rivalry between the brothers, which Livy develops, they reigned as co-monarchs. Attalus succeeded Eumenes in 158 and married Stratonice upon his brother's actual death. Eumenes' son (Attalus III) succeeded his uncle in turn in 138.

48 *King Ariarathes*: king of Cappadocia and father-in-law of Eumenes; he became a Roman ally after the war with Antiochus.

a ward of the state: this brief notice about Ariarathes illustrates Livy's pro-Roman bias and sources. By contrast, the account found in the Greek historian Diodorus Siculus makes the Romans into incidental pawns rather than world leaders. According to Diodorus, the boy (also named Ariarathes) was not the biological child of his parents, but one of two pseudo-heirs Ariarathes' wife procured when she could not have children of her own. When she subsequently produced two daughters and a son (originally named Mithridates), she had the first two boys shipped off to Rome and Ionia respectively to make way for Mithridates. In fact, the son sent to Ionia turned out so well that he ultimately won his 'father's' heart and inherited the kingdom (Diodorus Siculus 31.19). Prusias of Bithynia also sent a son to Rome, ostensibly for the upbringing he would receive but more probably to eliminate him as a rival. (See 45.44 and Appian, *Mithridatic Wars* 4.) A comparison with other sources thus reveals the many sides of Hellenistic diplomacy.

49 *columna rostrata*: this victory monument was a column decorated with the prows (Latin *rostra*) of ships taken in a battle off the coast of Sicily in 255. Shortly after this signal victory, almost the entire Roman fleet was destroyed in a storm (Polybius 1.36–7).

50 *the consulship of Quintus Fulvius and Lucius Manlius*: 179.

51 *the treaty established by Publius Scipio*: the peace settlement at the end of the Second Punic War in 201.

53 *having met with . . . on their departure*: there seems to be a pointed contrast here with the Romans' generous and even-handed treatment of the embassies from the Carthaginians and Gulussa as described at the end of the previous chapter. For Livy, one of Perseus' 'barbaric' characteristics is ignoring the rules of hospitality. Note also the interaction between the Senate and the Illyrians in the next chapter.

54 *worthy of record*: Livy's curt dismissal of the consuls' diplomatic achievements in this year epitomizes the Roman attitude towards 'foreign affairs'. Consuls earned recognition from military success and conquest, not responsible diplomacy.

envoys from Issa: Issa is an island off the coast of Illyricum (Map 2); the Greek city there was under Roman protection.

56 *at least 150 senators . . . at the time*: the Republican Senate traditionally consisted of 300 men, but the actual size at any point in time may have

been smaller, and full attendance was in any case unlikely, given the occupations and duties of the senatorial class. The general silence in the ancient sources suggests that there was no fixed quorum. The only two explicit references to a quorum in the second century occur here and in the regulations governing the worship of Bacchus, in which the Senate chose to interfere rather aggressively in 186: people seeking exemptions had to do so at meetings attended by at least 100 senators (39.8–19, confirmed by an inscription of 186 containing the text of the decree, the *Senatus Consultum de Bacchanalibus*, now in the Kunsthistorische Museum in Vienna).

56 *a shameful end*: Roman attitudes towards suicide varied with the circumstances: hanging was an ignoble route.

57 *Coele Syria*: in the Hellenistic period Coele (the Greek word for 'hollow') Syria comprised the valley running south-east from Tripolis (in modern Lebanon) to Damascus (in modern Syria). The area was a source of dispute between the Ptolemaic and Seleucid kings for centuries. This particular campaign (of Antiochus IV against Ptolemy VI) is known as the Sixth Syrian War (171–168).

58 *for the better part of the year*: the *lectisternium* is most frequently referred to as a discrete ceremony. From this passage and one other in Livy (36.1), however, it appears that some divinities were worshipped with semi-permanent *lectisternia*.

comitia centuriata: in origin, the military assembly of the Roman people, which alone had the power to declare war.

59 *in his absence*: see 41.15.

60 *in order of arrival rather than by experience*: in this period, centurions were officers selected from and by the ranks and received their positions according to their abilities. (For the different levels of centurions, see the note to p. 61 on the divisions of the army.) The objection here is that the military tribunes are not distinguishing among the different ranks of centurions when in fact—as will be illustrated in Spurius Ligustinus' speech in chap. 34—a centurion's position reflected his experience, skill, and achievement.

the official seats of the tribunes: in the Forum, near the Curia.

61 *of the Crustuminian tribe*: Roman tribes were voting districts, and to state one's tribe was a way of identifying oneself as a Roman citizen. The use of the word 'tribe' to translate Latin *tribus* is unfortunate since the English derivative connotes a political and social entity based on ethnicity. This meaning is anachronistic for Rome.

toga virilis . . . toga praetexta: see Glossary. By identifying which kind of toga his sons wear, Spurius Ligustinus is indicating their ages.

in the consulship of Publius Sulpicius and Gaius Aurelius: 200.

hastati: one of the main divisions of the Roman legion. In his history of Rome's conquest of the Mediterranean, Polybius describes in detail the army's organization. In ascending order of age, experience, and importance were the *hastati*, the *principes*, and the *triarii*. Each of these was subdivided into ten companies or maniples, each of which had two centurions. A centurion of the tenth company of the *hastati* was thus the least prestigious, and the first centurion of the first company of the *triarii* the most important in that tier of the legion. Spurius eventually became the highest-ranking centurion of all, the *primus pilus* (or chief centurion), who commanded the company of the *triarii* that stood on the right end of the line. For a longer account, see Book 6 of Polybius and L. Keppie, *The Making of the Roman Army*, rev. edn. (London, 1998), chap. 1.

the consul Marcus Porcius: in 195.

the praetor Quintus Fulvius Flaccus . . . the praetor Tiberius Sempronius Gracchus: Fulvius was governor of Nearer Spain in 182–180. (In 180 he vowed the temple to Juno that was subsequently his undoing.) Tiberius Sempronius Gracchus held the position for 180–178.

62 *six civic crowns*: a civic crown was the reward for saving a Roman citizen's life in battle.

four soldiers to take my place: i.e. his four sons.

The Latin Festival . . . earlier for their provinces: the Latin Festival did not have a predetermined date, but was set each year by the consuls. As they were the main participants, the ceremony normally took place before they left Rome for the campaigning season.

city legions: reserve troops.

63 *envoys from King Perseus arrived*: Livy describes this embassy again in chap. 48 below. Here his source is annalistic; there it is Polybius. The Polybian version is more reliable.

He brought forward as accusations . . . setting into motion: this is a pro-Roman version of events. Perseus' invasion of Perrhaebia, in northern Thessaly, is described as taking place only later (chaps. 53 and 54), and in the previous account of his trip through Thessaly (41.22 and 23), there was no mention of any towns being taken. Further, in chaps. 42 and 67 below Perseus appears to have alliances with three towns in Thessaly.

64 *as spoils of war*: in the first third of the second century, the Achaean League was the dominant political force in the Peloponnese. The Messenians and the Eleans became members in 191, after Antiochus III was defeated at Thermopylae.

the Orestae: these people lived on the borders of Epirus and Macedonia and had been under Macedonian control. They were granted autonomy by the Romans in 196, in the wake of the war against Philip; their freedom was a reward for having been the first to rebel against him (Polybius 18.47 and Livy 33.34). It is quite possible that the Romans wanted to hamper the Macedonians by supporting neighbours likely to be hostile to them.

65 *the Acarnanians*: they had sided with first Philip and then Antiochus against the Romans.

65 *Boeotian exiles*: Livy gives the background of these men in chap. 43. They and Ismenias, mentioned below, represent two different factions at Thebes.

to grant each city autonomy: Boeotia comprised multiple distinct city-states. These had been in a league of one kind or another almost continuously since the sixth century. Thebes was the largest and frequently most dominant city-state. In fostering autonomy among the cities, Marcius' desire was not to promote the liberty of the smaller ones, but to dissolve the league. The date of the formation of the alliance with Perseus is uncertain, but it was probably during the magistracy of Ismenias.

the gift of their freedom: in 196, after the war with Philip, the Thessalians were among the people declared free by the Romans.

the bond of amity and of the guest-friendship with Philip: there is almost certainly some confusion here. The guest-friendship was probably established between Philip and Marcius himself, not his father (as just noted).

68 *to go into exile*: neither the Greeks nor the Romans used long prison sentences to punish criminals. Exile or death served to remove wrongdoers from their community.

Grant that I was justified in fighting: according to Appian's summary of the events leading up to the war, the Romans renewed their treaty with Perseus after he defeated Abrupolis, so it appears that previously they had not regarded Perseus' behaviour as a violation of the treaty (Appian, *Macedonian Wars* 11.6).

70 *had been made public*: a reference back to chap. 38, where the Romans told the representatives of the Boeotian exiles that the cities in their league would soon be able to act independently and thus it would be clear whether they had supported the making of a treaty with Perseus.

a different factional quarrel: Livy gives a compressed and almost unintelligible account of a complicated political battle at Thebes that had consequences for the entire Boeotian League. There appear to have been pro-Macedonian and anti-Macedonian factions in the city. At the elections for the leading magistracies (the 'praetor' and the 'boeotarchs' or magistrates of the Boeotian League), the pro-Macedonians won. Some of their opponents managed to convince an assembly of the voters to pass a measure banning the victorious contestants from entering any population centre (effectively a vote of exile). Then public opinion swung back, and the newly elected officials were recalled. They retaliated by exiling the men responsible for driving them out. Consequently the Romans had two groups of Boeotians to deal with: Ismenias and his party, who supported a united Boeotia and the alliance with Perseus, and the 'exiles', who had initially resisted the election of Ismenias and who did not favour the alliance. The Romans backed the latter group.

71 *Coronaei and Haliarti*: Coronea and Haliartus are cities in Boeotia (Map 3).

72 *tainted with the suspicion of having taken bribes from the Illyrian kings*: unfortunately, there is no other evidence pertaining to Decimius' conduct.

73 *Thebes*: here a misreading for Thisbe, another Boeotian city; the mistake goes back to the text of Polybius (27.5).

74 *they could not recognize Roman practices in this embassy*: the passage that follows has interested students both of Roman history and of Livy's interpretation of it. To see the episode as marking a literal turning point is probably simplistic, but both Livy and Polybius (the source here) traced what they saw as the decline of Roman national character. Philippus' behaviour presents an excellent opportunity to moralize about that decline.

even to announce . . . to fight: Polybius praises the Romans for their honourable conduct in war (13.3). Traditional phalanx warfare generally required the opponents to determine when and where they would fight. Starting with the Peloponnesian War, Greek armies made increasing use of light-armed infantry, with its greater ability to manoeuvre. From Paris' archery in the *Iliad* on, however, men whose equipment (such as bows and arrows or the javelin) allowed them to fight from a distance were regarded as cowardly. It is possible that the style of warfare attributed to the Romans of 'the good old days' is simply a way of reinforcing the moral commentary and is not a literal account of tactics. (On the moral implications of Greek land warfare, see chapter 2 of Victor Hanson's *The Western Way of War: Infantry Battle in Classical Greece*, second edn., Berkeley, 2000.)

Pyrrhus' doctor . . . the Falisci: for Pyrrhus, see the note to p. 35. The attempt to betray him to the Romans was famous. Livy's fullest version occurs in one of the now lost books (Book 13). In the story of the Faliscan schoolmaster, as told by Livy, the teacher leads his pupils to the Romans and offers them as bargaining chips in the Romans' war against the neighbouring city of Falerii. Under the leadership of Camillus, the Romans nobly reject his offer and return the children to their families; the Falisci are so impressed that they surrender their city (5.27). See also 24.24.

artifice: Livy uses the word *ars* three times in this passage: Marcius boasts of breaking up the Boeotian League *arte* (skilfully); the old men reply that they cannot recognize Roman *artes* (practices) in his double-dealing; then they conclude that a true victory cannot be won *arte* (by artifice). Like its English cognate 'art', the Latin word has both positive and negative connotations, and Livy seems to be playing with them here.

Perseus' envoys: another version of the embassy Livy describes in chap. 36. Here he follows Polybius.

76 *a more belligerent cast of mind*: the paragraph that follows is an excellent example of Livy's ability to present events from a non-Roman perspective. The Macedonian war party is critical of Rome, regarding it as too oppressive and pointing out its vulnerability. Yet, at the same time, this anti-Roman view ends up revealing Rome's greatness: Macedonia is the last major power within striking distance of Rome, and it too will fall.

77 *Samothrace*: an instance of foreshadowing; this island became Perseus' last refuge. See the beginning of Book 45.

77 *attempt to take over the kingdom*: Perseus' rivalry with his younger brother
Demetrius is related in Book 40. Philip used his second son as an ambassador in his dealings with the Romans. Demetrius, however, became a Roman
sympathizer and apparently wanted to supplant his brother as their father's
heir. With Philip's connivance, Perseus had Demetrius killed in 180.

Alcidemos: an epithet meaning 'strength of the people'. Athena (Roman
Minerva) appears as a warrior on Macedonian coinage.

courtiers: the Latin word is *purpurati*, or 'men dressed in purple'. Because
the colour is hard to produce with natural dyes, it was expensive and associated with wealth and monarchy.

all the soldiers in a plain: the following list of forces is considered accurate
and authoritative, deriving ultimately from Macedonian sources,
specifically the so-called 'King's Journal', a daily record of what the
Macedonian king said and did. (See Hammond and Walbank, *History of
Macedonia*, vol. 3, pp. 18 and 515.) There are two types of infantry: the
phalanx, consisting of heavily armed foot soldiers with long spears that
could be wielded from a distance, and 'peltasts', who had lighter armour
and were consequently more mobile.

'agema': a Macedonian king's bodyguard.

Eulyestae: this name is almost certainly wrong (since it is otherwise
unknown). Editors and translators have suggested and sometimes printed
other names.

the young Demetrius: for Didas' role in Demetrius' death, see 40.21–4; Livy
sets up the rivalry between Perseus and his brother in Book 40 partly as
an introduction to the Romans' war against Perseus.

78 *a misleading conference*: Livy again gives a foreigner's perspective on
Roman behaviour. Perseus' characterization of the negotiators reinforces
the view of the older senators and so reminds Livy's audience of the
theme of Roman degeneracy.

79 *the Red Sea*: this is the usual term in Roman sources for the Persian Gulf
and the modern Red Sea; but it could be applied, as here, to bodies of
water even farther east.

80 *Larisa*: it had a Roman garrison at this point (chap. 47).

81 *a major reverse*: although Polybius' text for this period survives in fragments only, there is enough to show that he is Livy's main source for the
campaign that follows. Livy chooses to represent the consul, Publius
Licinius Crassus, and Perseus as foils for one another. Here the Roman
avoids a major defeat through Perseus' lack of initiative; in chap. 66 he
shies away from inflicting one on the king. Crassus is about to go on the
offensive because he hears that the Macedonians are raiding fields in
Thessaly; in chap. 64 Perseus reacts in a similar fashion upon learning of
Roman foraging. Throughout, the men's responses to success and failure
constitute an underlying message about the essential strength of the
Roman character and the corresponding weakness of the Macedonian.

82 *with his ships*: in chap. 47 Quintus Marcius Philippus was sent to Greece with a contingent of ships and a vaguely worded remit to do what 'seemed to him to be in the best interests of the state'.

'Hanging' Larisa: Larisa 'Cremaste' overlooks the northern shore of the entrance to the Euripus, the strait between Euboea and the mainland; it should not be confused with Larisa, one of the main Thessalian cities, which features elsewhere in the narrative.

83 *the enemy cavalry came into view*: i.e. the Romans.

84 *a small hill called Callinicus*: in modern treatments of the war, the ensuing cavalry battle is generally referred to as Callicinus, in accordance with the name that appears in V; Callinicus was conjectured by the nineteenth-century editor Madvig.

the Sacred Squadron: the men wore heavy armour and fought in formation with spears or lances, as opposed to the regular Macedonian cavalry which had lighter equipment and weaponry.

85 *with his first assault*: the apparently abrupt shift to Perseus' decisive cavalry charge results from the partially illegible condition of this section of the manuscript.

86 *the Aetolians*: according to Polybius, the Roman-backed leader of the Aetolians (see chap. 38) engineered the downfall of at least three of these men to enhance his position with the Romans (Polybius 27.15).

87 *the king went . . . camp there*: in contrast to this rousing speech that Livy has Perseus deliver, the king does not attack the Roman camp. The gap between word and deed implicitly undermines Perseus' credibility.

88 *spread through Greece*: almost all of the previous chapter and the first part of chap. 63 correspond closely to Polybius (27.8–9). The variations, however, add up to significantly different presentations. Livy, for example, intuits Perseus' motivation, saying that he was always receptive to advice and that he continued to negotiate with Crassus out of fear. These motives do not appear in Polybius. Together they portray Perseus as weak. Further, while Livy has adopted Polybius' explanation of the general reaction to the Romans' defeat, his version is considerably condensed. Polybius goes on to describe exactly how spectators respond at a boxing match and gives a particular example involving two famous boxers. Their names and the competition would have meant nothing to Livy's audience, and he omits them.

90 *the fields lay untouched*: as this section of the narrative makes evident, maintaining a food supply in hostile territory was a major undertaking for the Romans.

92 *The cestrosphondene . . . like a missile*: Livy's description is abbreviated and not easy to follow. According to Polybius (27.11), the firing device and the missile were each two hands (*c.*12 inches) long. The missile was, as Livy describes it, armed with three spines of wood like feathers on an arrow, and the main shaft had two straps, which held the missile in place.

They were twisted taut, and then one was released sending the missile to its target. A Thessalian coin from the period has been identified as representing the cestrosphondene. (See J. Warren, 'Two Notes on Thessalian Coins', *Numismatic Chronicle* (1961), 1–8 and plate 1.)

94 *Pteleum*: Roman spelling of Pteleon, mentioned at chap. 42.

BOOK FORTY-THREE

95 *The Senate . . . to so many peoples*: the Senate's reaction here sheds light on Roman governance. Magistrates had wide discretionary power while away from Rome, and no written provision precluded Cassius' action. His senatorial peers, however, clearly perceive his conduct as an abuse of his position and dereliction of duty.

96 *Marcus Porcius Cato . . . Gaius Sulpicius Galus*: at least three of these men had significant experience in Spain and may have been known personally to the members of the embassies. Cato was consul there in 195 and proconsul the following year. This Scipio was praetor for Farther Spain in 194, but in addition, his father, uncle, and famous cousin Africanus had all commanded Roman armies there. Paullus was praetor for Farther Spain in 191, and a promagistrate there the two subsequent years. Although there has been conjecture about a connection between Galus and Spain, it cannot be documented.

the consulship of Aulus Manlius and Marcus Junius: 178.

the consulship of Spurius Postumius and Quintus Mucius: 174.

the consulship of Lucius Postumius and Marcus Popillius: 173.

97 *to exact money*: an interesting episode in Roman provincial relations. On the face of it, Canuleius colluded with the accused, and they got off lightly: Praeneste and Tibur are both only about twenty miles outside Rome. At the same time, the public careers of both men came to an abrupt halt, and the Senate instituted measures to protect the Spaniards in the future. The passage epitomizes Livy's advantages and disadvantages as a historical source from a modern perspective. This is the first explicit reference to the fact that the Spaniards were required to sell 5 per cent of their grain to the Romans, but the practice almost certainly goes back to the 190s. Livy, however, mentions it only because he is tracing the increasingly corrupt behaviour of the Romans. This interest in morality, rather than the modern desire to understand provincial administration, accounts for his inclusion of the episode.

marriages recognized by Roman law: a critical point. The women, as foreigners by birth, did not have what the Romans termed *conubium*, the right to make a marriage whose offspring automatically received Roman citizenship.

a Latin colony: i.e. the inhabitants have the juridical status of Latins. They were partially enfranchised Roman allies with the right to make contracts under Roman law, the right to form a Roman law marriage (such as was unavailable to their parents), and possibly the right to move to Rome and be registered as Roman citizens in the census. The last component was problematic, as is apparent in 41.8–9. The creation of Carteia was a revolutionary step in Roman legal and constitutional history. For the first time the concept of Latinity was transported overseas. In addition, it appears from this passage that any former slaves of the colonists (the freedmen referred to) and current occupants of the city also could enrol as Latins and receive land and rights. Carteia was a unique foundation. (See J. S. Richardson, *The Romans in Spain* (Oxford, 1996).)

some Carthaginians: Livy here picks up a narrative thread last treated in 42.23 and 24.

99 *Antium*: modern Anzio, less than thirty-five miles from Rome, on the western coast of Italy (Map 2).

the same decree: in practical terms, this response probably means that the pro-Roman faction was put in charge of Abdera. Coronea was one of the three Boeotian cities not to cooperate with the Romans in this period. Somewhere in the lost section of Book 43 is the description of how Licinius attacked and took it. The Senate then issued a decree about its reorganization. A copy of part of this has been found. As an editor of the decree suggests, the Senate gave control of the city to Roman sympathizers (Sherk, *Roman Documents*, 32–3).

100 *he gave satisfaction*: there is no evidence Cassius ever had to face these accusations; he went directly from his consulship to service as a military tribune under Hostilius, the consul assigned to Macedonia for the following year (as noted at the beginning of this chapter and at 44.31).

101 *that divinity*: Alabanda, modern Arabhisar, in western Asia Minor (Map 4). This is the second earliest example (after Smyrna in 195, as noted in Tacitus, *Annals* 4.65) of a Greek community honouring Rome by recognizing the personified spirit of the state as a deity. Cults for individuals, cities, and abstractions were a regular part of Hellenistic religious practice. For Alabanda to honour Rome in this way does not mean that the inhabitants thought Rome was an actual goddess, but rather that it was important enough to be celebrated with a temple and a festival. In the Hellenistic world, establishing cults was a way of creating a bond with another community.

102 *his request had been denied*: any kind of severe physical handicap was considered an acceptable explanation for not undertaking public service.

103 *for the freedom of Greece*: by this point in Greek and Roman history, it was commonplace to claim freeing others as an explanation for war. The liberation of a people usually meant simply the exchange of one overlord for another. The liberation of the Greeks became a rallying cry in the late fifth century, but the idea probably goes back to the Ionian Revolt a century earlier. The Romans' use of the slogan illustrates their familiarity with the language of Greek diplomacy.

104 *Uscana*: about thirty miles north of Lychnidus (Map 3).

104 *the fourth watch*: the last quarter of the night, presumably here just as day broke.

106 *the Terminalia*: a festival for Terminus, the god of boundaries and thus of ends. He signified permanence and stability for the Romans because, according to a tradition reported by Livy (1.55), when the last king of Rome, Tarquinius Superbus, wanted to deconsecrate the Tarpeian Mount in order to dedicate it to Jupiter alone, Terminus' shrine was the only one which the auguries would not allow to be relocated. His festival took place on 23 February.

the augur, died <. . .>: there is no indication of his successor, and editors have posited that the manuscript is missing some text.

107 *meritorious of public attention*: one of the more famous passages in Livy. It has generally been cited to illustrate his traditional outlook and empathic (rather than analytical) attitude towards his subject. Levene has argued, however, that the passage must be read in its context, not as applying to the entire text. It introduces an unusually long and developed prodigy list at a time when Roman public morality was deeply flawed. Since Livy's stated intention is to trace the rise and fall of the Romans' greatness as expressed in their character and conduct, it makes sense that he dwells on signs of divine disapproval when the Romans are behaving deplorably. As Levene concludes, Livy relates the momentary moral decline in this period to the worse and more intractable collapse to come (D. S. Levene, *Religion in Livy* (Leiden, 1993), 113–16).

impluvium: a large basin set in the middle of the *atrium* (the central room of a Roman house); the *atrium* was open to the sky, and the *impluvium* was designed to catch and store rainwater. As this passage suggests, the word may sometimes refer not just to the basin itself, but also to the central area of the *atrium*.

wreaths: an extra measure, presumably to communicate to the gods just how seriously the Romans regard the prodigies. For example, at a two-day supplication in 180 the people wore wreaths and carried laurel branches (40.37).

108 *their censors*: here begins the first of three descriptions of these censors' activities (43.14–16, 44.16, and 45.15). This one concerns their efforts to promote conscription and the severity with which they handled the letting of contracts; the latter subject leads to their own trial for treason. The second is a more conventional summary of their actions. The third deals with the shifting of freedmen into a single urban voting district. Livy's decision to distribute the material in this manner is indicative of the free manner in which he treats so-called 'annalistic material'. The censors' term lasted one and a half years; Livy weaves their activities in at the relevant points in his narrative.

the younger men: (*iuniores*) those between 17 and 46. Ordinarily, they were the ones to perform military service. In this war, however, those over 46, the 'older men' (*seniores*), also served (see 42.31 and 32).

the consulship of Publius Aelius and Gaius Popillius: 172.

father or grandfather: a reference to the institution of *patria potestas* (paternal power). The *paterfamilias* or 'head of household' was the only person fully recognized by Roman law. He represented anyone under his power, ordinarily his children and their issue, and sometimes his wife (depending on the type of marriage). It is difficult to draw firm general conclusions about the evidence for the age at which most children, male and female, were likely to become legally independent, either by a formal ceremony or by the death of their *paterfamilias*. An adult male might well still be under his father's power; if so, the grandchildren were represented by the grandfather.

109 *Caepio*: Gnaeus Servilius Caepio, the consul just mentioned.

princeps senatus: leader of the Senate. It was an honorary title, with symbolic rather than constitutional significance. The censors conferred it on the man whom they listed first on the roll of the Senate.

the equestrians: for this class, see the Glossary. It is not known why the censors of 169 wanted to exclude men who had held contracts under their predecessors.

110 *Tiberius Sempronius*: up to this point Livy mostly calls the censor Tiberius Sempronius. His full name, however, was Tiberius Sempronius Gracchus, and in the following episode he is referred to as Gracchus and Tiberius Gracchus as well.

111 *suppliants*: presumably members of the Senate, whose rings and tunics with broad purple stripes distinguished them from ordinary citizens. By removing the visible signs of their status, they are putting themselves on the same level as the people whose mercy they seek.

114 *Conquerors*: Livy's word is 'Nicatores'; it apparently refers to an elite corps.

115 *for <. . . > days*: one, two, and three days have been conjectured.

BOOK FORTY-FOUR

118 *a single day's march for someone lightly equipped*: Livy consistently treats thirty or thirty-five miles as the distance that can be covered in one day by someone travelling light. As he describes Marcius' campaign in Book 44, it is useful to keep this figure in mind as a comparison point; the regular army can advance about seven miles a day, depending on the terrain, while lighter-armed troops can cover twice that distance.

treated the allies . . . maltreatment: a favourable version of Hostilius' consulship. Because of the incomplete state of Book 43, he is relatively obscure for a consul. The information in Livy mostly concerns his dealings with the allies (e.g. 43.4, 9, and 17). Other sources record significant episodes of his consulship: Perseus' failed attempt to have him kidnapped, Perseus' victory over him at Elimea, and a subsequent challenge to combat that Hostilius declined.

118 *the gods smiled on dutifulness and constancy*: while Livy himself rarely invokes the gods as agents in human affairs, his characters do, and the gods certainly have a place in his world view and his understanding of historical explanation. It is always important to have the gods' favour. Here, since Livy is showing the war beginning to swing in the Romans' direction, it is appropriate to have an explicit reminder that the gods are on their side.

119 *which way each of them would take*: Marcius begins in southern Thessaly and must either cross mountains or go a long way to the west to reach Macedonia (Map 3). Geography favours Perseus, except that he cannot know the Romans' route in advance and must prepare for as many eventualities as possible.

a base between Azorus and Doliche: at this point Marcius was joined by Polybius, who came as part of an embassy from the Achaean League and ended up participating in the Roman invasion of Macedonia (Polybius 28.13). Thus the details of the invasion are based on an eyewitness account, but Livy was highly selective in his use of Polybius, omitting the diplomatic activity recorded by the Greek historian. For example, according to Polybius, in this period Rhodian envoys approached Marcius and were encouraged by him, on the sly, to continue their attempts to end the war between Perseus and Rome (Polybius 28.17). Livy says nothing about the episode, and scholars continue to debate whether it happened.

around Dium: Asclepiodotus is protecting a major pass through the Cambunian Mountains; Hippias is guarding the south side of Mount Olympus; and Perseus is blocking the coastal path.

before returning to Dium by the same route: Livy depicts Perseus as irrational but, as has been noted, Perseus may have been making systematic sweeps with the cavalry in order to intercept the Romans whenever and wherever they reached the coast (see Loeb edn., trans. A. C. Schlesinger (Cambridge, Mass., 1951), 97).

120 *where one of Perseus' generals had established his camp*: the Lake Ascuris route, monitored by Hippias.

121 *a course of action . . . in the end*: as Livy's language here and in subsequent passages reveals, Marcius' decision was not necessarily the most prudent one. He was in a difficult position since retreating would presumably have damaged his reputation and given him no tactical advantage. It is worth noting that a similarly rash campaign in his previous consulship resulted in defeat and 4,000 casualties (39.20). Apparently, Marcius did not learn enough from that experience. Livy, however, chooses to describe Marcius' decision in positive terms as part of his larger agenda of showing improvement in Rome's fortunes.

had boldly undertaken: Livy's analysis of the two leaders is moral rather than strategic. Philippus' advance has been considered both courageous and foolhardy; it was at least more effective than Hostilius' cautious approach the year before. As for Perseus, he simply did not foresee that the Romans would attempt such a difficult route.

122 *the more horizontal terrain of the valley floor*: although some of the mechanical details have been omitted or garbled, this feat of engineering is apparently factual. Scullard notes that elephants cannot bend their legs sufficiently to descend at steep angles, and Polybius, Livy's source, was with the Romans on this march. As remarkable as it sounds, the Romans forced their way over the shoulder of Mount Olympus and brought more than thirty elephants down to the Macedonian coast (see H. H. Scullard, *The Elephant in the Greek and Roman World* (Ithaca, NY, 1974), 182–4).

the enemy was nearby: the Romans were within thirty miles of Perseus, and their desperate push across the mountains must have been quite a shock.

123 *through Tempe . . . into Macedonia*: in other words, barring a retreat back over the mountains, the Romans would have met Macedonian forces whether they attempted to continue to invade north along the coast or decided to withdraw to the south through Tempe.

stolen the king's wits: another reference to the gods to indicate that the Romans again enjoy divine favour.

124 *any violation of its sacred area*: Marcius' instructions emphasize Roman piety.

Pieria: the district of Macedonia between the mountains to the south and the Thermaic Gulf to the east (Map 3). Marcius advances through it at a rate of approximately ten miles a day.

no safe way to proceed far beyond it: the emphasis on Marcius' difficulties with supplies probably reflects Polybius' first-hand experience. Here Marcius makes what appears to be a sound choice: he cannot guarantee a supply of food, and the penetration of Macedonia does not seem to bring him any strategic or military advantage.

125 *in extremely short supply*: Livy is not concerned with noting the duration of the invasion, but the narrative has enough references to the passage of time for a rough count to show that the troops must have nearly consumed the rations they were originally directed to bring.

126 *arms, siege-works, and machines*: Livy specifies three kinds of weaponry here. One type (*arma*) seems to be hand-held while the other two are larger artillery (*machinae* and *opera*). The latter two, however, are regularly paired in his narrative and are apparently used generically rather than to refer to particular siege engines. Equipment of this kind was highly specialized in ancient warfare, and technical treatises were written on the subject. See, for example, the discussion in Livy's contemporary Vitruvius, who concludes his 10-volume work on architecture with seven chapters on offensive and defensive machines (Vitruvius, *On Architecture* 10.10–16).

testudo: a Latin word meaning turtle or tortoise in particular and shell in general. To assault walls, troops of Roman soldiers encased themselves in their shields, thus forming a protective shell. Part of Polybius' description of the manoeuvre here survives (28.11). Where the Greek historian regards the *testudo* as a curiosity, Livy adapts its deployment on this occasion to fit into his tracing of the historical contours of Roman morality.

127 *Gaius Marcius*: a cousin of the consul (Quintus Marcius Philippus) and the praetor in charge of the fleet. Livy now turns to naval operations, and in chaps. 10–12, 'Marcius' refers to the praetor, not the consul.

128 *Cassandrea*: a city on the site of archaic and classical Potidaea, which was originally founded by Corinthians. In Thucydides' account of the Peloponnesian War, the city was a major source of friction. In the generation after Alexander the Great, the Macedonian king Cassander refounded it and named it after himself. The site is strategically located at the neck of the peninsula of Pallene (Map 3).

King Eumenes: he last appeared in the narrative when the Romans won their minor victory at Phalanna in 171 (42.65–7). He then returned to Pergamum. Elaea, on the coast of Asia Minor, was the port of Pergamum (Map 4).

decked vessels: warships; the term indicates that Livy has a Greek source (Polybius); when the source is Roman, this type of craft is called a 'long ship'.

Archways were pointed out to him: the relationship between the missing dirt and the archways—and between the praetor's question and the answer given—is unclear. Apparently the soil was made into bricks, and the arches were constructed from them.

129 *set out for Demetrias*: a radical change of direction. The fleet is returning to the Gulf of Pagasae in Thessaly (Map 3).

at the first assault: a striking and no doubt intentional contrast with Perseus' reaction to the Romans' arrival. Livy uses some of the same language to describe Perseus' fear and that of the Meliboeans. The Romans' siege of the city fails, thereby implicitly showing the rewards of fortitude (as opposed to Perseus' cowardice).

130 *did withdraw from the city*: Livy does not explore the question of whether or not Eumenes attempted negotiations. Polybius, on the other hand, discusses at length the relationship and motives of Perseus and Eumenes (29.5–9). Livy evidently still wants to maintain Eumenes' reputation (as is apparent in the following paragraph; see the next note) while Polybius thinks it is essential to understand the consequential actions of leaders, even if information about those actions is incomplete.

completely different stories about King Eumenes: an effective use of a variant tradition to influence the way the audience perceives events. After three chapters where Eumenes and Marcius Figulus have been coordinating efforts, Livy draws attention to a version where Eumenes was uncooperative and his brother Attalus assisted the Romans. This alternative version probably reflects the fact that Eumenes eventually lost the Romans' favour while Attalus remained a loyal ally. By mentioning it, Livy maintains the favourable presentation of Eumenes which is central to the attack on Perseus' character, but also prefigures his loss of popularity.

131 *philippei*: valuable coins introduced by Philip II of Macedon in the fourth century.

from the Rhodians: the Roman annalistic version of an embassy to Rome in 167. Livy relays Polybius' version at 45.3 below. Given the stunning conclusion here, it seems that Livy found the patriotic version too good to omit. It is also possible that he failed to recognize and/or reconcile information in two different sources.

132 *the liberation of the Carians and the Lycians*: Livy twice notes the Lycians' resentment of their position (41.6 and 42.14), but the Senate's action, which actually happened after the war (Livy 45.25 and Polybius 30.4), was designed to punish the Rhodians and to demonstrate the Romans' power over them, not to redress wrongs done to the Carians and Lycians.

133 *Publius Rutilius . . . in his capacity as tribune of the plebs*: see 43.16 and note to p. 109.

Publius Africanus: Publius Cornelius Scipio Africanus, the Romans' victorious general in the war against Hannibal a generation earlier; Tiberius Sempronius married his daughter after Africanus' death.

the statue of Vortumnus: an Etruscan god whom the Romans associated with trade; the general area referred to is south of the Forum (Map 1).

135 *which allies seemed faithful to us*: unlike the other major Roman historians, Livy rarely aligns himself verbally with the Romans and tends to refer to them in the third person. The switch to the first person here makes the summary of Paullus' request more vivid.

the twelfth of April: in chap. 22, Livy reports that the Latin Festival was celebrated on 31 March. That is the day before the Kalends of April; 12 April is the day before the Ides of April. There is no way to judge the source of the error.

136 *clutching olive branches*: the untidy garments, the unkempt hair, and the olive branch all indicate suppliant status. In Livy's time defendants routinely tried to look as shabby as possible. At 29.16, the carrying of olive branches is referred to as a Greek practice.

the Quinquatrus: a festival lasting from 19 to 23 March. It celebrated both Mars and Minerva. See H. H. Scullard, *Festivals and Ceremonies of the Roman Republic* (Ithaca, NY, 1981), 92–4.

137 *our side . . . to force an engagement*: here again Livy switches from the third to the first person to convey the perspective of the commissioners as they address the Senate.

Eumenes . . . Attalus' resolute constancy was remarkable: earlier, when Livy narrated the campaigning in 169, Eumenes was depicted as a full participant in the naval war (chaps. 10–13); here, the historian has shifted to endorsing Attalus over Eumenes; see note to p. 130.

138 *nourish rumours . . . responsibility*: here Livy has Paullus introduce explicitly a theme that runs throughout Books 44 and 45, the misleading nature

of rumour and talk as opposed to solid information and actions. The idea is already implicit in Paullus' insistence on getting a field report before deciding how to conduct his campaign. Throughout his consulship, the ability to evaluate accurately words and deeds distinguishes sensible and admirable figures from fools.

139 *as Quintus Fabius did*: an early hero of the Second Punic War. He pursued the unpopular but successful strategy of avoiding a major engagement with Hannibal after the Carthaginian general had defeated the Romans multiple times. In the traditional version, the Roman people voted to give equal power to Fabius' second-in-command, Marcus Minucius Rufus. Minucius was lured into a trap by Hannibal and rescued by Fabius. At that point Minucius surrendered the power he had been voted and resumed his position as Fabius' subordinate. See Book 22. Livy uses Fabius as a model for Paullus in the campaign of 168, mostly tacitly; but the episode with Minucius is invoked explicitly again at 45.37.

140 *Meanwhile, because Perseus . . . king of the Illyrians*: this sentence introduces a lengthy section (chaps. 23–7) on Perseus' diplomatic manoeuvres in the second half of 169 and early 168 when he was actively pursuing allies. According to Livy, these were the Illyrians under Gentius, Eumenes, Antiochus, and a group of Gauls (the Bastarnae, cf. Perseus' previous dealings with them at 41.19). These chapters are organized thematically rather than chronologically: Livy uses the ultimate failure of all of Perseus' initiatives to illustrate his avarice.

the Romans had entered the pass: a reference to Marcius' surprise invasion in 169.

a reciprocal exchange of hostages: the first time Livy refers to Hippias' successful embassy to Gentius. Perseus' dealings with Gentius in this chapter are a selective version of Polybius (29.3–4). Perseus had been trying to win the Illyrian king's support for at least a year, but previously had been unwilling to pay for it (43.20 and 23).

oaths, hostages, and money: the ancient sources offer little insight into Pantauchus' influence over Gentius. Gentius was apparently willing to throw in his lot with the Macedonians, but his motivation is never made clear. He was cautious enough to want to wait until Perseus had fulfilled his part of the bargain: hence the Illyrian king's instructions to his men to delay their departure for Rhodes until after Perseus had complied with the agreement.

Metrodorus . . . from Rhodes: a Rhodian representing the pro–Macedonian faction in that city. His arrival in Thessalonica indicates prior communication between Perseus and the Rhodians.

141 *greater regard for Prusias than for Eumenes*: apparently a reference to the fact that Prusias had provided the Romans with at least minimal support in the war (the five ships mentioned at the end of chap. 10).

openly to Antiochus: nothing is known about Antiochus' response, if there was any. Presumably he was occupied with his attempt to take over Egypt.

a rivalry of trickery and greed: here Livy embarks on the history of the alleged negotiations between Eumenes and Perseus. This section is particularly difficult to follow because Livy groups all of Perseus' diplomatic efforts together. Although the focus at Rome has already shifted to Paullus and the imminent campaign of 168, Perseus and Eumenes' intermediaries started meeting while Eumenes was still with the Romans the year before.

Cydas: mentioned previously at chap. 13. He is introduced here as a key figure in Perseus and Eumenes' dealings.

142 *generated nothing but disrepute*: the material covered in the previous three paragraphs is a condensed version of Polybius (29.6–9). There are disadvantages and advantages to Livy's brevity. Without Polybius, it would be harder to understand that Cydas, Menecrates, and Antimachus are agents for Eumenes and Perseus. At the same time, since Polybius is interested in the relationship between the two kings, he pauses to analyse it at some length. Livy prunes away Polybius' commentary to summarize the kings' interactions and to highlight their weaknesses, especially Perseus' avarice. Here he follows Polybius in seeing it as a decisive factor in the Macedonian's downfall. Modern scholars, on the contrary, have pointed out that Perseus may have been wise not to waste precious resources on unreliable allies (Hammond and Walbank, *History of Macedonia*, vol. 3, p. 535). Ancient historians, however, invoked moral explanations, not economic ones. Perseus' fatal flaw is his character. The problem of whether Eumenes really did try to sell his loyalty has been a matter of longstanding scholarly debate. Livy does not question the story; for him it meshes with Eumenes' loss of favour at Rome.

Gallic auxiliaries, who had streamed down through Illyricum: Plutarch identifies these Gauls as the Bastarnae (*Aemilius Paullus* 12). Livy has not mentioned the alliance previously, but there must have been negotiations since both parties acknowledge the validity of the Gauls' demand to be paid for their services.

144 *Marcus Perperna and Lucius Petillius, who happened to have come to him in that period*: according to Appian, Petillius and Perperna were sent to Gentius after he made an incursion into the part of Illyricum under Roman control (*Macedonian Wars*, 18.2).

the person who was transporting the money: just above Livy refers to multiple bearers of the money; here he may mean the person in charge. The reason for the inconsistency is unclear.

145 *cutters*: smaller ships, with pointed prows; the term is Greek and was used for various kinds of large marine life with sharp noses. Chaps. 28 and 29 concern the war at sea.

Antenor promptly sailed around the island: with this sentence, Livy switches to the singular, and although Antenor's name does not appear here, he subsequently seems to be the officer giving the commands.

Sigeum: in Asia Minor, at the southern end of the Hellespont, and less than forty miles from the island of Tenedos (Map 4).

146 *protected them from one another*: Delos had a long history as holy ground. The sanctuary of Apollo was the most important, but there were shrines to many divinities.

147 *a favourable response was given to the kings*: Polybius (29.11) reports that there was a vigorous debate at Rhodes between the pro-Macedonian and the pro-Roman factions. Apparent indications of Perseus' success—the galleys, Roman cavalry losses, and the alliance with Gentius—wore down the pro-Roman group, and the ruling council decided to intervene to stop the war. The contrast between Polybius' and Livy's accounts suggests at least two of Livy's objectives. First, the Romans punished the Rhodians severely after the war, and the suppression of any debate here makes the Rhodians look more culpable. Secondly, Livy substitutes the story of the Gauls' arrival for the cavalry losses to which Polybius refers. Since the Gauls' help never materialized, the story is effectively a rumour, and the Rhodians' ill-fated choice can be seen as another example of the unreliability of hearsay.

Gentius: Livy now narrates Anicius' campaign against Gentius to dispose of it before his more extended treatment of the confrontation between Paullus and Perseus, which dominates the end of Book 44 and most of Book 45.

150 *before word reached Rome that it had begun*: the residual operations were administrative (45.26); the capture of Gentius effectively ended the campaign in Illyricum.

153 *the Illyrian hostages*: an obscure sentence. It seems more likely that the hostages referred to are the Macedonians left with Gentius, rather than the Illyrians handed over to Perseus; but this interpretation stretches the meaning of 'Illyrian' hostages.

the garrulity of the king's underlings: with this comment, Livy points again to the danger of loose talk.

occupied by strong garrisons: Livy has not previously indicated that Roman troops successfully assailed any Macedonian fortifications in 169. The claim may be intended merely to illustrate the character of the younger men (see the edn. by W. Weissenborn and H. J. Müller (Berlin, repr. 1967), *ad loc.*). Their combination of eagerness and poor judgement stands in implicit contrast to Paullus' deliberate approach to warfare.

154 *his own son, Quintus Fabius Maximus*: Paullus married twice and had four sons and two daughters. The sons from the first marriage were both adopted into important families: the son mentioned here, Quintus Fabius Maximus Aemilianus, was adopted by a son or grandson of the great dictator in the war against Hannibal; the younger of the two, Publius Cornelius Scipio, was adopted by a son of Scipio Africanus, who ultimately defeated Hannibal. Both of Paullus' older sons fought at Pydna and feature later in the narrative (chaps. 44 and 45). Adoption for dynastic purposes was not uncommon among the Roman elite, nor do Paullus' family connections end here: his sister (Aemilia) married Scipio

Africanus; one of his daughters married the son of Cato the Elder, and the other married Quintus Aelius Tubero (mentioned at 45.7), whom Plutarch praises for his noble character (*Aemilius Paullus* 5). Paullus' niece Cornelia, who was the oldest daughter of Scipio Africanus and Aemilia, was married to Scipio Nasica Corculum. Livy generally does not give biographical details, but the fate of the two younger sons is an important part of his characterization of Paullus and is foreshadowed by the attention paid to the older sons during the campaign. (For the younger sons, see 45.40–1.)

155 *lightweight shields or the Ligurian type*: the first kind of shield is the *parma*, which was small and round and usually used by cavalry and light infantry. The Ligurian shield was a four-foot oblong that covered nearly the whole body.

after the summer solstice: in fact, the Romans arrived at Pydna just before the summer solstice. The battle itself took place on 22 June; the date is established by the lunar eclipse described in the next chapter. Since Livy's date for the eclipse is 3 September, the official calendar was more than ten weeks ahead of the natural year in 168.

156 *the consul needed no less skill outwitting his own men than his opponent*: Livy's description of this scene reflects his own positive view of Paullus, which is shared by almost all ancient sources. What Livy depicts here as shrewd procrastination was probably absolute necessity: as Hammond points out, the Romans were not expecting to come upon the Macedonians and were totally unprepared for battle (Hammond and Walbank, *History of Macedonia*, vol. 3, pp. 549–51).

157 *from the second to the fourth hour*: see the note to p. 30

160 *Fortune . . . precipitated the battle*: the first reference to Fortune in this section of the text. Although no corresponding passage survives from Polybius, Livy was probably influenced by the Greek historian, who was interested in the role of chance and fate in history. The motif resurfaces in Book 45 as part of Livy's portrayal of Paullus.

a mule . . . towards the far bank: the sources are not consistent about whether a horse or a pack animal started the battle or just how it did so. Plutarch reports the tradition that Paullus precipitated the battle by having a horse driven towards the enemy so that when the Romans pursued it, fighting necessarily began (*Aemilius Paullus* 18). After his victory, Paullus erected a monument at Delphi with a frieze of scenes from Pydna; one includes a stray horse that has been taken to represent the animal Plutarch refers to. Plutarch says also that Paullus sacrificed twenty-one oxen to Hercules before receiving a favourable omen; it indicated, however, that the side that started the fighting would lose.

161 *Paullus*: I have supplied his name from the context.

more than sixty years old: Paullus' energy in spite of his advanced years makes him similar to Marcius Philippus, the most successful commander to date in the war against Perseus (see chap. 4).

161 *the phalanxes*: the core of the Macedonian infantry. Designed to fight as a tight unit, a phalanx's main offensive power consisted of the sarissa, a pike with a standard length of twenty-one feet at the time of Pydna. A well-trained and well-drilled phalanx on level ground was nearly invincible since the sarissas prevented close combat. At the same time, the strengths of the phalanx were also its weaknesses, as the battle at Pydna shows. An insufficiency of even terrain and any disruption to the phalanx's formation rendered it inoperable and vulnerable. Polybius discusses the advantages and disadvantages of the Macedonian phalanx and the Roman legion in the context of the battle of Cynoscephelae in 197, the most recent occasion when the two forces met (Polybius 18.28–32).

the 'Bronze Shields': simple description of the colour of the unit's equipment, as with the 'White Shields' in the next sentence.

useless—a mere name: the moralizing about novelties is translated and adapted from Polybius (29.17). Although Livy does not mention it, other sources report that Perseus tried to train his men to face the elephants. These 'elephant-fighters' had helmets and shields with special studs on them. Further, Perseus attempted to accustom horses to fight around elephants by constructing artificial ones imbued with an unpleasant odour (see Scullard, *The Elephant*, 184).

the force of a phalanx is irresistible: both Polybius (29.17) and Plutarch (*Aemilius Paullus* 19) report that in later years Paullus spoke of how terrifying he found the sight of the Macedonian phalanx. The passage in Polybius is preserved out of context but according to Plutarch, Paullus hid his fear and tried to inspire courage in his men by riding in front of them without his helmet and breastplate. There are so many textual gaps in Livy's description of the battle that it cannot be determined whether he included this apparently well-known story and if so, how he handled it.

162 *by far the majority of them were Paeligni*: while the astounding difference in the number of Macedonian and Roman casualties may seem implausible, there are parallels in ancient warfare, as Hammond has pointed out (N. G. L. Hammond, 'The Battle of Pydna', *Journal of Hellenic Studies*, 104 (1984), 41 n. 32). Based on the accounts of the battle in Livy and Plutarch, the circumstances were right for slaughter: once the phalanx was broken apart, the individual fighters were vulnerable to the Romans' training and style of weapons.

163 *Euctus and Eulaeus*: according to Plutarch, fair-weather friends who criticized Perseus so much after Pydna that Perseus stabbed them himself (*Moralia* 70 A).

Royal Pages: Livy explains who they are at 45.6.

the women rushed to the temple of Diana (whom they call Tauropolos) to implore her aid: the appearance of women in public is generally for Livy a sign of disorder: for example, the women of Rome pour into the streets after the defeats at Trasimene and Cannae in the early years of the war against

Hannibal (22.7 and 55), and Cato the Elder points to their demonstrating against a sumptuary law as an indication of moral decay (34.2–4).

The Roman Diana was assimilated to the Greek Artemis, who was worshipped widely among the Macedonians. The epithet *Tauropolos* has been interpreted as having to do with Tauris the place or *tauros* the animal (the bull). According to the first-century Greek historian Diodorus Siculus, when Alexander the Great died in 323, among his plans was the construction of a temple to Artemis Tauropolos at Amphipolis, but none of the plans were carried out (18.4). The temple Livy refers to has not been identified in excavations.

165 *the stronghold of Phacus rises like an island*: the storehouse for Perseus' treasury, a small fortification on a hill just south-west of the main city. The topography of the region around Pella has changed considerably since antiquity: the city now sits in a low plain while in Livy's day it could still be reached by water (Map 3).

BOOK FORTY-FIVE

167 *its presentiment in their minds*: this dramatic opening has clear thematic connections with Paullus' admonition to the Romans not to trust information from anyone but himself (44.22).

an equal appearance of truth: this phrase reflects a crucial standard of ancient historical writing: plausibility. As it remains today, the subject matter of history was past events. The historian's job was to explain the past so that it made sense. While historians were not supposed to lie or fabricate, their modes of explanation could be inventive and still regarded as valid. This sentence also indicates that Livy was treating his sources selectively here, and indeed comparison with other authors (such as Cicero, *On the Nature of the Gods* 2.6, and Valerius Maximus 1.8.1b) reveals that he is suppressing the version where immortal beings, sometimes specified as Castor and Pollux, brought word of the victory. For Livy, the theme of reliable information is more important than the indication of divine favour.

summoned the Senate there: ordinarily the Senate met in the Curia or a temple; this impromptu gathering appears to take place outside.

168 *men who had taken the oath of loyalty*: their identity is uncertain; the context makes clear that they are a different category from forces that were part of regular conscription.

169 *Illyricum was under the control of the Roman people*: at the conclusion of the Illyrian campaign, Livy says that Marcus Perperna brought the news to Rome (44.32). While the statement here may contradict the earlier notice and indicate that Livy was using two sources and repeated both of them, it is also possible that this is a second, fuller, and official communication from the praetor to the Senate.

169 *Some sources report*: Polybius' version (29.19) of the Rhodians' embassy described at 44.14–15. Polybius is regarded as the more reliable source; the previous, annalistic account has more patriotic appeal.

as was noted above: this information must have been reported in the lost text at the end of Book 44.

a letter from Perseus: with this letter begins Livy's use of Perseus as a direct foil for Paullus. Throughout Book 45, each of Perseus' shortcomings—e.g. vanity, lack of self-knowledge, absence of dignity—is matched by a strength in Paullus' character.

172 *Quintus Aelius Tubero*: Paullus' son-in-law. Characteristically, Livy does not mention the family connection.

King Syphax: a Numidian king who supported first Rome, then the Carthaginians in the Second Punic War. For his arrival at the camp of Scipio Africanus, see 30.13.

173 *in Greek*: as seems to have been the case with most educated Romans by the first half of the second century, Paullus was functionally bilingual. The shift here from Greek to Latin is pointed. It shows Paullus' erudition and his ability to choose the appropriate language, based on the audience and content of his remarks.

174 *winter quarters*: at this point it was probably August and so on the surface early to send the army into winter quarters, but the fighting was over for the year, and there was no reason to perpetuate the expense and logistical challenges of keeping forces in the field.

in the consulship of . . . and Aulus Manlius: Quintus Fulvius Flaccus and Lucius Manlius Acidinus were consuls in 179; Marcus Junius Brutus and Aulus Manlius Vulso were consuls in 178.

its ultimate demise: in this account of the rise and fall of Macedonia Livy is following Polybius, who found the subject a striking illustration of a treatise on Fortune written by Demetrius of Phaleron, an Athenian states-man (Polybius 29.21).

Antenor: Perseus' admiral (44.28).

When Gaius Popillius: it is generally agreed that Popillius' timing is not coincidental and that Roman intervention in the warring between the Seleucid and Ptolemaic dynasties was postponed until after the Macedonian defeat at Pydna.

175 *a capital sentence*: either exile or death.

176 *taken over the rest of Egypt*: Antiochus' Egyptian campaign was based on his alliance with his nephew Ptolemy VI. At the time of the alliance, this Ptolemy had been sharing power with his sister/wife Cleopatra and his younger brother, Ptolemy VIII. They were both in Alexandria. What prompted the older brother to ally with his uncle against his siblings is uncertain. The alliance lasted less than a year. All three siblings were in their teens at the time.

177 'I will do as the Senate decrees': the confrontation between Popillius and Antiochus is a famous moment in Roman history. Now known as the 'Day of Eleusis', the episode was recounted for centuries afterwards. While Popillius seems to have had a strong personality, more noteworthy are the extent and power of the Roman Senate's authority. In comparison with other versions, Livy's is fairly understated. Though he is careful to depict Popillius' character consistently, the episode is narrated in context and without much commentary or judgement, except for the summary in the final sentence.

178 without having taken the auspices: as we have seen, the consuls had rituals to follow before they left on campaign. Compare Gaius Claudius at 41.10. Licinius seems to have committed the error inadvertently. It is, however, a mark of the Romans' renewed piety that the augurs are consulted and their opinion followed.

179 Pisa and Luna: Pisa was an old and formerly independent city. Luna was founded as a Roman colony (i.e. the inhabitants retained Roman citizenship) in 177 (41.13).

the people who conferred it on him: Roman law distinguishes between ownership and possession: Masgaba is saying that Masinissa recognizes that he has some kind of usufruct or lifetime-interest in property that technically belongs to the Roman people. Since it is highly unlikely that Masinissa was familiar with Roman law, Masgaba's speech is an easy example of Livy's Romanocentric perspective. It is more interesting, however, as a reflection of what the historian could assume about his audience's knowledge of civil law.

180 asked that . . . in place of <. . .>: any reconstruction of this sentence requires considerable speculation.

181 the four urban tribes: traditionally, when slaves were manumitted, they were assigned to one of the four 'urban' voting districts as opposed to one of the thirty-one 'rural' districts. Votes in the rural districts were more valuable because there were fewer people in them than in the urban ones. As this passage suggests, recent censors had, in some cases, departed from established practice. Because of the missing text at the beginning and the lacuna at the end of this sentence, there is no way to ascertain exactly what happened. For further discussion, see S. Treggiari, Roman Freedmen during the Late Republic (Oxford, 1969), 43–7.

The Esquilina was chosen by lot: from other sources it is clear that freedmen were assigned to all four urban tribes. Livy or his source may be wrong, or the procedure may have undergone further discussion and change.

The censors . . . previous censors had: Livy describes this part of the census earlier, at 43.15 and 16 and 44.16.

184 the Macedonian mines . . . the rural estates: these belonged to the Macedonian kings. Since the Roman settlement eliminated the monarchy,

some provision had to be made for these sources of income. This initial plan, subsequently modified, shut down these resources entirely.

184 *revenue-collector*: the Latin word is *publicanus*, which became the English word 'publican' (meaning both tax-collector, as in Latin, and the operator of a public house, or pub for short). The Romans' original mechanisms for managing conquered territory were minimal, and the most powerful Roman presence in a province was often that of the publicans, who had government contracts to collect taxes.

a federal council of the people: although the text in the manuscript does not contain the necessary negative, most scholars believe that the Romans did not install a federal council linking all four regions. The translation follows that interpretation.

185 *the son who subsequently ruled*: see 42.16 with the note to p. 46 on the complex domestic relations of Eumenes and Attalus after the supposed attempt to assassinate Eumenes at Delphi.

186 *impious brothers, as handed down by myth*: e.g. Polynices and Eteocles, the sons and brothers of Oedipus, and Atreus and Thyestes, the father and uncle of Agamemnon. Livy rarely refers to Greek myth and history, but the allusion is appropriate here because, as Macedonians, Stratius and Attalus are heirs to Greek culture.

(if there were any): an observation not found in Polybius' summary of Attalus' speech (30.2). The addition contributes to the doubts about Eumenes' role in the war. Livy started qualifying the portrayal of Eumenes back at the beginning of Book 44 (chap. 13, with note to p. 130).

when he left: Polybius' version of Attalus' trip is rather different. Most notably, he claims that the Senate expected Attalus to return to ask for more; in addition, the Senate promised him the two cities he requested, but then did not confer them when he failed to return (30.3). Livy's streamlined version makes both Attalus and the Senate appear more noble.

188 *rendered the Carthaginians your foes*: reference to the trigger for the First Punic War (264–241). Initially, three parties were involved: the Carthaginians, who controlled south-western Sicily, a group of mercenaries who had taken over Messana, directly across the straits from Italy, and the king of Syracuse. The Romans allowed themselves to be drawn in when the mercenaries requested their help. Because of that request, they could claim that they were not the aggressors in the war that resulted. For a fuller account, see Polybius 1.7–12.

made Philip your enemy: here the speaker refers to the ostensible causes for the Romans' war with Philip (the Second Macedonian War, 200–196). Livy gives a detailed account in Book 31.

he attempted to dislodge you from control of your empire: the war against Antiochus (192–189).

189 *as it approached from Syria*: the battles near Samos and Pamphylia are highlights of the Rhodians' contribution to the naval component of the

war against Antiochus. Hannibal commanded part of Antiochus' fleet in the second battle (Livy 37.8–24).

190 *that the Republic was not under your control*: in the Roman historical tradition, the plebeians seceded three times (494, 449, and 287), physically removing themselves from the city in their struggles with the patricians. (See Livy 2.32–3, 3.50–4, and *Per.* 11).

The Athenian people . . . total confidence: Astymedes is paraphrasing a famous passage in Thucydides, where the Corinthians sketch the respective natures of the Athenians and the Spartans (Thucydides 1.70).

our manner of speaking is inflated: Livy may be alluding here to a mid-first-century BCE literary debate over 'Attic' speech, which was associated with the best of fifth- and fourth-century Athenian prose, and 'Asiatic' speech, which was loosely connected to the more elaborate style used by the Greeks in Asia Minor during the Hellenistic period. Cicero, who was engaged in the debate (*Orator* 25), and Quintilian, who offers a later overview (*Institutes* 12.10.16–18), classify the Rhodians as using a rhetorical style in between the two perceived extremes.

192 *a man of harsh temperament*: the same phrase Livy used for Popillius earlier (chap. 10).

his Origines: comprising seven books, Cato's *Origines* was the first work of history written in Latin. Only fragments remain. Livy's refusal to reproduce Cato's speech is interesting. The only time he composed a speech for Cato is the *lex Oppia* debate at the beginning of Book 34. In that case, no trace of the original survives, and it looks as if Livy composed speeches only when the original (or a version of it) could not be known. The author of the *Periochae* notes when speeches of Cato do or do not survive. Passages from Cato's defence of the Rhodians are preserved in Aulus Gellius (*Attic Nights* 6.3.1–55); his style differs markedly from Livy's.

193 *treaty of alliance*: Livy here uses two terms (*amicitia*, or 'position of friendship', signifying an unofficial, mutually beneficial relationship, and *foedus*, or 'treaty of alliance', a more technical term for a treaty) that are often regarded as significant for understanding Rome's relations with other states.

In the same period: the following paragraph refers to cities and territories that Rhodes, for over a century an Aegean powerhouse, controlled in Asia Minor.

194 *the Illyrians should be free*: there is of course a paradox in ordering people to be free. In practical terms the Romans preferred not to create an administration for conquered peoples, but to leave them to look after themselves, provided that they did not interact with other states independently of Rome.

195 *victory statues of himself instead*: traces of Paullus' victory have survived at Delphi. In addition to a series of scenes from a frieze depicting the battle of Pydna, there is an inscription stating 'Lucius Aemilius, son of Lucius, general, took [this] from King Perseus and the Macedonians'. For the Latin,

see H. Dessau, *Inscriptiones Latinae Selectae*, vol. 3, pt. 2 (Berlin, 1954), no. 8884.

195 *whose shrine is there*: the second-century CE Greek travel writer Pausanias gives a detailed description of the shrine, its history, and the procedure for consulting Trophonius. After an elaborate sacrifice and ritual purification, the supplicant descends into a twenty-foot pit and then is sucked feet first through a hole from which he emerges feet first also. Pausanias states that he consulted the oracle and went through this process (9.39).

the Euripus and the island of Euboea: Artemisium, the beach on the northern tip of Euboea, at the end of the Euripus (the strait between Euboea and the mainland), was the site of a naval battle between the Persians and the Greeks in 480.

his daughter . . . as an offering: a reference to Agamemnon's sacrifice of his daughter Iphigenia.

the ancient prophet is worshipped as a god: Amphiaraus, a seer from Argos. He was one of the 'seven against Thebes' in the Argive campaign against that city. After the expedition was defeated, Amphiaraus was swallowed up by the earth, near Thebes. Enquirers at his shrine sacrificed a ram, slept in its hide, and were supposed to have a dream revealing the future. The shrine has been excavated and can be visited.

the walls linking Piraeus to the city: the famous Long Walls, originally built in the fifth century so that Athens would be connected by defensible walls to its port, Piraeus.

196 *before its destruction*: Corinth was destroyed by the Romans in 146 to punish the Achaean League for the revolt it staged against Rome that year. The punishment was also supposed to warn others against attempting to rebel. Carthage was razed that same year. Although there is no evidence to suggest a direct connection, the orders given by Lucius Mummius, the Roman commander at Corinth, and Scipio Aemilianus, the Roman commander at Carthage (and Paullus' companion on this trip), are often viewed together and regarded as emblematic of a new level of brutality in Rome's relations with others in the Mediterranean. It is interesting that Livy mentions the city's destruction, because he rarely adumbrates future events.

memorable . . . for its educational system and its institutions: apparently another echo of Thucydides. He contrasts the material grandeur of Athens with the paucity of monumental buildings at Sparta and comments that if one were to judge from the physical remains, it would not be possible to tell how powerful Sparta was (Thucydides 1.10).

as if the god were present: the statue of Zeus (Jupiter) at Olympia was one of the Seven Wonders of the World.

197 *the tiles to be returned and the exposed areas to be repaired*: this episode is not found in other sources, but its appeal to Livy is clear. Earlier in the pentad (42.3), Fulvius Flaccus stole the roof-tiles from the temple of Juno Lacinia. The Senate censured the act, but no one could reaffix the tiles.

Paullus, by directing the soldiers to undo the damage to the walls of Amphipolis, and thus looking out for the local community, is a counter-example to Fulvius, showing how a Roman commander should behave.

translated Paullus' words into Greek and repeated them: the fact that Paullus announced the policy in Latin and then had Octavius translate it when Paullus himself could have used Greek shows the complexity of Roman attitudes towards Greek culture in this period. This episode seems to be a display of power: official discourse, as opposed to the private interrogation of Perseus, takes place in Latin to remind the Macedonians that they are now subject to Roman policy.

198 *Pelagonia*: almost certainly shorthand for the region of the Pelagones, according to N. G. L. Hammond, *A History of Macedonia*, vol. 1 (Oxford, 1972, repr. New York, 1981), 74–5.

199 *the Aetolians were called in*: see chap. 28.

200 *Callicrates . . . would be endangered*: Callicrates was last mentioned in Book 41, where he speaks in favour of respecting the Achaeans' alliance with the Romans (chap. 23). From Polybius it is clear that Callicrates maintained his pro-Roman stance during the war. Since Polybius was one of the 1,000 Achaeans sent to Rome, an unintended consequence of this witch-hunt was his monumental history.

203 *There was so much plunder*: this one-day assault on Epirus resulted in the pillaging of seventy towns and 150,000 captives being sold into slavery. Livy minimizes its brutality and emphasizes Paullus' efficiency and the amount of booty. The latter point is important for subsequent events. There is a noteworthy contrast with Plutarch: he deplores the extent of the devastation, especially relative to the amount each soldier garnered (*Aemilius Paullus* 29); Livy offers considerably higher totals and indicates that the soldiers should have been satisfied.

204 *the law was to be presented*: while the text in the manuscript is continuous, editors concur that words have been omitted; the relationship between the troops' anger and their attitude towards the voting is not entirely clear. The idea seems to be that the soldiers were too exasperated to bother casting their votes for Paullus' triumph, which the Senate had already approved.

205 *consul*: his consulship was in 202, so he was presumably in his seventies in 167.

206 *shed his apprenticeship and to put his eloquence on display*: according to Polybius, in this period a Roman had to serve in the army for ten years before he was eligible for political office, and military tribunes (such as Galba was at Pydna) had to have at least five years of military service (6.19). Thus at the time of this debate Galba occupied the Roman equivalent of an entry-level position in public life. He went on to become praetor (151) and consul (144) and to achieve fame as an orator. Cicero identifies him as the first to draw on the full range of oratorical tricks (*Brutus* 82).

206 *he led you immediately in pursuit of the enemy*: while it is possible that Livy somehow forgot how he presented the sequence of events in Book 44, this seems unlikely since he makes rather a lot of the soldiers' eagerness to fight, Paullus' restraint, and the explanation the general offers. It seems more likely that Livy is making Servilius undermine Galba's credibility by repeating his misrepresentations; note that Servilius goes on to say that Paullus made the soldiers go directly from the battle to pursuing the enemy, while in Book 44 the Romans do not chase the survivors because it is dark and they are not familiar with the territory. I think we are supposed to remember Livy's presentation of events in Book 44 and see that the soldiers and/or Galba—as represented by Servilius—are lying.

207 *in the most recent Punic war*: see the note to p. 139.

208 *imitate the Athenian people, who make accusations against their leading men out of spite*: Servilius is probably referring to the fifth-century Athenian practice of ostracism, a publicly voted exile for ten years. The purpose seems to have been to limit the influence of outstanding individuals in the democracy, but the procedure was easily manipulated and was used for less than a century. As noted previously (note to p. 186), references to Greek history are rare in Livy. He may be adopting material from Polybius, who did not admire the Athenian democracy (e.g. 6.44), but it is not known whether or not Polybius gave Servilius a speech here.

Camillus . . . rescued our city from the Gauls: Camillus directed the successful conclusion of the Romans' campaign against Veii in the 390s. He was subsequently accused of distributing the booty inappropriately and went into exile. Nonetheless, when the Gauls occupied Rome, Camillus mustered an army and rescued the city. See 5.19–55.

it is Liternum where his grave is to be seen: Scipio Africanus was responsible for defeating Hannibal, but an alleged financial scandal compromised his reputation towards the end of his life, and he retired to Liternum. (Scipio's involvement in the Second Punic War is spread throughout Books 21–30; Livy covers the so-called 'Trials of the Scipios' at 38.50–60.)

209 *we preordained them for him*: see the end of 44.22.

210 *his swollen testicles provoked laughter in those closest to him*: Servius presumably had a herniated scrotum. As this passage suggests, generally speaking, public nudity was not acceptable in the first half of the second century. There was, however, also a long tradition of displaying wounds as proof of one's valour.

211 *when the amount was announced*: in fact, the bonuses Paullus distributed were extremely large by the standards of recent campaigns. As Scullard notes, in 194 Titus Quinctius Flamininus gave the infantry twenty-five *denarii* apiece, as did Lucius Scipio Asiaticus in 188 and Marcus Fulvius Nobilior in 187. Subsequent generals raised the stakes somewhat: in 186 Gnaeus Manlius Vulso distributed forty-two *denarii* per man, and in 180 Quintus Fulvius Flaccus gave out fifty *denarii* each. In each case the centurions and cavalry received higher amounts on the same scale proportionally

(see 34.52, 37.59, 39.5, 39.7, and 40.43, and H. H. Scullard, *Roman Politics, 220–150 B.C.* (Oxford, 1951), 218 n. 2). Thus Paullus' troops got twice as much as their most immediate predecessors. The bonuses were also larger than those given to the men serving under Octavius (chap. 42) and Anicius (chap. 43) in the same campaign.

213 *King Perseus with his son Alexander to Alba for safekeeping*: there is no trace of Perseus' subsequent fate in Livy, but other sources provide more information. The king and his family were initially imprisoned in a dungeon, and Perseus was encouraged to commit suicide (with first a sword and then a rope lowered to him). Eventually either Paullus or another Aemilius (the sources are not consistent) put pressure on the Senate to improve the king's situation, and he was relocated. He died two years later, reputedly because his guards grew angry with him and tortured him to death by keeping him awake (Diodorus 31.9). Plutarch notes this version but says that Perseus starved himself (*Aemilius Paullus* 37).

Bithys . . . the hostages: Livy has not mentioned Bithys or these Thracian hostages before, at least not in the extant text. The editorial supplement of his name here depends on the reference at the very end of this chapter. Cotys was Perseus' ally from early on and fought with him both at Callinicus (42.56–8) and at Pydna (44.42).

214 *Lucius Anicius . . . on the festival of Quirinus*: according to an inscribed list of triumphs surviving from the Augustan period, Paullus' triumph occurred on 27, 28, and 29 November. The festival of Quirinus fell in the middle of February, two and a half months later. Regardless of whether Livy knew the actual dates, his interest is in juxtaposing the triumphs to highlight Paullus'. (The celebration for Octavius, which did occur immediately after Paullus' triumph, was too small to serve the same purpose.)

216 *care . . . over the sons of allied kings*: the reference is to the current Ptolemy, whose interests the Senate had protected against Antiochus with the famous embassy of Gaius Popillius.

the total given to Masgaba: 100 pounds of silver; see chap. 14 above.

217 *degrade him*: see Polybius 30.18–19. By including Polybius' unflattering description here, Livy may be laying the groundwork for his own subsequent (apparently) critical depiction of Prusias. Nicomedes eventually overthrew his father, and according to Appian, Prusias' motive for depositing Nicomedes with the Roman Senate was his preference for his other sons (*Mithridatic Wars* 4). From the *Periocha* for Book 50, it appears that Livy's ultimate appraisal of Prusias was close to Polybius' view as reported here.

THE *PERIOCHAE*

221 *1a*: there are two summaries for Book 1. This first one is noticeably more telegraphic; the second one begins with the reign of Ancus Marcius, Rome's fourth king (1.33).

spolia opima: the spoils taken by a Roman general who defeats the enemy leader in single combat. This happened only a handful of times: see *Per.* 4 and *Per.* 20. The precise qualifications for achieving the honour came under debate in 29 BCE. when Marcus Licinius Crassus killed the leader of the Bastarnae; Octavian blocked his attempt to dedicate the spoils, probably wanting to deny him the concomitant glory of such an unusual distinction. One of the rare references to Octavian/Augustus in the extant books occurs when Livy discusses the dedication of the *spolia opima* by Aulus Cornelius Cossus (4.20).

221 *Ancus Marcius*: name supplied from context.

223 *vindicta*: a rod used in the ceremony for manumission.

225 *In the three hundred and second year after Rome was founded*: 448; the standard modern date is 451, but the epitomator uses 750 BCE instead of 753 for Rome's foundation.

this type of magistrate: the military tribunes with consular power, who, according to the tradition represented in Livy, replaced consuls as the chief magistrates for the years 448–368 BCE.

226 *the dictator Quintus Cincinnatus*: a mistake; this is Lucius Quinctius Cincinnatus.

227 *thrown from the Rock*: the Rock is the Tarpeian Rock, a steep cliff on the Capitoline Hill; being thrown from it was an ancient form of execution at Rome.

228 *the name of Corvus*: *corvus* is the Latin word for crow.

229 *devoted himself*: Decius offered himself and the enemy to the gods of the underworld and entered the battle intending to kill as many men as possible before dying himself, in exchange for a Roman victory.

231 *the Forum claque*: a derogatory way of referring to freedmen.

232 *Triumviri capitales*: a board of three men in charge of prisons and executions.

236 *watched the games in his toga praetexta*: i.e. he appeared at a public event in the garb of the office from which he had been compelled to step down.

238 *a sacred spring*: the practice of sacrificing everything born in the spring of one year; this dedication was limited to animals (though the full ritual involved exiling the human offspring of that year once they reached adulthood).

241 *Marcian verses*: prophecies attributed to one Marcius; see 25.12.

242 *Archimedes*: the great mathematician, a native of Syracuse, born around 287, and killed when the Romans took the city.

247 *the initiation rites*: the ceremony during which new members were inducted into the cult of Demeter (Roman Ceres) and Persephone at Eleusis, about thirteen miles from Athens in north-western Attica.

250 *before all the rest*: the dialogue is reproduced virtually verbatim from Book 35; it must have caught the epitomator's attention since it is just one passage in Livy, but roughly half the *Periocha* for 35.

the praetor of the Achaeans: here, as in Livy's text, the epitomator uses a Roman term for a foreign leader. The Greek title is *strategos*, or general.

the Mother of the Gods: another name for the Idaean Mother (*Per.* 29) and the Magna Mater.

254 *The books of Numa Pompilius*: Numa was Rome's second king; these books supposedly contained his sacred and philosophical writings.

256 *against his household instead*: in Livy, this sentiment is not expressed until 45.41.

258 *In the five hundred and ninety-eighth year from the founding of the city*: 153 BCE, i.e. 157 by standard modern reckoning.

259 *funeral masks*: elite Romans made masks of family members when they died; these masks were worn at subsequent family funerals to show the relationship between the deceased and his ancestors.

261 *in the six hundred and second year from the founding of the city*: 150; 149 is the usual date.

judged the best by the Senate: the epitomator has confused this Scipio Nasica with his father, the consul of 191; for the arrival of the Magna Mater in Rome, see 29.14.

Following an indication from the books: i.e. the Sibylline books.

games for Father Dis were held at the Tarentum: these are known as the 'Secular Games' because they were supposed to take place once in a *saeculum* (one hundred years). In Roman religion, Dis rules the underworld; the Tarentum referred to here is in the Campus Martius.

in the five hundred and second year from the founding of the city: 249 BCE by modern counting.

267 *the cognomen 'Serapio'*: according to Valerius Maximus (9.14.3), this name derived from Nasica's physical resemblance to a sacrificial attendant of that name.

placed under a furca: a Y-shaped piece of wood; it sat on the condemned man's neck, and his arms were bound to its arms.

270 *the optimates*: in the late Republic, people were identified as *populares* (populists) and *optimates* (the best men); the latter group overlapped with the Senate for the most part. These groups were not organized political parties; the terms indicate rather public stances, whether in favour of the privileged or of the general population.

271 *marriage among the orders*: 'orders' are similar to classes; in Augustus' time these included senatorial families, equestrians, Roman citizens in general, freedmen, and slaves. Legislation passed under Augustus regulated marriage between members of different orders. Other initiatives concerned raising the birth rate and punishing adultery. Augustus' social legislation was controversial during his lifetime and has greatly interested historians of his reign.

272 *whom the Greeks call the Gymnesians*: *gymnos* is the Greek word for naked; since Greek athletes trained naked, the original meaning of 'gymnasium' was a place where people exercised in the nude.

the trajectory of a missile: the Greek verb *ballo* means throw, and the related noun *belos* means something thrown.

273 *Aquae Sextiae*: modern Aix-en-Provence.

276 *a new man*: generally, someone who was the first in his family to become a member of the Senate, and, more narrowly, the first in a family to be elected consul.

the shields: twelve shields with a figure-of-eight shape. According to tradition, Mars sent the first one to Numa Pompilius. They were guarded and used by the Salii, special priests of Mars.

277 *forbade him water and fire*: an interdiction accompanying voluntary exile.

278 *the Social War*: the name given to the conflict between Rome and most of the rest of the Italian peninsula between 91 and 88 BCE. The Latin word *socius* means ally and is cognate with the English word 'social'. By the ancient meaning, however, a 'social' war is a war with allies.

282 *nobiles*: not a hereditary aristocracy *per se*, but individuals whose ancestors had held an important magistracy (typically the consulship).

284 *the city of Ilium*: this city claimed to be Troy and traded on its august heritage.

285 *Gnaeus Pompeius*: generally referred to in English as Pompey.

286 *the Civic Villa*: the oldest public structure in the Campus Martius, used for various activities (such as taking the census).

proscription list: Sulla invented the practice of proscriptions: a form of bounty-hunting where a magistrate posted a list of people who could be killed with impunity; their property was then at the disposal of the magistrate.

290 *Marcus*: from other sources we know that the epitomator must mean Marcus Perperna and not Marcus Antonius.

294 *the Senate changed its attire*: i.e. wore mourning, to protest the use of the tribunician veto to prevent the functioning of a Republican institution.

295 *Gnaeus Pompeius*: I have departed from Jal's text here by not translating the word *legato*.

<happened>: Jal uses this conjecture in his translation, but not in his text of the Latin.

298 *Pompeius Magnus*: one of two instances where the epitomator refers to Pompey with his honorific *cognomen* 'the Great'.

Marcus Antonius: generally known as Mark Antony.

299 *his own client*: a pervasive Roman social structure was the relationship between a patron (a more powerful, influential, and wealthy person) and his clients (people of lesser importance). Reciprocity was assumed, so there is an implication of betrayal here.

300 *sacrosanct*: inviolability of person was traditionally a right of the tribunes of the plebs.

running with the Luperci: priests who celebrated the Lupercalia, a fertility festival that involved nearly naked young men running around the Palatine Hill.

he assumed the name of Caesar: a crucial step for Octavius/Caesar/Augustus. As is apparent in this *Periocha*, Octavius' adoption of his great-uncle's name had outstanding tactical consequences. He conflated his identity with that of his great-uncle, and the resonance of the name gave him the backing of Caesar's army. The author of the *Periochae* refers to him as Caesar until the summary for Book 134, where he receives the name Augustus.

GLOSSARY

aedile four aediles (two 'curule' and two 'plebeian', without much distinction in this period) were elected annually to oversee public matters in Rome such as games, markets, the water supply, maintenance of roads, and fire prevention; they had some judicial powers, but their authority was less than that of praetors and consuls.

as, asses bronze coins, the least valuable denomination.

augur one of a board of nine priests responsible for divination, i.e. determining the gods' disposition either towards a particular event or over a longer period; the augurs interpreted the movements of birds, celestial activity, the sacred chickens (see note to p. 20), four-legged animals, and any unusual, ominous event.

boeotarch/boeotarchs title of the chief magistrates of the Boeotians.

Campus Martius an area outside the *pomerium*, originally with enough open space for elections, the census, and the mustering of troops (Map 1).

Capitol/Capitoline the Capitoline is the lowest of Rome's hills; the southern summit is the Capitol and the site of the temple of Jupiter Optimus Maximus.

censor two censors, elected every five years for an eighteen-month term, had several general areas of responsibility: taking the census, revising the membership of the Senate, reviewing the equestrians, regulating morals, and collecting revenue from state-owned property for activities such as building roads; revenue-collection extended to responsibility for taxes, the gathering of which they contracted out.

century the basic voting unit when the Romans assembled to elect their chief magistrates; despite the name, centuries were not uniformly comprised of 100 men each, but varied in size based on property qualification.

cognomen the third and usually most distinctive part of the tripartite name of a Roman citizen. Romans typically had a *praenomen* (of which there are only about a dozen for men: e.g. Gaius, Marcus, Titus), a *nomen* (the clan name, such as Cornelius or Aemilius), and then a *cognomen*; *cognomina* could arise from anything from a great accomplishment to a physical characteristic. Livy uses the term *cognomen* also for epithets that foreigners received, such as Ptolemy Apion.

college a board of a particular kind of priest: the four major priesthoods (augurs, decemvirs for sacred rites, *fetiales*, and *pontifices*, with the priests (*flamines*) of individual gods included in this last college) were all organized into colleges, and matters were referred to each college as a collective.

Comitium the open area next to the Roman Forum where public meetings were held (Map 1).

consul the two annually elected consuls were both the leading generals and the top magistrates; they had *imperium*, or the right to lead an army, they could convene the Senate to conduct public business, and they could veto each other; if a consul died in office, his replacement for the remainder of the year was known as a suffect consul.

crown in the Hellenistic world, ceremonial crowns (a diadem or headband) originally were a means of expressing honour or gratitude and came with gifts of cash. Romans awarded crowns for military accomplishments, such as saving a soldier's life in battle (the civic crown) and being the first to scale the wall of an enemy city under siege (the mural crown).

Curia the building where the Senate ordinarily met (Map 1).

curio maximus chief priest of the *curiones*, thirty men, each of whom was in turn the chief magistrate for one of the thirty divisions (*curiae*, sometimes translated as wards) in which the Romans originally voted.

decemvir literally a 'ten-man'; when Romans assigned a task to a team of officials, the team often took its name from the number of members; so a decemvirate is a board of ten (cf. duumvir and triumvir); the 'decemvirs for sacred rites' were responsible for consulting the Sibylline oracles and advising the Senate based on the prophecies they contained.

denarius, denarii the standard unit of silver coinage, introduced during the Second Punic War; one *denarius* was worth ten *asses*.

dictator originally a magistrate for emergencies, in whom all power was vested for a maximum of six months; the office was temporarily revived during the Second Punic War; the office as Sulla and Caesar used it in the first century resembled the original office only in the absolute power they wielded.

duumvir plural *duumviri*; a team of two men (cf. decemvir and triumvir); in this period there are *duumviri navales* responsible for patrolling the Adriatic.

equestrians exactly who comprised this order changed considerably over the history of the Republic. In the period covered by Books 41−5, they came from the top property class, and the status was a coveted one. By the last century of the Republic, as is evident from the *Periochae*, the equestrians were more important for their political identity and interests. In the second century many equestrians engaged in business, including Rome's crude system of taxation. The censors took bids on contracts for the collection of taxes, which was done by members of the equestrian class; they made their profit by swindling provincials beyond the official rate.

flamen Dialis, Martialis, Quirinalis these three priests were dedicated to Jupiter, Mars, and Quirinus respectively.

freedman/freedmen former slaves. The Romans were unusually liberal in the regularity with which they manumitted slaves and in the open manner in which they subsequently included them in public life. Freedmen could not hold office, but they could vote, and their children were full Roman citizens (provided that they were born free).

haruspices a type of priests, traditionally of Etruscan origin, whose expertise lay in reading entrails; they also interpreted prodigies and advised the Senate how to expiate them.

imperium a Latin word for power, specifically the power to command an army; normally held by consuls and praetors, it was invalid within the *pomerium*, and thus a consul needed special permission from the Senate to bring his army into Rome for a triumph.

intercalation the insertion of an extra month or days to bring the official calendar in line with the rhythm of the solar year. During the Republican period, the Roman civic calendar had twelve months totaling 355 days (the length of a lunar year). Since this was more than ten days shorter than the solar calendar, it was regularly necessary to add an extra month. (Even so, at this time the calendar was ten weeks ahead of the seasons.)

iugerum/iugera a *iugerum* was the standard unit of measurement for land; it is slightly less than two-thirds of an acre.

lictors public servants who accompanied magistrates with *imperium*; they carried the *fasces* (bundles of rods and axes that symbolized the magistrate's power; also the origin of the modern term Fascism).

lustrum in general a ritual purification; more particularly, the ceremony that closed the census taken every five years. The censors' *lustrum* purified the city and drove out evil; it consisted of a procession around the *pomerium* and ended with the sacrifice of animals. Livy describes the first one in Book 1 (chap. 44). The word can also mean simply the five-year period from census to census, e.g. at 41.8, 45.15, and *Per.* 5.

master of the horse traditionally the dictator's second-in-command and the general for the cavalry.

ovation a smaller version of the triumph; for example, the general entered Rome on foot or on horseback instead of in a chariot.

pomerium the sacred boundary of the city of Rome.

pontifex plural *pontifices*; the least specialized college of priests, the *pontifices* had responsibility for general religious matters such as public sacrifices, most festivals, and sacred law; the college included the *flamines* and was headed by the pontifex maximus (chief pontiff), by this period an elected official and the highest religious authority.

praetor (peregrine and **urban)** the second highest magistracy. In this period there were six praetors elected annually for a one-year term: the urban praetor (or praetor with urban jurisdiction) was in effect the mayor of Rome, running the city while the consuls were on campaign and overseeing the administration of civil law; the peregrine praetor (or praetor with peregrine jurisdiction) has traditionally been understood to have had responsibility for legal affairs that involved Romans and non-citizens (*peregrinus* is the Latin word for foreign and designates a person who does not have Roman citizenship); the other praetors received areas of responsibility that required a high-ranking Roman official and often an army but which were not considered as important as the commands allotted to the consuls.

proconsul a general who had previously been a consul (usually in the year just past) whose *imperium* was extended, to increase the number of generals available and/or to ensure continuity of command; promagistrates might also be private citizens specially empowered by the Roman citizen assembly or the Senate.

province area of responsibility; although the word tends to connote geographical territory, in any given year a province could be a task such as eliminating brigands or expelling pirates or, as routinely in the case of praetors, the administration of Rome and civil law.

quinquereme the standard warship of the Roman Republican navy.

Quirites formal name of Roman citizens.

Senate a council of approximately 300 men who had held at least one magistracy and who were officially selected by the censors; membership was ordinarily for life although individuals could be removed by the censors for egregious conduct; while technically the Senate's role was advisory, in this period it was in effect the standing government, as is clear from Books 41–5. See also the note to p. 16 for the use of 'fathers' and 'conscript fathers' as synonyms for senators.

sesterces (plural); the *sestertius* was a silver coin worth 2½ *asses* or a quarter of a *denarius*.

Sibylline oracles a collection of writings supposedly recording the sayings of the Sibyl, a prophetess near Cumae; according to tradition, they were acquired during the reign of Rome's last king. A special board of priests, the decemvirs, consulted them in public emergencies.

spolia opima the 'finest spoils', the booty stripped from an enemy leader when killed in single combat by the Romans' general; see note to p. 221.

toga the dress of the Roman citizen. Magistrates and males under 16 were entitled to wear the *toga praetexta*, which had a purple border. At the age of 16 or 17 the *toga virilis* (lit. toga of manhood) was assumed; it was a plain, undyed garment.

togate wearing a toga, i.e. formally dressed as a Roman citizen.

tribune/tribune of the plebs ten officers elected each year by the plebeians to protect their interests; although there are a few episodes in Books 41–5 where tribunes are called on as a college to act in this capacity, in this period they tended to be aligned more with the interests of the senatorial class than those of the general public, and the office was used as another stepping-stone to higher positions; in the last century of the Republic the tribunes became associated again with popular concerns rather than those of the elite. Military tribunes are junior officers.

triumph a victory parade, normally awarded by the Senate at the request of a general returning from campaigning. If the Senate granted a triumph, the general would be allowed to lead his army in a parade through the city. He wore a special costume, and booty from the campaign was displayed in the parade. The procession culminated on the Capitoline where the general paid tribute to Jupiter. The triumph was thus a source of honour for both the general and the gods. If the Senate refused the general's request, he could hold a parade outside Rome and offer the spoils to Jupiter on the Alban Mount. Because this form of the triumph was held outside the city and the Senate did not finance it, it was essentially a private celebration. The location also limited attendance, so it was altogether less prestigious.

triumvir plural *triumviri*; literally a 'three-man', but more importantly, the title given to Marcus Aemilius Lepidus, Marcus Antonius, and Gaius Octavius/Gaius Julius Caesar (Octavianus) Augustus in 43 BCE when they were constituted as a board of three (triumvirate) to re-establish the state.

Vestal priestess of Vesta; there were six at a time, and they lived in seclusion starting from childhood for at least thirty years; their chief duty was tending the fire in the shrine of Vesta, the Roman goddess of the hearth.

victoriatus a silver coin older than the *denarius*, struck outside Rome to Greek standards of three-quarters of a *denarius* in weight (though not in metal content).

INDEX

The index is comprised primarily of names of peoples and places. In cases of very similar or identical names, supplementary information is given in parentheses if possible. Prominent Romans are identified by the first year of the highest office they held and, in cases where they feature extensively in the narrative of Books 41–5, by offices held in that period. The dates provided are based on T. R. Broughton's *The Magistrates of the Roman Republic* (vols. i–ii, New York; vol. iii, Athens, Ga., 1951–86).

A SELECTION OF   **OXFORD WORLD'S CLASSICS**

THOMAS PAINE   **Rights of Man, Common Sense, and Other Political Writings**

JEAN-JACQUES ROUSSEAU   **The Social Contract**
Discourse on the Origin of Inequality

ADAM SMITH   **An Inquiry into the Nature and Causes of the Wealth of Nations**

MARY WOLLSTONECRAFT   **A Vindication of the Rights of Woman**